FrontPage® 2002 Developer's Guide

Mike Jennett

Osborne/**McGraw-Hill**

New York   Chicago   San Franci...
Lisbon   London   Madrid   M...
New Delhi   San Juan   Se...

Osborne/**McGraw-Hill**
2600 Tenth Street
Berkeley, California 94710
U.S.A.

To arrange bulk purchase discounts for sales promotions, premiums, or fund-raisers, please contact Osborne/**McGraw-Hill** at the above address. For information on translations or book distributors outside the U.S.A., please see the International Contact Information page immediately following the index of this book.

FrontPage® 2002 Developer's Guide

1234567890 CUS CUS 01987654321

Book p/n 0-07-213257-4 and CD p/n 0-07-213258-2
parts of
ISBN 0-07-213259-0

Publisher	Brandon A. Nordin
Vice President & Associate Publisher	Scott Rogers
Acquisitions Editor	Ann Sellers
Project Editor	Mark Karmendy
Acquisitions Coordinator	Tim Madrid
Technical Editor	Mark Hammock
Copy Editor	Bart Reed
Proofreader	Brian Galloway
Indexer	David Heiret
Computer Designers	Michelle Galicia, Lauren McCarthy, Roberta Steele
Illustrators	Michael Mueller, Alex Putney, Beth E. Young
Series Design	Roberta Steele
Cover Design	Greg Scott

This book was composed with Corel VENTURA™ Publisher.

FrontPage® 2002
Developer's Guide

About the Author

Michael Jennett is the executive vice president and COO of Spotlight Studios, an award-winning Internet development consultancy. Mr. Jennett oversees Spotlight Studios' overall business operations including technology development, system integration, and business strategy. In this role, he has served as executive producer for numerous corporate Web projects for clients such as HP, Levi-Strauss, Philips, Sybase, Sun Microsystems, and Visa International. In addition to his recognition as one of the Top 100 Producers of the Year by AV Video and *Multimedia Producer* magazine, Mr. Jennett authored *FrontPage 2000 Developer's Guide*, (Osborne/McGraw-Hill, 1999).

Prior to co-founding Spotlight Studios, Mr. Jennett worked as a technical writer and project manager producing and overseeing the development of Web interfaces, technical manuals, and online help systems for such clients as Sun Microsystems, Oracle, Visa International, and New York Life Insurance.

His educational background includes a BA degree in English Literature from the California State Polytechnic University in Pomona, CA.

Mr. Jennett currently lives in San Jose, California, with his wife Kim and two daughters, Deven and Tehya.

This book is dedicated to the three girls in my life. To my wife and soul mate, Kim. You have been there from the beginning and have always gotten me to take it one step further, whatever it may be. Your love and understanding are never taken for granted. To my daughters Deven and Tehya, who are the lights of my life and who make me believe, every day, that the world truly can be a better place.

Contents at a Glance

Contents

Part III   **Beyond HTML**

Acknowledgments

There are so many people that have made it possible for this book to be written, but there are also those special people who have been instrumental in the development and production of this project. I would like to thank Ann Sellers, Acquisitions Editor, who brought this project to life. Ann was there to kick-start this book and make sure that it lived up to its name. I would also like to thank Tim Madrid, Acquisitions Coordinator, who was there every step of the way making sure that I had what I needed and kept on schedule, even if it meant calling me while at the vet with my dog. I would also like to thank Mark Karmendy, Executive Project Editor, for taking each chapter and making sure that it became the final manuscript you see before you; as well as a thank you to Bart Reed, Copy Editor, for making sure that I stayed at least close to writing in English. Another person who was instrumental to the finished product you see before you is Mark Hammock, Technical Editor. This is the second book I have had the pleasure of working on with Mark, and he never ceases to amaze me in the knowledge he carries and can obtain. His expertise can be found throughout the chapters of this book as he made sure that all aspects were not only technically correct, but also carried the punch that a Developer's Guide should have. Thanks again, Mark.

I would also like to thank, as always, Kim Emerick, my partner in crime. Kim has always been there for me in business and personally. She has seen my potential even when I felt that I had nothing left to give. Her words of wisdom and her incredible talent have always made me go one step further, not only because she makes me feel like I can accomplish anything, but because she makes me a believer in myself and others. Kim, you are a shining star in this industry and in my life and I thank you for everything you have given me.

Last, I would like to thank my parents, William and Eugenia Jennett. Throughout my life they have supported me in every endeavor, even when they did not know if it would be successful or not. They have given me an appreciation for life, literature, and the arts that has been instrumental in my own personal and professional development. Thanks, Mom and Dad.

Introduction

Do you need this book? If you are developing Web sites, the answer is yes, you need this book. Whether you are an executive producer for a large development firm or simply taking your first steps toward creating a Web site, this book gives you the knowledge and tools to get the job done. Throughout this book you will find keys to the inside knowledge needed to create sites that take FrontPage and the Web to their extremes.

If you are an advanced user, you will find out not only how to use the tool to its greatest extent but also how to customize FrontPage, along with the code it generates for your sites. Within these pages, I show you how to create projects with FrontPage as well as how to take these projects one step further. You'll find great tips and tricks for tweaking your code to get the most out of the advanced capabilities of FrontPage.

If you are just getting started, this book will show you the basics and give you the tools to hone your skills and become a seasoned developer. You'll find out how to create sites with all the fancy fixings of the big guys, without the investment of years of learning. You'll also be able to use this book as a reference for your basic needs, such as the most commonly used HTML codes, and you will easily learn how to use the more advanced features of FrontPage.

How this Book Is Organized

To make it easier for you to make your way through the chapters, this book is divided into three parts. Each part works with a specific area of FrontPage 2002 and the concepts found within the product.

Part I: Cutting-Edge Design and Layout Techniques

Part I gives the background knowledge and reference material to get started on even the most complex of development projects. Once you've made it through the first few chapters, you'll dive right into some of the more advanced components of FrontPage, such as the new SharePoint Team Services, and you'll see how easy it is to implement them into your designs. The book doesn't stop there, however. Once you see how to implement cutting-edge techniques into your Webs, you'll find out how to take them to the next level, surpassing standard FrontPage integration to make your developments stand above the rest.

Part II: Creating Dynamically Driven Web Sites

No longer is the Web a place of static images and text. Today's sites are filled with dynamic content and layout. In this section of the book, you'll learn how to incorporate database and ASP technology into your Webs. Furthermore, you'll see how the Office XP suite of products can be merged to offer you intranet developers the ability to pop Office applications directly into your site. Using the chapters found in this section, you'll quickly begin to see how FrontPage 2002 can make activating your site with advanced technologies much less of a chore.

Part III: Beyond HTML

Part III tackles the most advanced topics of dynamic design. Throughout you will find out in a hands-on manner how to incorporate advanced scripting technology into your Webs, making them a truly active environment. Once you've seen how to create advanced custom Web implementations, you'll move on to find out how to customize FrontPage 2002 itself, using the integrated Visual Basic editor. Throughout this section you'll tackle the tough developments and learn how to create custom sites and environments in easy-to-follow steps.

What's on the CD

A CD-ROM is included with this book to further extend your capabilities when it comes to development. Within the CD, you will find a trial version of FrontPage to get you started.

You will also find all the code discussed throughout the book. This code is ready to use and can be incorporated directly into your sites, or it can simply be used to aid you while going through the exercises you'll find in the book.

Examples on the CD

The examples on the CD are accessible by viewing the directory that corresponds to the chapter you are working on in the book. Each chapter that contains sample code is found under the corresponding chapter directory. For example, you'll find the sample code in Chapter 16 under the CH16 directory on the CD-ROM.

You can also view all of the available pages through the use of your browser. An index page has been set up on the CD-ROM to allow you to see where files used in the examples can be found. To access the index, simply open index.html on the CD-ROM.

CAUTION

Many of the examples on the CD-ROM will not work properly unless they are imported into your current Web. If you find that an example is not working correctly, try importing that file into the Web you are currently working with.

Special thanks to:

▶ **Stephen Bullen**, developer of the AutoStart FrontPage Add-In
  Business Modelling Solutions Ltd.
  18 Lynmouth Crescent
  Furzton
  Milton Keynes MK4 1HD
  England
  phone: +44 (0)1908 340050
  fax: +44 (0)1908 340051
  http://bmsltd.co.uk/

▶ **Jenson Crawford**, developer of the Sequential Quote JavaScript
  Media Services
  500 S. Sepulveda Avenue, 4th Floor
  Los Angeles, CA 90049
  888-653-5300

Cutting-Edge Design and Layout Techniques

An Introduction to FrontPage 2002

IN THIS CHAPTER:

Review FrontPage 2002 Features

Work with SharePoint Team Services

Use Web Site Management Tools

Well, here we are again, talking about the latest release of FrontPage from Microsoft, FrontPage 2002. Luckily for us, *2002* doesn't stand for the year, at least I don't think so. Anyway, Microsoft has done it again with this latest release. The more I get into this product, the happier I am. Now, as I have said in the past, you can't use a WYSIWYG (What You See Is What You Get) editor for everything, but the crew at Microsoft is making it harder and harder for me to make that claim.

With the release of FrontPage 2002, Microsoft has taken an already good product and made it better. With previous versions, I would only use FrontPage for complex page layouts and then move over to a competing code editor for the really grueling stuff. With the release of FrontPage 2000, I found myself doing that less and less, and with this release, I find myself barely doing it at all. I know it is hard for a lot of the old-time developers to swallow this, but the days of needing to switch between editors is coming to an end. The raw HTML editing capabilities of this product give you the option to go to your roots for customized code, whereas the WYSIWYG "Normal" view of FrontPage allows you to create all the designs and layouts you can handle.

If you're just starting out in design, this product will allow you to create compelling sites, complete with navigation features, active elements, and custom graphics. For the seasoned developer, the new features of FrontPage 2002 will help you take your designs to the next level, or, at the very least, speed your development time considerably.

As we go through this chapter, you will begin to see what I'm talking about. A whole bunch of new features have been added to the product, and some great customization settings have also been incorporated. But before we get into the features, I want to spend a little time talking about the basic principle of a FrontPage *Web*. This will give those of you who are new to FrontPage some insight into what you will need as we move forward in the book.

FrontPage 2002 Webs

FrontPage 2002 works with what is called a *Web* to create and manage your site. A Web includes all the pages, images, and other content contained in your Web site, along with all the directories in which those files are found. It is also where FrontPage stores all the hidden configuration files necessary for implementing many of the advanced features in the program.

Think of a Web as your Web site as a whole. You will find later in this book, however, that you can have many Webs within a single Web site. The idea of a Web should be looked at as one type of Web site that can be nested within (or *incorporated into*) a larger Web site. By viewing it in this manner, you will see that a Web is really an administrative tool that allows you to create multiple layers for controlling the look and feel of your overall Web site as well as gives you control over who has access to what information within your Web site. We'll cover the details of managing your Web later in this chapter (see "Web Site Management Tools").

FrontPage 2002 Feature Overview

Now that you have a basic understanding of what a Web is, let's dive right into some of the basic features of FrontPage, along with some of the new and enhanced features you will want to check out while working with the product. This is not a complete features list, because many of the product features are dealt with in detail throughout the book. However, this section does give you a general overview of how FrontPage is set up and how to get started working with it.

Site Design Elements

With the release of FrontPage 2002, Microsoft has improved upon many of the features in the last release and has added an array of new features that allow you to do more than ever, all while using one tool. The latest release comes with a variety of new design elements that let you quickly put together presentations, add collaboration to your sites, and keep your documents looking the way you intended them to look (not the way the editor thinks you wanted them to look). This section takes a look at some of the new site design features incorporated into the product, many of which are described in detail in later chapters of this book.

Controlled Pasting

One of the biggest complaints I have heard from developers in my office who use FrontPage comes when they are cutting and pasting content from other programs such as Word. In the past, when someone would cut a page out of Word and paste it into FrontPage, it would go in with all the formatting code that Word uses in its system. This caused a lot of frustration because that person would then have to go into the HTML view and rip out all the unwanted code. The only way around this, previously, was to dump all the content into Notepad or some other simple text editor and then copy it again and paste it into FrontPage.

Thankfully, the group at Microsoft must have heard the developers' cries because they have added a new feature to the paste capability. Now when you paste content from Word, you will see a small clipboard icon appear on your screen. If you click the icon, it expands to display an option menu with the following three options:

▶ **Use Destination Styles**   Instructs FrontPage to use the styles you have in your current document to format this content

▶ **Keep Source Formatting**   Instructs FrontPage to use the styles found in the original document to format this content

▶ **Keep Text Only**   Instructs FrontPage to remove all formatting from the content

These new options allow you to control how your pasted code will look once it is placed in your FrontPage document, thus eliminating a lot of extra code and work.

Photo Gallery

The new Photo Gallery features incorporated into FrontPage give you the ability to create slideshow-style presentations within your sites with ease. This is a new feature to FrontPage 2002, and it has met with rave reviews from the developers and designers at my office.

Through the use of the Photo Gallery, you can create a number of layouts for your graphics on a page, complete with custom formatting of the pictures and the ability to add descriptive text, much like you would see in an actual Photo Gallery. This feature is great for the amateur creating pages to show off the new baby or the new house, but it really comes in handy for developers.

A couple of great examples of this new functionality for developers are the storyboarding of Web site conceptuals and the creation of presentations. Using the Photo Gallery, you can easily take all the conceptual layouts you have for a Web site and put them in a slideshow with descriptive text for each design you are displaying. The same can be said for presentations. The Photo Gallery gives you considerable control over layout, font usage, and coloring, and it offers a number of template layouts for you to use.

Web Components

With the release of FrontPage 2002, Microsoft has greatly expanded the number of Web Components included with the product. *Web components* are developed sets of code that work with FrontPage and allow you to create complex interfaces, such as searches, dynamic effects, and dynamic content, to your sites without needing to implement any custom programming on your own.

The great thing about the Web components in this release is that they are all available through the use of the Insert Web Component dialog box, shown here:

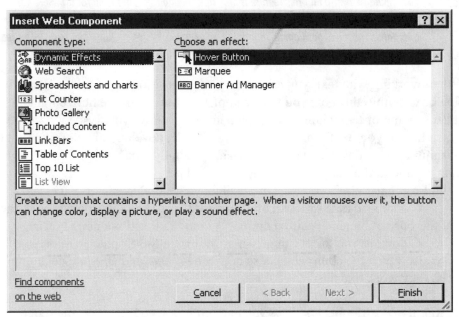

Using this dialog box, you can select and preview the contents of any component prior to customizing and implementing it, whereas in the previous version, the components were simply listed in the Insert menu and you actually had to start working with them prior to knowing what they did.

When you open this dialog box and select a component, you are shown a description of the component and what it does. Once you find the component that suits your particular need, you can click Finish to start customizing the component.

Upon opening the Insert Web Component dialog box, you will see that there is a component for just about every need, but it doesn't stop there. Microsoft has also included components and links from third parties that allow you to incorporate dynamic content into your site from other sites. These dynamic components are being added to regularly and allow you to make stock quotes, weather reports, current news, and much more available from your site without needing to program a thing.

Precise Positioning Within Your Document Layout

With FrontPage 2002, you have the ability to design your pages exactly the way you want, with pixel-precise positioning. This can be done with both text and images through the use of various settings within the editor portion of the program.

CAUTION

You should be aware that this feature is only functional on Internet Explorer browsers 4.0 and above and Netscape Navigator 6.0 and above. For this reason, you may want to find an alternative means of positioning your data (for example, tables, spacing, and so on). This feature is very useful if you are not concerned with browsers other than the latest browser versions.

When working with text, you can specify exact positioning using the Paragraph dialog box. Within this box, you have complete control over the horizontal and vertical spacing of text within your document. This allows you to specify the layout for each line of your text. This feature brings HTML development closer to desktop publishing capabilities than it has ever been, especially when you use it in conjunction with the image positioning discussed here.

With FrontPage 2002, you can simply click your graphic and drag it exactly where you want it to be positioned on the page. This is accomplished through the use of the Format menu's Position option. Within the Position dialog box are various selections allowing you to determine where you want the graphic positioned. But you are also given the ability to choose between relative and absolute positioning. Briefly, they work like this:

▶ **Relative positioning**   Allows you to insert image code in a specific spot on the page and then specify where you want the image to appear in conjunction with that spot. For example, you could insert your image code at the top left of the page and then set the image to be exactly one inch to the right of that position.

▶ **Absolute positioning**   Gives you exacting control over the layout of your image. You can select your image and drag it anywhere on the screen. When you then view your image in a compatible browser, the image will appear right where you put it.

Combined with layering and layer ordering (known as *zorder*), these features give more control than ever over the positioning of your text and graphics within your Web site. Unfortunately, they are not compatible with all browsers; therefore, for most of us, other means of placement need to be found. If you are designing for a multiplatform audience, you will probably want to avoid these features of FrontPage and use tables to position your text and images where you want them on your page.

Preserved HTML Editing Capabilities

One of the biggest problems with WYSIWYG editors is that they have this nasty habit of taking the code you put in and translating it to what they believe the code should be.

Over the years, I have seen FrontPage do this many times. This has caused many designers to stay away from FrontPage, especially at the professional level.

Luckily, the folks over at Microsoft have heard the cries and have set up FrontPage to preserve both the HTML code that you write and the code you bring in from other applications. With FrontPage 2002, you can modify the source code, and FrontPage will preserve it exactly the way you wrote it. This is extremely beneficial if you like to, or need to, work directly with your HTML code or are editing scripts within your HTML documents.

TIP

FrontPage now gives you a choice as to how your code will be preserved. Within the Page Options dialog box, found by selecting Page Options from the Tools menu, you can instruct FrontPage to reformat any code you implement following specific rules you set up.

Inserting code into your HTML using the toolbar icons and menu bar commands is done in the HTML view of FrontPage. This view displays your HTML code exactly as it will appear to the browser, with the addition of color coding for easy reference and error checking. With FrontPage 2002, the HTML view gives you more control than ever. You now have the ability to decide how FrontPage will produce your HTML code.

In the Page Options dialog box, you can set up the color coding that will be shown when you view your code, and you can set up various rules as to how FrontPage will save your code. These rules are especially nice because they allow you to create code that meets your criteria. With these rules, you can specify whether the code is capitalized, how far tags are indented, and many other options.

Custom Themes in FrontPage 2002

Many designers create their own styles for their Web sites. However, FrontPage does include a set of comprehensive styles, called *themes*, that can be applied to pages or entire sites. Themes allow you to create a Web site based on a predetermined set of images, page layouts, and formatting options. With FrontPage 2002, these themes have been updated, and you have the ability to customize the themes that come standard with FrontPage 2002.

The ability to customize themes allows you to take an existing structural layout and make it your own. The process for this customization begins by selecting a theme for your Web site. Once you have selected a theme, you are offered an array of options that allow you to modify the graphics that appear, along with the colors and the text layout, throughout the theme. This feature gives you ultimate control over the look and feel of your themes and allows you to create your own variations on themes.

SharePoint Team Services Webs

This is a feature that has been a long time coming as far as I'm concerned. SharePoint Team Services is an expanded set of FrontPage Server Extensions that are included with this version of FrontPage and Office XP. It allows you to create team-based Web sites where people can collaborate through the use of document libraries, custom discussions, event calendars, and many other tools. In days past, you would have to create these items through custom programming or buy another expensive product to place on your server to implement these types of custom services. With SharePoint Team Services, you can now create all this right from FrontPage, with no custom programming whatsoever. The following list takes a quick look at some of the new features available to you with the SharePoint Team Services that will make collaborative Web sites something you'll want to create right away:

▶ **Events**   With SharePoint Team Services, you can create an events calendar where people can quickly view what's on tap. You can also set it up so that users can add their own events to the system.

▶ **Announcements**   This type of feature comes in very handy for group collaboration. You can quickly add announcements for meetings, special occasions, and the like using the announcements section.

▶ **Shared Documents**   A great new feature for collaboration, the shared documents capability built into SharePoint Team Services allows groups to share various documents online, with full uploading, downloading, and editing capabilities.

▶ **Discussions**   FrontPage comes equipped with a wizard that allows you to create online discussions within your sites, but it is somewhat limited in the way it creates and displays topics, and is even more limited when it comes to editing and deleting posts. The SharePoint Team Services discussions feature allows you to create any number of discussions and comes with a much more robust interface for editing, deleting, and adding discussion topics.

▶ **Task Lists**   With SharePoint Team Services, you can easily keep track of projects using the task lists feature. The system allows you to add tasks to the list as well as assign responsibilities, display the status of the tasks, give tasks priorities, assign tasks due dates, and indicate the percentage of completion.

▶ **Contact Lists**   If you work with Outlook, you are probably familiar with contact lists that let you store information such as phone numbers and the like. SharePoint

Team Services allows you to integrate this capability right into your Web site, giving everyone access to the information they need right through their browser.

▶ **Subscriptions**   With SharePoint Team Services, you can set up subscriptions so that users who are subscribed to a particular Web site will receive e-mail notifications when specific items, such as documents or events, have changed. This keeps everyone up-to-date without having to go to the actual site.

▶ **Security**   SharePoint Team Services allows you to control who sees what as well as who can work with a particular feature of the Web site you have created. For more information on setting up the SharePoint Team Services security features, see Chapter 17.

These are some of the many new features you have at your disposal with the SharePoint Team Services. Along with these features, SharePoint gives you the ability to customize your Web site and its content to fit the look and feel you require—all from FrontPage's interface.

Site Management Elements

One of the most impressive features of FrontPage has always been its site management capabilities. These capabilities allow you to manage your entire Web site as well as run various reports and make global changes throughout the site with the click of a button. Unfortunately, many people do not take advantage of the site management capabilities that FrontPage has to offer.

With the release of the latest version of FrontPage, you will find that the site management features have been improved and expanded, which should, in turn, ensure that this is the one tool you will use for all your development needs.

Single-Page Publishing Control

One of the biggest problems with FrontPage has been its publishing capabilities. In FrontPage 2000, the features of this capability were enhanced to allow you to specify that certain pages were not to be published so that you could deem which pages went live and which pages did not. However, if you modified a single page in a very large Web site, you would then have to go through and select all the files—other than the one you just modified—and select Don't publish. This became very cumbersome when making a number of modifications. To solve this problem, Microsoft now allows for single-page publishing. This gives you the ability to select one or more files and publish only those files, without needing to flag any other files in your site.

To publish only selected files, follow these steps:

1. In the Folder view, select the page(s) you want to publish.

2. Right-click and select Publish Selected Files. This brings up the Publish Destination dialog box, shown here:

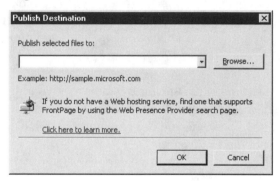

3. Type the destination URL where you want these files to be published and click OK.

Source Control Capabilities

Along with the ability to assign specific permissions to areas of your Web site, you have control over the pages that are being worked on, through the use of FrontPage 2002's source control capabilities. These capabilities allow individuals to check out files they are going to work on and then check them back in when they have completed their work. Using this type of system ensures that the files individuals are working on are not overwritten by someone else working on the same files. Checking out a file is easily accomplished when working with FrontPage 2002. Simply select the file you want to reserve and then select Check Out from the Edit menu. When you have completed your work on the file, you can check it back in by using the Check In command, also found on the Edit menu, without fear of overwriting someone else's work.

To activate the source code control feature, simply select Tools | Web Settings and click Use Document Check-In and Check-Out in the General tab.

Group Collaboration

Working in groups and assigning tasks is easy with the incorporation of workflow reports in FrontPage 2002. These reports allow you to assign responsibilities for certain pages to specific individuals within a project group. They also allow you to specify what category the particular page falls in (for example, jobs, products, and so on), along with the status of a given page.

Assigning status to files can be extremely useful when you are working with large groups. The use of this feature allows anyone working on the project to quickly find out where a file is in the production process and allows the publisher the opportunity to see what files are ready for publishing, without needing to contact the individual responsible for each file. Also, FrontPage allows you to choose from the default status settings or to create your own settings to match the naming conventions you use in your publishing process.

The reports are easy to set up and are available by selecting Properties from the File menu when working with a file. All the reports are found under the Workgroup tab, shown in Figure 1-1.

Browser-Specific Settings

A big concern when developing a Web site is making sure it works on the platforms it will be deployed on. If you are working with an Internet-based site, this problem is compounded by the fact that the people viewing your site may be viewing it using a

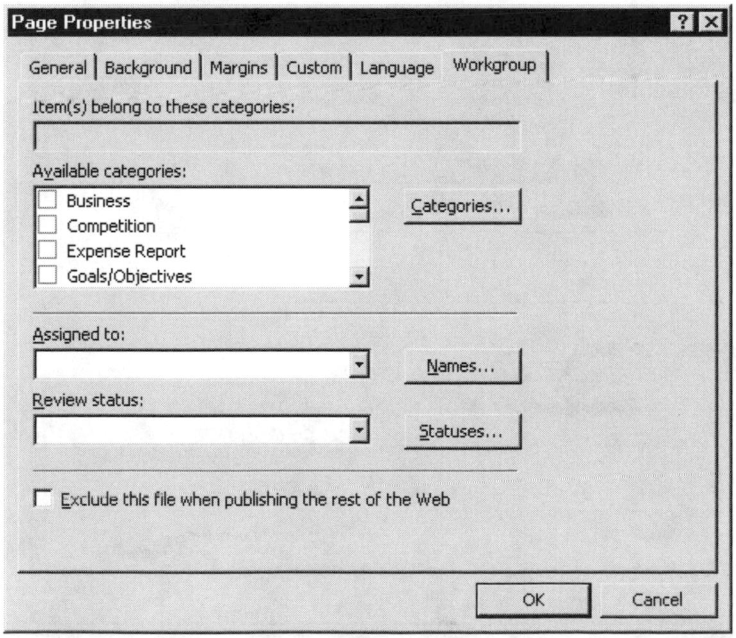

Figure 1-1   *The Workgroup tab of the Page Properties dialog box*

variety of browsers. This problem does not occur as much if you are in a controlled intranet environment, where you know exactly what the audience will be using to view your pages. In either case, though, the need for browser compatibility is a major issue.

Luckily, FrontPage 2002 has made it easy to create Web sites that are compatible with the audience that will be viewing them through the use of the compatibility options. These options are found in the Page Options dialog box, accessed via the Tools menu, as displayed in Figure 1-2.

By selecting your compatibility options, you can target specific browsers for the deployment of your Web site. Once an option is selected or deselected, FrontPage will alter its menus and coding to adhere to your selection. This way, you will not have users incorporating features into their pages that are not supported on the appropriate browsers.

Database Elements

Microsoft has a slew of database features to make database integration easier than ever. The following sections outline some of the database-integration features found in FrontPage 2002.

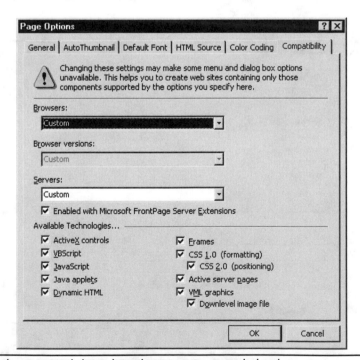

Figure 1-2   *The Compatibility tab in the Page Options dialog box*

Database Results Wizard

You don't have to be an advanced designer to integrate databases directly into your Web sites with the Database Results Wizard. This wizard takes you through the steps of retrieving the data sources, setting up the look for the database, and incorporating the data references into the page. This is an excellent way of incorporating dynamic data into your Web sites, and it's easily accessible via the Insert | Database menu.

NOTE

For the dynamic database information to be displayed, you must be serving your Web site on a server that supports Active Server Pages. For more information on Active Server Pages, see Chapter 11.

Database Publishing with the Click of a Button

Many people spend their entire careers working with databases. With a little programming knowledge, these people have no problem developing and implementing custom databases into their Web sites. But for Web designers, FrontPage gives you some great help in this area. You now have the ability to create databases by following a few simple steps:

1. Create a form in FrontPage with all the fields you want to send to a database.

2. Right-click the form and select Form Properties from the pop-up menu. This brings up the Form Properties dialog box, shown here:

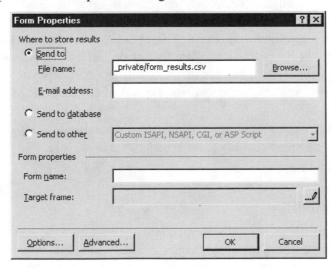

3. Click the Send to Database radio button and then click Options. This brings up the Options for Saving Results to Database dialog box, shown here:

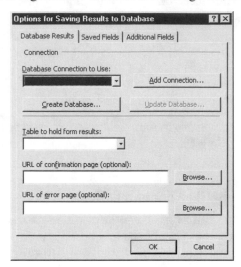

4. Click the Create Database button, and FrontPage 2002 will create an Access database, complete with tables populated with the information fields you designated in your entry form. This allows you to create a form and have the rest of the work done for you in the creation of the database.

Once FrontPage finishes creating the database, it posts the database to your Web and creates the necessary connections. Another nice feature worth mentioning is that you can choose to import an existing database. When doing so, FrontPage recognizes that it is a supported database format and offers to create the data connection for you. We will get into all this information in depth in various chapters of the book—this capability touches many aspects of advanced development.

NOTE

When the database is published, FrontPage sets it up so that no one is given permission to browse it.

Scripting Elements

Today, Web sites use scripts to accomplish many programmatic actions within a page. Microsoft has taken this into account and has added functionality to FrontPage to help you incorporate scripts into your Web sites. One of the most useful components that has been integrated into FrontPage is the Microsoft Script Editor (discussed in detail in Chapter 14). This editor is available from the Tools | Macros menu, and it allows you to add scripts directly into your pages.

When working within a page where you want scripts incorporated, you simply select the Script Editor. The page is then loaded into the editor, and you can input both JavaScript and VBScript into the page. The Script Editor shares the Visual Studio integrated development environment and includes IntelliSense and AutoComplete features. Experienced script authors will find the Script Editor a joy to work with, whereas beginners will find these features invaluable learning tools.

Programming Elements

A key element that many developers have asked for is an extensible and programmable tool to accompany FrontPage. Microsoft has answered this request with the incorporation of many programming features that enable developers to create macros for use within FrontPage and to design programs that automate various tasks within FrontPage.

FrontPage has Visual Basic for Applications 6.3 incorporated into its structure, allowing you to develop extensive macros that not only work with FrontPage but also can be incorporated to work in conjunction with your other Microsoft Office applications. This capability gives you the power to create application macros that cause FrontPage to interact with your other Office applications to help you automate content and generate pages.

Wizards

FrontPage 2002 comes equipped with a number of wizards to help you when creating your site. Wizards are programs that take you through a step-by-step selection process to create a specific item for your Web, such as a discussion group, or an entire Web site. These wizards create all the files and structures you need for the item you are creating, and all you do is answer some basic questions. Wizards can be extremely helpful, even for advanced developers, in creating basic structures to build upon within a Web.

FrontPage 2002 comes equipped with a variety of wizards to help you in your site creation. You will see references to them throughout this book, along with information to help you optimize their use.

Web Site Management Tools

The ability to manage your entire Web site is a key feature of FrontPage 2002. It not only allows you to create Web site pages but also gives you the ability to view, edit, and organize all your documents within your Web. You will find that the term Web is used extensively within the management side of FrontPage. Whenever you begin a Web site, FrontPage will create a new Web. This Web will contain all your Web pages, but it will also include the configuration files that FrontPage needs to manage your Web site.

Working with Webs

Whenever you work within FrontPage, you want to make sure you are working within a Web. Yes, you can open individual pages using FrontPage, but you lose many of the capabilities that come with working within a Web.

NOTE

To take advantage of the server extensions used for many items, such as discussion groups, you must be working through your Web server, not from your hard drive. You will know if you are working within your server if you see "http://" in front of the directory structure for your Web.

Once you have your Web open, you can work within various areas of your site. The main areas we will look at here involve the management side of a Web. This is the aspect of your project where you are not actually editing pages within your Web site but rather are organizing the structure behind those pages.

Working with Views

You manage your Webs through various views available within FrontPage. These views allow you to change the structure of your site, based on your criteria, as well as allow you to view your site's vital statistics and assign tasks for site development. The following views are your main tools when managing your Web site within FrontPage.

Folders   Folders work much like the folders in the Windows Explorer. They are for organizing where your files are stored within the Web. The difference between these folders and those found in Explorer is that when you move files between folders in FrontPage, the system will automatically update your hyperlinks to match the changes you make.

Reports   The reports view allows you to run reports on your current Web for an array of items. With these reports, you can check to see how your Web is set up and whether there are any problems (broken links, slow pages, and so on) that need to be taken care of. These reports are useful for validating your Web site prior to launching it, and they can also come in handy on an ongoing basis to see how updates are affecting your data. The following reports come standard with FrontPage 2002:

▶ **Site Summary**   Gives you a basic overview of the current Web by listing each of the individual reports and their summary information.

▶ **All Files**   Lists all the files within the current Web, along with their vital statistics.

▶ **Recently Added Files**   Allows you to view files added within a specific time frame that you select from the available options.

▶ **Recently Changed Files**   Allows you to view files changed within a specific time frame that you select from the available options.

▶ **Older Files**   Allows you to view files that have been in the Web for more than a specified number of days.

▶ **Unlinked Files**   Allows you to view all the files within your Web that are not linked to other files.

▶ **Slow Pages**   Allows you to view all files that take longer than a defined time to load. You define the time using the drop-down menu available within the report's toolbar.

▶ **Broken Hyperlinks**   Displays any hyperlinks that do not point to files within the Web. If these files are URLs outside the Web, they are marked as unverified by the system. If they link to files within the Web that do not exist, they are marked as broken.

▶ **Component Errors**   Lists any errors occurring within the components you have included in your pages. It displays the file containing the error, along with a description of the error encountered.

▶ **Review Status**   Displays all the files within your Web, along with any review information that has been entered by reviewers.

▶ **Assigned To**   Displays all the files within your Web, along with their assignments and who assigned them.

▶ **Categories**   Displays all the files within your Web, along with the category for the file.

▶ **Publish Status**   Shows the publishing status for each of the files within your Web site. The publish status is set to either Publish or Don't Publish, depending on the settings you have specified in the page properties. If the file is set to Don't Publish, it will not publish to your server during the publishing process. This is a very useful report to run prior to publishing your site.

▶ **Checkout Status**   Allows you to see who has which files checked out on the system for editing. This can be helpful if you are administering a site and you want to keep track of who has files checked out and for how long.

▶ **Usage Summary**   Gives an overall summary of site statistics for your Web site.

▶ **Time Based Summaries**   These include the Monthly, Weekly, and Daily summaries, which show the number visits, hits, and downloads you have had on your Web site.

▶ **Page Hits**   Displays the number of times each page in your Web site has been viewed, along with information about that page.

▶ **Visiting Users**   Displays available information about the visitors to your Web site.

▶ **Operating Systems**   Displays the type of operating systems the visitors to your site are using.

▶ **Browsers**   Displays the type of browser visitors are using when they view your Web site.

▶ **Referring Domains**   Displays the domain a visitor came from to view your Web site. This is especially useful because you can see where your visitors are coming from (for example, search engines, advertisements, and the like).

▶ **Referring URLs**   Displays the last URL the visitor was at prior to coming to your site.

▶ **Search Strings**   Displays the search strings visitors are inputting to find your Web site.

Navigation   The Navigation view allows you to see how your site works from a flowchart perspective. Through this view, you have the ability to see each aspect of your site in relation to the other pages. You can even expand or collapse nodes of the site tree to view specific sections up close or view the site as a whole.

This view can be very helpful when you are first setting up your site, because you can build the pages from start to finish within the view. You start with the default page and simply add pages from there by clicking the New Page icon on the toolbar and dragging the pages to the level you want them to appear. Once you have your site structure developed within this view, you can print it out to give yourself a complete flowchart of how the site will work.

If you have chosen to use shared borders with navigation bars, the navigation view's structure also controls the links within the navigation bars.

Hyperlinks   The Hyperlinks view gives you a complete look at the links you have going from page to page within your Web site. Unlike the navigation view, which just shows your layout from a hierarchical/navigation bar point of view, the hyperlink view shows every single link that goes into and out of specific pages on your Web site.

Using this view, you can see where your pages link to and how far the links go down into your structural layout, along with seeing where broken links, if any, appear within your Web site.

Tasks   Your tasks view displays all the tasks that you, other group members, and wizards have set up for the current Web. Within this view, you can check to see who has been assigned a task and what the status of that task is. Using tasks is a great way to manage your projects when developing a site—whether you are working with a team or just need reminders for yourself. Using tasks and the task view, you can keep track of where your site is going and how it is getting there.

Web Settings

The FrontPage Web Settings dialog box, reached by selecting Tools | Web Settings, allows you to set up your basic parameters for the current Web. These settings affect the underlying structure of the entire Web. This dialog box consists of six tabs, which are outlined next.

General   The General tab provides general information about the current Web and the server on which it resides. From this tab, you may change the Web's name (a FrontPage internal alias) and select to enable or disable document check-in and check-out.

Parameters   The Parameters tab allows you to insert variables into your Web for use with the FrontPage Substitution Component. Once you define your variable, you can simply insert it into a page using the component. This works well for information that is commonly used, such as copyright notices and phone numbers.

Advanced   The Advanced tab of the Web Settings dialog box allows you to customize these features:

▶ **Default scripting language**   Allows you to specify what the default client scripting language will be.

▶ **Options**   Specifies whether you want files in hidden directories to be visible while you're editing. Having hidden files visible is necessary when working with items such as discussion groups, where the individual message files are hidden as the default. New to FrontPage 2002 is the option to display a Web page view of available document libraries to Office users who open from or save to the Web. Use of this feature requires that users are running Office XP and that the SharePoint Team Services extensions are installed.

▶ **Temporary files**   Lets you safely clean up old temporary files that FrontPage has generated but not properly disposed of. This is new in FrontPage 2002.

Language   This tab allows you to select the default languages for multiple-language support within your Web. Within this tab, you have the following settings:

▶ **Server Message**   Determines the language used by FrontPage when returning various server errors and messages.

▶ **Default Page Encoding**   Specifies the default language you want to use for your HTML pages. The settings chosen here will determine the page encoding for your current Web.

▶ **Ignore Keyboard**   Instructs FrontPage to ignore the keyboard being used when deciding the encoding.

Navigation   This tab allows you to specify the names for the text labels associated with the default navigation buttons when using navigation bars within shared borders. The names chosen here will not affect the actual navigation; they just change the words the user sees when presented with these links.

Database   The Database tab displays all the current databases (if any) in use with your Web. Adding a database connection within this tab causes FrontPage to create a global.asa file, if none exists, and save the database connection information in it. This topic is covered in detail in Chapter 11.

Editing Your Web Site

The FrontPage editor is a fully functional WYSIWYG editor that allows you to create pixel-precise document layouts that you can then view directly in a browser. It works much like any standard word processing program, except that it also allows you to work with the actual HTML code and to preview your work in the built-in browser.

CAUTION

Many of the options available within the editor will not work with all browsers. When creating your pages, be sure to create them with your audience in mind. Although you will still want to test your pages on various browsers, FrontPage's new browser compatibility options will make this work much smoother and easier.

Throughout this book, you will find information on making the best of what the editor has to offer, but here we will take a look at the views available within the editor. When working with a document, you have the option of viewing it as a normal WYSIWYG document, viewing it as HTML code, or previewing it in the integrated browser:

▶ **Normal view (WYSIWYG)**   You will probably do most of your layout and editing in this view when working with documents. Using the normal view allows you to create documents exactly as you want them to appear in the browser, right down to pixel-precise positioning.

▶ **HTML view**   In this view, you work with the underlying code that the browser uses to display your pages to the viewer. Working in this view allows you to customize how specific items are positioned within your documents.

▶ **Preview view (browser)**   Choose this view to see your work as you are creating it. It is a great way to check items as you develop them without having to switch to another program to do so.

NOTE

The FrontPage Preview view displays the current page from a temporary file on your hard drive, not the Web server. For this reason, pages that rely on Web server functionality might not properly display for function within the integrated Preview view. When working with such pages, it is better to preview them using an external browser.

Summary

Upon completing this chapter, you should have a good understanding of the development features afforded to you by this latest release of the FrontPage product. Along with knowing what is new in FrontPage 2002, you should also have a basic grasp of the main concepts behind FrontPage and how it works to allow you to create comprehensive Web sites over which you have precise control.

CHAPTER
2

Advanced Layout

IN THIS CHAPTER:

Learn the Basics of HTML

Incorporate Images into Your Webs

Create Complex Table Layouts

Incorporate Frames into Your Webs

his is one of the most comprehensive chapters in the book because it tackles a number of basic areas of the Hypertext Markup Language (HTML). The concept behind this chapter is to give you a clear base understanding of HTML as a whole and to take a look at the implementation of HTML into your pages. Although we will not cover every basic element of creating HTML documents, we will cover the major tags and some advanced design techniques involving tables and frame layouts.

Along with looking at the HTML language as a whole, this chapter also incorporates some information about tags that I have found to be lacking in available documentation. Items such as the <META> tag, which can perform a number of functions that will help you in your development efforts, are explained with examples so that you can quickly and easily incorporate them into your pages.

I suggest you keep this chapter in mind as a reference while working with this book, and as a general reference while developing.

Developing with HTML

FrontPage 2002 is a development tool that allows you to create compelling Web sites without the need for programming in HTML—the language behind Web pages. Although this is true, it is a good idea to have a basic grasp of HTML and its components. The first part of this chapter outlines the basic tags available within HTML, along with some tricks for using HTML with FrontPage 2002. As you will see, the use of the FrontPage HTML view allows you to make changes and additions to your Webs that are customized to your exacting standards.

HTML Tags

For browsers to be able to interpret Web pages, they must contain some basic HTML tags. Some of these tags determine the fundamental structural layout of the page for the browser, whereas others control the formatting of text and images or make the browser aware of special, nondisplayed information. The following sections describe some of the more commonly used tags available to you when working with HTML. This is not intended to be a complete reference.

NOTE

Changes are constantly being made to the HTML standard. For the latest standards and tags, visit the World Wide Web Consortium at http://www.www3.org. You should also be aware that not all browsers support all standard HTML tags, and many browsers support additional tags that are not part of the HTML standard.

Basic Document Tags

We'll start with the tags that control the most basic structure of the page.

NOTE

You can view these tags in FrontPage through the HTML tab.

<!DOCTYPE...>   Although it's not really a tag, the *<!DOCTYPE>* declaration identifies to the browser the version of HTML being used within the document. This declaration is optional, but it is a good idea to include it in your documents, especially when it comes to analyzing your code, because it allows the analyzer to know what version of HTML you are working with. If included, this declaration must be the first thing to appear in your HTML document.

Here are a few examples of the <!DOCTYPE> declaration:

▶   **<!DOCTYPE HTML PUBLIC "-//W3C//DTD HTML 3.2 Final//EN">**   This is the declaration to use if you are working with HTML 3.2.

▶   **<!DOCTYPE HTML PUBLIC "-//W3C//DTD HTML 4.0//EN" "http://www.w3.org/TR/REC-html40/strict.dtd">**   This is the declaration to use if you want to be held to HTML 4.0 strictly, which means that deprecated tags cannot be used.

▶   **<!DOCTYPE HTML PUBLIC "-//W3C//DTD IITML 4.0 Transitional//EN" "http://www.w3.org/TR/REC-html40/loose.dtd">**   This is the declaration to use if you want to be held to HTML 4.0 with the ability to include deprecated tags.

▶   **<!DOCTYPE HTML PUBLIC "-//W3C//DTD HTML 4.0 Frameset//EN" "http://www.w3.org/TR/REC-html40/frameset.dtd">**   This is the declaration to use if you want to be held to HTML 4.0 while working in a frameset.

<HTML> </HTML>   Instructs the browser that the information within the beginning and ending tags is written in the Hypertext Markup Language.

<HEAD> </HEAD>   Contains information identifying the title of the document and other information stored in Meta tags. You may also include scripts within this tag.

<TITLE> </TITLE>   Identifies the title of the document to the browser. The title will be displayed in the caption bar of the browser.

NOTE

The <TITLE> tag is required to be within the <HEAD> tag.

<BODY> </BODY>   Defines the viewable portion of the document. All information that the browser interprets as being available for display in the browser's window is contained within this tag. This tag can also contain a number of page property identifiers.

Meta Tags

The term *meta* signifies a definition or description. Within the HTML <HEAD> section, the <META> tag is used in name/value pairs to define the content, format, and other nonvisible information about the page the tags are within. Although Meta tags are used to define anything from page expiration dates to author names, the two most common (and probably most important) uses of Meta tags involve the DESCRIPTION and KEYWORD tags. Many search engines use these tags when indexing and ranking sites.

There are two basic types of Meta tags: NAME and HTTP-EQUIV. The NAME attribute is used primarily for the inclusion of keywords and descriptions in your pages. Most of the major search engines will now view the <META> tag and use it to index your site. The <META> tag also allows you to set specific keywords that you think people will use to search for your site or the type of information it contains.

The three settings within the NAME attribute that allow you to incorporate these keywords into your site are listed and described here:

▶ **Keyword**   Use this to set your basic keywords that you want the search engines to use for indexing purposes. Here's an example:

```
<META NAME="keywords" CONTENT="dog, pet, pet food,
  dog food, parks, beaches, hotels">
```

▶ **Description**   Use this to incorporate a description of your page within the header. This description will be used by Meta-capable search engines when your page comes up in a search. Here's an example:

```
<META NAME="description" CONTENT="Dogs by the Bay
  is your one-stop resource for information about
  where to take your dog in the Bay Area.">
```

► **Robots** Use this if you do not want a description or any keywords indexed by the search engines. Traditionally, the robots.txt file on your server took care of this. You can, however, use the <META> tag to get the same effect. This is especially helpful if you don't have access to the robots.txt file on your server. Content options are INDEX, FOLLOW and NOINDEX, NOFOLLOW. Here's an example:

```
<META NAME="robots" CONTENT="noindex, nofollow">
```

HTTP-EQUIV tags are just what they sound like—HTTP header equivalents. They contain header block information that is interpreted by the browser when it loads the page. When the browser loads these HTTP header equivalent tags, it performs the function associated with the tags. These tags can be used to perform a multitude of operations on your Web site. You can insert them to perform actions, such as page refreshes and expirations, and to set cookies.

When working with the HTTP-EQUIV tag, you will create a Meta tag within your <HEAD> tags that looks similar to the following example. Here, we are telling the browser to load the page specified by the URL argument in 3 seconds:

```
<META HTTP-EQUIV="Refresh" CONTENT="3;
URL=http://www.yourpage.com">
```

Here are the operations that can be performed using this style of tag:

► **Expires** Instructs the browser that the current document is to be considered out-of-date as of the specified date. This will cause the browser to request the document from the server so as not to display a cached copy. The Expires tag looks like this:

```
<META HTTP-EQUIV="Expires"
CONTENT="Sun, 2 Dec 2001 11:23:00 GMT">
```

► **Pragma** Works much the same as the expires tag by causing the browser to request the document from the server when the page is loaded. However, rather than specifying an expiration date, it instructs the browser always to request a new page. It works with the content structure being set to "no cache", as shown here:

```
<META HTTP-EQUIV="Pragma" CONTENT="no-cache">
```

NOTE

This tag is now considered somewhat obsolete because it has no effect on Internet Explorer 4.0 or later.

▶ **Refresh**   Allows you to instruct the browser to send viewers from the current page to another page. This is one of my favorite tags—I use it whenever I make changes to page structures. Using this tag, you can simply leave a page that you know many people have bookmarked and have that page redirect them to the new content page.

With the Refresh parameter, you can also set a delay prior to refreshing the page. This delay causes the page containing the refresh to be viewable for a certain amount of time before the refresh takes place. The following is an example of a refresh containing a 10-second delay:

```
<META HTTP-EQUIV="Refresh" CONTENT="10;
URL=http://www.yourpage.com">
```

▶ **Set-Cookie**   Places a cookie on a user's machine. Using this style of Meta tag allows you to specify what the cookie is, along with any expiration date you would like associated with the cookie. In this example, *xxx* represents the information you would store in the cookie.

```
<META HTTP-EQUIV="Set-Cookie"
CONTENT="cookievalue=xxx;
expires= Sun, 2 Dec 2001 11:23:00 GMT; path=/">
```

NOTE

If you do not associate an expiration date with the cookie, it will automatically expire at the end of the current session.

▶ **Window-Target**   Allows you to specify that your page is always to be in the topmost window. This will instruct the browser to wipe out any frames that are attempting to display your page within them. Here's an example:

```
<META HTTP-EQUIV="Window-Target" CONTENT="_top"
```

Format Tags

Once you have your basic document set up, you will get into the creation of a page layout. This is accomplished by using a variety of tags to specify different headings and paragraph styles. The following information relates to the tags necessary for developing basic page layouts in HTML.

<BLOCKQUOTE> </BLOCKQUOTE>   Instructs the browser to indent the text from both the left and right margins.

<CENTER> </CENTER>   Centers the text on the page.

<DL> </DL>   Stands for *definition list*. It identifies the text as a definition (or *glossary*) list.

<DT> </DT>   Stands for *definition term*. It marks the entry as a term to be defined within the definition list. Use of this tag is only valid within a definition list.

<DD></DD>   Stands for *definition description*. It marks the entry as the definition for the term that comes before it. Use of this tag is only valid within a definition list.

<Hn> </Hn>   Specifies the standard heading style within HTML. The *n* stands for the heading number of the associated text. This tag can also have alignment properties associated with it using the ALIGN attribute, which can be set to CENTER, RIGHT, or LEFT alignment.

<P> </P>   Specifies the beginning and end of a paragraph. Within the paragraph tag, you may set alignment characteristics through the use of the ALIGN attribute.

<OL> </OL>   Represents an ordered list (a numbered list, for example).

<UL> </UL>   Represents an unordered list (a bulleted list, for example).

<LI> </LI>   Represents an item within an ordered or unordered list. This tag may only be used within a DIR, MENU, OL, or UL tag list.

Text Formatting

The following are the basic tags used for formatting text within the body of a document.

<ADDRESS> </ADDRESS>   Italicizes the text within it and, as the name implies, is normally used for address listings.

<BASEFONT>   Determines the standard font to be used within the document when displayed. When this tag is used, it should be the first tag within the <BODY> area of the page.

<CITE> </CITE>   Identifies citations within the text.

<CODE> </CODE>   Displays the text to logically represent computer code through the use of a monospaced font. This tag is generally the equivalent of the <TT> (teletype) tag. The <PRE> (preformatted) tag may also be used to display code and will prevent the browser from automatically wrapping the text within the window.

<EM> </EM>   Places emphasis on the formatted text through the use of italic font.

<KBD> </KBD>   Displays the text to logically represent keyboard input. This tag is often used in instructional text.

<PLAINTEXT> </PLAINTEXT>   Follows the same rules as the <PRE> tag (see the next entry), but no embedded tags may be used inside it.

<PRE> </PRE>   Specifies your text as preformatted. When this tag is used, all spacing is preserved within the text.

NOTE

You may embed tags within this tag, but not all will be recognized.

<S> </S> or <STRIKE> </STRIKE>   Causes the displayed text to have a strikethrough appearance.

<SAMP> </SAMP>   Changes the text to logically represent literal characters.

<SMALL> </SMALL>   Causes the text to appear one size smaller than the standard text, as specified in the <BASEFONT> tag.

<STRONG> </STRONG>   Boldfaces the specified text.

<STYLE></STYLE>   Used to determine various styles within a document. The use of the <STYLE> tag is discussed later in the book when I talk about cascading style sheets (CSS).

****   Gives the text the appearance of a subscript.

****   Gives the text the appearance of a superscript.

<TT> </TT>   Gives the text a teletype appearance.

<VAR> </VAR>   Changes the text display to logically represent that of a variable.

Image Tags

The following tags and attributes are used within the <IMG> tag for formatting and laying out images within your documents. An <IMG> tag might look something like this:

<IMG SRC="myimage.gif" BORDER="0" ALIGN="LEFT">

As you can see, the <IMG> tag can contain a number of attributes that will determine its display characteristics.

<IMG>   Specifies the insertion of an image into the document.

ALIGN   Specifies the alignment of the image on the page.

ALT   Allows you to specify alternative text to be displayed while the image is loading or in place of the image in image-disabled browsers.

BORDER   Determines whether the image will have a border. This is a numeric determination, with 0 equaling no border around the image.

HEIGHT   Specifies the height of the image.

HSPACE   Determines the number of pixels between the image and any text on the horizontal axis.

ISMAP   Informs the browser that this image is to be used as an image map.

LOWSRC   Specifies an optional low-resolution source of the image to be displayed.

SRC   Determines the source of the image to be used.

USEMAP   Specifies the image map name to be used with the image.

VSPACE   Determines the number of pixels between the image and any text on the vertical axis.

WIDTH   Specifies the width of the image.

Table Tags

The following tags are used for the insertion of tables into your document.

<TABLE> </TABLE>   Specifies the insertion of a table into the document. This tag may contain the following attributes:

- ▶ **ALIGN**   Specifies the alignment of the table to the left or right margin or to the center of the page.
- ▶ **BACKGROUND**   Specifies a URL for a background image within the table. This feature is supported in Internet Explorer 3.0 and higher and Netscape Navigator 4.0 and higher.
- ▶ **BGCOLOR**   Specifies a background color for the table.
- ▶ **BORDER**   Specifies the border thickness, in pixels.
- ▶ **BORDERCOLOR**   Specifies the color of a border. This feature is supported in Internet Explorer 3.0 and higher and Netscape Navigator 4.0 and higher.
- ▶ **BORDERCOLORLIGHT**   Specifies the color of the lighter shaded border. This feature is supported in Internet Explorer 3.0 and higher and Netscape Navigator 4.0 and higher.
- ▶ **BORDERCOLORDARK**   Specifies the color of the darker shaded border. This feature is supported in Internet Explorer 3.0 and higher and Netscape Navigator 4.0 and higher.
- ▶ **CELLSPACING**   Determines the number of pixels between cells within the table, in effect, widening the thickness of the internal borders.
- ▶ **CELLPADDING**   Determines the number of pixels between the cell outline and the content within the cells.
- ▶ **COLS**   Specifies the number of columns within the table.
- ▶ **HEIGHT**   Determines the overall height of the table, in pixels or as a percentage.
- ▶ **STYLE**   Allows you to define a style to be applied to the formatting of the table.
- ▶ **WIDTH**   Determines the overall width of the table, in pixels or as a percentage.

<TR> </TR>   Stands for *table row*. It specifies the beginning and end of a table row. This tag may contain the following attributes:

- ▶ **ALIGN**   Determines the horizontal alignment of the row within the table.
- ▶ **VALIGN**   Determines the overall vertical alignment for the content within the cells found in the row. This feature is not supported in Netscape Navigator 3.0 and 4.0.

NOTE

The <TR> tag supports all the following attributes described in the <TABLE> tag: BACKGROUND, BGCOLOR, BORDERCOLOR, BORDERCOLORLIGHT, BORDERCOLORDARK, HEIGHT, and STYLE.

<TD> </TD>   Stands for *table data*. It instructs the browser to insert a table cell. This tag must fall within the <TR> tag and may contain the following attributes:

- ▶ **ALIGN**   Determines the overall alignment of the content found within the cell
- ▶ **COLSPAN**   Determines the number of columns that this cell will span
- ▶ **NOWRAP**   Instructs the browser not to wrap the text within this cell
- ▶ **ROWSPAN**   Determines the number of rows that this cell will span

NOTE

The <TD> tag supports all the following attributes described in the <TABLE> tag: BACKGROUND, BGCOLOR, BORDERCOLOR, BORDERCOLORLIGHT, BORDERCOLORDARK, HEIGHT, and STYLE.

<TH> </TH>   Stands for *table header*. It instructs the browser to insert a table header cell, displaying the contents of that cell center-aligned and boldfaced. The following attributes are allowed within the <TH> tag:

- ▶ **COLSPAN**   Determines the number of columns that this cell will span
- ▶ **NOWRAP**   Instructs the browser not to wrap the text within this cell
- ▶ **ROWSPAN**   Determines the number of rows that this cell will span

NOTE

The <TH> tag supports all the following attributes described in the <TABLE> tag: BACKGROUND, BGCOLOR, BORDERCOLOR, BORDERCOLORLIGHT, BORDERCOLORDARK, HEIGHT, and STYLE.

<CAPTION> </CAPTION>   Specifies a caption for a table and may contain the following attributes:

▶   **ALIGN**   Determines the horizontal alignment for the caption.

▶   **VALIGN**   Determines the vertical alignment for the caption. This feature is only supported by Internet Explorer.

Frame Tags

The following tags are used to incorporate frames into your Web site.

<FRAMESET> </FRAMESET>   Determines the beginning and end of a frameset for use within your site. Use this tag on the main page where you want the frames to begin and incorporate all your frame tags within this tag set. Within the <FRAMESET> tag, you may set the following configuration attributes:

▶   **BORDERCOLOR**   Specifies the color of the border around the frame, if any. This feature is only available in versions 4.0 and higher of Netscape Navigator and Internet Explorer.

▶   **COLS**   Determines the number of columns that will appear within this frameset, along with their size attributes. The size attributes may be specified as relative or absolute values.

▶   **FRAMEBORDER**   Specifies whether the frames within the set will have borders. This can be either a numerical or alpha value (for example, 1 or Yes turns the frame border on, and 0 or No turns the frame border off).

▶   **FRAMESPACING**   Defines a set number of pixels to be placed between each frame within the set. This feature is not available when using Netscape Navigator.

▶   **ROWS**   Determines the number of rows that will appear within this frameset, along with their size and attributes. The sizing attributes may be specified as relative or absolute values.

<FRAME> </FRAME>   Specifies the beginning and end of a frame within the set. This tag may contain the following attributes:

▶   **MARGINWIDTH**   Sets the right and left margins for the frame, in pixels.

▶   **MARGINHEIGHT**   Sets the top and bottom margins for the frame, in pixels.

▶ **NAME**   Specifies the name to be used for this frame. This name is associated to the frame for allowing you to target links to this frame using the TARGET attribute.

▶ **NORESIZE**   Specifies that this frame is not resizable by the user.

▶ **SCROLLING**   Determines whether scrolling will be allowed within this frame.

▶ **SRC**   Specifies the source file for the content to be inserted into this frame.

NOTE

The FRAMESPACING, FRAMEBORDER, and BORDERCOLOR attributes may also be used within this tag.

<NOFRAMES> </NOFRAMES>   Inserts alternative information to be displayed to those browsers without support for frames.

TIP

You also want to include alternate navigation in this tag so that search engines will be able to see the other pages within your Web site.

<IFRAME> </IFRAME>   Specifies an inline frame, which is a frame that occurs within the content of a normal page. This tag is not supported by Netscape Navigator.

Special Characters

Because HTML is a markup language, it reserves several characters (called *markup characters*) for use within tags themselves. For this reason, certain keystrokes should not be used as content within paragraphs and should be replaced with their HTML-equivalent codes. Instead of typing the characters shown in the first column of the following list, type the codes in the second column:

Special Character	Replacement Code
<	&LT;
>	&GT;
&	&AMP;
"	&QUOT;
®	&#174;
™	&#153;
©	&#169;

NOTE

Many newer versions of browsers allow for these characters within the body of your text. It is a good idea, however, to avoid using them in case older browsers are used to view your material. Also be aware that although FrontPage allows you to insert many types of symbols, non-Windows-based browsers will likely misrepresent these special characters. For this reason, you should avoid placing nonstandard characters within your text unless you know your viewers will all be using Windows-based browsers.

Cross-Browser Compatibility

Browser compatibility is always a major issue when developing Web sites. Using FrontPage 2002, you can make your life a lot easier by setting up your environment prior to developing your sites. What's more, if you are administering a group that needs to abide by specific browser standards, you will find that doing this will save you the time of explaining why someone's work needs to be redone because it doesn't meet the standards.

Hands On: Setting Your Web Properties to Work with Specific Browsers

With FrontPage 2002, setting your environment to meet specific browser-compatibility standards is accomplished by following these steps:

1. Open or create the Web you want to specify the browser settings for in FrontPage.

2. Select Tools | Page Options from the menu bar. This brings up the Page Options dialog box.

3. Click the Compatibility tab in the Page Options dialog box to bring up the compatibility options, as shown in Figure 2-1.

4. Make your selections based on the criteria you have set up for your Web sites. Selecting from the drop-down lists for browsers, versions, and servers will automatically affect the options available to you when developing. If there are specific items you want to include or disallow, you can select them individually.

5. Click OK.

This takes care of the settings for browser compatibility. Now, when you (or other users) work with the pages within this Web, you will only have access to the commands that fit the compatibility settings you have specified. If you want to change these settings in the future, simply follow the same steps.

Incorporating Custom HTML into Your FrontPage Web

Although FrontPage 2002 allows you to work in a WYSIWYG environment without needing to work with the actual HTML, it also gives you the ability to insert and modify HTML while working in the editor. This can be accomplished in a variety of ways, as you will see in the following discussion.

Inserting HTML into Your Web Within the Editor

FrontPage allows you to insert custom HTML directly into your pages through the use of the HTML Markup dialog box. Using this method, you can insert HTML that will not be altered by FrontPage in any way.

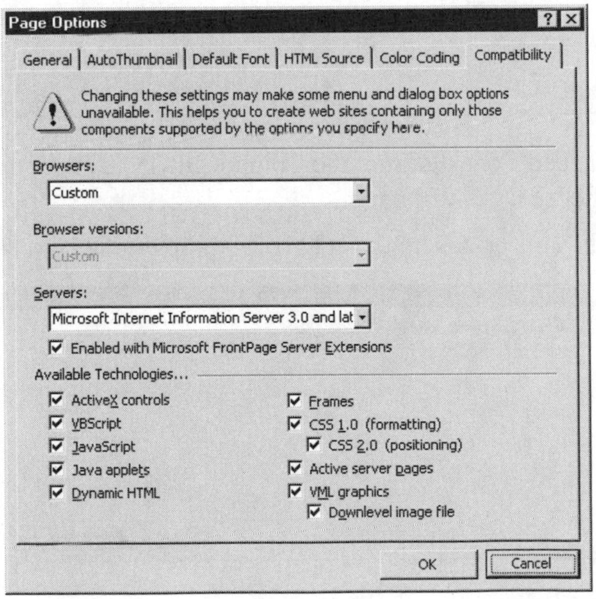

Figure 2-1   *The Compatibility tab of the Page Options dialog box*

NOTE

Incorporating HTML through the HTML Markup dialog box causes it to be ignored by FrontPage when it checks your HTML for accuracy. Be sure your HTML is clean before entering it this way.

To incorporate custom HTML into your pages, follow these steps:

1. Position your cursor where you want to include the HTML.

2. Select Insert | Web Component. This brings up the Insert Web Component dialog box, shown here:

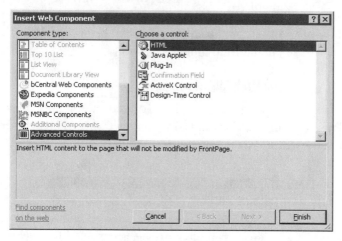

3. Select Advanced Controls from the Component Type pane; then select HTML from the Choose a Control pane.

4. Click Finish. This brings up the HTML Markup dialog box, shown here:

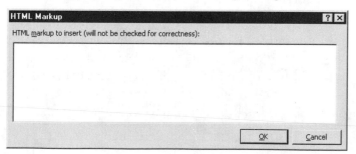

5. Type the HTML exactly as you want it to appear within your document and then click OK.

Your HTML is now embedded within your page as an HTML Markup component, and it will only appear as a yellow box with the characters <?> while in the Normal editor view. You will be able to see the code if you switch to the HTML view in your editor, and it will also appear when you preview the page. To edit the contents of an HTML Markup component within the Normal editor view, double-click it to display the HTML Markup dialog box.

Working with the HTML View

Although you have the ability to enter HTML code into your page using HTML Markup components, the preferred method is to use the HTML view in the editor. Entering your code this way allows you to see it immediately in the Normal view. This also allows FrontPage to check the code to make sure it is correct.

Although there have always been problems with WYSIWYG editors mangling manually edited HTML code, we saw with FrontPage 2000 that great leaps had been make in an attempt to preserve your code exactly as you enter it. This has been further improved with the release of FrontPage 2002.

Within the HTML view, you have all the capabilities of working with a standard text editor, along with many of the same features available when working in the normal (WYSIWYG) view. This way, you can still include all your extended features, and you can see how FrontPage implements them in the page in real time. Working in this view also gives you the ability to edit various aspects of your code directly without the need to open the various dialog boxes necessary when you are working in the Normal view. If FrontPage cannot accurately display your manually edited code, it will warn you before allowing you to switch from the HTML view to the Normal view. The gives you the power to decide whether to risk having FrontPage change your code or to limit editing of the page to the HTML view.

TIP

If you're unsure whether to proceed into the Normal view after being warned that FrontPage might have to change your code, you can always cancel the view change and save a backup copy of your page before continuing. This way, you have the opportunity to inspect FrontPage's code changes and determine for yourself whether they have had any adverse effects on your code. If problems arise, you can simply delete your altered page and rename the backup copy to the original page name.

Revealing Tags in the Editor

Starting with FrontPage 2000, you are given the best of both worlds when working in the Normal view. With the Reveal Tags capability, you can work in a WYSIWYG environment in the normal view while having many of the HTML tags displayed. Working in this view, you have more control over the environment.

One of the best features to come out of the Reveal Tags option is the ability to select the beginning tag in a tag set and have FrontPage highlight all the information that falls between the beginning tag and the ending tag for that set. This not only allows you to organize your layout better but also allows you to check your code layout while working in the WYSIWYG environment.

To view your HTML tags in the normal view, simply select View | Reveal Tags from the menu bar (or press CTRL-/ to toggle the display). When the tags are revealed, your page will look something like the one shown in Figure 2-2.

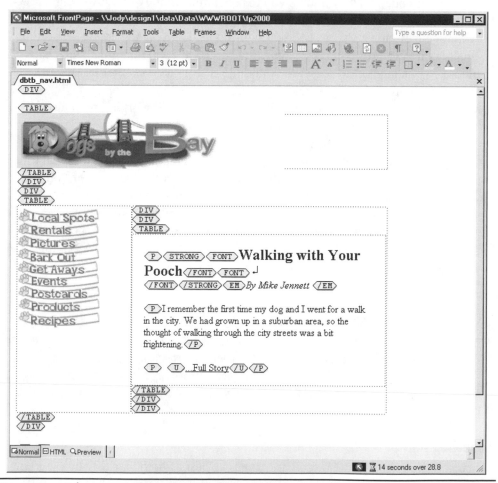

Figure 2-2   *Editor view of FrontPage with Reveal Tags turned on*

Images in Your Webs

As you know, graphics can be a great addition to any Web site. They can be used to display products, show your logo, or provide the navigational backbone of your site. However, there are many things you need to take into consideration when incorporating graphics into your Web site. For example, when you use graphics on a page, you add to the bandwidth necessary to transfer your page from the server to the browser. With higher-speed connections now in rampant use, you may decide that this isn't a problem. However, if you are developing for the Internet, you have to be conscious of the number of people who may still be viewing your site from a low-speed connection.

TIP

FrontPage 2002 includes a nice little addition to the status bar, found at the bottom of the application, that tells you approximately how long the page will take to load with modems of different speeds. The default for this is 28.8, but you can change it by simply right-clicking the modem speed and selecting a different speed from the list.

You also want to be aware that many people will not be viewing your site with a large monitor and a nice graphics card. For these reasons, you want to be sure to test any graphics you incorporate by using various browsers and screen settings to ensure that your images will appear just the way you want them to when someone views your site.

This part of the chapter looks at these problems, along with the best ways to incorporate graphics into your Web site. We will also take a peek at the various graphic formats and the Web-safe color settings that you will need to work with when incorporating your graphics.

Graphic Formats

Two formats are generally accepted for use with graphics on the Web today: the JPG and GIF image formats. Browser technology is moving toward accepting newer formats, such as Portable Network Graphics (PNG), as time goes on, but GIF and JPG are the two most common formats in the industry today. Although you may use either of these formats, there are reasons for using one over the other in certain situations.

GIF Images

GIF stands for *Graphic Image Format*, and it is a technology developed by Unisys for CompuServe for the purpose of compressing graphics down to manageable sizes.

This image format was adopted early by the graphical Web browsers and is one of the most popular formats in use today.

Generally, GIF images are best used to display small graphics, such as buttons, icons, and banners, or images that contain large blocks of solid colors and little detail. The compression used with the GIF format is a *lossless* algorithm, which means that no image information is lost when a graphic is compressed.

When working with the GIF format, you need to realize that it can display a maximum of 256 colors. Although this is the maximum number allowed, you may also create your images with fewer colors, which will cause the image size to be smaller. The set of colors contained in a GIF image is know as its *color palette*.

With GIF images, you can also create interlaced and transparent images. *Interlaced images* display as they load, with the image coming into focus as more of it loads, until the complete image appears. This allows viewers to get an idea of the image displayed as it loads rather than having to wait until the loading is complete. *Transparent images* are just that—transparent. With GIFs, you can choose a color that will not appear when the image is viewed, showing the background page wherever the transparent color appears. In effect, this allows you to layer the image on top of another image, which can be very useful when you are using backgrounds within your pages.

Along with the ability to create interlaced and transparent images, this format allows you to animate your graphic files. This is called *GIF animation* and is available when using the GIF89a format. You create animated GIFs in the same way traditional animations are created—with a sequence of images. You then use a software tool, such as the GIF Construction Set (http://www.mindworkshop.com) or Adobe ImageReady, to combine these images and turn them into an animation.

JPG Images

Unlike GIFs, JPGs can display up to 16.7 million colors (also known as *true-color*), which gives you a more detailed and lifelike look. This number of colors is not really necessary when you are incorporating buttons and icons, but it does become useful when incorporating photographic image work. Also, JPGs use a *lossy* compression method that shrinks the file size based on the quality of image you are looking for. The problem with lossy compression is that the more you compress the image, the less quality you retain.

JPG images also dither much better than GIF images. This means photographic images that should normally be displayed in true-color will look better on systems configured to display only 256 colors when presented in the JPG format.

TIP

A good rule of thumb is to use the JPG format for images that contain a high level of detail or colors and the GIF format for images that contain little detail and a limited color palette. Many of today's image editors provide the ability to preview the result of saving an image in the GIF or JPG format, allowing you to judge for yourself which format is better suited for a particular image.

Web Color Palette

One problem with developing graphics and displaying them within a Web is that the current browsers only support 216 nondithering colors when displayed on a computer configured to display 256 colors (considered the "lowest common denominator" and thus the targeted audience for public Internet sites). For this reason, you need to make sure that the colors you use match what is called the *Web-safe color palette*. Many of the popular graphics programs on the market today, such as Photoshop and Fractal Design Painter, come equipped with Web-safe color palettes for you to use when developing your graphics. If you are not working with a Web-safe color palette, you should be sure to check your graphics on various monitors, video adapters, and color depth settings to ensure that your images appear properly on the screen. By doing so, you will likely discover that when set at 256-color depth display, various video adapters dither colors differently. Higher-quality video cards will show nice solid colors, whereas the same colors will look rather grainy and blotchy on some less expensive cards.

Working with Images in FrontPage

FrontPage allows you to use images extensively when developing your Webs. Once you have created an image, FrontPage allows you to import it into your Web, make modifications to the image properties, and set up a variety of attributes for the image, through the use of the Picture Properties dialog box. This dialog box has three tabs: Appearance, General, and Video. These tabs allow you to set the attributes for the image as well as specify the location and size for the image. Let's look at each aspect of the dialog box and the options available to you while working in it.

The following options are available on the Appearance tab of the Picture Properties dialog box, shown in Figure 2-3:

▶ **Wrapping style**   Allows you to specify how the text appearing around the image will wrap. There are three settings to this aspect of the dialog box: None, Left, and Right.

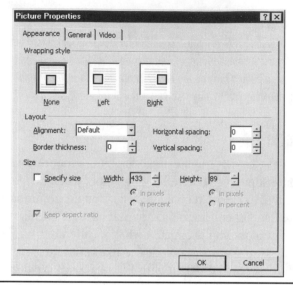

Figure 2-3 *The Appearance tab of the Picture Properties dialog box*

The None option specifies that the image should appear exactly where inserted with no text-wrapping attributes. The Left and Right options specify that the text should wrap to the left and right sides of the image, respectively.

▶ **Layout** Allows you to specify where the image will appear within the browser window compared to other items, along with the buffering space (horizontal and vertical spacing) that will be incorporated into the image. This spacing allows you to have a specific number of pixels between the image and any other content on the page. If you do not specify a certain number of pixels, any text will be placed right next to the image.

You can also set a border around your image in this area. You can use a border to identify the image as a hyperlink or to create a frame around the image.

▶ **Size** Allows you to specify the size of the image as it appears within the browser. You can set the size any way you want, but it is important to know that any change in size will affect the appearance of the image when viewed. Also, if you want your image to shrink but have the same proportional layout, you will want to select the Keep Aspect Ratio check box. This instructs FrontPage to size your image proportionally.

TIP

Due to bandwidth and Web site storage considerations, it is generally not good practice to set an image's size smaller than the actual image size. Instead, shrink the image to the actual size required. This way, the user doesn't have to download a 200KB image in order to view it in a size that could be accomplished with a 15KB image. See "When Not to Use Image Sizing," later in this chapter.

The following options are available on the General tab of the Picture Properties dialog box, shown in Figure 2-4:

▶ **Picture source**   Specifies the location of the image file you are working with. If you do not know the path for the image file, you may click the Browse button to select a file from your current Web, your hard drive, or the Internet. When selecting a file from your hard drive, FrontPage will automatically prompt you to save the file within your Web when saving the current page. Be aware, however, that FrontPage will not allow you to directly save an image that resides on the Internet within your Web. Instead, it will simply save the image source as the current URL (Web address) of the image. Although this may sometimes be desirable, you should make sure that such an external image

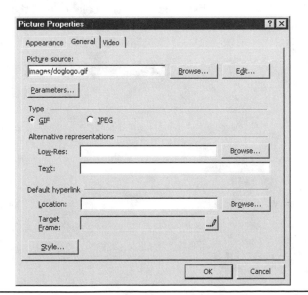

Figure 2-4   *The General tab of the Picture Properties dialog box*

will always be available at its specified URL before linking to it within your Web site. If that image is ever removed from that location, it will appear as a broken link within your site. When in doubt, save a copy of the image to your Web and then link to it within FrontPage.

▶ **Type**   Allows you to specify what type of image you are incorporating. In this section, you may specify that the image is in a GIF or JPG format. You may also specify the attributes associated with these image formats.

▶ **Alternative representations**   Allows you to specify a low-resolution image to be displayed while the main image is being loaded, along with alternative text to display in place of the image.

▶ **Default hyperlink**   Allows you to specify a hyperlink to be associated with the image. The hyperlink will be loaded when a user clicks the image.

The following options are available on the Video tab of the Picture Properties dialog box, shown in Figure 2-5:

▶ **Video source**   Specifies the path to the video file you are incorporating into the page. If you do not know the path, you may click the Browse button to select the file from the file list. The same file selection and save options that apply to standard images also apply to videos.

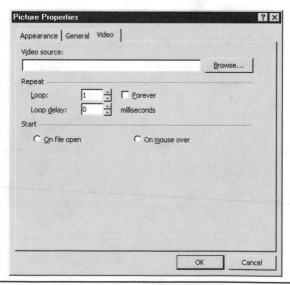

Figure 2-5   *The Video tab of the Picture Properties dialog box*

▶ **Repeat**   Allows you to specify how often the video clip will play when viewed in a browser. Within these settings, you may specify that the clip repeats (loops) a specific number of times or forever. You can also specify how long the browser should wait until reloading the clip in a loop sequence.

▶ **Start**   Allows you to specify when the embedded video clip will begin playing. This is useful if your clip does not appear in the uppermost frame of the page, because you can specify that the clip not begin playing until the user moves the mouse over the clip. This way, the user will not miss any of the action shown in the clip that would otherwise play out of view. The available options here are On File Open and On Mouse Over.

Image Sizing Tips and Tricks

FrontPage allows you to size your images in a number of ways, but there are some caveats to sizing images, along with a trick that will help you design a custom layout using image sizing.

When Not to Use Image Sizing   When working with a photographic image, you will rarely want to change the default display size of the image. If you increase the size, the image will look grainy. If you decrease the size, you will be adding needless image file size and thus increasing download time with no benefit to the viewer. You've probably experienced waiting an extremely long period of time for a page to load, only to find that an inexperienced designer has included a huge image in the page and simply lowered its display size instead of actually making the image smaller to fit the desired area. Don't get caught making this mistake.

Fun with One-Pixel GIFs   The true beauty of image size attributes is the ability to take a one-pixel, solid-color GIF and stretch it to fit your size needs. Because the color is solid and the image contains no additional details, you can display a 1x1-pixel GIF in any size without distortion or loss of any kind. What's more, because the source image is still only one pixel in size, the image takes less than 1,000 bytes (1KB) of storage space. This can be especially useful with horizontal and vertical lines.

You can also set an image size to be a mix of several fixed pixels by a percentage of the page height or width. For example, you can create a horizontal line that will stretch and shrink as necessary to cover 80 percent of the page, regardless of the browser's window size, while always maintaining its five-pixel height. Another particularly useful aspect of one-pixel GIFs is the ability to make their single color transparent, thus giving you an invisible spacer, which can be used to intercede in the browser's tendency to move things around to make them fit the way it wants, without regard to your design.

Working with Image Maps

Image maps allow you to create multiple links within a single image. This can be very useful when you're working with navigational layouts and diagrams. What they do is create a set of coordinates that the browser uses to determine what links you are incorporating on your image. Client-side image maps have become the standard for Web design today, replacing the old server-side style of image map, which required a call to the server to retrieve the link associated with your coordinates. Client-side image maps are embedded within the HTML code using the standard <MAP> HTML tag, which greatly enhances performance. Furthermore, when you use client-side image maps, users can see the actual link in the status bar when they move their mouse over the image. This is in contrast to the old server-side image maps, which only displayed the image coordinates in the status bar when users moved their mouse over the image.

FrontPage makes incorporating the maps into your Web easy through the use of the image map tools on the right side of the Pictures toolbar, as shown here:

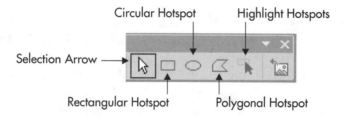

To incorporate an image map into your Web, follow these steps:

1. Insert an image into your page. For this example, we will use the navigation bar for the Dogs by the Bay page found on the CD.

2. Select the image by clicking it with your mouse. You will see the anchor points appear around the image, as shown in Figure 2-6.

3. You will now want to create links to various pages from this image. To do so, select the Rectangular Hotspot button.

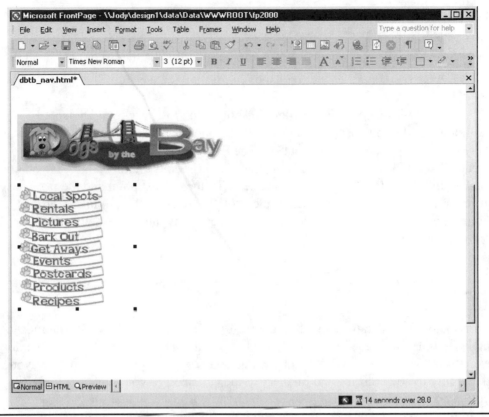

Figure 2-6   *Selected navigation bar image with anchor points*

4. Hold down your mouse button and drag the cursor across the portion of the image you want to create the hotspot for, as shown here:

5. Release the mouse when you have chosen the area you want for the hotspot. The Create Hyperlink dialog box now appears.

6. Select the file you want this hotspot to link to from the file list or type in a URL.

7. Repeat these steps for each hotspot you want to create.

You may also choose the Circular Hotspot button to create round hotspots (although the button's image is an oval, it can only make circular hotspots), or you may use the Polygonal Hotspot button. The Polygonal Hotspot tool allows you to create custom-shaped hotspots by clicking various points on the image. As you click each point, the hotspot will draw a line between the current point and the previous point. When you finally come full circle and click back on the original (starting) point, the Create Hyperlink dialog box will open, allowing you to select the target for your new image map hotspot link.

Table Layout

FrontPage 2002 is equipped with many features that allow you to make the most of table design within your Web site. The program allows you to create tables that look exactly the way you want them to by using a variety of methods. It also gives you the ability to add coloring and imagery to the table design you implement, giving you even more options when it comes to creating a look and feel for your page.

In this part of the chapter, we are going to look at the features available in FrontPage 2002 for creating tables, along with some advanced tips on using tables to create exceptional layouts within your pages.

Design Layouts Using Tables

Using tables to lay out a Web site has become pretty standard these days. Tables allow for much more control over the design elements of your page in the way of placement of text and graphics than was traditionally available with HTML. When we look at pages today, we see nicely organized text and graphics created using borderless tables that are transparent when viewed with the browser.

There are many uses for tables in designing your page layouts, especially when it comes to standard navigational layouts, such as those sites that have a sidebar navigation system. Using a table layout, you can create two columns—one holding your sidebar navigation and the other containing the body of your page.

Another common and more traditional use of tables is the columnar display of information. Tools such as Microsoft Excel and Microsoft Access use this format as a primary method of displaying volumes of categorized records. Because FrontPage is part of the Office family of products, it should come as no surprise that you can highlight portions of Access tables or Excel spreadsheets, copy them, and then paste them right into an open page within FrontPage's editor. With the addition of HTML as one of the native file formats in Office, FrontPage does an excellent job of maintaining the source table's formatting.

Hands On: Importing Delimited Text as a Table

If you work with databases, this Hands On exercise is for you. Have you ever had delimited database information that you needed to display on the Web? If so, you probably know how difficult it is to create the table layouts necessary, even in FrontPage. Well, here is a trick that will make creating tables from delimited text a problem that you are not afraid to face anymore.

Follow these steps to quickly change a set of delimited text into a nice clean table in FrontPage:

1. Open the file containing your delimited text.

2. Copy the text and paste it into your FrontPage document.

3. Select the text.

4. Select Table | Convert | Text to Table from the menu bar. This brings up the Convert Text to Table dialog box, shown here:

5. Select the delimiter from the available options and click OK. Your text now appears in an HTML table that you can edit using the various table tools.

Working with Backgrounds

More than likely you've seen colored backgrounds and background images used in HTML pages. As a matter of fact, they became almost as bad as the dreaded <BLINK> tag when people first started using them. But you will see that proper backgrounds can enhance the overall look and feel of a page. This same thinking goes into the use of background colors and images within tables. You can use various colors to emphasize the text within particular table cells. Also, you can add background images to your table cells to attain certain effects.

Using background images in your tables can be extremely useful when you are creating navigational layouts and certain layout effects. This example shows you how to incorporate a background image behind a navigational bar to continue the sidebar image found above it. For this example, we will be using images on the included CD-ROM. You can use these images or create a similar layout using your own images. Here are the steps:

1. Create a one-column table and insert the image doglogo.gif. This image contains a background design that we want to match on the navigation bar, which we will insert next.

NOTE

Be sure to set your cell padding and cell spacing to zero so that there will be no breaks between the cells.

2. Create a new table with two columns in your page. The left column will contain our background image, and the right will be used for our content.

3. Highlight the entire table and select Table | Table Properties | Cell from the menu bar. This brings up the Cell Properties dialog box. (The Cell Properties dialog box is described in more detail later in the chapter, in the section "Adjusting Cell Properties.")

4. Set Vertical Alignment to Top.

5. Select Use Background Picture and type the path for the background image you want inserted (for example, images/backgrounddbtb.gif found on the CD).

6. Specify the height and width for this table cell based on the size and height of the image.

NOTE

All background images tile when inserted (they repeat across the available space), so it is a good idea to match your cell size with your image size.

7. Click OK. Your image will now appear within the table cell, as shown in Figure 2-7.

   The image shown in Figure 2-7 looks as if it appears inside the table cell, but it actually appears behind the table cell. This allows you to place images within the cell, as you will see in the remaining steps.

   We now want to insert our navigation bar into the table cell. To do so, continue with these steps:

8. Select Insert | Picture | From File from the menu bar.

9. Select the image you want to use for your navigation bar. For this example, select navbardbtb.gif from the images directory (which you can import from the CD).

10. Click OK. Your navigation image now appears on top of the background.

11. As you can see in Figure 2-8, our navigation image covers the background image, so we need to make its background transparent. Select the image and click the Set Transparent Color button (represented by a pencil with an eraser) on the Picture toolbar.

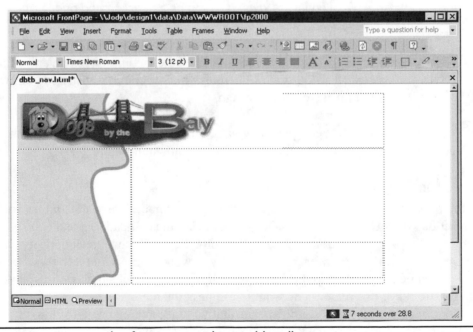

Figure 2-7   *An example of an image within a table cell*

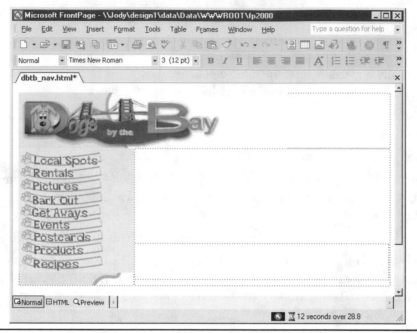

Figure 2-8   *An example of an image layered on top of the background prior to the transparency being set*

12. Move the pencil over the light blue portion of the navigation image and click it with your mouse. This portion of the image now becomes transparent, allowing the background image to show through.

You should now have a complete navigational layout containing a background that continues fluidly from the image above it, as shown in Figure 2-9.

Nested Tables

In the previous section, we discussed having images appear in separate tables with a continuous flow. This is accomplished by adjusting the cell padding and cell spacing options to zero. If the options are not set to zero, there will be a break between the images. This works nicely for images, but if you were to insert text into these tables, it would appear right next to the image, which is not a very clean way of displaying information. For this reason, you want to use nested tables.

The use of nested tables simply means that you incorporate one table into another. This allows you to determine the settings of specific elements of your page without affecting the other elements. I will demonstrate this using the same example used for incorporating background images into your pages, taking it one step further by incorporating content. Here are the steps to follow:

1. Working with the page created in the previous section, position your cursor in the table cell on the right, which was previously left blank.

NOTE

If you have not performed the Hands On exercise, you can import the files found on the CD-ROM in the directory DBTB2.

2. Select Table | Insert | Table from the menu bar. This brings up the Insert Table dialog box, shown here:

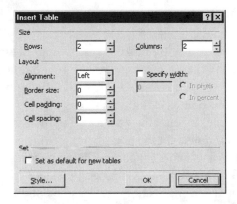

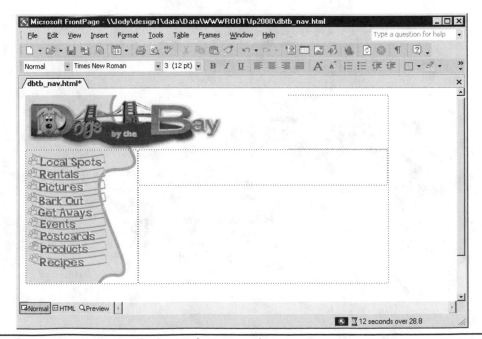

Figure 2-9   *An example of a layered image with transparency set*

3. Select one row and one column and then set the cell spacing to 5. This will give us a five-pixel pad between this table and the outside table.

4. Click OK.

5. Enter the text you want to include within this newly created table cell. As you can see from Figure 2-10, the text you enter here is spaced away from the parent table and does not affect the spacing between the graphics.

Table Properties

When working with tables, you will undoubtedly want to change them as you go along. In my experience, creating a table that works perfectly when it appears on the screen is a rare occurrence. I usually make about a hundred changes to the layout as I go along—anything from merging cells to removing columns. For this reason, the FrontPage 2002 Cell Properties and Table Properties dialog boxes are the most important tools you have when working with tables.

Yes, you can adjust tables by clicking and dragging their inner and outer borders within the editor, but you cannot get the pixel-perfect adjustments that are available within the Cell Properties and Table Properties dialog boxes. Furthermore, these dialog boxes allow you to add background images, specify exact width, and take advantage of many other options. The following sections outline the options available to you within these dialog boxes and how to work with them.

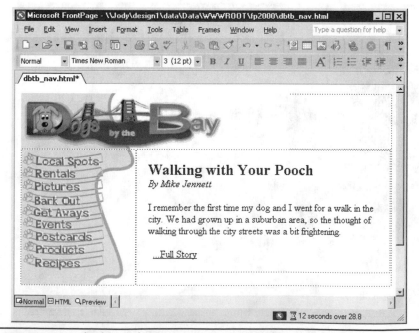

Figure 2-10   *A nested table within a page*

Hands On: Creating a Table to Align Your Forms

When you create a form on a page, the various elements appear on the screen in a linear fashion, causing them to wrap at the end of the available space in the browser. This may cause your forms to appear in a way you did not intend. For this reason, it is a good idea to create a table within your form that will hold the form elements. This way, you have complete control over the layout of the form on the page. To accomplish this, follow these steps:

1. Select the HTML view in your editor and select Insert | Form | Form. This will insert the <FORM> </FORM> tags into your HTML.

2. Position your cursor after the <FORM> tag and select Table | Insert | Table. This brings up the Insert Table dialog box. Select the settings you want for your table and click OK.

3. Switch back to the normal view in your editor. You will now see the table you created with a dotted line surrounding it. The dotted line represents the form.

4. You may now insert your form elements into the table as you would like them to appear on the page. Figure 2-11 displays an example of a form designed within a table.

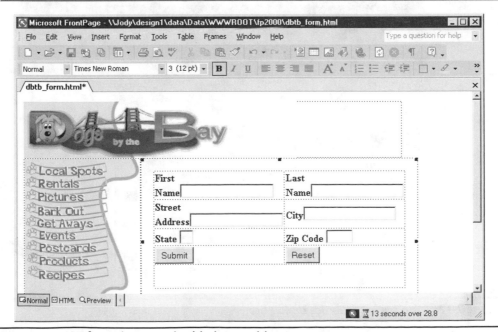

Figure 2-11   *A form design embedded in a table*

Adjusting Overall Table Properties

When working with a table, you will probably need to make adjustments and additions to the table as you go along. The bulk of this work is accomplished using the Table Properties dialog box, shown in Figure 2-12. Although many adjustments can be made using the Table toolbar, discussed a little later in the chapter, the Table Properties dialog box allows you to make changes and additions to your entire table layout. Within this dialog box, you have a variety of options, as outlined here.

Let's start with the options in the Layout section:

▶ **Alignment**   Determines where your table appears on the screen.

▶ **Float**   Allows you to create a table that lets text outside the table wrap around it. This is much like the alignment settings used for images.

▶ **Cell padding**   Allows you to specify the number of pixels of space inserted between the table border and the text inside the table cell.

▶ **Cell spacing**   Allows you to specify the number of pixels between the outer edge and the inner edge of the table cells.

▶ **Specify width**   Allows you to set the width of the entire table. This may be set to an exact number of pixels or as a percentage of the screen.

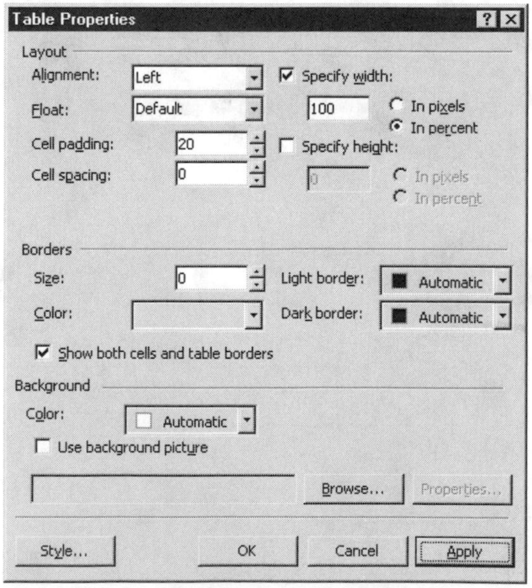

Figure 2-12   *The Table Properties dialog box*

NOTE

Setting your width to a percentage of the screen will cause the table size to adjust based on the viewer's screen size.

▶ **Specify height**   Allows you to set the height of the entire table. This may also be set to an exact number of pixels or as a percentage of the screen.

NOTE

When working within a nested table, these size percentages apply to the parent table cell instead of the overall screen.

The Borders options affect the colors associated with your table borders. The settings available to you are as follows:

▶ **Size**   Allows you to specify the size of the border around your table. If you select a border, you may also want to customize your border colors with the border color options.

▶ **Color**   Specifies an outline color for your entire border.

▶ **Light Border**   Overrides any color settings associated with the light shaded area of the table border.

▶ **Dark Border**   Overrides any color settings associated with the dark shaded area of the table border.

▶ **Show both cells and table borders**   Instructs FrontPage to display both your overall table border and the underlying cell borders.

▶ **Background**   Allows you to specify whether the table will have a custom color or a custom image. You can select a custom color from the Color drop-down list, or you can select Use Background Picture and enter the path for the image. The color or image will appear behind all table cells within the table.

NOTE

To view background images in tables or cells, the viewer must be using Internet Explorer version 3.0 or higher or Netscape's Communicator version 4.0 or higher.

Adjusting Cell Properties

Once you have developed your tables, you may find that you want to alter the look and feel of individual cells for better control over the layout of the table. FrontPage 2002 gives you the ability to modify many aspects of each cell you create within a table. These attributes are modified through the use of the Cell Properties dialog box, shown in Figure 2-13.

The Layout options control the overall placement of the text within your cell and specify the type of cell you are working with. The following options are available to you:

▶ **Horizontal alignment**   Specifies where within the cell your text will appear on the horizontal axis.

▶ **Vertical alignment**   Specifies where within the cell your text will appear on the vertical axis.

▶ **Rows spanned**   Specifies the number of rows, within the table, this cell will span.

▶ **Columns spanned**   Specifies the number of columns, within the table, this cell will span.

▶ **Header cell**   Instructs FrontPage to modify the code for the cell to the <TH> tag, turning the cell into a table header cell rather than a content cell. As described earlier in the HTML reference section of the chapter, the contents of table header cells are normally centered and boldfaced.

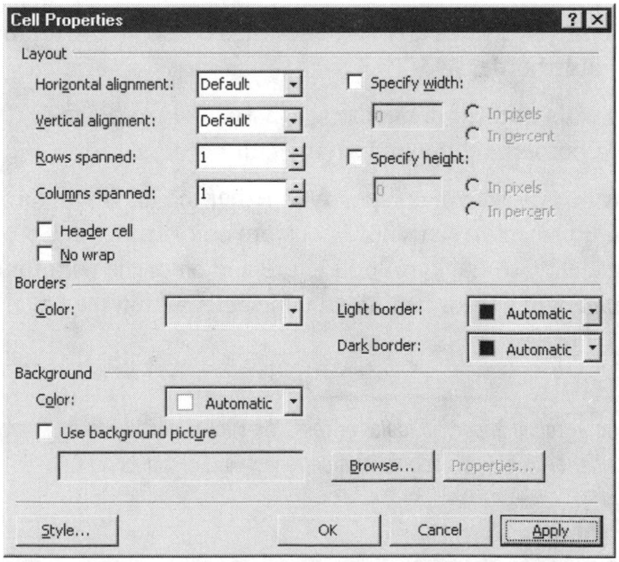

Figure 2-13   *The Cell Properties dialog box*

▶ **No wrap**   Instructs FrontPage not to wrap the text when it reaches the end of a line. Text breaks will only appear when a carriage return or line break is inserted into the code.

▶ **Specify width**   Allows you to set the width of the cell. This may be set to an exact number of pixels or as a percentage of the parent table.

NOTE

Setting your width to a percentage of the parent table will cause the cell size to adjust based on the viewer's screen settings and those of the parent table.

▶ **Specify height**   Allows you to set the height of the cell. This may also be set to an exact number of pixels or as a percentage of the parent table.

The Borders settings affect the colors associated with your cell's borders. There are three settings available to you:

▶ **Color**   Specifies an outline color for your entire cell border

▶ **Light border**   Overrides any color settings associated with the light shaded area of the cell border

▶ **Dark border**   Overrides any color settings associated with the dark shaded area of the cell border

Within the Background section, you have two options:

▶ **Color**   Specifies the color settings for the cell

▶ **Use background picture**   Specifies a background image for the cell

Table Toolbar

Using the Table toolbar, you can create a table and also edit many of its properties without having to open any property dialog boxes. Table 2-1 describes what each function of the Table toolbar accomplishes.

Button	Name	Description
	Draw Table	Allows you to create a table by drawing the various cells and columns.
	Eraser	Lets you remove specific columns and cells from your table.
	Insert Rows	Inserts a row above the current location of the cursor.
	Insert Columns	Inserts a column to the left of the current location of the cursor.
	Delete Cells	Deletes the currently selected cell(s).
	Merge Cells	Merges the currently selected cells.
	Split Cells	Brings up the Split Cells dialog box, allowing you to specify the number of rows or columns you want the cell split into.
	Align Top	Aligns the content to the top of the cell.
	Center Vertically	Aligns the content in the center of the cell.
	Align Bottom	Aligns the content to the bottom of the cell.
	Distribute Rows Evenly	Balances the size of all selected rows.
	Distribute Columns Evenly	Balances the size of all selected columns.

Table 2-1   *The Table Toolbar*

Button	Name	Description
	Autofit	Removes the width setting from the HTML code.
	Fill Color	Allows you to specify a color for the current cell(s).
None ▼	Table AutoFormat Combo	A drop-down menu that allows you to select from various predetermined look-and-feel settings for your table.
	Table AutoFormat	Brings up the Table AutoFormat dialog box, allowing you to select a look and feel for your table.
	Fill Down	Allows you to fill a selected column with the content in the topmost selected cell. Only available when multiple cells are selected.
	Fill Right	Allows you to fill a selected row with the content in the row furthest to the left of the selection. Only available when multiple cells are selected.

Table 2-1   *The Table Toolbar* (continued)

Advanced Frame Layout and Development

Frames are coming into use more and more as the Web matures. In the early days, the use of frames was an exciting addition to browser capabilities that quickly turned into a monster. Like background images and many other new innovations, frames became overused and improperly used. This led many developers to abandon frames altogether. Now that things have settled down a bit, it has become apparent that the proper usage of frames can add a great deal of functionality to your Web site. Whether you use them simply for navigational purposes or to create a complete design layout, frames can be a useful addition to your pages, when used properly.

In this part of the chapter, you will see, hands on, how to create a framed site through the use of the FrontPage templates, but we will also delve into the advanced Web applications of frames. This includes the incorporation of inline frames within your site and the development of controlled frame layouts within new site windows.

You will also see some ways of making the most of what FrontPage has to offer for frame creation, setup, and editing, along with some tricks you can do using FrontPage that might surprise you or, at the very least, be useful in your developments.

To Use or Not to Use Frames

Many people have come to believe that frames should not be used under any circumstances. This was definitely the case in the early days of frames when designers incorporated them just because they had the capability to do so. The overuse and incorrect use of frames caused a backlash that the technology has had a lot of trouble overcoming, even though frames can be extremely useful within certain site structures.

One of the most useful aspects of incorporating frames into a Web site is that of navigation. With the use of frames, you can create a navigational layout that appears when users first enter your site and remains throughout their stay. Frames are also useful when items such as large images or your company's logo are loaded into a Web site and remain throughout the site. Loading these items when users first enter the site and keeping them there allows your visitors to move throughout the site without using up bandwidth every time they load a new page.

Frames are not always the answer to a Web site's needs though, and they should not be used just for the sake of incorporating the technology. One prime example of when frames should not be used is when your navigation system changes every time the user enters a new section of the site. If the navigation changes, you end up reloading the page containing the navigational information anyway. Unless you have a page that causes the user to scroll quite a bit within the site, this use of frames is extraneous, at best.

If you do choose to incorporate frames into your site, be sure to create them in a way that will add value to the site and its content. Check the frame structure on various browsers to ensure compatibility, and whatever you do, don't overuse them.

Reserved Frame Names

You can use just about any name you want when you name the frames in your set. It is a good idea, however, to keep in mind that you need to remember these names when linking from frame to frame. Also, some frame names are reserved (have special meanings) when specified as a link's target. Because of their special meanings, they should not be used as frame names. The functionality of these reserved target names is described here:

Target Name	Description
_blank	Using this target name causes the browser to open a new blank window and loads the linked document into that window
_self	Using this target name loads the linked document into the same frame as the link
_parent	Using this target name loads the linked document into the parent frame of the frame containing the link
_top	Using this target name loads the linked document into the whole window, removing the frameset from the screen

Working with Frames in FrontPage 2002

FrontPage 2002 comes with various frame templates that allow you to easily and quickly create a frameset for your Web. The following sections cover frame integration using these templates, along with some tips on optimizing your layout using FrontPage.

Creating a Frame Layout

Creating a custom frameset is easily accomplished through the use of the FrontPage templates. We'll use one of these templates to step through the creation of a basic frameset here. Once you have created your frameset, take a look through the rest of this chapter to see how you can optimize your frames. Here are the steps:

1. Select File | New | Page or Web from the menu bar. This brings up the New Page or Web pane.

2. Click Page Templates to bring up the Page Templates dialog box.

3. Select the Frames Pages tab to bring up the various templates available to you. For the purposes of this example, select the Banner and Contents template.

4. Click OK. FrontPage will now create a frameset based on the template you selected.

   As you can see, FrontPage has created placeholders for the pages that will appear within your frameset. It has also added some extra editor views to the tab list at the bottom of the screen (for more information on these tabs, see "Frames Tabs in the Editor," later in this chapter). It is now necessary for you to set up the frameset you have just created by selecting the files that will be contained within the set. For this example, we will set up the top banner frame with a new page.

5. Click New Page. A blank page will appear within this frame. You may now edit this page as you would any other page within the Editor tab. Although it may sometimes be tempting to leave a frame's starting page undefined, doing so will break an empty frame's functionality in many browsers. Therefore, if you want a frame to start out blank (containing no content), create and save a blank document and specify that page instead of leaving the Initial Page attribute empty.

6. Repeat step 5 for the other two pages.

NOTE

If you already have a page that you want to appear in the frame, click Set Initial Page and select a page from your Web.

7. Save your pages by clicking File | Save. FrontPage will prompt you to save the individual frame content page(s) first and then the main frames page.

Setting Frame Properties

Once you create a frameset, FrontPage allows you to modify the look and feel of each of the frames appearing within your frameset. With FrontPage, you can set your initial frame page, along with the size of the frame and other features associated with the frame's page. You accomplish this through the use of the Frame Properties dialog box, shown in Figure 2-14.

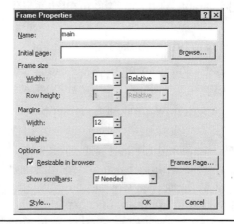

Figure 2-14   *The Frame Properties dialog box*

To adjust your frame page layout, follow these steps:

1. Create a frameset within FrontPage and select or create content pages for each of the frames.

2. Once your frameset is in place, in the Normal view, select the frame page whose properties you want to adjust.

3. Right-click to bring up your options menu.

4. Select Frame Properties from the menu. This brings up the Frame Properties dialog box, shown in Figure 2-14.

5. Adjust your frame page options and click OK. The following list explains the options available to you:

   ▶ **Name**   The target name for the selected frame. The target name is used by links within your frameset to determine where to display a particular page.

   ▶ **Initial page**   The page that will load when you load your frameset. As previously mentioned, leaving this setting blank may cause your frameset to misbehave in some browsers. Always specify a page here, even if it's just a dummy blank page.

   ▶ **Frame size (Width and Row Height)**   The width and height you want this frame to occupy within your frameset. You may set the width in any of the following ways, keeping in mind that adjusting a frame within this dialog box will have a direct effect on the other frames in your set:

      ▶ **Relative**   Specifies that this frame size will be set in relation to the other frames in the same row, as long as the other frames have specified settings in them. If you select Relative, you will normally want to set the left-hand box (containing numbers) to 1.

      ▶ **Percent**   Specifies that the corresponding frame dimension should load as a percentage of the entire page. This setting is best used if you do not know what resolution the user's screen will be set to and you want your frames to take up a specific portion of the available browser window.

      ▶ **Pixels**   Specifies that the frame should be sized to an exact number of pixels on the screen, regardless of the user's screen resolution or window size. This option is particularly useful in top or side navigation frames where you always want a persistent size, regardless of the user's screen resolution or browser window size.

NOTE

These adjustments can also be visually made within the Normal tab of the FrontPage editor by dragging your frame borders to the desired size. Do this by positioning the cursor over a frame border until the double arrow appears. Hold down the left mouse button and drag the frame to the desired position on the screen. Unlike previous versions, FrontPage 2002 will not change your frame's measurement style (Relative, Percent, or Pixels) when you drag it to its desired position.

▶ **Margin Width**   The amount of space that will appear between the left and right edges of the frame and the content within. This option works in conjunction with the content page's left margin setting.

▶ **Margin Height**   The amount of space that will appear between the top and bottom of the frame and the content within. This option works in conjunction with the content page's top margin setting.

▶ **Resizable in Browser check box**   When checked, this option instructs the browser to allow users to resize the frame when viewing your pages. Frames are resizable by default, and this option should only be unchecked if you are sure you do not want to allow users to change the look of your frameset. Nonresizable frames should normally only be used in conjunction with the Pixels measurement style, because auto-resizing frames are much more likely to require user intervention for proper viewing.

▶ **Frames Page button**   Clicking this button brings up a special version of the Page Properties dialog box containing a Frames tab. In addition to specifying normal page properties for the frame's page, you can also set the frame's spacing (frame border width) and select whether to display the frame borders with the Show Borders check box.

▶ **Show scrollbars**   Specifies whether and when scroll bars will appear within your frame. You may choose one of the following settings:

 ▶ **If Needed**   Instructs the system to display scroll bars only when the content of the frame appears outside the viewable area of the page.

 ▶ **Never**   Instructs the system not to display scroll bars at all.

▶ **Always**   Instructs the system to display scroll bars whether they are needed or not. Once again, nonscrolling frames should normally be used only in conjunction with the Pixels measurement style.

CAUTION

Setting the Show Scrollbars option to Never may cause users to miss important information inside your page. If there is any chance that a user will not be able to see all the information within the page, select an option other than Never.

Editing Frame Layouts in FrontPage

As a developer, you know how important it is to properly lay out your frames to avoid a mass of unwanted e-mails from users who do not like frames. Careful editing of your frames will help you to create layouts using FrontPage that will enhance your Web site.

Frames come with visible gray borders. In the early days of frames, this was one of the great drawbacks of using frames within your site. Even though they allowed for extended navigation and other interesting effects, the fact that you had to have a gray border between each layer of content impeded their usefulness with graphical layouts and the like. With the onset of newer browser technologies, you can now create cohesive graphical layouts using frames, without the hindrance of forced visible borders. To remove or adjust your frame borders, follow these steps:

1. Open your main frameset file.

2. Select Frames | Frame Properties from the menu bar. This brings up the Frame Properties dialog box, shown previously in Figure 2-14.

3. Click the Frames Page button to bring up the Page Properties dialog box. This will default to the Frames tab.

4. Uncheck Show Borders and click OK. FrontPage will now remove borders from your frameset by adding the Frameborder="0" tag to your frameset.

If you have multiple nested framesets, you have the option of removing the border from specific frames. This must be done in the HTML, though, because FrontPage's option controls the entire frameset. If you want to have a frameset that, say, has a border between the top and bottom frames, but no border between the left and right frames, you would want to adjust your frameset's code to look like what's shown here:

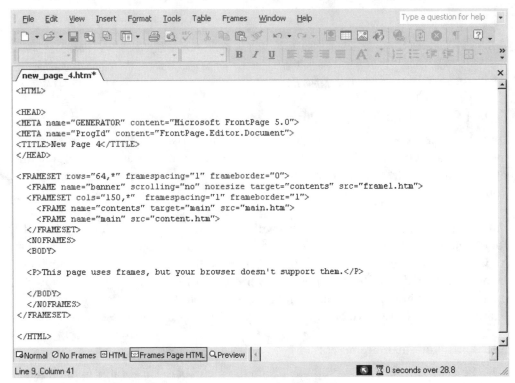

As you can see, the main frameset contains the frameborder="0" tag, whereas the subset contains a border setting of frameborder="1". This allows you a bit more control over how your frames are displayed.

If you want to display frame borders, but wish to alter their thickness, you may do so by leaving Show Borders checked and adjusting the Frame Spacing attribute. Also, you can adjust the spacing for your frames the same way by unchecking Show Borders but assigning a number to Frame Spacing.

Frames Tabs in the Editor

When you create a frameset in FrontPage, you will see two extra tabs added to the editor window: the No Frames and Frames Page HTML tabs. These tabs allow you to control the way your frameset is displayed within frame-supporting browsers and those that do not support frames. These special views are used as follows:

▶ **No Frames**   Allows you to input information that will display if the browser viewing your page does not support frames. This is usually a notice informing users that their browser does not support frames, but it is a good idea to include some form of alternative navigation to allow those visitors to view the information within your Web site. As you will see in the section "Making Sure Search Engines Find Your Information," later in this chapter, this is also what search engines will read when encountering your frameset.

▶ **Frames Page HTML**   Allows you to view and modify the page containing your frameset definition. This is the information that tells the browser which pages to bring up in the frames, along with the frame layout, sizing, and other attributes.

Creating Inline Frames in Your Web Site

With inline frames, you can have a standard HTML page with an embedded frame, allowing the user to scroll through material without having to scroll through the page.

CAUTION

Inline frames will only work in Internet Explorer 3.0 and higher and Netscape Navigator 6.0 and higher. They are not currently compatible with other browsers.

Because inline frames only work within Internet Explorer and Netscape's latest browsers, they have all but been ignored by most of the development community. However, if you work exclusively with Internet Explorer or are not worried about incompatibility with Netscape's older browsers, inline frames are a great feature to add to a Web site.

Many intranet projects I have worked on have been based on Microsoft products being used in a controlled environment. Inline frames have allowed me to create cutting-edge designs that would have been extremely difficult, if not impossible, to create without them. The following sections explain, in detail, how to integrate inline frames into your site, along with some interesting integration techniques.

How Inline Frames Work

An inline frame is a Microsoft HTML extension that works only in IE 3.0 and higher and Netscape Navigator 6.0 and higher. It consists of an embedded tag that instructs the browser to bring up a page that you have specified in the Inline frame tag. The following illustrates the inline frame tags:

```
<IFRAME NAME="body" width="400" height="244" SRC="body.html">
Inline frames are used in this site, and can only be seen
by IE 3 or above and Netscape Navigator 6 or above</IFRAME>
```

The frame SRC instructs the browser to place the file specified into this position in your document. If the browser viewing the document is not inline frame enabled, it will display the message between the <IFRAME> tags—in this case, "Inline frames are used in this site, and can only be seen by IE 3 or above and Netscape Navigator 6 and above".

CAUTION

Test your inline frame in a noncompliant browser to ensure that it does not affect your layout.

Because inline frames are not compatible with many of the browsers in use today, it is a good idea to have a substitute in place just in case your inline frame isn't visible. Luckily, FrontPage 2002 gives you exactly the tools you need to take care of this. With the use of the Include Page Component, you can create a page that will display your inline frame for those who can see it, and you can also afford those who can't an alternative way of viewing the information without changing browsers.

Using the Include Page option works quite well if your page is small enough so that the user will not be scrolling within the frame, or you do not mind the layout changing a bit if the user is not working with Internet Explorer. If, however, you are working with a large document that will be included within the frame, you will want to take another approach. For this problem, you would want to use a bit of JavaScript to detect the user's browser type and version and then direct the user to a different page. The page the user is directed to can be set up as a standard frame page that displays the text in a manner suited for the browser.

This may seem like quite a bit of extra work just to incorporate a feature that is unsupported by many browsers, but it can add a new dimension to your Web site if you are willing to put in the effort.

Integrating Inline Frames

The following instructions demonstrate how to go about integrating inline frames into your Web site. The Hands On exercise that follows covers the added features necessary to allow all browsers to view your content when they are not inline frame enabled. Here are the steps:

1. Lay out your page as you want it displayed in the browser. For this example, we will be creating a two-column table with a width of 600 pixels. The first column will contain our inline frame, with a width of 315 pixels, and the second will contain an image, with the column having a width of 285 pixels.

2. In the right column, insert the picture puppy.jpg, found on the CD included with this book.

    Now it is necessary to create the description page that will be included within our page. To do so, create a normal HTML page within FrontPage with some descriptive information about the picture we just added to our main page. Then save it with the name description.html. Once the description page is created, we want to create our inline frame, which will include the description of the picture we have just added to our table.

3. Position your cursor in the left column of the table and select Insert | Inline Frame from the menu bar. You will now see a frame placeholder inserted into the page.

4. Within the placeholder, click the Set Initial Page button. This brings up the Insert Hyperlink dialog box, where you can select the page you previously created.

5. Select the description.html page and click OK. Your description page will now display within the frame.

    We now need to make modifications to our new inline frame so that it will display in the page as we want it to.

6. Click one edge of the frame so that the frame's anchor points appear.

7. Select Format | Properties from the menu bar. This brings up the Inline Frame Properties dialog box, shown in Figure 2-15.

8. Adjust the inline frame using this dialog box by setting its width to 315 pixels. Then click OK.

9. Click the Preview tab to preview your new inline frame. Your page should look like the one shown in Figure 2-16.

NOTE

If you view this same page in an older Netscape browser, you will be given the alternative text that FrontPage placed between the <IFRAME> tags.

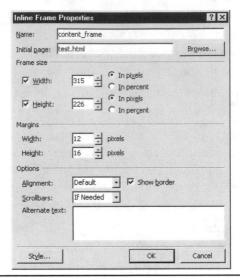

Figure 2-15   *The Inline Frame Properties dialog box*

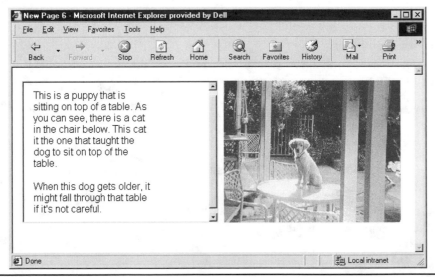

Figure 2-16   *A complete inline frame preview*

If you look at the example in Figure 2-16, you will see that the text of our frame is short enough so that very little scrolling is necessary to view it. Because of this, we can use FrontPage to allow browsers that do not recognize inline frames to view the same information on this page, without causing the page display to alter too much. This is done by way of incorporating the Page Include Component available in FrontPage between the frame tags. To use this feature, follow the next series of steps:

1. If you have not already created an inline frame, follow the previous steps to do so.

2. Position your cursor on an area of your main page where there is no content.

3. Select Insert | Web Component from the menu bar. This brings up the Insert Web Component dialog box.

4. Select Included Content from the Component Type list. This displays your options for including content on your page in the Choose a Type of Content list.

5. Select Page from the Content Type list and click Finish. This will bring up the Include Page dialog box.

6. Type the filename **description.html** in the dialog box and click OK. FrontPage now inserts the Include Page component onto your page.

   To finish up this exercise, you will need to copy and paste your Include Page component over the default alternative text display for the inline frame. Continue with these steps to do so.

7. Switch to HTML view.

8. Locate and highlight the newly created Include WebBot. The code should appear as so:

   ```
   <!--WebBOT bot="Include" U-Include="description.html" TAG="BODY" -->
   ```

9. Cut this code and paste it over the alternative text appearing between the <IFRAME> tags.

10. Save your document and preview it in a browser that does not support inline frames.

NOTE

If you preview this page in IE 3 or higher or Netscape 6 or higher, you will see your inline frame. This is because the Include Page component only appears if the browser does not support inline frames.

Hands On: Using JavaScript to Reroute Noncompatible Browsers

You may find that your inline frame contains a large document that does not display well using the Include Page component in browsers that do not recognize inline frames. If this is the case, you can add some JavaScript in your page that will detect whether the browser is inline frame compatible. That way, if the browser is not compatible, you can redirect it to a standard frames page that includes the same information, just not as pretty. To insert the detection script, follow these steps:

1. Create an inline frame as shown back in "Integrating Inline Frames."

2. Create a standard frame page that includes the same information as the inline frame page.

TIP

You can use the same page that appears within your inline frame for your frame page.

3. Create an introduction page that contains the following JavaScript. This script will detect the browser in use and direct it to the proper page. Within the JavaScript, replace the HTML files listed here with the HTML files that contain your pages:

```
<script language="JavaScript">
<!--
// hide the script from browsers that do not work with
javascript var page = "framepage.html";
if (navigator.appName == "Microsoft Internet Explorer") {
    if (parseFloat(navigator.appVersion) >= 3) {
      page = "floater.html";}
}
if (navigator.appName == "Netscape")
    if (parseFloat(navigator.appVersion) >= 5) {
      page = "floater.html";}

window.location.href= page;
// end hide
// --></script>
```

> **NOTE**
>
> *You probably noticed that I'm checking for Netscape Navigator version 5 and higher in the preceding code example. This is not a typo. Netscape Navigator version 6 reports that it is version 5 when queried with the appVersion method. Although this may seem a bit confusing, it causes no problem because there never was a version 5 of this browser.*

Advanced Linking Within Frames

Frames offer you numerous avenues for displaying content to users. There are, however, drawbacks to using frames. Tasks such as having two new pages load and changing the information that displays within a page cannot be accomplished using standard HTML. This is where JavaScript and VBScript can become really useful tools for your Web site. Both these scripting languages have their own pros and cons, which I will outline later in this book. For now, I just want to point out a trick you can integrate into your framed Web site to give it that extra polish it needs.

Many sites use multiple frames for their content. Usually, when multiple frames are used, the site is laid out with a left-frame navigation bar, a top frame containing the title, and the right frame containing copy. One of the biggest problems I have faced with this style of layout is creating my links so that the title frame will change with the copy frame from a link in the navigation frame.

Setting up this type of link system can be very helpful in your overall navigation scheme. If you have a Web site that contains multiple core areas, you will want users to see the title for each of those areas when they enter them.

Integrating JavaScript into your frame structure allows you to accomplish this by changing the top frame (the title) and the copy frame with one link from the navigation frame. This is accomplished through the following steps:

1. Create a frameset that uses the Nested Hierarchy template. This page will contain a top frame, named rtop, and a two-pane bottom frame, named left and rbottom, respectively.

2. Rename the left frame *contents*, the rtop frame *banner*, and the rbottom frame *main* by right-clicking each frame, selecting Frame Properties, and changing the Name attribute.

3. Either create a new page in each frame by clicking the New Page buttons or load existing pages using the Set Initial Page buttons.

4. In the left frame (contents), enter some text to be later used as a hyperlink.

5. Switch to the HTML tab in the FrontPage editor.

6. Insert the following JavaScript into the <HEAD> or <BODY> section of the page containing your navigation system (the page displayed in the contents frame). This JavaScript will be used to change the links within your site:

```
<script language="JavaScript">
<!--
// hide the script from browsers that do not work with
javascriptfunction Link()
{
    parent.banner.location.href = "banner.html";
    parent.main.location.href = "copy.html";
}
// -->
</script>
```

    As you can see, this script instructs the browser to open the banner.html page in the banner frame and copy.html in the main frame of the frameset. Of course, you can replace the banner and main frame names with those of your choosing.

7. Replace the filenames with those that you want the link to open when the user clicks.

    We now need to create the link that will cause these pages to open when a user clicks it.

8. Switch back to the Normal view tab in the FrontPage editor.

9. Return to the page containing your navigational link text entered in step 4 (displayed in the contents frame).

10. Highlight the text and click Insert | Hyperlink from the menu bar.

11. In the Insert Hyperlink dialog box, insert the following code in the Address field:

```
javascript:parent.Link();
```

    This hyperlink is actually code that instructs the browser to use the JavaScript you entered earlier to accomplish its goal.

12. Save your pages, remembering to save the pages within the banner and main frames using the names you specified in the script back in step 6.

13. Test the link by previewing the frames page in your browser and clicking the hyperlink in the contents frame.

TIP

You can create as many links as you want by following these same steps. To create more than one link in this manner, all you have to do is increment the word "Link" in each aspect of the JavaScript (for example, to create a second link script, change Link to Link1, and so on) and copy the new code below the first instance. If the page contains many links, you will likely want to create an array of URLs and pass the array indexes to a common link(x,x) function.

Making Sure Search Engines Find Your Information

One problem with the use of frames is that search engines can have a hard time indexing the information on your site. At the time of this writing, a large percentage of search engines still cannot penetrate a framed site. When their robots are sent to your site, they will simply index the first page and not find anything below it.

To combat this problem, be sure to use the <NOFRAMES> tag on your main frame page. This is the tag that appears to browsers that are not frame capable, and it is what a good percentage of the search engine robots will see. Within the <NOFRAMES> tag, put text links to the various areas of your site. If you have a main navigation page, you may just want to link to that. This way, the robot will go to that main navigation page and then be able to find the rest of your pages. Unfortunately, this will cause the engine to link to individual frame source pages. For this reason, you may also want to provide a link to the master frame page within each of your indexed pages. Additionally, several search engines now only index the home page of the site (the page displayed when you only type the site's domain name—http://www.somedomain.com). In addition to providing links to your main navigation page or individual frame source pages, you should also seriously consider entering descriptive text that contains lots of key words and phrases about your site.

Summary

This chapter has discussed many of the basic ideas behind developing Web sites using HTML, along with how to create advanced design layouts when working with FrontPage 2002. After reading this chapter, you should have a good grasp of how to lay out and design a basic Web with features such as tables and a frameset design. Although this chapter will not give you all the knowledge necessary to create award-winning Webs, it can be used as a basic reference for your development and while working with the other chapters within this book.

Upon completing this chapter, you should have a good understanding of how HTML works and how to create layouts and pages using FrontPage. Using the methods shown in this chapter, you can now develop sites by incorporating the features of HTML with FrontPage's capabilities. This understanding will give you the knowledge necessary to tackle many of the more advanced aspects of Web creation found later in this book.

CHAPTER 3

FrontPage Themes and Styles

IN THIS CHAPTER:

Learn How to Create Style Sheets for Your Webs

Incorporate Shared Navigation System

Create and Incorporate Themes into Your Webs

B y now you know that FrontPage XP allows you to create Web sites without needing to know HTML. What you may not know is that FrontPage gives you the capability to develop compelling Web sites without needing to create graphics or know much about navigational layout.

If you are new to Web design, the information in this chapter will allow you to begin creating sites like the pros in no time. If you are a seasoned developer, you can use this chapter as your guide to the ins and outs of developing consistent layouts and styles using FrontPage.

Throughout this chapter we will take a hands-on look at developing themes and style sheets for use within your Webs. Each section looks at a different aspect of style development and how to optimize your styles for use within your development environment.

Cascading Style Sheets

Style sheets allow you to create documents that work as templates for the styles found in your Webs. These templates are viewed by the browser upon opening your pages, and they determine the various styles that appear within your pages.

The styles in your style sheets can specify various aspects of your layout and design, including, but not limited to, the font properties, background colors, and paragraph layouts. Through the use of style sheets, you can create a consistent look and feel without worrying about setting the properties on each and every page.

Using style sheets also gives you the ability to create a layout for specific sites that you can then hand off to other individuals. This works well if you have a group environment where certain layout standards need to be met. For example, you can create a style sheet specifying that all body text within a page is set to a specific font and font size. Furthermore, you can specify the heading layouts, text colors for areas of the page, and paragraph layouts, along with many other aspects of your page layouts.

Creating a Style Sheet

Style sheets are text files that contain configuration information for use by the Web browser to determine the overall look and feel of a page. Although you can create style sheets in any text editor, FrontPage lets you create your style sheets without having to know the necessary layout information. You see, creating style sheets is much like creating Web pages. You need to have a certain understanding of the language behind your style sheets to make them work.

However, once again FrontPage comes to the rescue, allowing you to create comprehensive style sheets without the knowledge necessary for programming them. All you need to do to create a style sheet is to follow the steps given here:

1. Select File | New | Page or Web from the menu bar. This brings up the New Page or Web dialog box.

2. Select Page Templates from the options; this brings up the Page Templates dialog box.

3. Select the Style Sheets tab. As you can see, you can select from a variety of templates in this tab. These templates refer to the various themes found in FrontPage, which are discussed later in this chapter.

4. Choose the Normal Style Sheet icon and click OK. A new page appears on your screen. You are now ready to begin creating your style sheet.

5. When opening a style sheet, FrontPage displays the single-button Style toolbar. By clicking this button, or selecting Format | Style, you bring up the Style dialog box shown in Figure 3-1. Here is a brief description of the parts of this dialog box:

   ▶ **Styles**   Lists all the HTML tag styles you can modify. The tags shown in this list are determined by your selection in the List option's drop-down box.

   ▶ **List**   Allows you to select between all available HTML tags and your user-defined tags. This is a helpful distinction if you are making modifications to several styles and want to view only those you have modified.

   ▶ **Paragraph preview**   Shows how the paragraph properties are set for the current style.

   ▶ **Character preview**   Shows how the character properties are set for the current style.

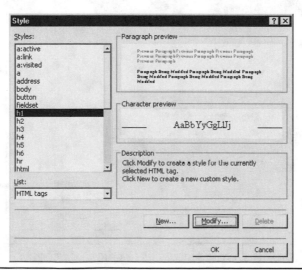

Figure 3-1   *The Style dialog box, used to view attributes of your HTML tags*

▶ **Description**   Displays any modifications you have made to the selected style.

▶ **New**   Allows you to create a new style for use within your page. Continue reading in this chapter for more information on creating new styles in FrontPage.

▶ **Modify**   Allows you to modify an existing HTML tag, or user-defined style, as discussed in this example.

▶ **Delete**   Allows you to delete a selected style.

6. Select the style you want to customize for your style sheet. For this example, we will modify the <H1> tag.

7. Click the Modify button to bring up the Modify Style dialog box shown in Figure 3-2. This is where you will specify the basics of the style. We will create various aspects of this style by clicking the Format button and selecting from the available options.

8. Begin with the Font option. This brings up the Font dialog box, where you can specify the style of the font that will appear in your <H1> tag. Select Arial from the Font list and 18 pt from the Size list. Click OK.

9. Now select Paragraph from the Format list. This brings up the Paragraph Properties dialog box. For this example, we want to set the alignment of the paragraph to center. Once you've done this, click OK.

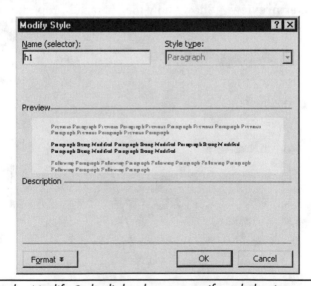

Figure 3-2   *Using the Modify Style dialog box to specify style basics*

10. We want to include a border around our <H1> tags, so choose the Border option from the Format list. This brings up the Borders and Shading dialog box. Select a dashed border with a width of one pixel and click OK.

11. Click OK to close the Modify Style dialog box. Click OK again to close the Style dialog box. Your screen should now have text appearing as shown here:

```
newpage1.css                                                              ✕

h1            { font-family: Arial; font-size: 18 pt; text-align: Center;
              border-style: dashed; border-width: 1 }
```

12. Repeat this procedure for each style you want in your style sheet and save the file to your Web.

Although the style sheet editor in FrontPage is very handy and easy to use, it is somewhat limited. As new HTML and style tags come into use, you'll likely find that the graphical style editor is missing some desired features. Handily, FrontPage also allows you to edit your style sheet's code directly within the text editor window.

After you click OK within the Style dialog box, the customizations you have made are shown in the text-based style sheet editor window. Based on the changes you made in the exercise, your style sheet code should include the following line:

```
h1 { font-family: Arial; font-size: 18 pt;
text-align: Center; border-style: dashed; border-width: 1 }
```

To make manual changes and additions to your style sheets, you will eventually need to understand what code like this means. Slightly different from HTML, a basic style definition consists of a style name (h1 in this case), followed by a bracketed ({}) set of arguments. Within these brackets, you may enter as many or as few attributes as you wish. The basic structure of these arguments is as follows: attribute name, followed by a colon, followed by the attribute value. If you want to include more than one attribute in the style definition, you separate the attribute declarations with semicolons (;). We'll delve further into creating your own styles and classes as the chapter progresses.

Once your file is saved, you will want to link it to the pages in your Web. This way, all your pages will have a consistent look and feel.

Linking Style Sheets to Your Pages

A style sheet does not do you much good on its own. What you need to do is link it to the various pages within your Web where you want your styles to appear. This causes the Web browser to read the file and apply the styles to a page when the browser displays that page on the user's screen. To link your style sheets to your pages, follow these steps:

1. In the editor, open the page you want to contain a style sheet link.

2. Select Format | Style Sheet Links from the menu bar. This brings up the Link Style Sheet dialog box shown here:

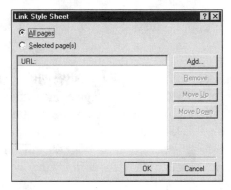

3. Click Add to select the location of your style sheet.

4. Select the style sheet you want to link to your page and click OK. Your style sheet link now appears in the Link Style Sheet dialog box.

5. If you want to have this style sheet reflected throughout your Web, select the All Pages option and click OK. If you want the style sheet to apply only to selected pages, click the Selected Page(s) option and click OK.

   The style sheet is now linked to your page (or pages) and will cause your text to be displayed based on the settings you have specified.

TIP
_____

You can view the style sheet link by selecting the HTML view in the editor.
The style sheet link appears in your document header in the following form:
<link rel="stylesheet" type="text/css" href="[your style sheet's filename]">

Adjusting Internal Styles in Your Web

Although style sheets allow you to control the overall look and feel of your pages through linked templates, you still have the ability to make modifications to specific pages within your Webs through the use of various properties dialog boxes. Unlike with style sheets, the changes you make to individual styles within a page affect only that page. This allows you to create custom looks within specific pages of your site when developing your Webs. The drawback to this type of developing is that you need to assign the styles for each page, whereas you only have to assign a link to a style sheet to have that style propagate throughout the page.

CAUTION

Styles created within specific pages will overwrite any style sheet linked to those pages.

FrontPage allows you to easily format various HTML tags to meet specific style requirements. To make adjustments to your styles, simply follow these steps:

1. Open a page in your Web.

2. Select Format | Style from the menu bar. This brings up the Style dialog box shown in Figure 3-1.

3. For this example, we will modify the Heading 1 HTML tag. From the Styles list, select h1.

4. Click Modify to bring up the Modify Style dialog box (shown in Figure 3-2).

5. Now that we have the Modify Style dialog box on our screen, we can begin formatting our style. For the purposes of this example, we will only be modifying the font properties for this tag. Once you complete this modification, you can go back and modify other aspects of the tag in the same way. Click the Format button and select Font from the available options. This brings up the Font dialog box.

6. Adjust your font to Arial, with a Bold font style and a 14 pt size.

7. Click OK. You will now see your selections appear in the Description field of the Modify Style dialog box.

8. Click OK once more to close the Modify Style dialog box. If you want to modify other fonts, you may select them now. Otherwise, click OK one more time to close the Style dialog box.

Your style change is now embedded in the HTML document you are working with, and you can view it by selecting the HTML tab at the bottom of your screen. You should see the following code:

```
<style>
<!--
h1              { font-family: Arial;
                 font-size: 14 pt; font-weight: bold }
-->
</style>
```

Hands On: Creating New Styles

Along with modifying existing styles, FrontPage lets you create your own styles for use within your pages. Creating your own style within a page can save you a lot of time when formatting your various headings and the like.

When you create your own style, the name you assign to the style appears in the Style drop-down list on the Formatting toolbar. Using this drop-down list, you can assign the style to any text within your page.

NOTE

Creating a style within a specific page will cause the style to appear only when you edit that page. To have your style available throughout your Web, you should create a linked style sheet.

To create a new style within a page:

1. Open a page in your Web.
2. Select Format | Style from the menu bar. This brings up the Style properties dialog box shown in Figure 3-1.
3. Click New to bring up the New Style dialog box shown next.

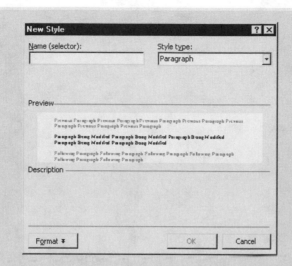

4. Assign a name to the style you are creating. For this example, we will create an italic version of our h1 style, so we will name it h1.Italic. This style version is known as a *class*.

5. Click Format to bring up the format options. For this example, we will be editing the font properties for this style, so we will select Font from the drop-down list. This brings up the Font dialog box.

6. Select Arial for the font, with a Bold, Italic font style, and an 18 pt size.

7. Click OK to close the Font dialog box and then click OK once more to close the New Style dialog box. You will now see your new style appear in the Styles list of the Style Properties dialog box.

8. Click OK to close the final dialog box and return to your page.

We now want to take a look at the new style we have created. You can do this by clicking the HTML tab in your editor. Your style should look like the one shown here:

```
<style>
<!--
h1              { font-family: Arial;
                  font-size: 14 pt; font-weight: bold }
h1.italic       { font-family: Arial;
                  font-size: 18 pt; font-style: italic;
                  font-weight: bold }

-->
</style>
```

As you can see, we have two styles listed. The h1 style is the one created earlier in the chapter by making a modification to the existing Heading 1 style, and the h1.italic style is a new class we have just created from scratch. To use your new style, simply select your text and then select h1.italic from the Style drop-down menu in the Formatting toolbar.

Classes, Inheritance, and Global Classes

A *class* is a variation or modification of a style. The class code created by FrontPage's Style dialog box is technically correct, but it is also a little redundant. Because our italic class is simply a variation of the parent h1 style, all that is really necessary is to specify the changed font-style parameter: h1.italic { font-style: italic }. This concept is known as *inheritance*—the child class inherits all the parent style's attributes by default. This is a powerful feature of the CSS1 (cascading style sheets) specification.

In the previous example, we created a class of the Heading 1 style (h1.italic). Although this implementation of classes is useful, it can be made more flexible through the use of global classes. A *global class* is a class that has no parent style. Instead of creating the style-specific class h1.italic, we can simply create a global .italic class. This global class will then be accessible to all styles that contain its specified attribute(s).

FrontPage fully supports the use of global classes, but it makes you work a little to use them. Because the .italic global class may be applied to any supporting style, you must first select the style that you want to apply from the Formatting toolbar's

Style selection box and then select the class using this same selection box. Although you must select these items separately, FrontPage recognizes your combined formatting and displays Heading1.italic in the Style selection box.

"Cascading" Style Sheets and Precedence

Now that we've discussed the creation and use of style sheets and the modification of styles, you're probably wondering what makes them "cascading" style sheets. The answer to this question is quite simple. *Cascading* means that multiple style sheets may interact with each other on a single page. This ability to specify multiple sheet links within a page allows standards to be set for an entire Web site, while allowing additional styles to be added to certain sections or areas of the site without interfering with the entire site's look.

So, what happens when you use multiple style sheets that contain conflicting style definitions? Simply put, the loser (that is, the later or final declaration) wins and has precedence over other duplicate definitions. The Link Style Sheet dialog box allows you to set the order that sheets are linked for this very reason. Although this is the default method for setting precedence, you, as the designer, also have control over this conflict precedence. By inserting "! important" after a parameter definition, you make that specified value the presiding or most important declaration. For example, h1 { font-style: italic ! important } specifies that the h1 style should always appear as italic, even if another style sheet contains a conflicting definition for the h1 style's font-style attribute.

Links and Pseudoclasses

Within the collection of standard HTML tags that may be modified through style and class declarations, the <A> (anchor) tag is somewhat unique. Because this tag is used to specify a hyperlink, it also contains a state or condition known as its *pseudoclass*. Anchor tag pseudoclasses are identified by a separating colon (:) and consist of the following:

Pseudoclass	Description
A:link	A standard link.
A:visited	A link that has already been visited.
A:active	A link that is currently active (clicked and waiting for the target to load).
A:hover	Slightly different from the other pseudoclasses, hover is triggered whenever the user's mouse moves over the link.

Other than their declaration as pseudoclasses, these link states may have all the same attributes set as the standard anchor style. One common use is to specify a different color in the A:hover pseudoclass. Because this use is so popular, FrontPage also lets you set this style in the Page Property dialog box's Background tab. The Enable Hyperlink Rollover Effects option adds the following style definition to a page:

```
<style fprolloverstyle>
A:hover {color: red; font-weight: bold}
</style>
```

The *fprolloverstyle* flag has no meaning to the browser and is just a FrontPage-specific identifier that tells FrontPage the style to edit when you toggle the Enable Hyperlink Rollover Effects option on or off. Of course, you may also customize this tag with your own attribute values.

Incorporating Shared Borders

So far, we have been looking exclusively at the development of styles for your Webs and how to incorporate those styles by embedding them into your document or linking them via cascading style sheets. This part of the chapter looks at creating a consistent look and feel through the use of a FrontPage proprietary feature known as *shared borders*.

Shared borders allow you to add consistent borders to your Web site pages. These borders can be used to display information that is the same throughout your Web site, such as your navigation system or logo information. By using shared borders, you can create and change single sections, with the change reflected throughout your entire Web site once it is saved. This saves you the time of changing each page in your site just because you updated a navigational element.

It is through the use of shared borders that FrontPage's graphical site creation and link management system is implemented. Within the navigation view, you can create new pages and manage their links in an organizational diagram. Not only does this diagram facilitate the quick and organized creation of a large site, but it also continues to serve as a site-management tool. With the use of shared borders and navigation bars, you may simply drag a page to another location within the diagram, automatically updating the entire site's hyperlinks to accommodate the change. This site diagram may also be zoomed, rotated, and printed for further analysis.

Along with creating a standard navigation system, you also have the ability to add any other aspect of information you want to shared borders. This may include information that you want to be consistent throughout your site, such as copyright information. A drawback to shared borders is that you can only include one per Web. This is in contrast to frames, which allow you to set up your links to any page and change styles wherever necessary.

For those of you who find that shared borders will work for the style of site you are creating, the following sections walk you through the creation and alteration of shared borders, along with some tips for getting the most out of this FrontPage technology.

Inserting a Shared Border

Inserting a shared border is done within the Editor tab of FrontPage. To insert a border, follow these steps:

1. Open the Web in which you want your shared border to appear.

2. Select Format | Shared Borders from the menu bar. This brings up the Shared Borders dialog box shown here:

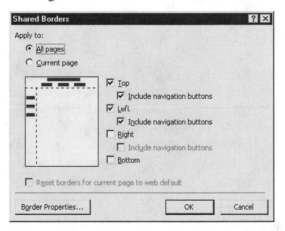

3. Select the type of border you want your Web to have. You may choose as many borders as you like.

4. If you want your borders to include standard site navigation, check Include Navigation Buttons for the border that is to include the navigation buttons.

NOTE

You may only include navigation buttons if you are setting the shared borders for the entire Web.

5. Click OK.

A dotted line now appears with comment text at the location of your shared border on the page. You may replace the comment text with any information you want to appear within the border.

Editing Shared Border Information

Although you have the ability to edit the information in your shared borders directly within a page in your Web, it is best to edit the actual shared border pages that FrontPage will be substituting when the pages are viewed. Shared border files are stored in hidden directories within your Web. To access them, you must first change your Web settings to allow you to view hidden files. Here are the steps:

1. Select Tools | Web Settings from the menu bar. This brings up the Web Settings dialog box.

2. Click the Advanced tab to bring up the advanced properties.

3. Check the Show Pages in Hidden Directories option.

4. Click OK. FrontPage confirms that the specified change will take place once the Web is refreshed. To refresh your Web, click Yes.

Once FrontPage has refreshed your Web, you will see a folder titled "_borders" within the folder view. This folder contains all the files associated with your shared borders. As you can see, their names are associated with the appropriate borders (for example, right.htm equals the right-hand border in your Web).

Once you have set FrontPage to allow you to view your shared border pages, you can begin editing them within the editor tab. Edit these pages as you would any standard page within the editor.

Using the Navigation View

One of the nicer features of shared borders is the navigation bar component. If you have chosen to have FrontPage automatically include navigation buttons within a shared border, a navigation bar is included on each page. The navigation view, which can be displayed by selecting View | Navigation from the menu bar, provides a simple and intuitive method of maintaining this component. You simply build the navigation structure of your site by dragging individual pages onto the navigation view and placing them so that they fall within the desired hierarchy. Additionally, FrontPage allows you to define how your navigation system is to be linked with its Link Bar Properties dialog box that gives you options as to how the links will be implemented.

To configure the link bar, follow these steps:

1. Open any page within the Web.
2. Double-click the WebBot that reads "[Edit the properties for this link bar to display hyperlinks here]." This opens the Link Bar Properties dialog box shown in Figure 3-3.

Within this properties dialog box are two tabs. The first tab contains all the information you will need for setting up your Web's navigational structure. The second tab allows you to specify the styles you want to use for displaying the navigational elements of your Web.

You will notice that as you click each of the options under Hyperlinks to Add to Page, the sample navigation tree diagram changes to display the results of your selection. Keep in mind, however, that you may only select one of the options, because that selection will then be applied to the entire Web. You may change this option at a later time, and this change will then be applied to the entire Web. Although this might seem restrictive at first, you'll soon realize that this site-wide option forces you to use a consistent navigation system throughout the site.

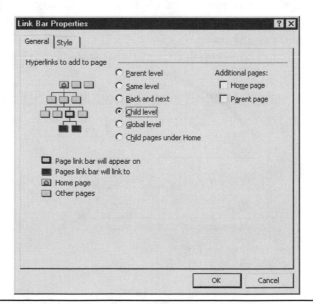

Figure 3-3   *The Link Bar Properties dialog box makes it easy for you to set up navigational links for your Web pages.*

A consistent navigation system makes getting around a site easier for visitors and is a mark of a professionally designed site. The navigation style options are as follows:

▶ **Parent level**   Hyperlinks will be provided to pages within the navigation tree level immediately preceding each page's level.

▶ **Same level**   Hyperlinks will be provided to pages within the same navigation tree level.

▶ **Back and next**   Hyperlinks will be provided to pages within the same navigation tree level that immediately precedes and follows each page.

▶ **Child level**   Hyperlinks will be provided to pages that reside in the next level under a page's navigation tree level.

▶ **Global level**   Hyperlinks will be provided to pages in the top level of the navigation tree structure.

▶ **Child pages under Home**   Hyperlinks will be provided to pages residing in the first navigation tree level under the home page.

Besides these six navigation style options, the Additional Pages options let you add pages to each page's navigation bar. These additional pages are the site's home page and each page's parent page. In most cases, it is both helpful and considered good design to add these links to each page.

Clicking the Style tab brings up the navigational-style layout information for your link bar, as shown here:

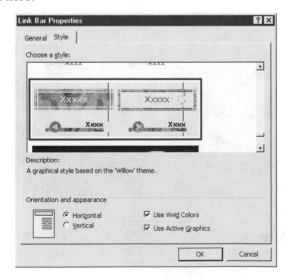

The Style tab consists of three areas that allow you to specify how you want your navigation to display in a particular pane:

▶ **Choose a style**   This portion of the screen gives you a scrollable list of all available layouts on the system. You can select from the available styles. Alternatively, if you have created your own theme, you can select it from the list.

▶ **Description**   The description gives a brief introduction to the selected style in the Choose a Style pane.

▶ **Orientation and appearance**   This section of the dialog box allows you to specify whether you want your navigation to display in a horizontal or vertical fashion. You may also specify whether the links should appear as buttons or simple text links. Also, if you have selected image-based navigation buttons, you can choose to optionally display them in vivid colors and/or as animated (active) graphics.

Once you have configured the way your pages will be linked, you may then build your site's navigation structure by switching to the navigation view and dragging your pages into position, as shown in Figure 3-4.

Limiting Shared Borders to Certain Pages

FrontPage offers you the opportunity to eliminate shared borders from specific pages within your Web without affecting the other pages. This can come in handy if you are working with a Web that has some pages with alternative content. One such case

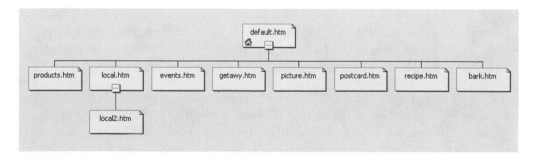

Figure 3-4   *FrontPage navigation view*

that I have run into is a site that had a consistent look and feel and a standard navigation bar, except for one section that contained a single navigation frame on the left side. Because of this, shared borders would not work. The only solution was to remove the shared borders from that particular area of the site. This can be accomplished by following these steps:

1. Open the page or pages in your Web where you do not want the shared border to appear.

2. Select Format | Shared Borders from the menu bar. This brings up the Shared Borders dialog box.

3. Click the Current Page radio button and uncheck any borders that are checked in the dialog box.

4. Click OK. The border will now be removed from the current page. Do this for each page on which you do not want the border to appear.

Behind Shared Borders

Shared borders are really nothing more than tables inserted into your HTML code by FrontPage during development and by the FrontPage server extensions when the page is viewed in a browser. This is accomplished using a Meta tag recognized by FrontPage. When you save the page, FrontPage inserts the appropriate tables into each of your pages based on the Meta tag appearing at the top of each page. When FrontPage reads the Meta tag, it knows to look in the hidden borders directory and basically include those pages within the displayed page, much like FrontPage's Include Page component.

NOTE

When FrontPage creates the underlying HTML code, it will space the top and bottom tables at 100 percent, so you will need to lay out your code with this understanding. The left and right borders will contain tables that match the width and length of the actual content.

Because FrontPage creates the underlying HTML code for your borders, you don't have complete control over the layout. This can be annoying to many developers, including this one, but there are ways around this snag. Your best bet for control of the shared borders is to work within the border page itself and lay it out exactly as you want it to appear. Here's how to do this:

1. Open the page containing your border.

2. Create the layout of the page exactly as you want it to appear. Remember that this border will appear on a specific part of the page, so you will want to lay out the content accordingly.

3. Save the page. Now when you view the page in the Normal view, your borders will appear as you have designed them.

Incorporating FrontPage Themes into Your Designs

Themes can be looked at as fully developed style templates for you to use when creating your Webs. FrontPage XP comes equipped with over 60 themes, and many companies on the Internet create and sell theme packages. Using a theme allows you to create a consistent look and feel for your Web so that all the images, fonts, and so on are the same throughout all your pages.

With FrontPage, not only can you select from the included themes, but you can also customize the themes you are working with. Along with this, FrontPage gives you the capability to create your own themes to use in your Webs. This is accomplished through the use of the theme-modification dialog boxes incorporated within FrontPage.

Using the theme-modification dialog boxes, you can create complete layouts for your Webs that you can use with your projects. This is a great way of getting individuals without experience started if you are working within an intranet system.

Because FrontPage is now integrated into Microsoft Office, you can use these themes throughout your system—in essence, sharing them with the other Office applications you work with. This way, if you create a page in Microsoft Word, you can give it the same appearance as your HTML pages in FrontPage. The same goes for all the Office applications you work with, and you will find that PowerPoint has some nice presentation themes that may work well with the Webs you create.

Developing Webs Through the Use of Themes

Themes are detailed style sheets and .inf (information) files that contain all the information you need to automatically format your Web pages. Themes also make extensive use of the shared borders capabilities found within FrontPage (discussed earlier in this chapter). With FrontPage themes, you have all the formatting elements necessary for creating consistency throughout your Web, as well as all the graphical elements you need for creating your Web.

When working with a FrontPage theme, you can have the theme layout either incorporated directly into each of your pages or linked to your pages as a cascading style sheet. Both of these methods have benefits, as outlined here:

▶ **Incorporated themes** Incorporating theme elements directly into your Web pages allows your pages to be viewed by the widest variety of browsers. This is useful if you do not know what browsers your users will be using to view your pages, because older browsers do not support CSS.

▶ **Themes as style sheets** Linking to an external theme controlling a cascading style sheet instead of modifying the style attributes of each page to incorporate the theme provides more centralized control. If you know that the majority of your users will be viewing your pages with newer browsers that support externally linked CSS, you should use this method. This way, you can modify your styles in the sheet and have them change your entire Web.

Incorporating a Theme into Your Web

Using FrontPage, you can quickly and easily incorporate professional looking layouts and graphics through the use of themes. Incorporating a basic theme into your Web is a fairly simple task, which is explained here. Once you have incorporated a basic theme, you will want to check out the remaining sections, which discuss how to customize your themes and how to create your own themes for use with your Webs.

To incorporate a theme into your FrontPage Web, follow these steps:

1. Create or open a Web in FrontPage. If you want to apply a theme to specific pages within your Web, switch to the folder view and select the pages you want your theme applied to by clicking them while holding down the CTRL key on your keyboard.

2. From the menu bar, select Format | Theme. This brings up the Themes dialog box shown in Figure 3-5. The settings on this dialog are as follows:

   ▶ **Apply Theme to** Use this option to specify whether you want this theme applied throughout your Web (All Pages) or associated with specific pages within your Web (Selected Pages). If you choose Selected Pages, the theme will be applied to all the pages you have selected.

   ▶ **Available themes** FrontPage comes equipped with 60 predefined themes that you can choose from to format your Web. You may also choose to install new themes in FrontPage by selecting Install Additional Themes from this list of available themes.

   ▶ **Vivid colors** When you select a theme, it appears with standard color settings. If you like the theme you have selected but want to add more

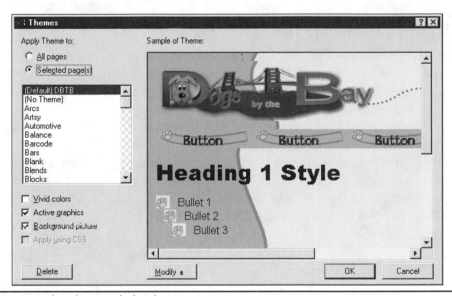

Figure 3-5   *The Themes dialog box*

color, select this option. You will see a change in the colors associated
with the theme in the preview window.

▶ **Active graphics**   Selecting this option incorporates animated images into
your theme.

▶ **Background picture**   If this option is selected, a background image
will appear within your theme. You will see this background image in
the preview window.

▶ **Apply using CSS**   Selecting this option causes the theme to be saved to a
.css file, which is then linked to the pages within your Web. Once again, this
option is not supported by older browsers and should be used with caution.

▶ **Modify**   Use this button to make modifications to the currently selected
theme. Information on modifying your themes is presented later in this
chapter.

▶ **Delete**   Use this button to delete a custom theme that you have created
on the system.

3. From the Themes dialog box, you can select any one of the available themes as
well as select from a variety of options for the selected theme. Once you have
selected a theme, click OK. Your theme is now applied to the current Web.

Customizing FrontPage Themes

You can use the standard themes available with FrontPage, but they will give your site a look and feel that may be found in many other Webs throughout the Internet. For this reason, FrontPage gives you the ability to customize your themes to contain your own style of design and layout.

If you worked with FrontPage 98, you might have heard about an undocumented feature, called the *Theme Designer*, that allowed you to create FrontPage themes for use with your Webs. Starting with FrontPage 2000, the ability to create and modify themes was incorporated directly into the Themes dialog box. From this dialog box, you can select one of the available FrontPage themes and use it as a template for designing your own custom themes, which you can then save for use throughout your Web.

Working with Theme Colors

When working in the Themes dialog box, shown in Figure 3-5, you can adjust the colors associated with a chosen theme to fit the color scheme you want for your Web. Adjusting your color settings is as easy as following these steps:

1. Select Format | Theme on the menu bar to bring up the Themes dialog box.

2. Select a theme that resembles your desired result.

3. Click the Modify button in the dialog box. You will see a new set of buttons appear.

4. Click the Colors button to bring up the Modify Theme dialog box shown in Figure 3-6. This dialog box has three tabs that allow you to specify the color settings for your currently selected theme:

   ▶ **Color Schemes**   Allows you to select from available color schemes already on the system.

   ▶ **Color Wheel**   Allows you to specify a select color range to use for your theme. You can also adjust the color brightness in this tab.

   ▶ **Custom**   Gives you complete control over the color settings for your theme's text. You may select each text style from the list and specify the color you want for that element.

5. At the bottom of this dialog box is the Normal Colors and Vivid Colors option. By toggling these options, you can modify color selections for each option.

6. Make your selections and click OK.

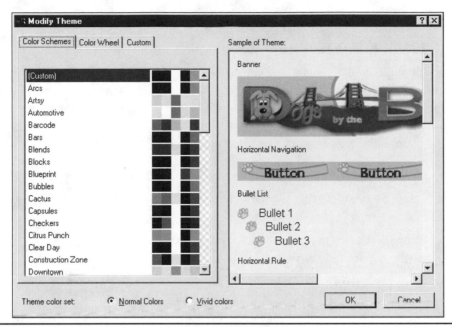

Figure 3-6   *The Color Schemes tab of the Modify Theme dialog box*

Working with Theme Graphics

Now you may be wondering how the graphics within a theme will work with your site, especially when you have your own titles for banners, buttons, and the like throughout your Web. Well, you will be happy to know that when you create a Web using a theme, FrontPage will automatically take the information from the <TITLE> tag on your page and use it to fill in the various banners and buttons. All you have to do is select a theme, set up the navigation through the use of your shared borders (discussed earlier in this chapter), and name your pages. FrontPage takes care of the rest.

That works great if you like what you see in the current theme, but you also have the ability to make changes to the graphical look by changing the colors, as described previously in this chapter. In addition, you can change the font layout within the graphic, which is outlined in "Hands On: Reworking Text in Your Theme Graphics." A bit later, when we talk about creating your own themes, you will find out how to incorporate your own graphics into a theme.

Hands On: Reworking Text in Your Theme Graphics

Working with themes can make your life a lot easier when developing Web sites, but you may find that you do not like some aspects of the themes presented to you in FrontPage. This Hands On section shows you how to easily change the textual layout for all the graphics in a given theme.

To change the way text appears in a theme, follow these steps:

1. Open a Web in FrontPage.

2. Select Format | Theme from the menu bar. This brings up the Themes dialog box shown in Figure 3-5.

3. Choose a theme pattern to work with. For this example, we will be working with the Arcs theme.

4. Click the Modify button in the dialog box. This brings up the modification icons.

5. Click the Graphics button to bring up the Modify Theme dialog box for graphical properties.

6. Select the Font tab to display the font properties, as shown here:

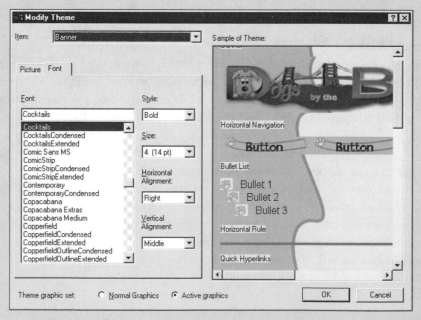

TIP

When changing font layouts, it is a good idea to use a consistent font and style throughout.

7. From the Item list, select each graphic you want to change the font for, and make your adjustments for both the Normal Graphics and Active Graphics theme sets (specified at the bottom of the page). As you make your changes, they will appear in the preview window on the right side of the dialog box. You can use this window to verify that this is the exact style you want to use for your fonts.

NOTE

When you save this theme, your changes will be made directly to the images used within the theme. Because of this, you can use any font on your system and not worry about users having the same font when they view your pages.

8. When you have completed all your changes, click OK. You will be returned to the Theme dialog box.

9. Click OK again to return to your page. FrontPage will ask if you want to save the changes made to this theme. If you choose Yes, you are then asked to give the theme a new name. This way, you will not overwrite the old theme and can come back to it later. In fact, FrontPage will not allow you to overwrite the original theme.

10. Save the theme under a new name and click OK. Your new information is saved to the system, and your theme is applied to your current Web.

NOTE

If you want to save your new theme but do not want to apply it to your site, use the Save or Save As button and click Cancel. On the flip side, you cannot make changes to a theme and apply it to your site without saving the theme.

Working with Theme Styles

Each FrontPage theme has a set of user-defined styles that are created to go along with it. When working with your theme, you have the capability of modifying its styles to fit your tastes by adjusting various aspects of these styles.

When you first click the Modify button in the Themes dialog box (Figure 3-5), you are presented with the Modify Theme dialog box for fonts, shown in Figure 3-7. This dialog box allows you to modify the font associated with a specific style within the theme by selecting the style from the Item list and then selecting a different font.

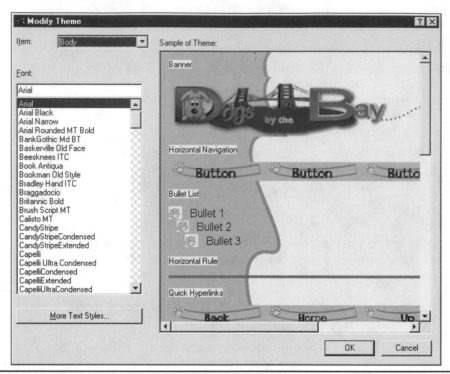

Figure 3-7   *The Font list in the Modify Theme dialog box*

NOTE

Be careful when selecting specific fonts, because the font you select will need to be on the user's system for the user to be able to view it. Although it is possible to embed your own fonts, this feature is only available with Internet Explorer 4.0 and above and should only be used in private intranets where browser compatibility can be ensured.

If you want to make more extensive modifications to your styles, or the style you want to work with is not listed in the Item list, you can click the More Text Styles button. This brings up the Style dialog box (Figure 3-1), which allows you to make more extensive modifications to the styles in the selected theme.

Hands On: Creating Your Own Theme

Having the ability to use themes is a great help when you are developing Webs, but what if you are a developer who needs to create custom layouts for your clients? Well, with FrontPage, you not only have the ability to use themes, but you also have the ability to create your own themes. The following steps take you through the process of creating a custom theme within FrontPage.

1. Create a new Web in FrontPage.

2. Select Format | Theme from the menu bar. This brings up the Themes dialog box, which we have discussed throughout this chapter. For the purposes of this exercise, we will be working with the Blank theme and modifying it to meet our needs.

3. Select Blank in the list of themes and click the Modify button in the dialog box. You will see a group of icons appear. These are the icons we will use to make our modifications.

4. First off, we want to modify the color coding for our text. To do so, click the Colors button to bring up the color options, as shown in Figure 3-6.

5. For our new theme, we want to modify the colors for the default hyperlinks and our Heading 1 tags. Click the Custom tab.

6. From the Item list, select Hyperlinks. Change the color to Green in the color palette.

7. Now select the Heading 1 style and change the color to Navy.

8. Click OK. You will notice that your changes appear immediately in the preview window.

9. The next step is to incorporate your own custom graphics into this theme. These graphics will replace the one currently shown in the preview window. For this example, we will be working with the Dogs by the Bay images found on the CD-ROM.

10. Click the Graphics button to bring up the graphics options, as shown here:

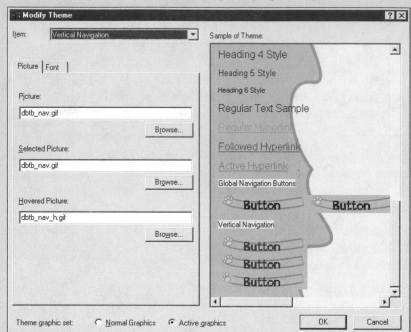

At this point, we want to change all the images that go with this theme to our own images. To save time, I will only give the steps for changing a few of the images and then show what they look like in the finished product.

NOTE

When you are substituting images, don't forget that you may have multiple sets of images that perform the same function, such as the vertical and horizontal image pointers.

Select the various images you want to substitute with your own images. Here we will substitute the banner and navigation images.

11. First off, select Banner from the Item list. You will see the default file for this theme—ablbnr.gif. Replace this file by browsing to and selecting the dbtb_banner.gif from the CD-ROM. You will see the new banner appear in the preview window.

12. Click Vertical Navigation in the Item list.

13. If you have selected Active Graphics, you will see three image links appear, as follows (if the Active Graphics option is not selected, select it now):

    ▶ **Picture**   The image that appears when the page is viewed

    ▶ **Selected Picture**   The image that appears when the user clicks the image

    ▶ **Hovered Picture**   The image that appears when the user moves a mouse over the image (only available with Java-capable browsers)

14. For this example, we will change all three of these. In the Picture field, enter the file **dbtb_nav.gif**. In the Selected Picture field, also enter **dbtb_nav.gif**, and in the Hovered Picture field, enter **dbtb_nav_h.gif**. These entries will cause the picture to appear the same when the user views the page and clicks the image, but they will cause the image to change when the user's mouse moves over it. Once your images are linked, they will appear in the preview window. As you will see, the image dbtb_nav_h.gif has a different colored paw.

    We now want to change the fonts that appear on the image as well as align them so that they appear where we want them to.

15. Begin with the banner titled dbtb_banner.gif. As you can see, the text appears in the center of this banner and can hardly be seen. We want to move this text into the circle on the right side of the graphic. To do this, select the Font tab.

16. In the preview image, use the bottom scroll bar to scroll over to the circle on the right side of the image. You are now ready to adjust your text. Set the size to 14 pt, with Horizontal Alignment set to Right and Vertical Alignment set to Middle.

17. For this example, I have chosen to use the Cocktails font in bold, but you can use any font you like.

18. We now want to adjust the text on our navigation buttons. Select Vertical Navigation from the Item list, and your navigation buttons will appear in the preview window.

19. Once again, I am using the Cocktails font in bold. Set the font size to 12 pt, with Horizontal Alignment set to Center and Vertical Alignment set to Bottom. You will again see your changes appear as you make them.

20. Click OK to close the graphics window once you have made all your graphical adjustments.

    Now it is time to set your text styles for this theme. This is accomplished through the text options, which are shown in Figure 3-7.

21. Click the Text button to bring up the font properties in the Modify Theme dialog box. Here you have the option of setting your styles by selecting them from the Item list. For this example, we will only modify two styles.

22. Select the font you want to use for your style's body text. I have selected Arial for this theme.

23. Select Arial Black for your Heading 1 tag.

24. Adjust any other styles you want changed and click OK.

You have now created a custom theme in FrontPage. All that is left to do is to save your theme with a unique name; then you can begin using it for your Webs. An example of the theme we just created is shown here, and you can find the completed theme on the CD-ROM:

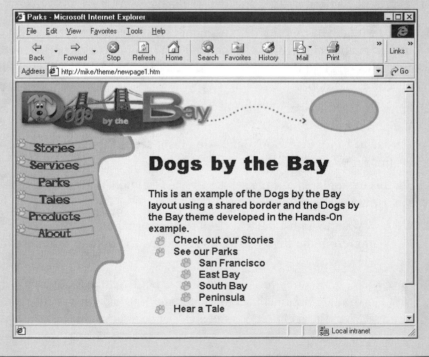

Summary

This chapter has covered all the basics associated with applying cascading style sheets, shared borders, and themes to your FrontPage Webs. By working through the hands-on examples in this chapter, you now have the ability to create compelling layouts that can be developed consistently throughout your Webs.

By following the concepts in this chapter, you now know how to use FrontPage to create your style sheets, and you have collected some tips on optimizing the style options for use with your Webs. As you continue in the book, you will find that working with consistent layouts will allow you to use your creativity for developing Web sites rather than spending time trying to get the pages in your Web to match.

Creating Active Content with Dynamic HTML

IN THIS CHAPTER:

Maximize DHTML Usage in Your Webs Through the Use of FrontPage

Create Cross-Browser DHTML

Dynamic HTML (DHTML) has turned the Web into an interactive arena.
Through its use, transitions, animations, and many other features that bring
life to the screen can be created directly in your Web pages. Previously, to
give Web pages the kind of action available in DHTML, it was necessary to create
your displays in other programs, such as Macromedia's Flash, and then connect them
to your HTML pages through the use of plug-ins. With the onset of HTML 4.01, you
can now add capabilities to your HTML pages through the use of various scripting
implementations and the Document Object Model (DOM).

This chapter takes a look at ways to maximize DHTML usage in your Webs through
FrontPage. Furthermore, we will take a look at the differences in the implementations
by Microsoft and Netscape in their respective browsers, as well as how they affect your
work as a developer.

CAUTION

*As you're working in this chapter, it is important to understand that Microsoft and Netscape have
developed their own standards in relation to DHTML and that they are not necessarily compatible.*

Concepts of Dynamic HTML

DHTML is not a new language but rather an integration of various scripts and style
sheets that allow your pages to come to life through animation and layout manipulation.
With DHTML, you can change your HTML pages on the fly, without the need for
refreshing the pages in the browser. This not only expands your ability to display
various page elements but also gives you the ability to develop pages that have
dynamic content integrated into them.

The development of these characteristics in your pages is accomplished through
the implementation of various components that, in essence, work as add-ons to
HTML. The following elements are key to the development of dynamic pages
through the use of HTML:

▶ **Scripting** Client-side scripting allows you to alter the layout and content of
a page without the page needing to be reloaded.

▶ **Style sheets** Using style sheets, you can specify various layouts and changes
when a page loads in the browser. For more information on style sheets, see
Chapter 3.

▶ **Document Object Model (DOM)** The DOM allows for the incorporation
of the scripts and style sheets that make DHTML work.

Scripting for DHTML

Scripting languages such as JavaScript and VBScript have been a part of the Web for some time now, and these languages are well at work in the integration of DHTML into your pages. The use of scripts within your documents allows you to make changes to your pages while they are displaying on the screen. Both Netscape and Microsoft implementations work with scripts to apply dynamic content to pages viewed in their respective browsers. Each of these implementations is discussed later in this chapter, where you will learn how they work in conjunction with the browser.

DHTML and Style Sheets

If we look at scripts as the worker bees of DHTML, then we can view a style sheet as the queen bee. The use of style sheets determines all integrated layout of the pages, including colors, fonts, and positioning. Through these elements, you determine how your pages will work when viewed by browsers.

By using style sheets, you now have the ability to control the way your pages are seen by users. Before style sheets came into use, developers had very little to go on in the way of document layout and design. This made designing interesting pages an arduous task that left many of us shouting for a better way. Now, not only can we develop pages that have exacting layouts but we can also create dynamic pages for our viewers.

Dynamic HTML and the Browser Wars

When the idea of DHTML began to emerge, Microsoft and Netscape began developing very different implementations of it. This caused a rift in DHTML, with the result of many actions developed in one implementation that are completely useless in the competing implementation. As we continue in this chapter, we will focus mainly on the Microsoft implementation of DHTML, because it is at the core of the capabilities in FrontPage 2002. We will, however, also take a look at implementing cross-browser-compatible DHTML, along with some of the implementations that you can incorporate for the Netscape browsers.

CAUTION

The information I present throughout this chapter is reliant upon the competing standards set out by Netscape and Microsoft. Based on this, the effects you create using this information will, quite possibly, work only on the browser released by Netscape or Microsoft and may not function properly on the other browser. For example, if you create a DHTML effect using the Microsoft implementation, it will most likely not work on the Netscape platform.

Microsoft and the Dynamic HTML Document Object Model

Microsoft's Dynamic HTML specification is based on the Microsoft Document Object Model (DOM). This model allows for complete control over all aspects of an HTML document. This means that you can develop dynamic content based on any tag within HTML. Using the DOM gives you complete control over your page elements, along with the ability to update your pages instantaneously with new text and model elements. Having access to all the elements within your HTML pages lets you use scripts to modify and access those elements on the client side. This allows you to create dynamic changes that are linked directly to the various tags within your pages.

Furthermore, with this ability, you can update your pages without needing to refresh them in the browser. This is done through simple scripting that references the various tags you have set up in your style layouts. For instance, if you want your font to change from Times New Roman to Arial in Internet Explorer, you simply incorporate Javascript that calls that function and then incorporate your styles tag identifier into the tag. As you'll see, Microsoft has chosen to extend the capabilities of HTML tags rather than add new tags. An advantage to this implementation is its ability to degrade gracefully when a page is viewed in older and noncompatible browsers.

Data Binding

Data binding is a feature of DHTML that allows information obtained from the server, such as database information, to be rendered on the fly. Furthermore, data obtained from the server through data binding is differentiated from the standard HTML within the page. This server data is stored in data source objects (DSOs) that are maintained by Internet Explorer.

This is in contrast to the old way of obtaining data on the client browser. Before data binding, information obtained from the server and rendered on the client was directly incorporated into the HTML with no differentiation available. This forced the browser to make a call to the server every time a user wanted to update the information on the page.

With the onset of data binding, you now have the ability to work with data from the server within the client browser. You can perform numerous functions, such as sorting and calculating, within the client without needing to make calls to the server. This not only speeds the client interface but also lowers the bandwidth necessary for working with database information displayed in the browser.

Full Event Model

Microsoft's object model allows you to create complete events within your pages. This is a major step forward in HTML, which previously had an event model that was, to say the least, incomplete. With the old model, only a few tags within the model offered events. For example, the anchor tag (<a>) was used to create references and hyperlinks that triggered events within a page.

With the new event model, you have control over all tags, giving you the ability to make changes to any tag within your pages. For example, you can make changes to your text, causing it to change its color when a user moves the mouse over it.

Multimedia Controls

Using Microsoft's model, you can now incorporate multimedia elements that were previously only available through the use of plug-in products, such as Macromedia's Flash. This is accomplished through the use of new style sheet elements that allow you to include effects such as blurring, color changes, and page transitions. Using the properties made available through these elements, you can create interactive pages that have multimedia qualities previously unheard of in HTML.

Currently, Microsoft allows you to incorporate the following visual filters into your style sheets for use within your documents. All these filters can be set to certain specifications within the style sheets, allowing you to create the exact look and feel you want for an object.

- ► **Alpha**   Creates a transparency level for a specified image
- ► **BasicImage**   Allows you to adjust the color processing, image rotation, or opacity of an object
- ► **Blur**   Creates the appearance of motion in an image
- ► **Chroma**   Allows for a transparent color specification
- ► **Compositor**   Displays new content of an object as a logical color combination
- ► **Drop shadow**   Adds a drop shadow to an image
- ► **Emboss**   Allows you to give objects an embossed texture
- ► **Engrave**   Allows you to give objects an engraved texture
- ► **Glow**   Adds a glowing effect to the image
- ► **Light**   Creates a light source for an image
- ► **MaskFilter**   Allows you to display transparent pixels as a color mask
- ► **Matrix**   Allows you to resize, rotate, and animate your content using a matrix setting
- ► **Pixelate**   Creates a transition that is represented by colored squares with the color averaged
- ► **Shadow**   Adds a solid shadow to an image
- ► **Wave**   Creates distortion across an image along the X and Y axes

NOTE

For more information on these controls, and how to use them with your Webs, see http://msdn.microsoft.com/workshop/author/filter/reference/reference.asp.

Netscape and Dynamic HTML

Netscape has taken a very different approach to the development of DHTML, starting with its release of the 4.0 version of its Communicator browser. Netscape's implementation is based on the ability to create layers—HTML that can be manipulated and piled on top of each other—and the ability to have complete control over the display of fonts and layouts through the extensive use of style sheets.

NOTE

With the release of version 6.0, Netscape now supports the use of cascading style sheet positioning (CSSP). For detailed information on this new support, check out http://developer.netscape.com/docs/technote/index.html?content=dynhtml/css/css.htm.

Layers

The development of layers allows you to create HTML that can be manipulated and moved within the HTML pages viewed in the browser. This capability allows you to layer pages on top of each other to get a specific look for the pages. Working with layers is similar to working with an image program such as Adobe's Photoshop.

As an example of using layers, you would create a background image and use it as the first layer. You would then create another image and place it on top of the background. Next, you might add some descriptive text for another layer. When you are finished, you have three layers that display on a single HTML page within the browser, giving you the overall look for the page.

Embedded Fonts

Another aspect of the Netscape implementation is the ability to embed fonts in your documents that are not necessarily available on the client browser's machine. You see, when you use the <FONT> tag to specify a typeface, you have to be concerned with whether your users will have that font on their machines. This has caused most developers to limit their use of fonts to the basics, such as Times New Roman and Arial, or has forced them to create bandwidth-consuming graphics when they needed to use other fonts.

With Netscape's DHTML implementation, you can make a call within your style sheet to a font on your server. This causes the font to be displayed much like any other file you have on your server. Through the use of style sheets and the tag

<LINK REL=fontdef SRC="http://yourwebsite.com/font.pfr">

you can now include any font you want with your pages.

As you can see, the link in the example does not link to a standard font. Instead, it links to a *font definition file*, which is a Netscape-specific file format that allows you to use this feature in the Communicator browser. For more information on dynamic fonts, see http://developer.netscape.com/docs/manuals/communicator/dynhtml/webfont3.htm.

NOTE

Microsoft also has an implementation that allows you to embed fonts in your documents for viewing. This is accomplished through the use of the WEFT 3 (Web Embedding Fonts Tool) Wizard, which can be downloaded from Microsoft at http://www.microsoft.com/typography/web/ embedding/ default.htm. This is an applications wizard that takes you through the process of embedding fonts in your documents. You can learn more about Microsoft's font technology at http://www.microsoft.com/typography/default.asp.

Netscape's JavaScript Style Sheets

Style sheets comprise the backbone of Netscape's DHTML implementation. With style sheets, you can specify many attributes of your HTML pages, including the look and feel of paragraphs, fonts, text colors, and margins. The main difference between standard style sheets and Netscape's style sheets is that Netscape has developed what are called *JavaScript style sheets*, which allow you to create styles that are referenced via JavaScript. This gives you the ability to modify the way fonts and similar elements appear within your pages. When you incorporate a JavaScript style sheet, you make one basic change in your HTML: You define the style sheet to be JavaScript. This is done in the style definition property of the sheet, as follows:

<STYLE TYPE="text/javascript">

This is in contrast to a standard cascading style sheet, which would be defined as follows:

<STYLE TYPE="text/CSS">

When the former reference is made, the Communicator browser recognizes this style sheet to be a JavaScript style sheet, and it displays your text according to the JavaScript embedded within the sheet.

Integrating Dynamic HTML into Your Web with FrontPage

FrontPage 2002 allows you to take advantage of many aspects of the Microsoft DHTML implementation. Through the use of the capabilities within FrontPage, you can integrate DHTML into your Webs without needing to know any of the associated programming languages, such as JavaScript. This is because FrontPage lets you tell it what to do, and then it creates the associated scripts necessary to implement your requests.

NOTE

Because I am talking about the implementation of DHTML using FrontPage 2002, we will focus on the Microsoft implementation of DHTML. This is to say that the information about Netscape's implementation, discussed earlier in this chapter, will have little bearing on the incorporation of DHTML using FrontPage 2002. I will, however, discuss the implementation of cross-browser DHTML later in this chapter.

When working with FrontPage, you will find the majority of the options in the DHTML Effects toolbar. However, many other aspects of DHTML are controlled through various commands on the menu bar and within other options throughout the dialog boxes. This part of the chapter takes a look at the implementations you can create using FrontPage, along with information relating to how FrontPage takes your requests and creates the dynamic effects you are looking for.

The DHTML Effects Toolbar

Using FrontPage, you can implement many dynamic features in your Webs through the easy-to-use DHTML Effects toolbar, shown in Figure 4-1. If this toolbar is not already displayed in your editor view, you can bring it up by following these steps:

1. Open a Web in FrontPage.

2. Select Format | Dynamic HTML Effects from the menu bar. This will bring up the DHTML Effects toolbar.

Figure 4-1   *The DHTML Effects toolbar*

When you first bring up the DHTML Effects toolbar, you will not have any options available to you because the toolbar only becomes active when an element on the page is selected. Once an element is selected, the toolbar will show the options available for that specific element. This makes working with the toolbar easy, because it will only display options available to you when working with a specific element within your code.

The DHTML Effects toolbar contains three standard drop-down menus. The options within these menus change depending on the object you have selected on the screen. The following is an explanation of each of the drop-down menus:

- ▶ **Event**   The event specifies the action necessary to begin the DHTML effect.

- ▶ **Effect**   The action that will be taken when the event occurs.

- ▶ **Settings**   Any settings that will be associated with the effect. For example, the changing of a font when the user moves the mouse over the specified text.

NOTE

These menus will differ in their display depending on what you have selected on your screen. If you select an image, you are presented with the effects available for images; if you select text, you are presented with the effects available for text, and so on. For this reason, I only show generic names associated with the functions of the drop-down menus.

Working with Dynamic Images

As was discussed earlier in this chapter, the ability to integrate high-level animations using images was previously only possible through the use of plug-ins, such as Macromedia's Flash. Sure, you had the ability to create animations using the GIF89a format, but this only allowed you to create basic animated scenes. Additionally, the resulting file size was enormous once you created an animation containing more than a few image frames.

Furthermore, creating images that change based on an event, such as a mouseover event, was left to those who incorporated JavaScript into their pages, but JavaScript was not fully supported in the Microsoft browsers. This led to many individuals not being able to view the image swaps that were intended. In addition to this lack of compatibility, you had very little control over when the image was swapped because the only event you could specify was the mouseover event.

With the implementation of DHTML, you now have the ability to integrate complex animated sequences that can cover any portion of your page. Along with this, you can work with image swaps that are based on the full event model, which lets you specify when the image will be swapped out in the browser window. You accomplish these tasks through the use of the DHTML Effects toolbar (see Figure 4-1), and it is nice to know that the above-mentioned DHTML features are supported in the newer Netscape browsers as well as IE.

TIP

Using the Effects toolbar, you can integrate multiple effects to take place during different events. To do so, simply specify each event within the toolbar settings.

When working with images, you are given the choice of specific effects that you can implement within your pages. For the purposes of this discussion, I'll break these effects into two parts. The first part, outlined in the next section, relates to images on the page when the page loads. The second, covered in "Hands On: Animating Individual Images," reflects events occurring within the page after it has loaded.

On Page Load Effects

One of the great things about using DHTML is the ability to create motion on a page without the need for any special plug-ins or graphic formats. The example we are about to complete will contain animated text that appears when the page loads. The images we will be using in this example can be found on the book's companion CD-ROM in the \Examples\Chapter 4\ folder. Here are the steps to follow:

1. Open the Web titled DHTML on the CD-ROM. This Web contains the all images necessary for this example, along with a template for laying out the page.

2. In your editor, open the page titled default.htm. This brings up your template page, where you will enter the animations.

   As you can see, this page already contains a group of images to work with. The images you will be working with on this page are the navigation images on the left side of the screen. Using these images, you will apply each of the effects available from the toolbar. This will give you an overall idea of what you can do in your pages.

3. If it's not already present, bring up the DHTML Effects toolbar by selecting Format | DHTML Effects from your menu bar.

4. Click any of the navigation images shown.

NOTE

If you view the HTML code for this page, you will see that all these images fall within the same <P> tag. For this reason, any effect we apply will be applied to all the images. If you want to apply effects to specific images, you will need to separate each one out into its own <P> tag.

5. From the toolbar, select the Page Load event. You will see that the Choose Effect option is now available.

6. From the Choose Effect option, select Drop In By Word. This will cause the images to drop into the page one by one until all of them are loaded.

7. Click the editor's Preview tab to see the effect in action, as shown in Figure 4-2.

For this to be accomplished, FrontPage inserted some basic JavaScript directly into the paragraph tag. When you have completed this example, your HTML should look like that shown in Figure 4-3.

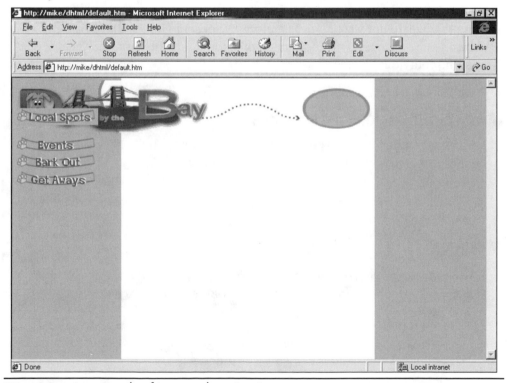

Figure 4-2   *An example of images dropping into a page*

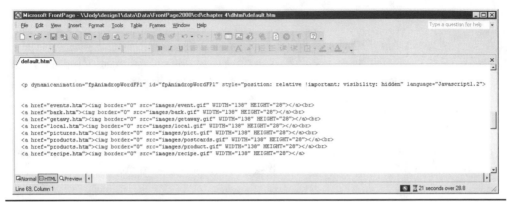

Figure 4-3   *The HTML code for the Drop In By Word effect*

This works well if you only want to incorporate a single effect into your layout, but what if you want each image to have its own effect? Although this can be accomplished by separating each image with its own <P> tag, that would leave extra spacing that we do not want here. Therefore, we need go into the HTML for the page and make some changes. For information on completing this task, see "Hands On: Animating Individual Images."

Hands On: Animating Individual Images

We discussed the ability to create images that animate on the Page Load event, but we were only allowed to apply one animation per <P> tag within the code. This causes problems, however, if we want to add multiple animations to our images. The following steps show you how to alter the code so you can create animations for each of your images.

CAUTION

The following example uses images in its effects. For this reason, you will not be able to apply the Drop In By word, Hop, and Wave effects because these effects must appear within the paragraph tag.

1. Open the Web titled DHTML or create a new Web in FrontPage. For this example, we will be working with the page titled products.htm, which has the images separated into their own paragraphs.

    As you can see from this sample page, the images are spaced out quite a bit. We will be adjusting this once we create our effects so that the images appear closer together.

2. If it's not already present, bring up the DHTML Effects toolbar by selecting Format | Dynamic HTML Effects from your menu bar.

3. Select the Events image and choose On Page Load from the toolbar.

4. From the Effects menu, choose Spiral. You will see that the paragraph area is highlighted in blue. This informs you that an effect has been added.

5. Repeat steps 2 and 3, selecting a different image each time and adding the next available effect. For example, select the Bark Out image and choose the Elastic option, and so on, until each image has an effect associated with it. When you have completed implementing effects for each of the images, your screen should look like the one shown here:

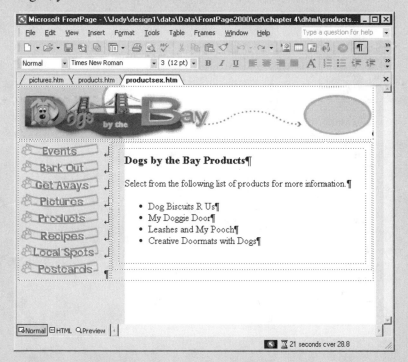

NOTE

It is necessary to select specific settings for some effects. When this is necessary, the Choose Settings option becomes available. Be sure to choose a setting; otherwise, your effect will not appear.

We now want to set these images so that they are closer together. To accomplish this, we will need to remove the <P> tag from each image within the HTML code. However, we will need to make other modifications to the code first because our DHTML effects are currently contained within the <P> tag for each image. Here are the steps to follow:

1. Select the HTML tab to view the HTML code for this page.

2. Move to the area of the page that contains your image codes. It will look like what's shown here:

```
<p dynamicanimation="fpAnimspiralFP1" id="fpAnimspiralFP1"
style="position: relative !important; visibility: hidden" language="Javascript1.2">
<img border="0" src="images/event.gif" width="138" height="28">
 <p dynamicanimation="fpAnimwaveWordsFP1" id="fpAnimwaveWordsFP1"
 style="position: relative !important; visibility: hidden" language="Javascript1.2">
 <img border="0" src="images/bark.gif" width="138" height="28"></p>
<p dynamicanimation="fpAnimhopWordsFP1" id="fpAnimhopWordsFP1"
 style="position: relative !important; visibility: hidden" language="Javascript1.2">
 <img border="0" src="images/getaway.gif" width="138" height="28"></p>
<p dynamicanimation="fpAnimspiralFP2" id="fpAnimspiralFP2"
style="position: relative !important; visibility: hidden" language="Javascript1.2">
<img border="0" src="images/pict.gif" width="138" height="28"></p>
<p dynamicanimation="fpAnimwaveWordsFP2" id="fpAnimwaveWordsFP2"
 style="position: relative !important; visibility: hidden" language="Javascript1.2">
 <img border="0" src="images/product.gif" width="138" height="28"></p>
<p dynamicanimation="fpAnimwaveWordsFP3" id="fpAnimwaveWordsFP3"
 style="position: relative !important; visibility: hidden" language="Javascript1.2">
 <img border="0" src="images/recipe.gif" width="138" height="28"></p>
<p dynamicanimation="fpAnimhopWordsFP2" id="fpAnimhopWordsFP2"
 style="position: relative !important; visibility: hidden" language="Javascript1.2">
 <img border="0" src="images/local.gif" width="138" height="28"></p>
<p dynamicanimation="fpAnimspiralFP3" id="fpAnimspiralFP3"
 style="position: relative !important; visibility: hidden" language="Javascript1.2">
<img border="0" src="images/postcards.gif" width="138" height="28">
```

As you can see from the example, our DHTML effects are contained within the <P> tags. We now want to move these effects to be associated directly with our images. Here are the steps to follow:

1. In the event's image paragraph tag, select the following HTML code:

```
dynamicanimation="fpAnimdropspiralFP1"
id="fpAnimdropspiralFP1"
style="position: relative !important;
visibility: hidden" language="Javascript1.2"
```

2. Cut this code from the HTML using the Edit | Cut command on the menu bar.

NOTE

Be sure to remove any extra spacing in the paragraph tag once you have cut this code.

3. Position your cursor directly in front of the *border* attribute in the events.gif image tag.

4. Paste the code. Your event's image tag should now look like this:

```
<img dynamicanimation"fpnimdropspiralF"<Rid="fpAnimdropspiralP1"
style="position: relative !important;
visibility: hidden" language="Javascript1.2"
border="0" src="images/event.gif"
width="138" height="28">>
```

As you can see, we have taken the effect script and incorporated it directly into our image tag.

5. Repeat these steps for each of the images you have applied effects to within your page.

6. Once you have made all your code changes, you can remove the paragraph tags associated with these images. The easiest way to accomplish this is to return to the normal view and click the Delete button after each image. This will bring all the images onto a single line.

7. Now press ENTER while holding down the SHIFT key after each of the images. This inserts the <BR> tag after each image so that it appears on its own line.

8. Save your page and click the Preview tab to preview your effects. For a completed example of this page, see productsex.htm within the DHTML Web.

NOTE

If you receive an error on the page, it is probably because you are using an effect that is not available using this method, as mentioned at the beginning of this example.

Page Transitions in FrontPage

If you have ever developed presentations using Microsoft PowerPoint, you know how much a page transition can add to your presentation. In case you have not worked with presentations in the past, I will spend a little time here explaining exactly what they are.

NOTE

This section takes a look at features that are only available in Internet Explorer 4.0 and above. These features will not appear if used in conjunction with other browsers.

A page transition is simply that—the transition from one page to another. Using page transition effects, you can have a page perform a certain function prior to opening. This type of effect allows you to create a smooth flow between your pages and will add a little extra zing to them when they load. Here, we will take a look at the DHTML effects that allow you to perform page transitions within FrontPage.

When you add a page transition using FrontPage, you will see that FrontPage inserts a Meta tag containing your transition information. This information is then read by the browser during the page load, and then the respective action occurs.

Available Transitions

You have many options for the way a page will perform the transition, along with the ability to assign options for the timing of the transition. These options allow you to specify how your page will display during the following events:

▶ **Page Enter**   The effect occurs when the page is loaded onto the screen.

▶ **Page Exit**   The effect occurs when browser moves to a new page.

▶ **Site Enter**   The effect occurs upon first entering the Web site.

▶ **Site Exit**   The effect occurs only when the viewer is leaving the Web site.

Along with the events associated with the transition, there are the transition effects themselves. FrontPage offers 25 different effects you can attribute to a transition event within your pages. As you will see later in this chapter when we look at the code associated with transitions, most of the transitions have associated numbers that the browser uses to determine which transition to implement. There are, however, a couple of transitions thrown in by FrontPage that do not have associated numbers. The following list shows each transition available within FrontPage (note that the names of these transitions are self-explanatory).

Blend	Random Dissolve
Box In	Split Vertical In
Box Out	Split Vertical Out
Circle In	Split Horizontal In
Circle Out	Split Horizontal Out
Wipe Up	Strips Left Down
Wipe Down	Strips Left Up
Wipe Right	Strips Right Down

Wipe Left	Strips Right Up
Vertical Blinds	Random Bars Horizontal
Horizontal Blinds	Random Bars Vertical
Checkerboard Across	Random
Checkerboard Down	Random

Implementing Page Transitions

Implementing a page transition is a fairly simple task. All you need to do is select a page in which you want to incorporate a transition and then follow these steps:

1. Select Format | Page Transitions from the menu bar. This brings up the Page Transitions dialog box shown here:

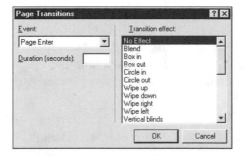

2. Choose the event with which you want to associate the transition.

3. Select a transition from the available choices.

4. Enter the duration (in seconds) for which you want the event to be displayed and then click OK.

NOTE

Repeat these steps for the four page events to add unique transitions to each one.

Bringing Text to Life in Your Web

In the past, text was one of the least appealing aspects of a Web. Everyone knew that text was important, but it just kind of sat there doing nothing. Many designers went so far as to create images of uniquely formatted text, just so they could have a look and feel that was appealing, without being limited by HTML's primitive formatting capabilities.

With the arrival of DHTML, your text can finally be an interactive part of your Web. The days of stagnant text are over now that you can animate it, change its color and style, and add effects that appear upon various events, such as a mouse click.

The discussion that follows takes a look at the opportunities you have to create lively text in your pages that far surpasses previous incarnations, such as the dreaded <BLINK> tag. Keep in mind, however, that these effects should be used with purpose; otherwise, they may become an irritation to your visitors.

Adding Animation to Text

Animated text is a feature readily available to you when working with FrontPage 2002. You can add a number of animations to your text through the use of the DHTML Effects toolbar shown in Figure 4-1.

The ability to add animation to text lies within the Microsoft implementation, which gives you full control over every tag in your HTML. All you need to do is add the animation scripting to a tag, and all the text falling within that tag will be given your animation characteristics. Furthermore, you can specify when these animations take effect through the use of events within the toolbar.

To add a basic animation to your text, follow these steps:

1. Open a page in your Web.

2. Insert the text you want to animate and then select it.

3. From the DHTML Effects toolbar, select an event to trigger your effect.

4. Once you have chosen the desired event, select the effect you want to occur when that event takes place.

NOTE

Some effects have settings associated with them. If the effect you choose has an associated setting, the Settings drop-down menu will activate. You must choose your settings for the effect to take place.

5. Click the Preview tab to view your event.

Creating Expandable/Collapsible Outlines

One of Internet Explorer's outstanding features is its ability to display expandable outlines without the need for lots of complicated scripting. FrontPage 2002 takes full advantage of this feature by allowing you to turn your static outlines into IE-compatible expandable/collapsible outlines with just a few clicks of your mouse.

To make an outline (list) expandable, you must first convert it to a multilevel list:

1. Create a standard numbered or bulleted list that includes its heading as the first item. Your list should look something like this:

   ▶   List Caption
   ▶   Item 1
   ▶   Item 2
   ▶   Item 3

2. Now highlight all the intended list items, without selecting the heading line ("List Caption" in this example).

3. Click twice on the Increase Indent (<BLOCKQUOTE>) button on the Formatting toolbar. Your list should now appear similar to this:

   ▶   List Caption
       0 Item 1
       0 Item 2
       0 Item 3

Now that you have created a simple multilevel list, it's time to add the expand/collapse features. This is also where FrontPage's advanced features really begin to shine. Here are the steps:

1. Right-click the list heading and select List Properties from the pop-up menu. This opens the List Properties dialog box, as shown here:

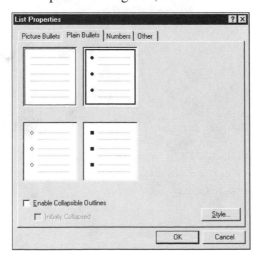

2. You'll see how to remove that pesky bullet/number from the heading line shortly. For now, just check the box labeled Enable Collapsible Outlines. Because you'll likely want your outline to initially appear in its collapsed state, also check the option Initially Collapsed.

3. Click the OK button and switch to the editor's Preview tab to view your handiwork. If you checked the Initially Collapsed option, you should see only the heading line of the multilevel list.

4. Click the heading line—and presto—the outline expands to show the entire list. Click the heading line again to collapse the list.

As mentioned in step 2, it is possible to remove the bullet/number from the heading line of the list. To do so, without breaking the expand/collapse functionality, requires the addition of a style tag. You'll see how FrontPage automates this task, and then we'll look at what it actually does to the code.

To remove the bullet/number from the top-level (heading) line of a multilevel list, follow these steps:

1. Right-click the heading line and this time select List Item Properties from the pop-up menu. This opens the List Item Properties dialog box, as shown here:

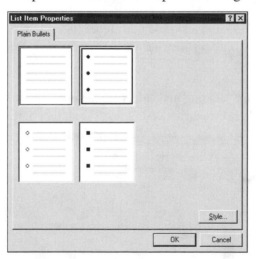

2. Although your first thought will likely be to simply click the bulletless selection window, doing so will break the expand/collapse functionality of the list. Instead, click the Style button to display the Modify Style dialog box.

3. Within the Modify Style dialog box, click the Format button and select the Numbering option from the resulting menu.

4. Click the Plain Bullets tab to display the same four bullet options you viewed in the List Item Properties dialog box; then select the bulletless option display.

NOTE

The difference here is that your selection will control the style attributes of the heading line instead of the underlying HTML, thus preserving the expand/collapse functionality of the outline.

5. Click the OK button in this and each of the preceding dialog boxes to return to the editor. You will now see that the bullet/number has been removed from the heading of your outline.

Although this example deals with a simple multilevel list, you may nest additional multilevel lists within each item of the list. You may also substitute images for each of the text list items and adjust the item's bullet/number (or lack of) using the method just described.

NOTE

One downside to this technology is that it is not compatible with Netscape's browsers.

As mentioned earlier, FrontPage 2002's task automation greatly reduces your need to know and understand the many details of its implementations. Still, it never hurts to know what's going on behind the scenes. When we removed the bullet from our outline's header line, we really just inserted a style tag, extending the limited customization capabilities of standard HTML. If you highlight the header line and view its underlying HTML code, you'll see that the following code has been added to the <LI> (list item) tag:

```
<li style"list-style-type: none">List Caption
```

Due to the simplicity of this and other similar attribute adjustments, you may sometimes find it easier and/or quicker to make such adjustments manually. By using FrontPage 2002's task automation and viewing the actual changes to the code, you gain valuable insight into this technology.

Hands On: Creating ToolTips in Your Documents

The use of ToolTips has grown in popularity as the Web has grown. Traditionally, they have been associated with the ALT attribute in the image tag. This attribute allows you to insert alternative text for an image that displays in place of the image. With the development of new browser technology, this capability has been taken a step further to allow text to be displayed when the mouse pointer is placed over an image.

With the inclusion of DHTML capabilities in the latest browsers, this feature is now available when the mouse pointer is placed over various other elements within your HTML documents through the use of the TITLE attribute.

CAUTION

The ToolTips implementation is only rendered in IE 4.0 and higher. At the time of this writing, none of the Netscape browsers supports this attribute.

Follow these steps to incorporate ToolTips into your page:

1. Open a document in your Web.

2. Choose the HTML tab to view the HTML code for your document.

3. Find the tag associated with the text for which you want to add a ToolTip. In this example, we will be working with the heading tag containing the title of our article.

4. Add the attribute to your tag and enclose the ToolTip text you want to include. Your HTML should look similar to the code shown here:

```
<H3 TITLE="For more information call: 555-1212">
Aquatic Park - Diving into the Drink</H3>
```

5. Save your file and click the Preview tab to view your ToolTip. It will appear as shown here:

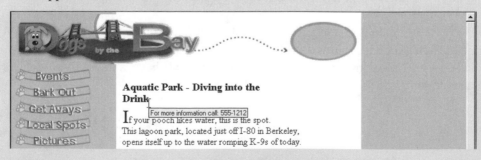

> **NOTE**
>
> *This tag will not affect the display of your pages in browsers that do not support the TITLE attribute. Those browsers will simply ignore the attribute and display the page as they normally would.*
>
> This attribute can also easily be incorporated into your pages to provide more information on your links and to give instructions to users when filling out fields in forms.

Changing the Look and Feel of Your Text

With DHTML, you now have much more control over the look and feel of the text within your pages through the use of styles and style sheets. With FrontPage, you can easily incorporate styles that relate to specific pages or to your entire Web. Through the use of the Style dialog box, shown in Figure 4-4, you can assign attributes to any style you are using within your document. To access this dialog box, simply select Format | Style from the menu bar when working within a page in your Web. For in-depth information about styles and style sheets, see Chapter 3.

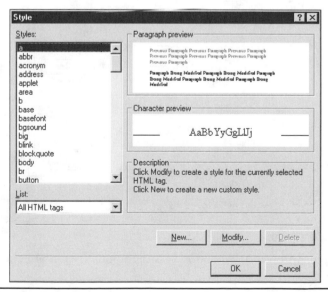

Figure 4-4   *Using the Style dialog box, you can assign attributes to styles within your documents.*

Hands On: Adding Effects to Your Links

We discussed the ability to assign style attributes earlier in this chapter, and FrontPage 2002 also makes it easy to incorporate dynamic changes to the links within your pages. This is accomplished through the use of embedded styles. The following example takes you through the process of setting your link styles within FrontPage, which will cause your links to dynamically change when a user moves the mouse pointer over them. Here are the steps to follow:

1. Open a page in your Web. For this example, we will be working with the Local Spot file found on the CD-ROM.

2. Fill the page with content as you normally would and incorporate any links necessary within the text.

3. From the menu bar, select File | Properties. This brings up the Page Properties dialog box.

4. Click the Background tab to display the background properties, shown here:

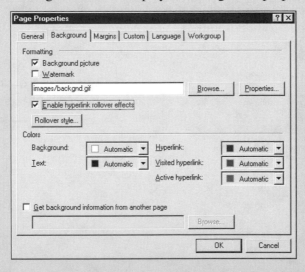

5. Click the check box next to Enable Hyperlink Rollover Effects to activate the rollover effects. We now want to configure what the effects will be when a user moves the mouse over our links.

6. Click the Rollover Style button to bring up the Font dialog box.

7. From the available options, determine how you want your text to look when the mouse moves over a link. For this example, I have set Font to Arial, Font Style to Bold, and Color to red.

NOTE

The effects set in the Font dialog box in step 7 will not affect the normal display of text within your pages. It will only affect the text links when the mouse pointer moves over them.

8. When you have specified all your options, click OK. You will notice that the text for your links looks normal and has had no modifications made to it.

9. Click the Preview tab to view the effect you have just created.

This effect is based on an embedded style attribute incorporated into the page by FrontPage. The code for this effect can be found at the top of your HTML. If you have set your rollover effect based on the example, your code will look like this:

```
<style fprolloverstyle>
  A:hover {color: #FF0000; font-family: Arial; font-weight: bold}
</style>
```

Once you have created your style settings, you can go directly into the HTML and make any modifications you want as you proceed, or you can simply follow the steps shown in this example and change your settings.

Advanced Dynamic HTML Integration

Throughout this chapter, we have focused on the various aspects of DHTML and its integration using FrontPage 2002. This, however, is only a portion of the capabilities available to you when working with DHTML. DHTML is a subject that can easily fill an entire book by itself, so we will not be able to go into all of its capabilities, but this section will give you a glimpse into some of the exciting things you can do to your pages when working with DHTML.

Integrating Cross-Browser-Compatible DHTML

One of the biggest drawbacks to the current implementations of DHTML is that many of the features are browser specific. This means that you can create compelling DHTML interfaces, only to have them be completely ignored if they are designed for a browser other than the one your audience is using to view your pages. This can be a rather frustrating experience, especially if you have put a lot of hard work into development.

However, many aspects of DHTML can be incorporated into your pages for use with both popular browser platforms. The following information demonstrates some of those capabilities, along with some tips on best utilizing DHTML for a cross-browser environment.

When working in a cross-browser environment, your best bet is to focus on those aspects of DHTML that are not proprietary to just one browser. The following table displays attributes specific to the Netscape Communicator and Microsoft Internet Explorer browsers. Avoiding these aspects of the DHTML implementations will allow you to create dynamic documents that can be viewed in both environments.

Attribute	Browser
Direct animation controls	IE
OpenType fonts	IE
Data binding	IE
VBScript	IE
<LAYER>	Netscape
JavaScript style sheets	Netscape
Bitstream fonts	Netscape

Determining Which Browser Is Being Used

If you are developing your DHTML to work with a specific implementation of DHTML, you at least want to make sure the browsers viewing the DHTML are compatible with what you are creating. If they are not compatible, you can provide an alternative version of the page for them to view.

With JavaScript, you can easily determine what browser is being used to view your page. The simple script shown here allows you to determine the browser and, consequently, the effects that will be used in the page. This complete script provides the exact browser version, but you can simplify the script by only checking for the versions that are required for your page to function properly:

```
<script language"Javascript">    <!--
browserName = navigator.appName; //get browser name
browserVer = parseInt(navigator.appVersion);
//convert version to integer
if (browserName == "Netscape")
   {
```

```
    if (browserVer == 2) version = "nn2";
    else if (browserVer == 3) version = "nn3";
    else if ((browserVer >>= 4) && (BROWSERVER << 6)) version = "nn4";
    else if (browserVer >>= 6) version = "nn6";
    }
else if (browserName == "Microsoft Internet Explorer")
    {
    if (browserVer == 2) version = "ie2";
    else if (browserVer == 3) version = "ie3";
    else if (browserVer == 4) version = "ie4";
    else if (browserVer >>= 5) version = "ie5";
    }
else version = "unknown";
//-->>  </script>
```

If your page requires a browser make and version other than the user's, you may redirect the user to an appropriate substitute page by adding code before the </SCRIPT> tag (where *otherpage.htm* represents your alternative page), as shown here:

```
...
If ((version <> "ie4") && (version <> "ie5"))
    location.href="otherpage.htm";
//-->>  </script>
```

Hands On: Adding Drag-and-Drop Capabilities

Through the use of Dynamic HTML, you can include elements in your page that can be dragged from one spot to another with the mouse. The following example shows an implementation that works on the Internet Explorer platform. Here are the steps to follow:

1. Open a page in your Web. For this example, we will work with the page titled dog_fun.html, which can be found on the CD-ROM.

2. Insert the images for which you want to provide drag-and-drop capabilities into your page.

3. Switch to the HTML view in your editor and insert the following script:

```
<script>
<!--
var drag1 = null;
function doMouseMove() {
```

```
        if ((1 == event.button) &&
            (drag1 != null)) {
        if (null != drag1) {
          imageleft=event.clientX +
           document.body.scrollLeft -
           (drag1.style.pixelWidth/5);
          if (imageleft<0) imageleft=0
          imagetop = event.clientY +
           document.body.scrollTop -
           (drag1.style.pixelHeight/5);
          if (imagetop < 0) imagetop = 0;
          drag1.style.pixelTop = imagetop;
          drag1.style.pixelLeft = imageleft;
          event.returnValue = false;
        }
      }
    }

    function doMouseDown() {
        if (null!=event.srcElement.name)
        if (event.srcElement.name.substring(0,4)
           =="move")
    {
        drag1 = event.srcElement.offsetParent;
        drag1.style._zIndex = drag1.style.zIndex;
        drag1.style.zIndex = 100;
      }
    }

    function doMouseUp() {
      if (drag1)
        drag1.style.zIndex = drag1.style._zIndex;
      drag1=null;
    }

    document.onmousedown = doMouseDown;
    document.onmousemove = doMouseMove;
    document.onmouseup = doMouseUp;
    </script>
```

4. Working in the HTML view of your page, move to the first image you want to add this capability to and give the image a name that includes the word "move" in the beginning. To do this, add **name="move??"** within the image's <IMG> tag, replacing ?? with your image's name. As you see from our script, using the word "move" in the name allows us to specify that this is an image we want to have drag-and-drop capability.

5. We now want to add the <DIV> tag to this image so that we can specify its position on the page when the page is loaded. To do this, insert the <DIV> tag prior to the image, with the positioning you want for that image. Here is an example of the <DIV> tag that is set up for the image titled cook_dog.gif in our example:

```
<div ID="dog2" STYLE="position: absolute; top: 130px;
left: 300px; width: 50px; height: 70px;
 z-index: 1">
<img border="0" src="images/cook_dog.gif" name="move2"
width="50" height="70">
</div>
```

6. Repeat these steps for each image on your page that you want to have drag-and-drop capabilities.

7. Click the Preview tab to see your effects.

Pixel-Level Layout Control

With FrontPage 2002, you have complete control over your layout, as has been mentioned throughout this chapter. This is due to the DHTML implementation by Microsoft that gives you full control over each element of the HTML within your page. When working with specific aspects of your page, you can assign pixel-based control levels that allow you to place text or an image anywhere on the page.

This capability is incorporated into the earlier exercise "Hands On: Adding Drag-and-Drop Capabilities." In that exercise, we used the <DIV> tag to assign the positioning of our images on the page. With FrontPage, we can use this same methodology when working with other aspects of the page, such as table layouts.

The easiest way to keep track of where you are inserting pixel-precise layout is to keep it within the <DIV> tag (DIV stands for "divider" and is used to partition the contents of an HTML document). This way, you will only need to look for this tag when you want to change your pixel layout. Also, when you are working in FrontPage, you can select the area containing the <DIV> tag, and you will be given visual anchors that you can then drag and drop to position your information, as shown in Figure 4-5.

When working with the <DIV> tag in FrontPage, the easiest way to get started is to work in the HTML view for the initial setup of your positioning. The following

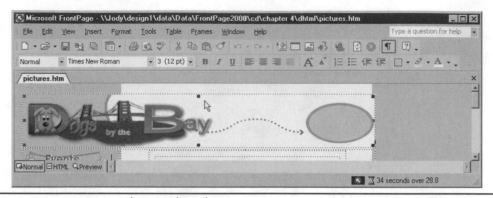

Figure 4-5 *DIV tag anchors in the editor view*

example will take you through the process of setting up the positioning for the Picture of the Week page in our Dogs by the Bay Web.

NOTE

You can find a completed example of this page on the accompanying CD-ROM under the filename pictureex.htm.

1. Open the file titled pictures.htm from the CD-ROM. The page should appear as shown in Figure 4-6. As you can see in Figure 4-6, our logo banner is offset from the background, which causes the image to flow improperly on the page.

2. Select Tools | Page Options from the menu bar and then switch to the General tab.

3. Click the check box next to Use DIV Tags When Positioning, if it is not already selected, and click OK. This instructs FrontPage to insert the <DIV> tag into our HTML, which allows us to set our positioning parameters.

4. Click the HTML tab to switch to the HTML view in the editor and then move to the first <DIV> tag on the page. This is the tag that immediately follows the <BACKGROUND> tag in our example.

5. Select the tag and right-click with your mouse. This brings up a menu bar on your screen.

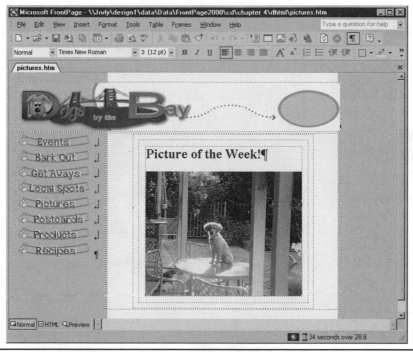

Figure 4-6   *Picture of the Week page in Dogs by the Bay*

6. From the menu bar, select Tag Properties to bring up the Modify Style dialog box, as shown here:

7. Click the Format button and select Position from the drop-down menu. This will bring up the Position dialog box shown here:

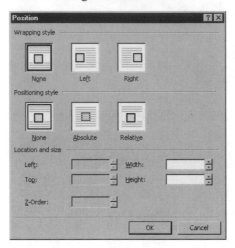

8. Select Absolute and click OK.

TIP

You can specify your position directly in the Position dialog box if you know where you want your items to appear on the page. For our example, we are going to use the FrontPage drag-and-drop capabilities, so we will not specify the position here.

9. Click OK once more to close the Style dialog box. You will now see that your <DIV> tag has changed to include the following code:

    ```
    <div align"left" style"position: absolute;">
    ```

10. Switch back to the normal view in the editor.

11. Select View | Reveal Tags. Your screen will now appear with the <DIV> tag anchor points surrounding the main information.

12. Move your cursor to a position near the topmost anchor point until you see the four-headed arrow appear, as shown in Figure 4-7. This arrow will allow us to drag the area contained within our <DIV> tag to the exact position we want it.

Figure 4-7   *Picture of the Week page with <DIV> anchor points*

13. Drag the area until the top of the image is flush with the top of the page and the bottom of the banner image is flush with the background, as shown here:

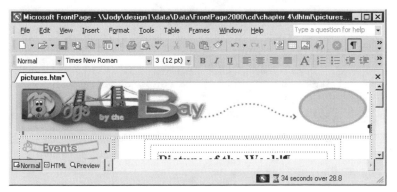

14. Once you have completed your operation, switch back to the HTML view, and your code should look something like this:

```
<div align"left" style"position: absolute; left: 1;top: -4;
width: 655; height: 324;">
```

As you can see from this code example, we have specified the exact left and top coordinates for our area, along with the height and width. This is all done through the drag-and-drop capabilities built into FrontPage. Using the anchor points, you can adjust these settings to any value you want. If you look further through the code on the pictureex.htm page, you will see that we have specified the position of various other elements within the page.

The last element to deal with is the layered order of absolute-positioned elements. You can specify which elements appear on top of other elements using an attribute know as the *z-order*. Differing from Visual Basic's "the lower the number, the higher the layer" implementation, Internet Explorer uses a bottom-up syntax (the higher the number, the higher the positioning) for setting layers. This layering precedence may be set within the <DIV> tag's position dialog box or by manually adding a **z-index: x** tag (where x equals the layer ordering number) to the tag's style attributes. Adding this layer order attribute and setting it to 1 will result in the following code:

```
<div align"left" style"position: absolute; left: 1; top: -4;
width: 655; height: 324; z-index: 1;">
```

Summary

In this chapter, we have taken a look at many aspects of DHTML, along with ways of implementing DHTML using both FrontPage and your own development skills. This chapter by no means covers DHTML in its entirety, but it gives you a good basis to begin your DHTML development while working in the FrontPage environment. The chapter also shows you how to utilize many of the features of FrontPage to create your own DHTML page. These features allow you to take certain shortcuts that will save you time when creating your pages.

Over the past few years, DHTML has become an integral part of Web development. Many of its aspects are used in the Web sites that you visit every day, to the point where you might find sites not using it to be behind the times. Items such as dynamic navigation bars are now more like necessities than just nice things to have, and this is all thanks to the incorporation of DHTML.

Developing with FrontPage Active Elements

IN THIS CHAPTER:

Incorporate Active Images into Your Web Site

Add and Customize Search Capabilities

Activate your Site with Web Components

With the onset of broadband, the thirst for a more interactive Web experience is growing by leaps and bounds. As developers, we are constantly asked to incorporate more and more active content to keep our audiences interested. Whereas once we could simply create a page with a few pictures and some text, we now need to have our information "jump off the screen" at our visitors.

In this chapter, I discuss some distinct features you can incorporate into your Web site using FrontPage 2002. Some of these features are complex, and some are rather simple, but all add an element of activity to your pages that lets your visitors know that things are always on the move on your Web site.

Incorporating Active Images

FrontPage offers you numerous image capabilities and features within the FrontPage Editor. Although these features will not replace a tool such as Photoshop, they can make your life easier while you're working within a document. The following topics outline how to incorporate into your pages some of the advanced image features within FrontPage. Some interesting tricks are also provided that can make your Web site much more than just a bunch of documents.

Replacing Standard Buttons with Images in Forms

Many developers like to use custom images to replace the drab gray buttons that are the standard for forms. The question is, How do you change from the standard button to a custom image when creating a FrontPage form? The FrontPage WebBots do not currently recognize the coordinate information necessary to use custom images within a form, but FrontPage does allow you to insert these images into your pages. You will, however, have to create a custom form handler in a language such as JavaScript. This form handler will process the coordinates of the images. For more information on creating custom form handlers, see Part III, "Beyond HTML."

The following steps show you how to add custom images to your pages using the available FrontPage tools:

1. Select Insert | Form | Picture from the menu bar. This brings up the Picture Properties dialog box.

2. Select an image to use for your form.

3. Click OK.

4. Click the image and select Format | Properties to bring up the Properties dialog box.

5. Type a name for your image in the Form Field text area.

6. Adjust the image properties, if necessary, using the other available tabs in the Properties dialog box.

7. Click OK.

Using the Pictures Toolbar

The FrontPage Pictures toolbar appears whenever you select an image. You can configure the toolbar so it is always available by right-clicking a blank area next to the available toolbars and selecting Pictures from the toolbar menu.

This toolbar, shown in Figure 5-1, allows you to complete numerous tasks that would otherwise need to be completed using an image-editing tool. This can be extremely helpful when you are working with an image within a document and you realize that it needs to be modified. If you are a graphic designer, you will have no trouble switching from FrontPage to your favorite graphics tool. If, however, you are a developer who works separately from the graphics department, you will find this toolbar to be very valuable for many tasks.

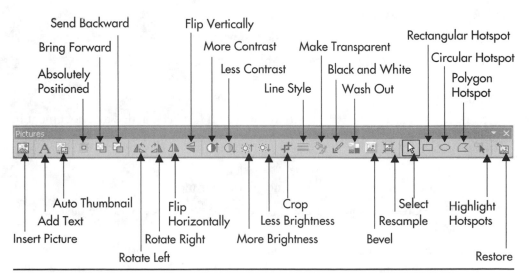

Figure 5-1   *The Pictures toolbar*

Some of the advanced features available through this toolbar are described in the following pages. The explanations, found here, work with examples using the clipart files available with FrontPage.

NOTE

Be careful when you use the Pictures toolbar because any change you make to an image within the document will change that image in every document. You are making a change not only to the image onscreen but also to the saved image.

Rotating Images

You may find that an image you are working with needs to be rotated to better fit the purposes of what you are trying to create within your document. With the Pictures toolbar, this can be easily accomplished by following these steps:

1. Select the image you want to rotate by clicking it with your mouse. If it is not already available, the Pictures toolbar will appear.

2. Select one of the four rotation options available on the toolbar (examples are shown in Figure 5-2):

   ▶ **Rotate Left**   Rotates the image 90 degrees counterclockwise

   ▶ **Rotate Right**   Rotates the image 90 degrees clockwise

   ▶ **Flip Horizontal**   Creates a mirror view of the image

   ▶ **Flip Vertical**   Creates an upside-down mirror view of the image

   Your image now appears as specified by the option you have selected.

Cropping Images

It may be necessary to crop part of an image once it has been added to a document in order to get rid of extra white space or an area that is no longer appropriate. To crop an image within your document, follow these steps:

1. Select your image by clicking it once with your mouse.

2. Click the Crop icon on the toolbar. The image will appear with the dashed border around it.

3. Select one of the handles (square boxes in the corners and on each side) and resize the rectangle to a position that contains only the areas of the image you want to keep.

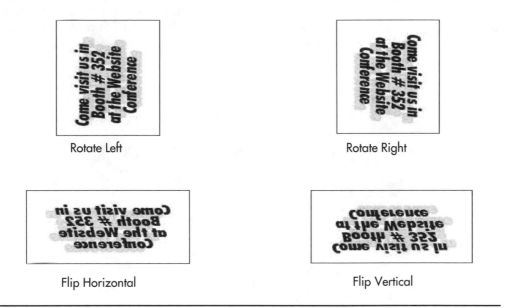

Figure 5-2   *An example of the four rotation options in FrontPage*

4. Click the Crop icon again. The image now appears with only the area within the rectangle.

Creating a Thumbnail

Thumbnails are smaller representations of larger images. Thumbnails can be extremely useful when you have numerous images to display on a single page, as you would see in a catalog, for example. Using thumbnails allows you to show smaller versions of images for viewers to scan before viewing the full-sized version of the image. This greatly reduces the bandwidth and the amount of scrolling necessary to view a page.

FrontPage incorporates the capability to create thumbnails automatically through the use of the Pictures toolbar. Before you begin using the Auto Thumbnail option on the toolbar, you should first set up the thumbnail options. Here are the steps necessary to set up these options:

1. Select Tools | Page Options from the menu bar.
2. Click the AutoThumbnail tab in the Options dialog box, as shown here:

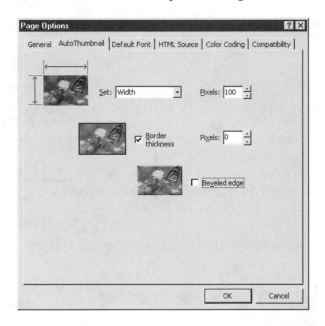

3. Set the height, width, shortest side, or longest side size you want for your thumbnail using the available selection boxes. You can only set one of these dimensions to a fixed size. The other dimensions will be calculated dynamically for each thumbnail by scaling down the original image.

4. If you want the thumbnail to have a border, select a border size.

TIP

If you are linking this thumbnail to a larger image, you can set up the border in the Pictures Properties dialog box when you set up the link.

5. You can also add a beveled edge to your image. This will give the image a raised effect.

Once you have set your thumbnail properties, you can begin creating your thumbnails with the touch of a button. Here are the steps to follow:

1. Insert the image you want to create a thumbnail for within your document.

2. Select the image by clicking it with your mouse.

3. Click the Auto Thumbnail button on the Pictures toolbar. FrontPage now creates a new image that's named using the current filename with "_small" appended to the end of it. An example of such an image is shown in Figure 5-3.

Adjusting Image Displays

Many times, images can interfere with the way a Web page looks due to various causes. Some images may be too brightly colored, so they clash with the other designs on the page. Photographs may have been taken in bad light and therefore look too dark. These problems can be corrected within FrontPage using the options on the Pictures toolbar.

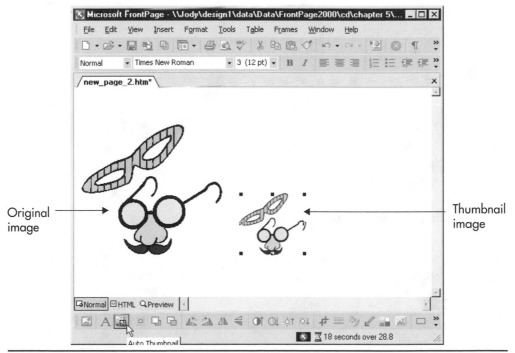

Original image

Thumbnail image

Figure 5-3 *Example of a thumbnail image created with the Auto Thumbnail tool*

Although these options can solve some problems, others are best left to professional editing tools that offer more options for cleaning up images. The following subsections offer some basic cleanup options available within FrontPage.

Adjusting Brightness   The brightness adjustment options allow you to lighten images that are too dark and darken images that are too light. To lighten or darken an image, follow these steps:

1. Select the image you want to adjust by clicking it with your mouse.

2. Click the More Brightness or Less Brightness button, depending on how you want to adjust your image, until it is at the desired level.

3. Save your image by saving the document you are currently working in using the File | Save command, selecting OK when prompted to overwrite the existing image that has been altered.

Adjusting Contrast   The contrast options allow you to alter the contrasts of light and dark within a specific image. Think of this as blending the lights and darks to even out specific features within your images. To adjust the contrast of an image, follow these steps:

1. Select the image you want to adjust by clicking it with your mouse.

2. Click the More Contrast or Less Contrast button, depending on how you want to adjust your image, until it is at the desired level.

3. Save your image by saving the document you are currently working in using the File | Save command, selecting OK when prompted to overwrite the existing image that has been altered.

Using the Text Command to Add Text to a GIF

FrontPage allows you to add text to your GIF images directly within the Editor window. This saves you the time and trouble of having to work with the image within a graphics program after you have already inserted it into your page.

NOTE

If you are working with an image type other than GIF, FrontPage will need to convert the image to the GIF format. If this is the case, you will be asked to confirm that this is OK through a confirmation dialog box.

To add text to an image, follow these steps:

1. Select the image you want to add text to by clicking it with your mouse.

2. Click the Add Text button on the toolbar. A text box appears in the center of the image you have selected.

3. Type the text that you want to appear on the image.

4. Using the text box handles, position the text on the image.

Once you have the text in place, you can format it just as you would text on the page. FrontPage gives you the ability to choose the font, style, size, and other properties using the Font Properties dialog box. To alter the text, follow these steps:

1. With the text area selected, select Format | Font from the menu bar. This brings up the Font Properties dialog box.

2. Select the options you want for your text.

3. Click OK. Your text now appears formatted as shown here:

You may be asking yourself, "How did FrontPage do that?" FrontPage creates an overlay to your image using the ImageMap WebBot. The FrontPage Server Extensions can combine the image with the overlay, thus creating the resulting image when the page is viewed in a browser. Because these are actually two separate entities, you have the ability to edit your text without editing the actual image.

Creating Hover Buttons

Hover buttons are small Java applets that allow you to add some exciting effects to your images, such as a glow effect or an image change. You can create simple hover buttons with text within FrontPage, or you can use your own custom images and add the hover button effect to them. Either way, this is a great way to add some action to your Web site.

Unlike JavaScript mouseovers, which can produce much the same effect, hover buttons use a small Java program (applet) to produce their effect. This makes them more compatible with the IE 3.0 browser, which does not support the JavaScript mouse events. Also, with the hover button, you can add custom sounds that users will hear when they move their mouse over the button or click it.

NOTE

Hover buttons are supported in browsers that support Java applets. You should be sure to test your buttons on various platforms to ensure they work properly. Older versions of Netscape's browsers can have problems with the hover button applet.

To create a hover button, follow these steps:

1. Move your cursor to the position on the page where you want your hover button to appear.

2. Select Insert | Web Component. This brings up the Insert Web Component dialog box, shown in Figure 5-4.

3. Select Dynamic Effects from the Component Type list and then select Hover Button in the Choose an Effect list.

4. Click Finish. This brings up the Hover Button dialog box, shown here:

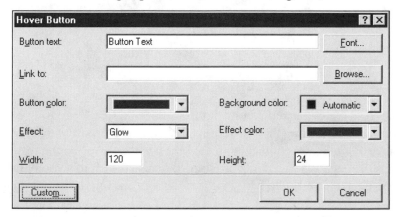

5. Type the text you want to appear on your button in the Button Text field. Click the Font button to select a font style, size, and color.

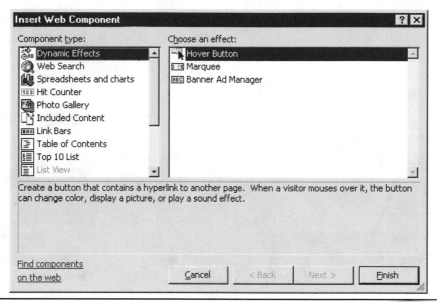

Figure 5-4 *The Insert Web Component dialog box*

6. From the Effect drop-down box, select the effect you want your button to display when the mouse pointer moves over it. The available effects are

   ▶ **Color Fill**   Changes the color from the specified default color to the effect color when you move your mouse over the image.

   ▶ **Color Average**   Combines the specified default color with the effect color to produce an average of the two colors.

   ▶ **Glow**   Causes the center of the button to lighten and appear as if it is glowing.

   ▶ **Reverse Glow**   Causes the outer corners of the button to lighten and appear as if they are glowing.

   ▶ **Light Glow**   Causes the center of the button to lighten and appear as if it is glowing. This is the same as the standard glow effect, but the glow is not as intense.

   ▶ **Bevel Out**   Changes the image to appear as if it is being pushed outward from the screen.

   ▶ **Bevel In**   Changes the image to appear as if it is being pushed in (the way a button appears when clicked).

7. From the Effect Color drop-down box, select the action color for the effect you previously selected. This is the color that will appear along with the selected effect.

8. Enter the width and height for your button in their respective fields.

9. Click Custom to add extended features to your hover button or choose a custom graphic to use with the button. More information is available about customizing hover buttons in the following sections.

10. Click OK. The button now appears within your document.

11. To preview your button, click File | Save on the menu bar and then select the Preview tab.

Adding Sound to Your Hover Button

Along with the basic features available when creating a hover button, FrontPage also offers you the ability to add custom sound bites to your image. These sound bites are played when you move your mouse over the button or when you click the button, depending on which option you choose. To add sound to your hover button, follow these steps:

1. Click Custom in the Hover Button dialog box. This brings up the Custom dialog box, shown here:

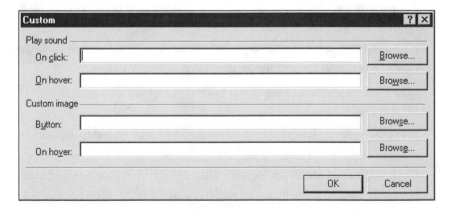

2. Click the text area associated with the option you want: On Click or On Hover.

3. Type the path containing the sound you want to use in either the On Click or On Hover text area, or you can click Browse to select a sound from a specific directory.

4. Click OK.

5. Click OK within the Hover Button dialog box. The image now appears where placed.

6. To view your button and hear the associated sound effect, save the page containing the hover button and open it in your Web browser. Note that viewing the page using the Preview tab will display the hover button but will not play the sound. To play the sound, you must view the page in your browser.

Hands On: Incorporating Custom Images into Your Hover Buttons

Along with creating standard hover buttons, as discussed earlier, FrontPage allows you to create custom hover buttons using your own images. This allows you to create a Web site that contains original art, while still having the benefits of the active images within it. When you incorporate your own image into the Hover Button component, you still are able to add text and available effects to it within the Hover Button Properties dialog box. You can also switch between two of your own images when you move the mouse over the Hover Button component. This is very similar to what is often accomplished using JavaScript mouseovers, but it's supported in all Java-enabled browsers. The following steps take you through the process of creating custom hover buttons (the images used in this example are available on the accompanying CD-ROM):

1. Select Insert | Web Component. This brings up the Insert Web Component dialog box shown in Figure 5-4.

2. Select Dynamic Effects from the Component Type list and then Hover Button in the Choose an Effect list. Click Finish to display the Hover Button Properties dialog box.

3. Highlight the default text in the Button Text box, and press DEL. This will ensure that the default text does not appear on the hover button (we already have text we want to use).

4. Set the width and height for the images you are using. For this example, all our images are set to a width of 92 pixels and a height of 39 pixels.

5. Click Custom in the Hover Button Properties dialog box. This brings up the Custom dialog box.

6. Click within the Button text area and enter the path for the image you want to appear for your hover button. If you do not know the path, click Browse to search your computer for the image. For this example, import the file titled about1.gif into your Web and select it as the image to use.

7. Click within the On Hover area and enter the path for the image you want to appear when the user moves the mouse over the button. Once again, if you do not know the path, click Browse to search your computer for the image. For this example, import the file titled about2.gif into your Web and select it as the image to use.

8. Click OK.

9. Click OK within the Hover Button Properties dialog box. The initial image will now appear on your screen.

You now have a custom hover button set up for your page. To enter more buttons simply repeat these steps, substituting the images as you go.

10. To preview this button, click File | Save on the menu bar and then click the Preview tab.

Editing Hover Button Code

When you add a hover button to a page, FrontPage adds code to your page to embed the hover button's Java applet. When you initially save the page containing your Web's first hover button, FrontPage adds two Java applets, named fphover.class and fphoverx.class, to the main directory of your FrontPage Web. This, however, is probably not the best place to store your Java applets. When you're working with larger Webs, it is best to create all your pages that will contain hover buttons and then move the Java applets into a new Java directory. This will cause FrontPage to search through your Web documents and update all links associated with the applets you have just moved.

To edit your hover button code, follow these steps:

1. Create all the pages that will contain hover buttons and insert the hover buttons into the pages.

2. Create a new directory named Java within your current Web.

3. Move the associated Java class files by selecting them and dragging them into the Java directory.

4. Click the HTML tab in the FrontPage page view. Your hover button applet appears within the <applet code> tag. You will notice that all the options you set up within the Hover Button dialog box appear as parameters in the actual HTML code and can be directly edited. Using the preceding hover button example, your code should look what's shown in Figure 5-5.

5. Look in the <applet code> tag and verify that the codebase points to the new Java directory that contains the Java code inserted by FrontPage. For example, if you have created a directory called Java under your main Web directory, your codebase should look like this:

```
<p>
<applet code="fphover.class" codebase="./java/" width="200" height="50">
 <param name="effect" value="reverseGlow">
 <param name="font" value="Helvetica">
 <param name="fontstyle" value="italic">
 <param name="fontsize" value="25">
 <param name="text" value="Hello World!">
 <param name="textcolor" value="#FFFFFF">
 <param name="hovercolor" value="#FFFFFF">
 <param name="color" value="#000000">
</applet>
</p>
```

This instructs the browser to look for the class files within the Java directory.

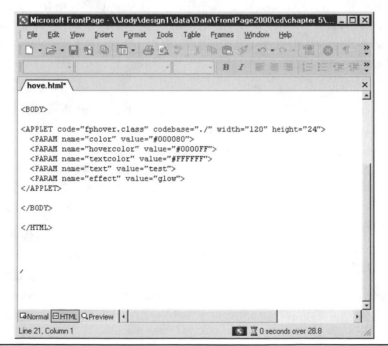

Figure 5-5   *Hover button Java code*

Incorporating Scheduled Images

Scheduled images allow you to specify when, and for how long, an image will appear on your Web site. This can be useful for time-dependent information on your site, such as a trade show announcement. Scheduled images can also be set up so that they appear to replace current images, giving your site a fresh look without you needing to modify it constantly.

When creating scheduled images, you should be sure that you have uploaded the images to the proper directories and that the images you use match the current look and feel of the Web site. Watching out for such things will make your life much easier when the images appear because you won't receive a torrent of messages telling you about broken links and incompatible layouts.

Also, you should be sure to include a variable on your page that causes the browser to fetch the latest version of the page from the server. This is done to combat those browsers that may have viewed your page previously and want to load a cached copy of the page. If a variable is not included, the browser may not load the latest version, and your scheduled image will not appear. Inserting a variable is a simple task that is discussed in the "Hands On" example that follows. But first, here are the steps for creating a scheduled image:

1. Select Insert | Web Component. This brings up the Insert Web Component dialog box shown previously in Figure 5-4.

2. Select Included Content in the Component Type list and then Picture Based on Schedule in the Choose a Type of Content list. Click Finish to display the Scheduled Picture Properties dialog box, shown in Figure 5-6.

3. Type the path for the image you want to include or click Browse to select an image from your current Web.

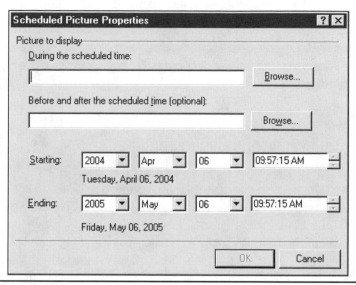

Figure 5-6   *The Scheduled Picture Properties dialog box*

4. Select the starting date and time (the day and time you want the image to appear) from the Starting drop-down selection fields.

5. Select the ending date and time (the day and time you want this image to expire) from the Ending drop-down selection fields.

NOTE

The starting and ending dates and times are determined by the server. If a user accesses your page from another time zone, the scheduled image display will be controlled by the Web server's clock, not the user's.

6. Type the path for a placeholder image you want to include or click Browse to select an image from your current Web. Be sure to include an alternate image as a placeholder before and after the scheduled image appears. This ensures that you will have a consistent-looking page and not receive any errors. If you do not choose an alternate image, a text-based message appears on your page, and the area will appear blank when viewed using a browser.

7. Click OK.

If you have selected an alternate image to appear before the loading of your scheduled image, that image appears within your document.

NOTE

It is a good idea to include a variable that updates your Web daily to ensure that your scheduled image appears on the day you want it to appear. Including a variable will cause the page to refresh whenever it is viewed.

Hands On: A Scheduled Image Example

Now that you know the basics behind inserting a scheduled image into your Web, we are going to insert a scheduled image into a page using specific examples. This example demonstrates one of the ways in which a scheduled image can be used in the creation of a Web site. Two images have been chosen for this example. The first one is the alternate image that appears on the page, and the second is the scheduled image that appears on the day and time we specify. These images will be used to inform visitors of an upcoming trade show. The scheduled image informs the viewer which booth the company will be in at the trade show, whereas the alternate image displays a "coming soon" message instructing visitors to check back soon to find out more information about where the company will be located at the trade show.

The following steps provide an example of scheduling an image:

1. Import the following images into your Web from the CD:

   ▶ tradeshow_coming_soon.jpg

   ▶ tradeshow_include.jpg

2. Select Insert | Web Component. This brings up the Insert Web Component dialog box shown previously in Figure 5-4.

3. Select Included Content in the Component Type list and then Picture Based on Schedule in the Choose a Type of Content list. Click Finish to display the Scheduled Picture Properties dialog box, shown previously in Figure 5-6.

4. Type the path to the image you will be using as your scheduled image or click Browse to select the image from your current Web. Two images have been created for this example, as mentioned earlier.

5. Select the day and time the scheduled image will appear. I've chosen Oct. 10, 2001, at 12:00 A.M. as our scheduled date.

6. Select the day and time that the scheduled image will expire. I've chosen Oct. 20, 2001, at 12:00 A.M. as the expiration date for this image.

7. Type the path of the alternate image or click Browse to select the image from your current Web.

8. Click OK. The alternate image now appears in your document.

   We now want to add a variable to the page that will cause it to refresh daily, as discussed previously in this chapter.

9. Position your cursor at the bottom of the page.

10. Select Insert | Web Component. Once again, this brings up the Insert Web Component dialog box.

11. Select Included Content in the Component Type list and then Substitution in the Choose a Type of Content list. Click Finish to display the Substitution Properties dialog box.

12. Select a variable from the list. For this example, select Author. This instructs FrontPage to display the page author's name where specified in the document.

13. Click OK. The page author's name now appears at the bottom of the page.

14. Save your page. The alternate image will now appear when viewed in a browser, and the scheduled image will appear on the day and time you have specified.

Scheduled Image Code

When you insert a scheduled image into your document, FrontPage inserts a WebBot component that instructs servers with FrontPage extensions installed to substitute the images you have specified on certain days and times. The specific code can be edited directly within the HTML code and is shown here:

```
<h2>
Inserting Scheduled Images
</h2>
<p>
<!--webbot bot="ScheduledImage" u-src="images/tradeshow_include.jpg"
u-else-src="images/tradeshow_coming_soon.jpg"
d-start-date="10 Oct 2000 00:00:00" d-end-date="20 Oct 2000 00:00:00" -->
```

As you can see, the code specifies what images are to be used and when they are to be used. The following table explains each of the attributes found with the WebBot:

WebBot Code	Description
bot	This is the name of the specified WebBot. In this case, we are working with the ScheduledImage WebBot.
u-src	This is the source of the scheduled image. This includes the directory where the image resides and the name of the image, which, in this case, is images/tradeshow_include.jpg.
u-else-src	This is the source of the alternate image. This includes the directory where the image resides and the name of the image, which, in this case, is images/tradeshow_coming_soon.jpg.
d-start-date	This is the day and time when the scheduled image, specified in u-src, should appear within the document.
d-end-date	This is the day and time when the scheduled image will expire, reverting back to the default image specified in u-else-src.

Incorporating Photo Galleries into Your Webs

FrontPage 2002 has added a great new feature that allows you to quickly and easily add photos and other images to your Web pages without having to create thumbnails for each image or complete any serious layout. Using the new Photo Gallery component, you can incorporate a number of different gallery styles right into your Web site.

To use the Photo Gallery component, follow these simple steps:

1. Position your cursor where you want the gallery to appear on the page.

2. Select Insert | Web Component from the menu bar. This brings up the Insert Web Component dialog box, shown previously in Figure 5-4.

3. Select Photo Gallery from the Component Type list. You then see a number of different gallery layouts appear on the right side of the dialog box in the Choose a Photo Gallery Option list.

4. Select the layout you want and click Finish. This brings up the Photo Gallery Properties dialog box, shown in Figure 5-7.

5. To add photos to your gallery, click Add and select the location from where you want the images to come. Here are your choices:

   ▶ **Pictures from Files**   Allows you to select pictures from your hard drive.

▶ **Pictures from Scanner or Camera**   Allows you to retrieve images directly from an outside source attached to your system.

TIP

If you are selecting images from your hard drive, you can select multiple images using the SHIFT and CTRL keys.

6. Once you have selected the images you want to display in your gallery, you have the ability to determine how they will be displayed with the following options:

   ▶ **Edit**   Brings up a rudimentary editing screen that allows you to make minor modifications to the image.

   ▶ **Move Up/Move Down**   Allows you to determine the order/position of a particular image in the gallery.

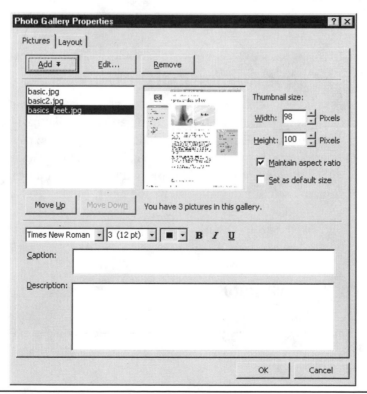

Figure 5-7   *The Photo Gallery Properties dialog box*

- ▶ **Thumbnail size**   Allows you to specify the size of the thumbnails that will be displayed on the page. This can be set for each individual image or as the default size by checking the Set As Default Size box.

- ▶ **Font layout settings**   These settings allow you to determine the font, size, color, and weight of the caption and description that will accompany each image.

- ▶ **Caption**   Allows you to add a caption to each image.

- ▶ **Description**   Allows you to add a description to each image.

7. Once you have specified how each image is to be displayed, click OK. Your gallery now displays on the page.

If you'd like to switch to another gallery layout option or change your image settings, double-click anywhere within the gallery to redisplay the Photo Gallery Properties dialog box. You can then edit any image settings or click the Layout tab to change your gallery layout.

Using the Page Inclusion Tools

FrontPage allows you to include pages within pages in your Web site. This can be useful if you have navigation or other information that changes on a regular basis. Using page inclusions allows you to make changes to the included file only and to have the changes reflected throughout your Web site in pages that contain the inclusion tag.

Page inclusion can be accomplished on a constant basis so that a page is included within your document each time a visitor views the page. Alternatively, you can create a page inclusion that appears only on a specific date, at a specific time. The following sections discuss each of these options and how to implement them. I also discuss ideas about when and how these can be used within your Web site.

Include a Page in Your Document

Including a page within your document is a useful way to add information that changes often throughout multiple pages. This type of inclusion can be especially useful for items such as dates or for navigation. To add an include page to your document, follow these steps:

1. Position your cursor where you want to insert the include page.

2. Select Insert | Web Component. This brings up the Insert Web Component dialog box, shown previously in Figure 5-4.

3. Select Included Content in the Component Type list and then Page in the Choose a Type of Content list. Click Finish to display the Include Page Properties dialog box, shown here:

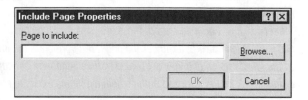

4. Type the path to the file you want to include or click the Browse button to select a file through the directory listing.

5. Click OK.

6. The page is now inserted into the Editor view. The text of the page cannot be modified within your current document; if you need to edit the text of the included page, right-click the text and select Open.

Include Page Code Explained

The Include Page code consists of a FrontPage WebBot. Although it is not really necessary to modify this code within the HTML—because it does not have many options—it is still a good idea to know what the options represent. Here is an example of the code, with the options explained in the following list:

```
<!--webbot bot="Include" u-include="include.html" tag="BODY" -->
```

WebBot Code	Description
bot	This specifies which WebBot the system should use. As you can see from the example, the Include WebBot is used here.
u-include	This specifies the path and filename to include within your document.
tag	This specifies that the document is to be included with the body of this page.

Include a Page at a Scheduled Time

You may want to include a page in your document at a specific time. This can be useful if you have an upcoming event that you want to publicize. You can create the page containing the information to publicize and then have it appear within your document at a time you specify within the Properties dialog box.

NOTE

As mentioned in the discussion of scheduled images earlier in this chapter, it is a good idea to include a variable in your page that will cause the browser to fetch the latest version of the page from the server. This is done to combat those browsers that may have viewed your page previously and want to load a cached copy of the page. If a variable is not included, the browser may not load the latest version and your scheduled include page may not appear. Inserting a variable is a simple task that is discussed in the scheduled image example earlier in this chapter.

To include a page at a scheduled time, follow these steps:

1. Position your cursor where you want the included page to be placed within your document.

2. Select Insert | Web Component. This brings up the Insert Web Component dialog box, shown previously in Figure 5-4.

3. Select Included Content in the Component Type list and then Page Based on Schedule in the Choose a Type of Content list. Click Finish to display the Scheduled Include Page Properties dialog box, which is almost identical to the Scheduled Picture Properties dialog box shown in Figure 5-6.

4. Type the path and filename for your page or click the Browse button to choose a page from the directory structure.

5. Set the day and time you want the page to appear within your document.

6. Set the day and time you want the page to stop appearing within your document.

7. Specify an optional page to appear before and after the scheduled page appears. Be sure to include the alternate page—this will ensure consistency within your document layout.

8. Once you have selected all your options, click OK.

The alternate page you specified in the Scheduled Picture Properties dialog box now appears within the Editor view of your document. You cannot modify the text of this included file directly. To edit the file, right-click the file and select Open.

Scheduled Include Page Code Explained

When you insert a scheduled include page into your document, FrontPage inserts a WebBot component that instructs servers with FrontPage extensions installed to include the text of the page you have specified on certain days and times. The specific code can be edited directly within the HTML code and is shown here, with the options explained in the following table:

```
<!--webbot bot="ScheduledInclude" u-include="our_promotion.html"
u-else-include="alternate.html" d-start-date="12 Oct 1998 16:01:53"
d-end-date="11 Nov 2000 15:01:53" -->
```

WebBot Code	Description
bot	This is the name of the specified WebBot. In this case, we are working with the ScheduledInclude WebBot.
u-include	This is the source of the scheduled page. This includes the directory the page resides in, along with the name of the page.
u-else-include	This is the source of the alternate page. This includes the directory the page resides in, along with the name of the page.
d-start-date	This is the day and time when the scheduled page should appear within your document.
d-end-date	This is the day and time when the scheduled page will expire.

Include a Page Banner in Your Document

Page banners allow you to create pages that contain embedded headers that you control. Working with a page banner becomes truly useful when you use the Shared Borders feature in your Web site. Using Shared Borders and the Navigation view allows you to create an entire layout for your Web. You can add all your page names to be displayed prior to ever opening up a page.

To see what I mean, follow these steps:

1. Create a new empty Web.

2. Switch to the Navigation view by selecting View | Navigation.

3. Because your new Web is empty, you will be directed to add a new page by clicking the New Page icon on the toolbar. Once you have created your first page, your screen should look something like this:

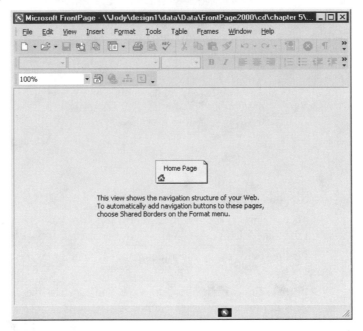

4. You will now want to add all your subpages. This is easily accomplished by right-clicking the Home Page icon and selecting New | Page from the menu. A new page will appear below the Home Page icon.

5. Before moving on, it is probably a good idea to name the page you have just created, because this is what will be displayed in the page banner. To accomplish this, select the page you have just created. The name will now be highlighted with a white background.

6. Once you have selected the page, click the name one more time and it will become editable.

7. Type the new name for the page.

8. Repeat steps 4 through 7 for each page you want in your Web. If you want pages that are children of secondary pages (fall beneath them in the Navigation view), simply right-click the page you want to assign a child to and select New | Page.

   Now it is time to create the shared border that will contain all our page banners. To do this, continue on to the next step.

9. Select Format | Shared Borders from the menu bar. This brings up the Shared Borders dialog box, shown here:

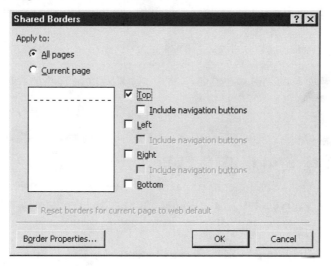

10. For this example, we are going to place a shared border with navigation at the top of the page. Select the All Pages and Top options (no other options should be selected) and click OK.

    You have now added a border that will display in all the pages. To complete this task, we now need to move to the Page view.

11. Double-click the home page in Navigation view. Your home page now displays with the Shared Border comment at the top of the page.

12. Click the comment area and select Insert | Web Component from the menu bar. This brings up the Insert Web Component dialog box, shown previously in Figure 5-4.

13. Select Included Content in the Component Type list and then Page Banner in the Choose a Type of Content list. Click Finish to display the Page Banner Properties dialog box, which already contains the title for your page.

14. Select the Text option because we're not working with an image banner. Then click OK.

15. Save the page.

That's all there is to it. Now, each of your pages will display the name you have given them in the navigation view. To use a Picture type page banner, you must apply a theme to the page(s). Selecting Picture as the type of banner in the Page Banner Properties dialog box will display the image specified in the theme if one has been applied to the page. Plain text is used if the page does not have a specified theme.

NOTE

If you want to use page banners on individual pages, not throughout the entire site, you may also add one directly within those individual pages.

Integrating Video into Your Web

Video integration is becoming a useful aspect of Web sites because it allows full presentations to be given, full of life and action. Embedding videos into your FrontPage Web site is accomplished in the following manner:

1. Select Insert | Picture | Video from the menu bar. This brings up a standard dialog box that allows you to choose a video from your system.

2. Select the video clip you want to insert into your document and click OK. The video clip now appears in your document.

Once you have inserted the video into your document, you will want to edit the video's properties. These properties allow you to adjust how the video displays on the page when a visitor sees it. To adjust the video properties, follow these steps:

1. Double-click the inserted video clip to display the Picture Properties dialog box. Make sure the Video tab is selected, as shown in Figure 5-8.

2. Using the dialog box options, adjust your settings for displaying the video onscreen when a visitor views the page. The following options are available:

   ▶ **Loop**   Specifies the number of times the video should replay. The default for this is 1, which instructs the video to replay one time.

   ▶ **Forever**   Instructs the video to loop continuously while the visitor is on this page.

   ▶ **Loop Delay**   Specifies the number of milliseconds the video should wait before beginning a looped playback.

   ▶ **On File Open**   Instructs the video to begin playback as soon as the file is loaded into the browser.

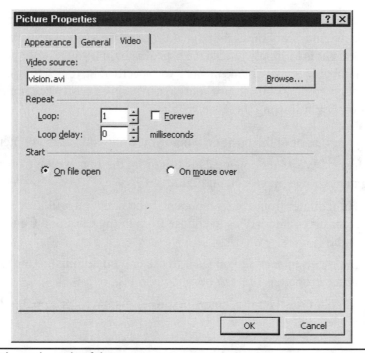

Figure 5-8   *The Video tab of the Picture Properties dialog box*

▶ **On Mouse Over**   Instructs the video to begin playback once the visitor has moved his or her mouse over the initial frame.

3. Once you have set your options, click OK.

4. You can now preview your video with the Preview tab in the Editor mode or with your browser.

Adding Page Counters

Page counters provide a fun way of informing your visitors of the popularity of your page. The counter displays a new number each time the page is accessed via a browser. This is also a tool that you can use to see how many people are visiting specific pages on your Web site, without the need for analysis tools. This is not to say that a page counter is a replacement for analysis tools, which give you much more detailed information, but it does offer you a quick glimpse into the popularity of specific pages.

Also, the page counter we look at here does not track individual users on your site. All it tracks is the number of times the page is accessed by a browser. An easy way of testing your counter is to simply refresh the page. Each time you refresh the page, you will see the number increment in the manner you specified in your settings.

Inserting page counters into your FrontPage Web is an easily accomplished task and can be done by following these steps:

1. Move your cursor to the position where you want your page counter to appear.

2. Click Insert | Web Component. This brings up the Insert Web Component dialog box, shown previously in Figure 5-4.

3. Select Hit Counter from the Component Type list. You will now see a number of different hit counter styles to choose from in the Choose a Counter Style list on the right.

4. Select the hit counter style you want to use and click Finish. This brings up the Hit Counter Properties dialog box, shown in Figure 5-9.

5. You will again see the hit counters that were displayed in step 3 with your counter selected.

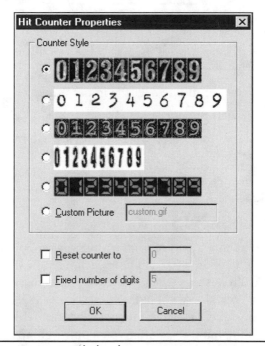

Figure 5-9 *Hit Counter Properties dialog box*

NOTE

You can also select a custom image to be used for your counter in this dialog box. If you are using a custom image, click the Custom Picture radio button and type the path and filename for the image you want to use. Custom counter image files must be GIFs and include the numbers 0 through 9 in an equally spaced rectangle, meaning that each number must be spaced equally in proportion to the other numbers. The FrontPage Server Extensions then load this single image and read in the digits by dividing the image into ten equal vertical slices. The FrontPage Server Extensions then combine the appropriate image segments into a single image that is sent to the user.

6. To have the counter display a specific number of digits (for example, displaying three digits causes the counter to show the number 001 the first time the page is viewed), click the Fixed Number of Digits check box and type the number of digits you want to appear on the page.

7. Click OK.

8. Your page now appears with the text "[Hit Counter]" in the spot you defined.

9. Save your document and view the page in your browser. The hit counter does not appear in the Preview tab of FrontPage because it requires interaction with FrontPage Server Extensions, which the Preview tab cannot accommodate.

10. Reload your page to see the number change in the counter.

Resetting Your Hit Counter

You may find that you want to reset the initial number displayed by your hit counter from time to time on certain pages of your Web site. This is a simple task that is explained in the following list of steps:

1. Open the page containing your hit counter.

2. Select the text "[Hit Counter]".

3. Select Format | Properties from the menu bar. This brings up the Hit Counter Properties dialog box.

4. Select Reset Counter To and type the number you want your hit counter to be set to on the page.

5. Click OK.

6. Save the page and preview it in your browser to ensure that the counter is reset.

Hit Counter Code Explained

The hit counter consists of a FrontPage WebBot that is inserted into your HTML code. An example of the code that may be used by the Hit Counter WebBot is shown here, along with an explanation of the code in the following table:

```
<h2>
Working with Page Counters
</h2>
<p>
<!--webbot bot="HitCounter" u-custom b-reset="FALSE" i-digits="0" i-image="0"
preview="<strong>[Hit Counter]</strong>" i-resetvalue="0" s-html -->
```

WebBot Code	Description
bot	This is the name of the current WebBot. As you can see from the example, this is the HitCounter WebBot.
u-custom	This displays the name and path of any custom image you are using for your hit counter.
b-reset	In the example, this is set to FALSE. This instructs the WebBot to continue counting from the number that it currently has stored. If this is set to TRUE, the WebBot will refresh the image to display the number indicated in the i-resetvalue option (see the last entry in this table) the next time the page is viewed.
i-digits	This instructs the WebBot as to how many digits should appear when the hit counter displays. For example, you may want your hit counter to display a three-digit image when the page is viewed. Therefore, if the page has been viewed five times, the image would display as 005 rather than just 5.
i-image	This number is associated with the image you chose in the Properties dialog box. The number shown in the example (0) refers to the first image in the dialog box.
preview	This is the text that displays in your FrontPage editing view. You may want to change this text to something that more appropriately refers to your counter.
i-resetvalue	This instructs the WebBot to reset the counter to the specified number if the b-reset option is set to TRUE.

Using Marquee Text in Your Site

The marquee consists of scrolling text that does not require a Java applet or JavaScript to operate. It is incorporated using a simple HTML tag. Unfortunately, this is a browser-specific tag that only works in Internet Explorer. It is not supported in the Netscape browsers currently available.

If you are not worried about browser compatibility, marquees provide an easy and interesting way to display active information. To insert a marquee into your Web, follow these steps:

1. Select Insert | Web Component. This brings up the Insert Web Component dialog box, shown previously in Figure 5-4.

2. Select Dynamic Effects in the Component Type list and then Marquee in the Choose an Effect list. Click Finish to display the Marquee Properties dialog box, shown in Figure 5-10.

3. Type the text you want to appear in your marquee in the Text box.

4. Select the direction you want your marquee to travel on the screen.

5. Adjust the speed of the text moving across the screen using the following Speed controls:

   ▶ **Delay**   Allows you to specify the amount of time, in milliseconds, that the marquee waits between each movement. You may adjust this setting so that the marquee moves faster or slower, depending on the effect you want to achieve.

   ▶ **Amount**   Determines how many pixels the marquee text travels after each delay. If you want your marquee to move smoothly across the page, select a lower number; if you want the marquee to move quickly across the page, select a higher number, keeping in mind that larger movements may appear jerky.

NOTE

Remember that the fewer pixels the marquee text travels across the page in each movement, the longer it takes for the message to appear. Test the speed to be sure you achieve your desired effect so that users don't scroll down the page without ever reading the message.

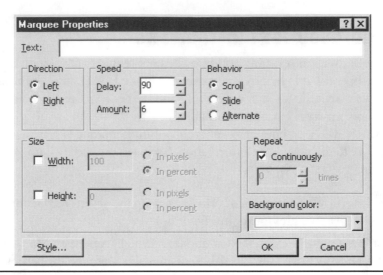

Figure 5-10   *The Marquee Properties dialog box*

6. Choose the behavior you want your marquee to have while it moves across the screen. Here are the options available to you:

   ▶ **Scroll**   Causes the text to appear on one side of the screen, move across, and disappear on the other side.

   ▶ **Slide**   Causes the text to appear on one side of the screen, move across, and stop in place on the opposite side of the screen.

   ▶ **Alternate**   Causes the text to bounce back and forth between the borders you set in the Width box of the Size category. The number of times the text bounces is controlled by the Repeat option. Setting Repeat to 1 causes the Alternate behavior to perform a single slide.

7. Type the width and height you want for your marquee in the appropriate boxes. The sizes you specify here are much the same as an image's width and height. The width determines how far the marquee moves from the right or left side of the screen, depending on what option you select under Direction. The height determines how many pixels appear above and below the text.

8. You may select the number of times this marquee repeats by adjusting the Repeat options. The default for this is to have the marquee repeat continuously, but you can specify an exact number of times you want the marquee to appear by typing a number.

9. Select a background color for the marquee using the Background Color drop-down box.

10. Once you have made all your selections, click OK.

Your marquee appears as static text within your editor, so you will want to preview it by clicking the Preview tab.

NOTE

You may also format the marquee's text by selecting the marquee and then setting the font properties, just as you would for any other text.

Adding Search Capabilities

FrontPage offers an integrated search capability that allows you to add search functions to your entire Web or to specific areas of your Web (such as a directory). Adding search capabilities to a Web site allows your visitors to quickly and easily obtain the information they are looking for without needing to search through the pages in your Web.

With FrontPage, you can create a search form using the Search Page template. Using this template allows you to have a page all set up that you can simply customize with your own text. This may be useful if you just want the basics. If you want to create your own search interface, you will need to incorporate a search box into the document.

Creating a Simple Search Form

FrontPage allows you to easily incorporate search capabilities into your Web through the use of the Search Page template. Here are the steps to follow:

1. Select File | New | Page or Web from the menu bar. This brings up the New Page or Web pane.

2. Click Page Templates under the New from Template section of the pane.

3. Select Search Page from the Page Templates dialog box.

4. Click OK. A basic search page now appears in the Editor view.

5. Customize the text on this page and select File | Save from the menu bar to save the page. If you want to modify the search box options, see the next section.

Creating Your Own Search Interface

By incorporating a search box in your document, you control everything from the words on the search button to what type of information the search will return. Here is the procedure:

1. Position the cursor where you want the search box to appear on your page. Remember that your search results will appear in the same page, immediately following the search form and before anything that follows the search form.

2. Select Insert | Web Component. This brings up the Insert Web Component dialog box shown in Figure 5-4.

3. Select Web Search in the Component Type list and then Current Web in the Choose Type of Search list. Click Finish to display the Search Form Properties dialog box, shown in Figure 5-11.

4. In the Label for Input text area, type the words you want to appear in front of your search box (for example, **Search for:**).

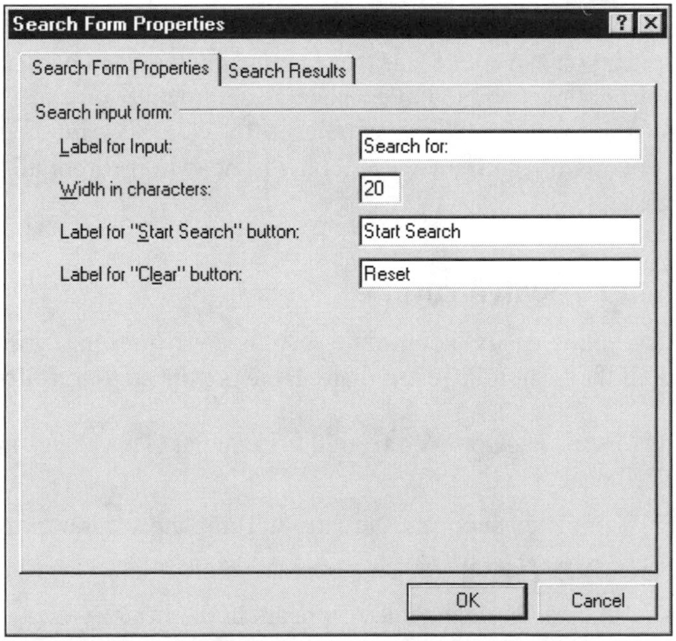

Figure 5-11 *The Search Form Properties dialog box*

5. Specify a width for your search box in the Width in Characters text area. This is the actual length, in characters, of the search box as it will appear on the screen. However, this setting does not limit the number of characters the user can enter.

6. Type a label for the search button in the Label for "Start Search" Button text area. This is the word or phrase that will appear on the button users will click to begin their search.

7. Type a label for the clear button in the Label for "Clear" Button text area. This is the word or phrase that will appear on the button users will click to erase the text from the search box prior to performing their search.

8. Click the Search Results tab. This brings up the Search Results options of the Search Form Properties dialog box, as shown in Figure 5-12.

NOTE

The Search Results tab varies depending on the OS you are currently working with. For this example, I am working with the Search Results tab in Windows 98.

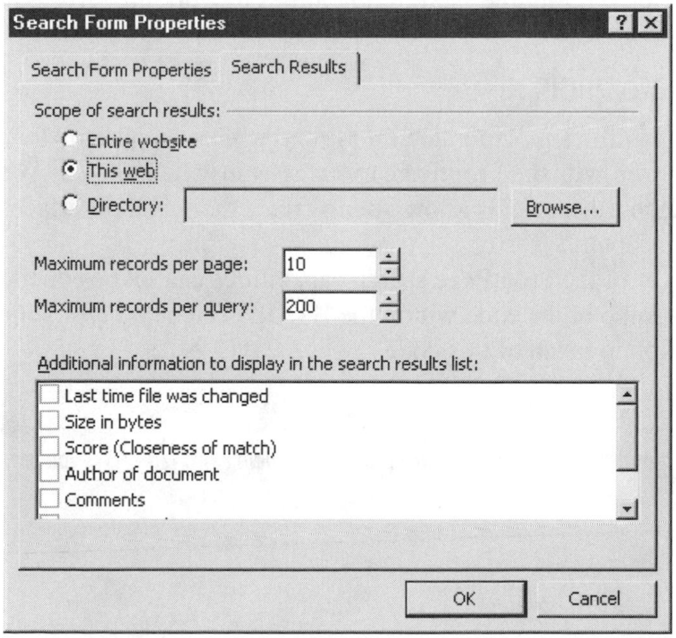

Figure 5-12   *The Search Results tab of the Search Form Properties dialog box*

9. Select what areas you want searched by selecting one of the available radio buttons in the Scope of Search Results area.

10. Enter the maximum records you want displayed per page, along with the maximum number of records that will be displayed for each search query.

11. The Search Results dialog box also allows you to specify what type of information you want displayed when a visitor receives search results. Select from the following display options:

   ▶ **Display score**   Displays a percentage in the search results that tells users how closely each document matches the text specified in their search.

   ▶ **Display file date**   Allows you to display the date and/or time that the file was last modified.

   ▶ **Display file size**   Displays the size of the file (in kilobytes) found during the user's search.

12. Click OK. Your search box now appears within your document.

13. Save your document and preview it in a browser to test your search. Remember that you must have the FrontPage Server Extensions set up on the server you are working with for the search capabilities to work properly.

Search Code Explained

The search capabilities incorporated into FrontPage use a system DLL (dynamic link library) associated with the FrontPage extensions installed on your Web server. Working together, these items allow you to create the search interfaces mentioned earlier in this chapter.

   Many aspects of the FrontPage search capabilities cannot be edited, but you can view and edit some of the code within the HTML. The next bit of code and table display and explain much of this code.

NOTE

The information listed in the search code may contain extra features if you are working with Index Server.

Hands On: Displaying Results from a Search on Another Page

One of the drawbacks of using the FrontPage search component is that it automatically assumes you want to display your search on the same page as your search box. As a developer, there are probably a number of times when you have had to put a search box on a page where you would not want the results to appear. This example shows you a little trick that allows you to use the FrontPage search component and have your results appear on a separate page. For this to work, you will need to create two pages—one that will display the search box and another that will display a search box and your search results. Along with this, you will need to alter the code a bit outside of FrontPage. Here are the steps:

1. Position the cursor where you want the search box to appear on your page.
2. Select Insert | Web Component. This brings up the Insert Web Component dialog box, shown previously in Figure 5-4.
3. Select Web Search in the Component Type list and then Current Web in the Choose Type of Search list. Click Finish to display the Search Form Properties dialog box, shown previously in Figure 5-11.
4. Enter your search options as you want them to appear in the search form.
5. Click OK.

Now it is necessary for you to create the page that will contain your search results. To do so, follow these steps:

1. Create a new page within your Web.
2. Insert a search form as specified earlier.
3. Save your page to the Web.

We now have the pages that we need to make this work. From here, you will need to close the pages and open them in a text editor. This is necessary because all that appears in FrontPage is the WebBot information. What we need to edit is the actual path information that the browser will see. To do so, follow these steps:

1. All that needs to be edited is the path that will appear in your original search form. This is the form on the page where you want your search box to appear but not your results. When you open this file in a text editor, you will see the following information within the form:

    ```
    <form action="_vti_bin/shtml.dll/index.html" method="POST">
    ```

    This path instructs the form to be submitted through the FrontPage DLL for processing and then post its results to the specified page. In this case, that page is index.html, because I have added the search box on my index page.

2. You need to change this filename to point to the search results page you created earlier in this example. In my case, I am going to change this to search.html, because this is the page where I want the results to appear. So, your code should look like this:

    ```
    <form action="_vti_bin/shtml.dll/search.html" method="POST">
    ```

3. Save this page and preview it in your browser.

4. Enter a search term into your search box and click Submit. Your results should now post in the secondary search page you have created.

NOTE

You will need to be careful when using this trick because FrontPage will want to change this back to the default page. If you make this change, do not save the page again in FrontPage.

```
<h2>
Incorporating Search Boxes
</h2>
<!--webbot bot="Search" s-index="All" s-fields s-text="Search Our Website:" i-size="30"
s-submit="Search Now" s-clear="Clear" s-timestampformat="%m/%d/%y %I:%M:%S %p"
tag="BODY"-->
```

WebBot Code	Description
bot	This is the name of the WebBot component currently in use. As you can see from the example, this is the Search WebBot.
s-index	This option tells the bot where it should be searching. In the example, the ALL option is selected, instructing the bot to search all files within the Web site. If you are searching private directories, those directories beginning with an underscore (_) will be specified here. To specify multiple directories, enter each one separated by commas.
s-fields	This option specifies the items you have set up in your Search Results tab. The example shows that the bot should display a timestamp (TimeStamp), the document size (DocumentK), and the percentage match for the retrieved documents (Weight).
s-text	This option instructs the bot to display the specified text in front of the actual search box.
i-size	This option instructs the bot to create a search box that is made up of the specified number of characters.
s-submit	This option instructs the bot to display the specified text on the "search" button.
s-clear	This option instructs the bot to display the specified text on the "clear" button.

Using Index Server and the WAIS Search Engine

If you are working with a server that has the default NT 4.0 Option Pack or a Windows 2000 install of IIS, Index Server is installed. The FrontPage Server Extensions see this and automatically set FrontPage search components to use Index Server for their searches instead of the built-in WAIS search engine. Many ISPs that support FrontPage Server Extensions leave Index Server enabled for the FrontPage Server Extensions, causing FrontPage searches not to work, unless the ISP specifically sets up an Index Server catalog for the Web. This is also the case in many intranet environments and will be so for any users running Windows 2000 (any version). This being the case, an additional attribute is added to the search bot code: b-useindexserver="1". Also, opening a search bot page in Notepad displays the form action for the preceding example as this: action="_vti_script/index.html0.idq".

This assumes that an Index Server catalog has been created for your Web on the server you are using.

To turn off the use of Index Server, making FrontPage use its built in WAIS search engine, requires a change to the registry. After making this change, you must then recalculate hyperlinks for the Web to have FrontPage build the necessary WAIS search indexes. To make your changes to the registry, follow these steps:

WARNING

To accomplish this task, you must edit your system's registry. Only edit the registry if you feel completely comfortable doing so. Also, be sure to back up your registry using the export command prior to making any changes so that you can import your old registry if problems occur.

1.   Click the Start button on your Windows taskbar and select run.

2.   Type **regedit** in the box and click OK. This brings up your system registry.

3.   Open the registry tree to the following location:

   HKEY_LOCAL_MACHINE\SOFTWARE\Microsoft\Shared Tools\
   Web Server Extensions\All Ports

4.   Right-click on All Ports and select New | String Value from the menu. You will now see a new string appear in the pane on the right.

5.   Give this string the name **noindexserver**.

6.   Double-click the string and enter **1** for the Value data.

7.   Exit the registry and recalculate your hyperlinks in FrontPage.

Using the Banner Ad Manager

More and more Web sites are using banner advertisements. Many of these ads are incorporated using complicated database-driven systems, or they are just added to the page as a single image. With FrontPage, you can incorporate banner ads into your site without the need for complicated systems, maintaining the ability to display multiple images with built-in effects and a link to a specific URL. Also, you can create multiple-frame banners using JPEG images, thereby creating animated JPEGs. Animation is something that has always been left to GIF images, which have many limitations when it comes to photographs. FrontPage supports this feature through the inclusion of a Java applet Web Component called the Banner Ad Manager.

Unfortunately, the Banner Ad Manager does not allow you to incorporate multiple URLs for your images, which is an option that you want if you have multiple banner ads for different companies. When creating an ad, you only have the ability to create a single link for all the images you are including. This somewhat limits the capabilities of the tool. However, the Banner Ad Manager allows you to add some interesting effects to the images you are displaying.

To insert banner ads using the Banner Ad Manager, simply follow these steps:

1. Position your cursor where you want the ad to appear on your page.

2. Select Insert | Web Component. This brings up the Insert Web Component dialog box, shown previously in Figure 5-4.

3. Select Dynamic Effects in the Component Type list and then Banner Ad Manager in the Choose an Effect list. Click Finish to display the Banner Ad Manager Properties dialog box, shown in Figure 5-13.

4. The first options you will want to set are Height and Width. When creating multiple images for banner ads, you should always create them all with the same height and width. Failure to do so will result in larger images being

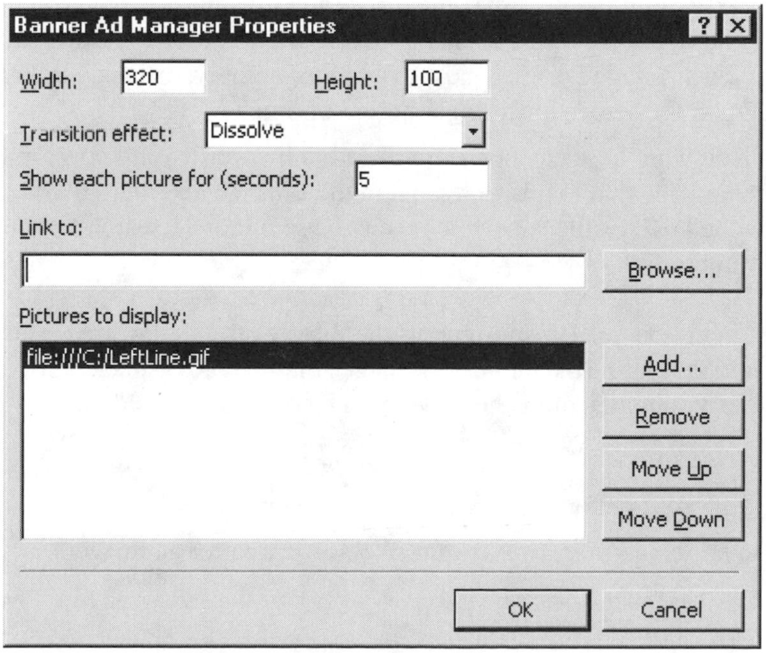

Figure 5-13   *The Banner Ad Manager Properties dialog box*

cropped and smaller images exposing the gray background of the applet. Accordingly, set the width and height to match that of your banner ad image.

5. Next, select the transition you want to have for your images. You can select a single transition that will be consistent throughout the images. The following list explains each Transition Effect option:

   ▶ **None**   Changes from image to image with no effects.

   ▶ **Blinds Horizontal**   Creates a Venetian blind effect horizontally that cuts up the image with horizontal lines as it transitions to the next.

   ▶ **Blinds Vertical**   Creates a Venetian blind effect vertically that cuts up the image with vertical lines as it transitions to the next.

   ▶ **Dissolve**   Dissolves the image into particles as it transitions from one image to the next.

   ▶ **Box In**   Creates a box effect that closes in on the image as it transitions from one to the next.

   ▶ **Box Out**   Creates a box effect that begins in the center of the image and boxes out as it transitions to the next image.

6. The next option involves the amount of time the image remains on the page. If you are working with a banner containing a lot of text, you will want to set Show Each Image For (Seconds) to a higher number, causing the image to remain on the screen for a longer period of time.

7. Now you want to select a page for the ad to link to. If you know the URL or filename you want to link to, type it in the Link To text area. If you do not know the URL or filename, click the Browse button to search for the path you want to link to.

The last item you need to configure is the Pictures to Display area. This area allows you to determine the number of images that will be displayed in your ad. It also allows you to determine how they will be ordered. To add pictures to your banner ad, follow these steps:

1. Click the Add button. This brings up the Image dialog box.

2. Select an image from your current Web or search for an image.

3. Click OK. The image path now displays in the Pictures to Display field.

4. Repeat steps 1, 2, and 3 until all the images you want to use are listed.

5. You can adjust the display order of the images to your liking by selecting the image you'd like to move and clicking the Move Up or Move Down button.

6. Once you have configured all your options, click OK. Your banner ad now appears in your editor.

Creating a Table of Contents for Your Web Site

There is nothing more frustrating than entering a large Web site and not having any resources for finding information. No matter how well you have designed your navigational layout, there is no substitute for a strong table of contents. This is one of the first areas I visit at any Web site when I'm trying to gather specific information. Even when sites have a search engine incorporated, I still make my way to the table of contents because it provides a hierarchical overview of the entire site.

FrontPage makes it easy to incorporate a detailed table of contents within your Web site. Furthermore, the table of contents created via FrontPage updates when you update your site, allowing you to create the table once and letting FrontPage do the editing every time you make a page change. To create a table of contents, follow these steps:

1. Select File | New | Page or Web from the menu bar. This brings up the New Page or Web pane.

2. Click Page Templates under New from Template to bring up the Page Templates dialog box.

3. Select Table of Contents from the available templates and click OK. The page appears with instructions embedded within the document.

4. Erase the information text down to the horizontal rule.

5. Click the text titled "Table of Contents Heading Page".

6. Select Format | Properties from the menu bar. This brings up the Table of Contents Properties dialog box, shown next.

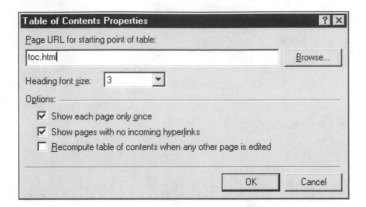

7. Type the path and filename of the first document in the table of contents. This will normally be your home page document. If you want to have a table of contents that only shows a specific section of your site, enter the name of a lower-level document.

NOTE

If you select a lower-level document, be sure that it doesn't link to all the other areas of your site. If it does, all your files will be shown in the table, but the order will not make sense.

8. Select the font size for the headings when they display in your table of contents.

9. Select from the available options, as explained here, by clicking their respective check boxes:

   ▶ **Show each page only once**   This instructs the WebBot to display each page only once within the table of contents no matter how many times it is linked to from the various documents.

   ▶ **Show pages with no incoming hyperlinks**   This instructs the WebBot to display pages in the table of contents that are not linked to by any of the other documents in your site.

   ▶ **Recompute table of contents when any other page is edited**   This is one of the most important features if you want your table to be up-to-date.

It instructs the WebBot to update the table whenever you edit another document on the site. This is especially important if you have multiple headings displayed in your table and you edit your pages often.

10. Once you have selected all your options, click OK.

11. You will see that the text appearing on your page does not seem to change when you change the options. This is because this page is created dynamically once loaded. Save the file and preview it in your browser.

Incorporating Top 10 Lists into Your Web Site

Top 10 lists allow you to show your visitors all the information about who is viewing your site, how they are viewing your site, and where they are coming from. Now you might be saying, "Why on earth would I want to show my visitors any of this information?" Well, you probably wouldn't, but you can create a page on your site that is not visible to the visitor that includes any, or all, of these Top 10 lists so that you can go to it and see how people are viewing your site.

Creating this type of page will allow you to see vital information about your visitors and let you customize your site to better accommodate their visiting trends. For instance, if a good percentage of your visitors are going to a specific page, you might think about incorporating more banner ads on that page.

Installing these Web Components is simple, and there is not much in the way of customization options, except for how they display on the page.

To install a Top 10 list, follow these steps:

1. Select Insert | Web Component. This brings up the Insert Web Component dialog box.

2. Select Top 10 List from the left pane and then select the type of list you want from the right pane.

3. Click Finish.

Once you select a list you want to insert, you are presented with the Top 10 List Properties dialog box, shown next.

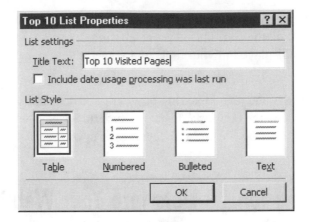

All you need to do is select the way you want the list displayed on your page and then click OK.

NOTE

When incorporating any Top 10 list, you need to make sure you have the FrontPage Server Extensions on the server you will publish the page to. Also, you will only be able to view the information once you have published the list.

Inserting Third-Party Components

FrontPage now comes with a variety of third-party Web Components that you can add to your site. These components allow you to quickly and easily incorporate information, such as banner ads and stock quotes, from outside sources. This section lists the types of components available to you in FrontPage 2002 and the basic steps necessary to insert them:

- ► bCentral Web Components
- ► Expedia Web Components
- ► MSN Web Components
- ► MSNBC Web Components

To insert one of these components, simply select Insert | Web Component and select a component from the list in the left pane of the dialog box.

Summary

This chapter contains various elements you can add to your Webs to give them that extra bit of creativity and interactivity through FrontPage. It also demonstrates how you can use FrontPage to create your initial layouts and then maximize those layouts by editing your code directly, as shown with the "Hands On" search example.

The techniques described in this chapter will be helpful to any developer who is looking for alternative means of creating better Web sites. This chapter has offered something for all types of developers. Whether you are a graphically inclined designer who wants to swap out original art with the Hover Button component or a fast-paced marketing webmaster who needs content to be automated, freeing you up for other tasks, this chapter gives you the tools you need.

6

Creating
Collaborative Webs

A s the Internet becomes more and more of an everyday tool at home and in business, it is only natural that we want to find ways to use it to interact with each other. This has often been a daunting task that requires the installation of additional software or the development of custom scripts and programs that allow for the type of interactivity we want. During my years as a developer, I have worked on many projects that entailed a client wanting to create something such as an interactive calendaring system or a document management system, and our development team would spend weeks, and sometimes months, creating custom interfaces that allowed the client to have the requested features.

This, however, like many other aspects of development, is being simplified by new and expanded features in FrontPage. This chapter will guide you through some of these features, which allow you to create truly interactive Web sites that enable teams of people to collaborate and communicate through the sharing of documents, information, and ideas. And the best part of all this is that it can all be done with FrontPage and a server with FrontPage Server Extensions, or in combination with one of the other .NET Enterprise Servers from Microsoft, such as SharePoint.

Using Discussion Groups to Collaborate on Projects

One of the best things about the Web is that it allows you to collaborate with people in different locations. The problem is, how do you give everyone access to the same information without having countless meetings and conference calls? Well, the use of discussion groups is a great answer to this problem, and FrontPage makes it easy through the use of the *project Web*. Although this style of Web site covers many areas of project implementation, this chapter will focus on the discussion group aspects.

I discuss, in this chapter, the creation of a Web solely for the use of discussion groups, but, there are times when a discussion group can easily fit within the Web you are working with. The project Web is a prime example of this type of discussion. The project Web comes complete with two discussion groups built into it for use while working on a group project. These are the Requirements Discussion and the Knowledge Base. Although these two types of discussions may be modified for use within your particular project, they give us a good starting point for seeing how a discussion group can work for collaborating on projects.

To see what I am talking about, you will first need to create a project Web. Do this by following these steps:

1. Select File | New | Page or Web from the menu bar. This brings up the New Page or Web sidebar.

2. Click Web Site Templates to bring up the Web Site Templates dialog box.

3. Specify the location and name for the new Web, such as http://localhost/
    myprojectWeb.

4. Select the Project Web icon and click OK. FrontPage will now create a project
    Web consisting of many of the standard elements of a project. Within these
    elements are the two discussion groups mentioned earlier.

Once the Web is created, you can view the site in your browser. On the navigation
system, you will see a link to Discussions. Click this link to be taken to the main
discussion page with the default Requirements Discussion and Knowledge Base
topics. This is a key example of how discussions are integrated into Web sites for
use with your projects. You can now modify these pages within your editor to fulfill
the requirements for your particular project by following the instructions in the
"Inside Discussion Groups" section, later in this chapter.

Making Your Intranet an Interactive Tool

Another useful application of discussion groups is for collaboration within a
company via the company's intranet. Although many companies have intranets that
display information about their various departments and services, many do not fully
utilize the capabilities of their systems with tools such as discussion groups.

Within the company I work for, discussion groups have become one of the main
forms of communication among employees. All employee tasks are listed on the
"Tasks" discussion group, and this is where questions and requests are passed back
and forth. It not only allows people with different schedules to easily communicate
information to each other, but it also creates a written record of the activities going
on within the company. Whenever an individual has a question about a particular
task being performed, she simply goes to the discussion group set up for that area
and views the latest notes and information about the task.

Building Communities Through Discussion

Today, the Internet has become not only a place to obtain information but also a
place to share information with people who have similar interests. There are many
tools for sharing information with others on the Web, but discussion groups are one
of the most widely used of these tools. Countless Web sites contain discussion areas

where individuals can come and share their questions with a wide variety of people. Some answers spark entirely new discussions, whereas others seem to lie dormant. When you create a discussion group for a community on the Web, there are a few things you need to be aware of.

First of all, you need to design the discussion group so it makes sense to the users. That is, include detailed instructions as to what the topics within the discussion group are, and what the dos and don'ts are for posting on the discussion group. Also, make sure you keep an eye on the discussion group. There is nothing more frustrating for a person posting a question than to have that question sit for days with no response from anyone. Even if you don't know the answer to a question, offer some sort of response, whether it be a short sentence about where else to look, or just some enthusiasm for what the person is asking. If you monitor your groups and keep the answers flowing, you'll be amazed how many people come back to see what's been posted, and to post more messages.

Discussion Web Wizard

FrontPage allows you to quickly integrate a discussion group into your Web via the use of the Discussion Web Wizard. When you create a discussion group, you have two options. You can create a new Web that consists only of the discussion group, or you can add the discussion group to your current Web.

Creating a New Web

In most cases, it is a good idea to create a new Web for your discussion group, even if it is going to be linked to the Web you are currently working with. Many times when creating discussion groups, I have attempted to incorporate them into the current Web, only to find that I was restrained by what I already had within that Web. In other words, the back-end organization leaves quite a bit to be desired when you incorporate a discussion group into your Web, especially if you are creating multiple discussions.

To combat the organizational problem, I always create my discussion groups within their own subWebs. This allows me complete control over the look and feel of the discussion group, without having to worry about the effects on any other Webs I'm working with. It makes further sense due to the fact that you can easily link your discussion groups into any Web you create.

Incorporating Your Discussion Group into Your Current Web

There are a few cases when incorporating a discussion group into your current Web makes sense. The most obvious one is when you are creating a rather small Web and just want to add some simple discussion capabilities to your site. If this fits what you are attempting to do, you will follow the same instructions described in this section, with one exception. When you are working in the New dialog box, you will simply check the box next to Add to Current Web. Checking this box will instruct FrontPage to incorporate all the discussion files and directories into your current Web.

Using the Discussion Web Wizard

The following steps outline how to use the Discussion Web Wizard within FrontPage:

1. Select File | New | Page or Web from the menu bar. This brings up New Page or Web sidebar.

2. Click Web Site Templates to bring up the Web Site Templates dialog box.

3. Click the Discussion Web Wizard icon.

4. Select the base location for your new subWeb from the Specify the Location of the New Web drop-down menu. If your base Web is in a location other than those listed, type the path for your discussion group Web in this box and append the name of your new discussion subWeb onto the base address.

5. Click OK. FrontPage will recognize that this new subWeb does not exist and automatically create it for you.

NOTE

If you are adding this discussion Web to your current Web, click the Add to Current Web check box. Also, if you are connecting to a secure HTTP address, click the check box next to Secure Connection Required if your system requires Secure Sockets Layer (SSL) connections. FrontPage now goes through the process of creating your discussion Web. Once this process completes, you are presented with the first page of the wizard, which contains information about the process.

6. Click Next. You are now presented with the requirements for your discussion. The requirements include various optional items you can use in your discussion group, as follows:

    ▶ **Submission Form**   Sets up the form that users will fill in to post messages to the discussion group. This is a required element of the discussion group.

▶ **Table of Contents**   Displays all the messages in the discussion group. This is highly recommended, because it will be difficult for visitors to view the topics if they do not appear on any page.

▶ **Search Form**   Allows visitors to enter a keyword search to look through the discussion topics. This is especially useful if you are planning on having a lot of information input into this group.

▶ **Threaded Replies**   Instructs FrontPage to allow users to reply to existing messages using the Reply option while viewing individual messages. When messages are replied to in this way, they are displayed on the contents page in a hierarchical format; replies to messages are indented an additional level, as compared to the source message. If this option is turned off (unchecked), users will not be given the option to reply to existing messages. In this case, they can only post new messages that appear in a unitary (nonindented) level within the contents page.

▶ **Confirmation Page**   Allows visitors to ensure that their messages were posted to the discussion group. This is simply an HTML page that displays a confirmation message informing visitors that their messages were posted.

7. Select the components you want your discussion group to include and then click Next.

8. The next step asks you to provide a name for the discussion, along with a name for the discussion folder. Enter this information and click Next.

9. Next, you need to enter the fields that will appear within your discussion form. These are the fields visitors use to enter their messages. The options for this form are outlined here:

▶ **Subject, Comments**   Allows visitors to enter only their name, a subject, and a set of comments into the discussion form

▶ **Subject, Category, Comments**   Allows visitors to enter their name and a subject, select a category (which you will populate in the Wizard), and enter comments into the discussion form

▶ **Subject, Product, Comments**   Allows visitors to enter their name and a subject, select a product from a list (which you will later populate in the Wizard), and enter comments into the discussion form

10. Select from the options you want and click Next.

11. You are now asked who will have permission to enter comments into this discussion. If you want control over who can input comments, click Yes; if

anyone will be able to add to this group, click No. If you select Yes, FrontPage will require users of your discussion to enter proper Windows authenticated login information upon entering the discussion (see the note at the bottom of this dialog box instructing you to change your Web). If you decide to select Yes, you will need to change your permissions for this Web. To do so, you will need to open Computer Management and deselect Allow Anonymous Access in your Web site properties. For more information on changing Web site properties, see Chapter 17.

NOTE

Although selecting Yes allows you to monitor who posts messages in a discussion, it is only an appropriate method for an intranet because FrontPage requires that users use their Windows login. If you are working on an Internet-based site, you should select No for this option or implement your discussion using the SharePoint Team Services capabilities discussed later in this chapter.

12. Click Next.

13. The next step is to decide how your group's table of contents is sorted. FrontPage gives you the option to sort your table of contents in two ways:

    ▶ **Oldest to newest (default)**   Causes the topics in your discussion group to be listed with the oldest message appearing on top and the newest message on the bottom.

    ▶ **Newest to oldest**   Causes the topics in your discussion group to be listed with the newest message on top and the oldest message on the bottom. As new threads (subjects) are started, they will appear at the top of the table of contents page. However, if you have selected the option that allows threaded replies, threads will still be presented in oldest-to-newest order.

14. Select your option and click Next.

15. If you want the table of contents to be this Web's home page, click Yes. If you have another page that you want visitors to access before entering the discussion group, click No.

CAUTION

Selecting Yes in step 15 will overwrite any existing home page.

16. Click Next to bring up the search information page. This page lets you specify search options to allow visitors to search through the various discussion topics.

Your choices, as explained here, will determine in what format the search results are displayed when a visitor searches the area:

▶ **Subject**   The subject of the message

▶ **Size**   The size of the message file, in kilobytes

▶ **Date**   The date the article (message) was submitted

▶ **Score**   A matching score, which gives visitors an idea of how closely the results match the keywords they entered in the search form

NOTE

Although the wizard forces you to select the search result display options in an inclusive manner, you can later fine-tune these options from the Search Form Properties window's Search Results tab. For more information on the Search Form Properties dialog box, see "Adding Search Capabilities" in Chapter 1 of this book.

17. Select your choices and click Next.

18. You are now given the opportunity to choose a theme for your discussion group. If you want to add a theme, click Choose Web Theme. This brings up the Choose Theme dialog box, shown in Figure 6-1.

19. Select from the available themes and click OK. (For more information about using themes in your Webs, see Chapter 3.)

20. Click Next. You now need to decide on a page layout for your discussion group. Select one of the following options and click Next:

▶ **No frames**   Use this setting to have your discussion group displayed on single HTML pages. Each time a user views a different area of the discussion (for example, table of contents, search, and so on), a new page loads, displaying the information. When you choose this option, a table of contents page will be the default starting page, and the welcome/instructions page will not be created.

▶ **Dual interface–use frames if available, or normal pages if not**   Use this setting to have the discussion group displayed using a dual-pane frame interface. With this interface, the contents page will display in the top frame of the interface, with a welcome/instructions page in the lower pane. When the user clicks a message in the contents pane, the message is displayed in the lower pane, leaving the list of messages in full view for further selection. This is also true when pages for posting and searching are initially displayed. If the user's browser does not support frames, the display will gracefully degrade to the No Frames interface.

▶ **Contents above current article**   Use this setting if you want the name and navigation of your discussion Web to always display at the top of the page. This interface consists of three frames. The top frame displays the title for the Web, along with a navigation bar. The second frame contains the contents of the discussion Web, and the third frame initially displays the welcome/instructions page for the group. As messages are viewed, searched for, or posted, they are also displayed in this bottom pane of the frameset.

▶ **Contents beside current article**   Like the previous option, this setting places the name of your discussion group at the top of the screen, with the contents on the left and the forms on the right.

21. At this point, you can simply click Finish, or you can click Next to read some basic information about the new discussion Web you have just created.

Once you click Finish, FrontPage will go through the process of creating all the pages necessary for your discussion. After FrontPage has created all the pages, you may edit them directly within FrontPage.

Figure 6-1   *The Choose Theme dialog box, used for selecting themes to incorporate into your Web*

Inside Discussion Groups

Because FrontPage creates your discussion group through the use of a wizard, you may feel a bit confused about what actually goes into the creation of the discussion group. In this section, we will go over the insides of the discussion group and what FrontPage uses to put it together.

HTML Pages

FrontPage puts together various HTML pages for use within the discussion group. These HTML pages comprise all aspects of the discussion, including any frames necessary and the pages that will contain your forms and contents.

All the HTML pages within a discussion can be edited through the editor within FrontPage. You may, however, notice that messages posted to the discussion groups do not seem to appear for editing. If this is the case, it is because they are found in hidden directories within your Web. When creating the Web with the Discussion Web Wizard, the default name for the discussion folder begins with an underscore (_). This tells FrontPage to make this folder a hidden folder. If you don't see the discussion folder within your Web, it is hidden. To work with these files, you must first instruct the system to show the files in the hidden directories. Here's how to do this:

1. Select Tools | Web Settings from the menu bar. This brings up the FrontPage Web Settings dialog box. If it is not already showing, click the Advanced tab, shown in Figure 6-2.

2. Click the check box next to Show Hidden Files and Folders. This instructs FrontPage to display all directories, including the hidden ones where your discussion group files are found.

3. Click OK. Your previously hidden folders containing the discussion group articles will now display after the Web reloads.

Forms

Two forms are available when working with discussion groups. The first is the article-posting form, and the second is the search form. The Post Article form page allows you to specify what information a visitor can enter when creating a topic. Although the name of this page varies, it will always be made up of the name of the discussion, followed by *_post.htm*. Within this page, the fields that must be included are the Subject and Comments fields. If you have chosen to use a registration Web,

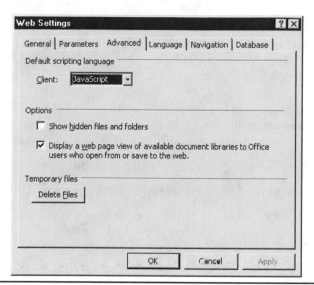

Figure 6-2   *The Advanced tab of the Web Settings dialog box*

the user's name will automatically carry over from the login form. If not, a From field will also appear on the Post Article form. These fields are the most basic of the discussion input fields.

In more complex discussion groups, you can add fields such as the Category and Products. These fields allow visitors to specify certain information about a topic. The information options are determined by you by editing these fields after setting them up in the wizard. Here's how to edit these fields:

1. Double-click a drop-down box form field to display the Drop-Down Box Properties dialog box.

2. Select one of the default choices and click Modify. This will bring up the Modify Choice dialog box.

3. Enter the name you want this choice to have. By default, FrontPage will give the choice the same value as the name. This will work for most operations. If you need to change this, select the Specify Value check box and enter a value for this choice.

4. Repeat this for each choice. If you need to add more choices, simply click Add and repeat step 3 for each addition.

5. Click OK when you have finished entering your choices. Your form will now contain the choices you have entered.

The Discussion Form Handler is a FrontPage-specific form handler that specifies how the forms for the discussion group are dealt with in your Web. This handler specifies the inputs and outputs of the form, and its properties can be edited by you. To edit the form handler, follow these steps:

1. Open the file containing the form for which you want to edit the handler. In the discussion group, this page will follow the naming convention of having the word "post" at the end of the filename (for example, disc1_post.htm).

2. Right-click within the form to bring up the available menu options.

3. Select Form Properties from the menu options. This brings up the Form Properties dialog box.

4. Click the Options button. This brings up the Options for Discussion Form Handler dialog box, shown in Figure 6-3. This dialog box allows you to specify many of the options available for the discussion group input form.

5. On the Discussion tab of the dialog box, select the main discussion options you want for this form:

   ▶ **Title**   Allows you to specify a descriptive title for the discussion group. This title will appear within the text of each posting, directly beneath the subject.

   ▶ **Directory**   Allows you to specify the directory where you want the discussion group articles to be stored. These are the actual messages entered by visitors.

   ▶ **Form fields**   Shows the fields that will appear in the table of contents when a message is posted. The defaults for these fields are the subject of the posting (Subject) and who the posting is from (From). You may modify these fields to display items such as the specific product associated with this posting. List each field you want to display, separated by a space.

   ▶ **Time**   Causes the time the message was posted to display in the table of contents.

   ▶ **Date**   Causes the date the message was posted to display in the table of contents.

   ▶ **Remote computer name**   Causes the name of the computer that posted the message to display in the table of contents. On the public Internet, this will normally be the IP address of the person posting the message.

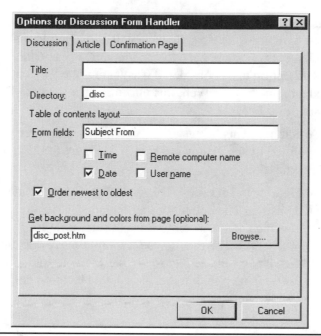

Figure 6-3   *The Options for Discussion Form Handler dialog box, containing options for setting up your discussion forms*

▶   **User name**   Causes the name of the user posting the message to display in the table of contents. If the user has logged onto a restricted-access Web (that is, a non-anonymous Web), this option will display his authenticated username. If the user was not required to log onto the Web, selecting this option will result in a blank username.

▶   **Order newest to oldest**   Determines the sort order of the messages. When this option is selected, it will cause the newest message to be posted first. As mentioned previously, threaded replies will still be displayed in oldest-to-newest order if you select this option and have activated the Threaded Replies option in the Discussion Web Wizard.

NOTE

Once the first message has been posted to the discussion Web, this option will have no effect.

▶   **Get background and colors from page**   Allows you to specify a page containing the theme elements you want for your postings. Because you will likely wish to maintain a consistent look throughout your discussion Web, designating a single style page will allow you to make changes to these elements once and have them automatically updated everywhere. This is an option to be considered if you are not using a theme. If you have applied a theme to your Web, this information will come from the theme, not a single style page.

6. Click the Article tab. This brings up the options available for your articles (what is submitted by the visitor), as shown in Figure 6-4. Each option is listed and explained next:

   ▶ **URL of Header to Include**   This is the path of the header that is included with each posting. The default header includes basic navigation for moving between postings. If you want to use a different file for your header, simply click Browse and choose the file you want to use. By default, the Discussion Web Wizard creates the header file in the *_private* folder. If you selected a theme for your Web within the wizard, this location default becomes the *_borders* folder.

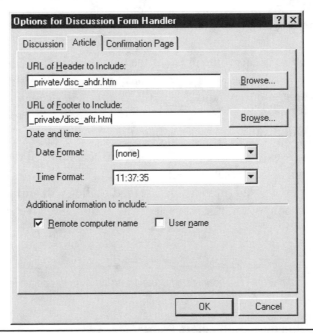

Figure 6-4   *Article properties*

▶ **URL of Footer to Include**   This is the path of the footer that is included with each posting. The default header includes a horizontal rule and a last-modified date. If you want to use a different file for your header, simply click Browse and choose the file you want to use. Like the header, the default location of this file is determined by your choice of whether or not to use a theme.

▶ **Date Format**   This is the format in which the date will appear within the actual posting. The default for this is None, which means the system will not display a date with the posting.

▶ **Time Format**   This is the format in which the time will appear within the actual posting. The default for this is None, which means the system will not display a time with the posting.

▶ **Remote computer name**   Selecting this option causes the system to display the name of the computer that posts the message. This name normally comes in the form of the computer's IP address.

▶ **User name**   Selecting this option instructs the system to display the authenticated username of the person posting the message. This information is only available in restricted-access Webs where the user is required to log in.

7. Select the options you want for your articles and click the Confirmation Page tab. This brings up confirmation page information, which contains the following options:

   ▶ **URL of confirmation page**   This is the path to the confirmation page informing visitors that their postings have been accepted. To change this path, simply type a new one or click Browse to select a new file.

   ▶ **URL of validation failure page**   This is the path to an optional failure page. This page displays if the posting is not accepted by the system. The default form is supplied, but you are allowed to substitute your own page by typing in a new path or clicking the Browse button to select a new file.

8. Enter your options for the Confirmation Page tab and click OK. Your changes will now take effect for all future postings in the discussion group.

Discussion Group Code Explained

FrontPage uses various components to make the discussion groups work. The following information relates to those components within the HTML code with explanations as to how FrontPage uses them. This is helpful if you are working directly in the HTML code to make changes.

WebBot	Description
Include	The Include WebBot (also referred to as the *Include Page WebBot*) instructs FrontPage to include a file within the current HTML layout. This is used for such aspects as the header and footer, and it simply targets a specific path and file for FrontPage to include. For more information on the Include WebBot, see Chapter 1.
Discussion	The Discussion WebBot consists of various settings for the actual discussion group. This WebBot is inserted into the article-posting form HTML page, and it consists of the following attributes: **s-discussion-description** The description that will appear below the subject in posted articles. **s-dir-name** The directory containing the articles for the discussion group. **s-article-format** The format in which the article will appear onscreen. **u-style-url** The link to the file FrontPage will use to determine the styles that will be used within the articles. **b-reverse-chronology** The order in which articles are displayed onscreen. Setting this to TRUE instructs FrontPage to display the articles from newest to oldest. **s-toc-fields** The fields that will be displayed on the table of contents page when a visitor enters the discussion group. **u-header-url** The path to the file that will be used as the header for all articles. **u-footer-url** The path to the file that will be used as the footer for all articles. **s-date-format** The format in which the date will be displayed within the discussion group. **s-time-format** The format in which the time will be displayed within the discussion group. **s-builtin-fields** The fields listed here are the ones that will display when a visitor views a posting. **u-confirmation-url** The path to the file containing the confirmation page shown once a user's posting is accepted.
ConfirmationField	The ConfirmationField WebBot is used to display the contents of a submitted form field as specified in its "s-subject" attribute.

WebBot	Description
Reply	The Reply WebBot allows visitors to reply to specific messages within the discussion group. This bot contains the configuration information necessary for the system to know which message the user is replying to, and it appears within the HTML of that message. The bot consists of the following components: **I-Article** Determines the number for the reply that a visitor is entering. FrontPage then pads this hexadecimal value with leading zeros to make up an individual eight-character article page name in the form 0000000x.htm. **I-ParentArticle** Informs FrontPage as to which article the visitor is replying to. **U-Discussion-Url** Contains the path to the HTML page containing the posting form for the discussion group. **S-DIR-Name** Points to the directory containing all articles within the discussion group.
FormInsertHere	The FormInsertHere WebBot is used to instruct the system where posts are to be placed on the page.

Administering Discussion Groups

Much of the administration of discussion groups is done within the HTML code and the editor options described earlier in this chapter.

NOTE

If you do not see the folders or files discussed in this section of the chapter, it means that your directories and/or files are hidden. To have these items display, you will need to change the settings for your Web, as described earlier in this chapter in the section titled "HTML Pages."

Rather than removing articles that you do not want viewed (if they contain inappropriate language, for example), you may want to open the articles and edit their contents. Doing this will ensure that all the hyperlinks within your discussion group continue to work properly. Although Microsoft does not recommend it, you may also delete articles, with a few precautions. Before attempting to remove articles, you should back up the discussion Web in case you make a mistake and need to start over.

If your Web server is running FrontPage 98 Server Extensions or later, you may simply delete articles, and they will be removed from the contents page, with Previous, Next, and Reply links being automatically repaired. Be aware, however, that if you remove an article with its own replies, the replies will be linked to the removed article's parent (preceding) article, possibly creating some discontinuity within the group's flow.

> **NOTE**
> *If you are running an earlier version of the Server Extensions, you will need to upgrade.*

Working with SharePoint Team Services

With the release of Office XP, Microsoft has added a new portal service that truly allows you to create collaborative Webs with a few clicks. The new SharePoint Team Services are what Microsoft calls a "prebuilt team Web site solution." After working with them for a while, I have to agree.

For years, I have had issues with the intranet at our office. It always seemed like the evil stepchild to our development projects, but nonetheless, a necessary tool. With the release of the SharePoint Team Services in Office XP, we now have the power to create an intranet system that allows us to share documents, create calendars, and collaborate on our projects, all with a few clicks. SharePoint also integrates directly with SQL Server. You just tell it the server to use and the server login, and it creates databases for you as required, totally automating the process. We can now get rid of all the custom programs we threw together over the years to handle calendaring, scheduling, and the like.

This section of the chapter takes a look at the new SharePoint server and how you can use it to create truly collaborative Web sites.

> **NOTE**
> *To work with the examples discussed in this chapter, you must have the SharePoint Team Services installed on a Windows 2000 Server. For more information on installing the SharePoint Team Services, see the SharePoint Team Services documentation.*

Creating a SharePoint-Based Team Web Site

Microsoft has made creating a new team Web site easy by incorporating a SharePoint template directly into the Web Site Templates dialog box.

To create a SharePoint-based Web site, follow these steps:

1. Select File | New | Page or Web from the menu bar. This brings up the New Page or Web sidebar.

2. Click Web Site Templates to bring up the Web Site Templates dialog box.

3. Select SharePoint-based Team Web Site from the available templates.

4. Specify the location where you want the new Web site to be stored.

NOTE

Remember that the location of your new Web must be on a server that has the SharePoint Team Services extensions installed.

5. Click OK.

FrontPage will now take a few minutes to create your SharePoint Web site. That's all there is to it. You now have a completely customizable collaborative Web site for documents, discussions, lists, calendars, and so on. Now you are probably thinking that there has got to be more to this, and you are right. However, it isn't anything as difficult as you may be thinking. Once you have created the site, you will want to add your own look and feel, along with customizing all the various items available to you. Customization is taken care of just like any other site in FrontPage, but it takes a little effort in your browser.

Customizing Your SharePoint Web Site

Once you have created a SharePoint Web site, you will want to customize it for your purposes. The type of customization I'm talking about is not changing images and the like. This can be handled just like any other Web site in FrontPage. What I'm talking about is more on the administration side. Because this is a book about FrontPage, we won't get into too much detail about administration of this type of site, but here are the steps to get you where you need to go:

1. Open your Web site home page in FrontPage and switch to Preview mode.

NOTE

You can also open your Web in your browser.

2. Click Site Settings in the menu bar. This brings up the Site Settings page of the Web site, as shown next.

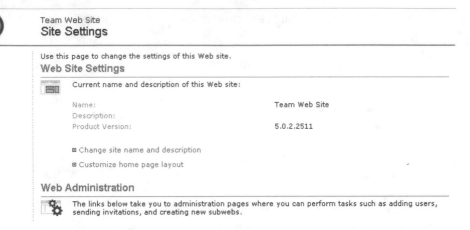

In this page, you have all the tools necessary to set up your site just how you want it.

Developing Informational Lists

Informational lists are a great addition to your Web site because they allow your viewers to quickly and easily scan information that you have put together. We discuss informational lists in this section because they require you to have the SharePoint Server Extensions installed. To create an informational list, follow these steps:

1. Create or open a SharePoint Web site with FrontPage.

2. Select Insert | Web Component from the menu bar. This brings up the Insert Web Component dialog box, shown in Figure 6-5.

3. Select List View from the Component Type pane. This fills the Choose an effect pane with various styles of lists for you to choose from.

TIP

You can always change the list style after you have inserted the Web Component by double-clicking the component itself in the Normal view.

4. Click Finish. This brings up the List View Properties dialog box, shown in Figure 6-6, and then the Choose List dialog box, shown here:

5. Select the type of list you want and click OK. You are now presented with the List View Properties dialog box, shown in Figure 6-6.

6. Click the various option buttons to determine what your list should display. When you are done customizing your list, click OK.

The component now displays in your window.

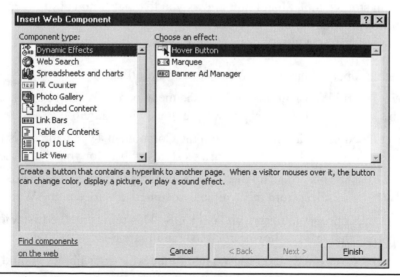

Figure 6-5   *The Insert Web Component dialog box*

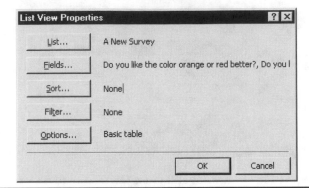

Figure 6-6   *List View Properties dialog box*

Working with Document Libraries

Document libraries are a great addition to any collaborative Web site as they allow multiple individuals to work with, edit, and save various documents using the Web as their main storage tool. SharePoint allows you to quickly and easily create document libraries for use in your Web sites.

To create a document library, follow these steps:

1.   Create or open a SharePoint Web site with FrontPage.

2.   Select Insert | Web Component from the menu bar. This brings up the Insert Web Component dialog box, shown previously in Figure 6-5.

3.   Select Document Library View from the Component Type pane. This fills the Choose a View Style pane with various styles of lists for you to choose from.

4.   Click Finish. This brings up the Choose Document Library dialog box, which allows you to select from the available document libraries in the Web.

5.   Select the appropriate library and click OK. This brings up the List View Properties dialog box, shown previously in Figure 6-6.

6.   Click the various option buttons to determine what your library should display. When you are done customizing your list, click OK.

The component now displays in your window.

Creating SharePoint-Based Discussions

Earlier in this chapter, we discussed the FrontPage Discussion Web Wizard. Although this tool can be used effectively, it doesn't hold a candle to the new discussion capabilities that come with SharePoint. With SharePoint, you can create new discussions, modify discussion groups, and filter discussion information, all within the browser window. SharePoint discussion groups are truly a collaborative tools for today, and they are simple to implement.

To create a new discussion group with SharePoint, simply follow these steps:

1. Create or open a SharePoint Web site with FrontPage.

2. Open the default.htm page and switch to Preview mode by clicking the Preview tab.

3. Click Discussion Boards in the Web site's navigation area. This will bring up the Discussions Boards page, shown in Figure 6-7.

4. Click the New Discussion Board icon. This brings up the New Discussion Board page, shown here:

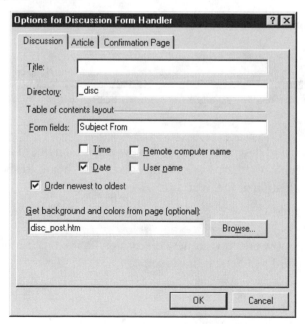

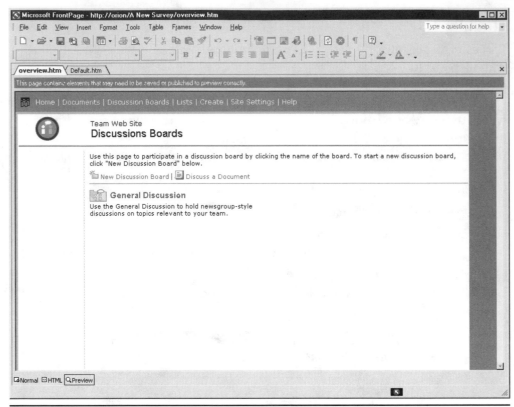

Figure 6-7   *The SharePoint Web site's Discussions Boards page*

5. Type a name and description for your new discussion board and then click Yes or No to specify whether you want this discussion board to show up on the left-side navigation of the Web site.

6. Click Create.

SharePoint will now create your new discussion board. Once it is created, your new discussion board will appear on screen.

Modifying Settings

Once you have created a discussion board in a SharePoint site, you can modify it by following these steps:

1. Click the discussion board you want to modify in the Discussion Boards page (refer to Figure 6-7). This brings up the selected discussion board.

2. Click Modify Settings and Columns to bring up the Customize General Discussion page, shown in Figure 6-8.

You can now select from the various options to modify your discussion board as I will show you in the following sections.

Changing General Settings   Once you have created a discussion board, you may find that you want to make modifications to it. To do so, follow these steps:

1. Click the discussion board you want to modify in the Discussion Boards page (refer to Figure 6-7). This brings up the selected discussion board.

2. Click Modify Settings and Columns to bring up the Customize General Discussion page, shown in Figure 6-8.

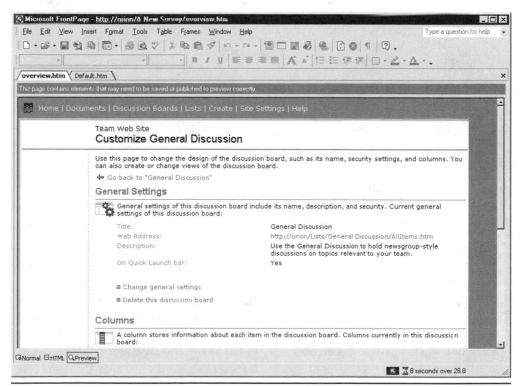

Figure 6-8   *A SharePoint discussion group's Customize General Discussion page*

3. Click the Change General Settings link on the Customize General Discussion page to bring up the Discussion Board Settings page, shown here:

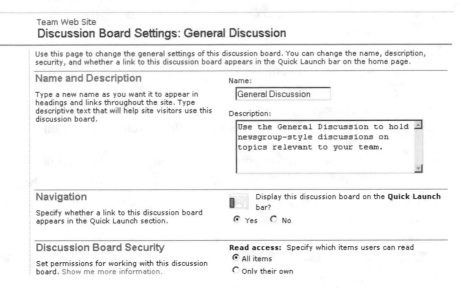

On this page, you have the option to modify the following settings:

▶ **Name and Description**   Allows you to rename the discussion board and change the descriptive text for the board.

▶ **Navigation**   Allows you to determine whether the board will appear on the site's navigation bar.

▶ **Discussion Board Security**   Allows you to set various aspects of the security for the discussion board, including what items users can read and edit, along with who has the rights to make modifications to the settings for this board.

4. Make your changes to the settings and click OK. The changes will now take effect.

Deleting a Discussion Board   You may find that you want to delete a discussion board that has been created on the Web site. This is accomplished by following these steps:

1. Click the discussion board you want to modify in the Discussion Boards page (refer to Figure 6-7). This brings up the selected discussion board.

2. Click Modify Settings and Columns to bring up the Customize General Discussion page, shown previously in Figure 6-8.

3. Click Delete this Discussion Board on the Customize General Discussion page. You are prompted to verify whether you want to actually delete the discussion board.

4. Click OK. The discussion board is now removed from the system, and you are returned to the main Discussion Boards page.

Filtering Information

Once a discussion board gets to a certain size, it can become rather unruly and difficult to find information in. The SharePoint system handles this problem with a filtering option that allows you to display only the information that you want.

To filter the information in a discussion group, follow these steps:

1. Click the discussion board you want to filter in the Discussions Boards page (refer to Figure 6-7). This brings up the selected discussion board.

2. Click Filter to bring up the filtering options shown here:

You may now filter the discussion using the available drop-down lists described here:

▶ **Subject**   Allows you to display topics based on the subject matter

▶ **Modified By**   Allows you to display topics based on the person who modified them

▶ **Modified**   Allows you to display topics based on date

Creating Online Surveys

Surveys can be an extremely useful tool in any group environment. They allow you to gather large amounts of information through the use of questions. The SharePoint

Team Services offer two great survey tools for use with FrontPage—both of which are available by selecting File | New | Survey from the menu bar:

▶ **Survey**   A basic survey outline where FrontPage creates all the necessary pages for the survey and you can then go in and add your questions

▶ **Survey Wizard**   A wizard that takes you through the entire process of creating the survey and allows you to create your questions, answers, and the way they will be displayed

For the purposes of this discussion, I will focus on the use of the Survey Wizard because it automatically creates all the questions and answers. Later in this section, you will see how to modify your survey, which you can use if you create a new survey using only the Survey option.

Using the Survey Wizard

The Survey Wizard allows you to create surveys, complete with questions and answers. To use the Survey Wizard, simply follow these steps:

1. Select File | New | Survey from the menu bar. This brings up the New Survey dialog box.

2. Select New Survey Wizard and click OK. You are now presented with the first step in the Survey Wizard.

3. Click Next to bring up the next step in the Survey Wizard, shown here:

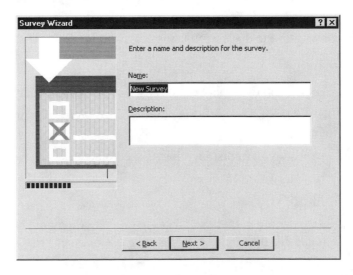

4. Enter a name and a description for your new survey in the available fields and click Next.

5. You are now asked to define the questions for your survey, shown here:

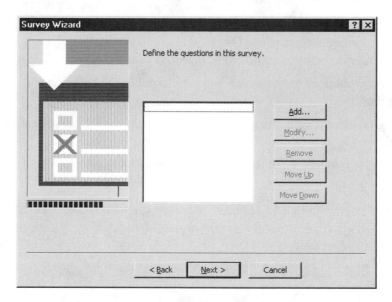

6. Click Add to begin defining your questions. You are now presented with the Add Question dialog box, shown here:

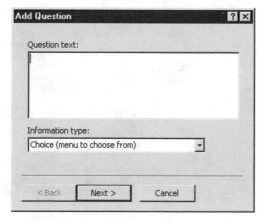

7. Type the text for your question.

8. Now select the information type for your question and click OK. For the purposes of this discussion, choose the Choice option.

NOTE

There are a number of different Information types. Depending on the information type you select, your next steps may vary slightly.

9. Because we have decided to select Choice as the information type, we are now presented with the Add Question dialog box once again, but now it asks us to enter the choices available in the survey.

10. Enter any number of choices, being sure to put each choice on a separate line.

11. Assign a default value for your choices. This will be the preselected value on the page.

12. Select the way you want the choices to display on the page.

13. Click Finish.

14. Repeat step 9 through 13 for each question you want to add. Once you have added all your questions, the dialog box for defining your questions will look something like this:

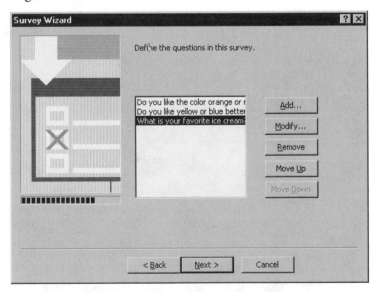

15. Click Next to move to the next step in the wizard, where you will specify how users will interact with the survey, as shown here:

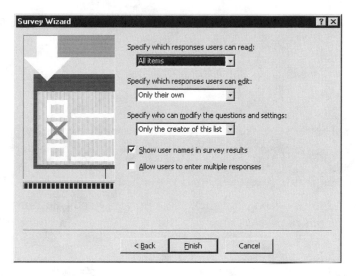

16. In this step, you can specify a number of settings that determine how your users will interact with the survey. The available options are as follows:

   ► **Specify which responses users can read**   Allows you to specify whether users can view the responses in the survey.

   ► **Specify which responses users can edit**   Allows you to specify whether users can modify responses that have been entered in the survey.

   ► **Specify who can modify the questions and settings**   Allows you to specify who has the right to modify the survey settings and questions.

   ► **Show user names in survey results**   Determines whether users' names will appear in the results.

   ► **Allow users to enter multiple responses**   Allows you to specify whether users have the ability to respond to the survey more than once.

17. Click Finish. FrontPage now creates your new survey and adds it to your current Web.

Modifying Surveys

Once you have created a survey, FrontPage makes it easy to modify your survey. To do so, follow these steps:

1. Open the page titled overview.htm in your new survey with FrontPage.

2.   Switch to Preview mode and click Modify Survey and Questions. This brings up the Customize page for your new survey, as shown in Figure 6-9.

From here, you can make modifications to your survey as I will show you in the following sections.

Changing General Settings   Once you have created a survey, you may find that you want to make modifications to that survey. To do so, follow these steps:

1.   Open the page titled overview.htm in your new survey with FrontPage.

2.   Switch to Preview mode and click Modify Survey and Questions. This brings up the Customize page for your new survey, as shown in Figure 6-9.

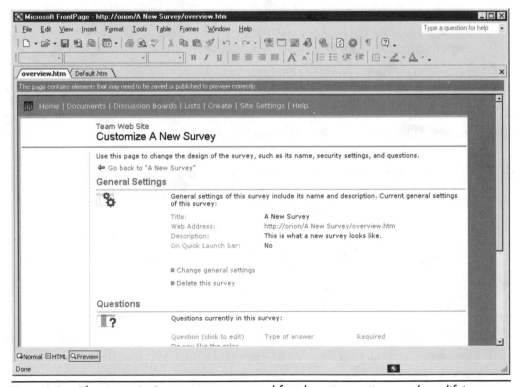

Figure 6-9   *The survey's Customize page, used for changing settings and modifying questions*

3. Click the Change General Settings link on the Customize page to bring up the Survey Settings page, shown here:

Team Web Site
Survey Settings: A New Survey

Use this page to change the general settings of this survey. You can change the name, description, security, and whether a link to this survey appears in the Quick Launch bar on the home page.

Name and Description

Type a new name as you want it to appear in headings and links throughout the site. Type descriptive text that will help site visitors use this survey.

Name:

A New Survey

Description:

This is what a new survey looks like.

Navigation

Specify whether a link to this survey appears in the Quick Launch section.

☐ Display this survey on the **Quick Launch** bar?
○ Yes   ◉ No

Survey Options

You can specify options for this survey.

Show user names in survey results?
◉ Yes   ○ No

On this page, you have the option to modify the following settings:

▶ **Name and Description**   Allows you to rename the survey and change the descriptive text for the survey

▶ **Navigation**   Allows you to determine whether the survey will appear on the site's navigation bar

▶ **Survey Options**   Allows you to determine whether the user's name will appear on the survey and whether a user can respond more than once

▶ **Survey Security**   Allows you to set various aspects of the security for the survey, including what items users can read and edit, along with who has the right to make modifications to the settings for this survey

4. Make your changes to the settings and click OK. The changes will now take effect.

Deleting a Survey   You may find that you want to delete a survey that has been created on the Web site. This is accomplished by following these steps:

1. Open the page titled overview.htm in your new survey with FrontPage.

2. Switch to Preview mode and click Modify Survey and Questions. This brings up the Customize page for your new survey, as shown previously in Figure 6-9.

3. Click the Delete This Survey link on the Customize page. You are prompted to verify whether you want to actually delete the survey.

4. Click OK. The survey is now removed from the system.

Exporting Survey Information to a Spreadsheet

Your online survey gives you the ability to view and edit information submitted through your Web browser, but you may find that you want to export this information to a spreadsheet so that you can compile the data. This is easily accomplished by following these steps:

1. Open the page titled overview.htm in your new survey with FrontPage.

2. Switch to Preview mode and click Export Results to a Spreadsheet. The system now processes your request and displays the standard File Download dialog box.

3. Select Save This File to Disk and click OK. You are now presented with the standard Save As dialog box.

4. Browse to the location where you want to save the file and click Save.

NOTE

You will notice that the survey is not saved as a standard Excel file. It is, in fact, a Microsoft Excel Web Query file.

5. Now open Microsoft Excel and select File | Open from the menu bar.

6. Browse to the directory where you have saved your file.

7. Select Query Files from the Files of Type drop-down menu in the Open dialog box. You will now see your file displayed.

8. Select your file and click Open. Excel now opens your file and requests the data from the server. Once the requested data has been obtained, it displays in the spreadsheet.

Summary

As you can see from this chapter, FrontPage offers quite a bit in the way of creating and maintaining collaborative Web sites. This is especially true if you add the capabilities of the SharePoint Team Services into the mix. This chapter covers how to set up basic discussions, along with optimizing them for your varied uses, and how to create project-based and collaborative Web sites. It also shows you how to use a number of the features available with the SharePoint Team Services.

With the information contained here, you now have the ability to create comprehensive Web sites that will add to your company's productivity and information-sharing capabilities.

Advanced Form Integration

IN THIS CHAPTER:

Understand How Forms Work

Create Custom Forms in FrontPage

Them use of forms has become an indispensable part of today's Web sites. Through forms, we can gather information about our visitors, obtain information about products, and allow visitors to become active users in the development of our Web sites. The feedback and information gathered through the use of forms can be used to develop databases, offer customer support, and even create new aspects of our sites on-the-fly. Along with the ability to gather information from our visitors, forms enable us to create dynamic sites that allow for the integration of e-commerce systems. Through the use of forms, visitors can fill out orders and use shopping cart systems that we develop in our sites.

In this chapter we will take a look at the basics behind forms and their use, but we will also go a few steps further. You will see how forms can add great value to your Web sites, and you will find out how to create extensive data-collection forms in FrontPage. We will also look at the capabilities FrontPage offers you when creating forms and how you can easily integrate complex forms into your sites through the use of FrontPage and its server extensions.

Anatomy of a Form

The core concept behind forms is the collection of data from users. You put a form on a Web site expressly for that purpose. How you use that information can differ greatly, depending on what your form's front end is created for. It may be that you are creating an online survey or are simply asking visitors for feedback on your site. Whatever the reason, you must keep in mind some of the following basic principles when creating your forms.

What Does the Form Tag Do?

The <FORM> tag instructs a browser that the tags found within it are to be used for the purposes of a form. This tag also contains the basic configuration information necessary for your form. It includes items such as the form action, which is the action that will be performed when the user submits the form, and the method in which that action will take place.

When you're working with FrontPage, by default, a <FORM> tag is automatically created when you add the first form field (such as a text box) onto a page. The form is displayed on your screen as a dotted line that encompasses all the fields, as shown in Figure 7-1.

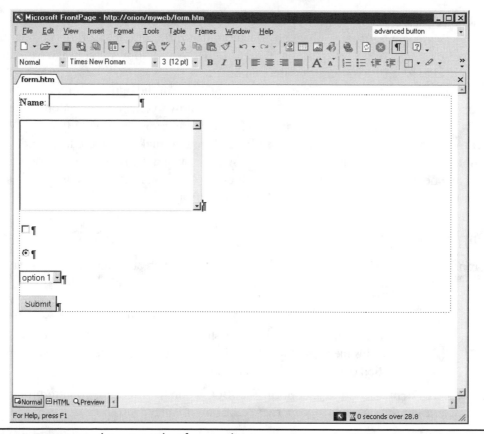

Figure 7-1 *A sample page with a form outline*

NOTE

If you are using your form fields for custom scripts, such as JavaScript, you can instruct FrontPage not to include the <FORM> tag when you insert a field. For more information, see "Using Scripts with Forms," later in this chapter.

Creating Forms in FrontPage

FrontPage gives you many options for creating forms. You can create forms quickly and easily using its wizards, or you can simply begin adding form elements to pages and configuring them on-the-fly. Much of what you do within FrontPage is meant for use with standard forms that can add submitted information to a file, send an e-mail message, or access a database, but FrontPage also allows you to incorporate form fields for use with scripting languages.

This part of the chapter takes a close look at many of the options you have when working with forms in FrontPage. You will learn how to create forms, along with how to configure and customize them to fit your requirements. You will also learn some great tricks you can use in FrontPage that make form creation and implementation painless, to say the least. Whether you are a seasoned programmer or have never touched the back end of a Web application, FrontPage has the tools you need to get moving in your data-collection efforts.

Form Menu Options

FrontPage comes with a complete selection of options for creating forms. These options are found under the Insert menu on the FrontPage menu bar and are described here:

▶ **Form**   Instructs FrontPage to insert the <FORM> tag into your document, which appears in your editor as a dotted box, as shown in Figure 7-1. FrontPage, by default, also adds the Submit and Reset buttons to get you started. These buttons can be modified or removed, depending on your requirements.

▶ **List Form**   Inserts a List Form WebBot. Upon its insertion, you are prompted to select the list and its properties (add, edit, display, and so on).

▶ **List Field**   Inserts a List Field into a List Form. List Fields are used to display and modify list data fields. This field is only available when in a List Form's Layout Customization View.

▶ **Text Box**   Inserts a single-line text input box into your page.

▶ **Text Area**   Inserts a multiline text input box that users can scroll through.

▶ **File Upload**   Inserts a WebBot that creates a "type=file" form field when viewed in a browser. This field appears as a single-line text box with a Browser button. Using this control, you can allow users to anonymously upload files to a folder within your site.

▶ **Check Box**   Allows users to select one or more options through the use of a check box. This is known as a Boolean (True/False) field.

▶ **Option Button**   Allows users to select one of many options. Option buttons can be grouped so that selecting an option deselects all other options within the group.

▶ **Drop-Down Menu**   Allows for a selection from a list of options. Drop-down menus can be used to perform auto-searches by selecting the first matching item in the list when the user presses a letter on the keyboard.

▶ **Push Button**   Inserts a button into your form.

▶ **Advanced Button**   Inserts an IE-specific <button> form element into your form. This new type of button allows you to format its text and add images. This form element will not work with Netscape's browsers.

▶ **Picture**   Inserts an image that can be used in place of the Submit button.

▶ **Label**   Allows you to create a label associated with your form item. This way, a visitor can click the item's associated text to select the item (see "Adding Labels to Form Fields," later in this chapter, for more information).

▶ **Form Properties**   Brings up the Form Properties dialog box, shown in Figure 7-2. This option is only available if you are working within a form that has already been created. (This dialog box will be referred to throughout the chapter.)

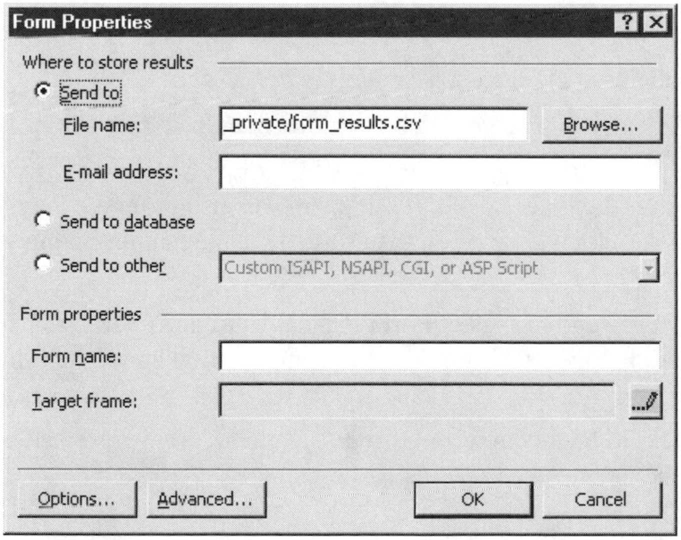

Figure 7-2   *The Form Properties dialog box*

FrontPage Form Wizard

The FrontPage Form Wizard is a great starting point for anyone developing forms for use with FrontPage. It really doesn't matter if you are an advanced developer or are just getting started; this wizard will prove to be one of your favorite tools in the FrontPage arsenal. Through the use of the wizard, you will easily be able to create the basic front end of just about any form you can imagine. Once you have completed the basics of the front end, the wizard gives you the ability to send the form via e-mail, insert it into a Web page, or even hook it into a custom Common Gateway Interface (CGI) script that has nothing to do with the wizard. (CGI uses server-side or client-side scripting and server applications.)

This section examines each step in the wizard and provides some interesting ways of extending the wizard to meet your development needs. This wizard, like many of the other wizards in FrontPage, makes your life easier. It takes you, step by step, through the process of setting up the various elements in your forms. This process allows you to configure the front end of your forms exactly as you want them. Once you have set up a form in the wizard, you can then cut and paste it into any document in your Web.

The following takes you through each step of the wizard along with everything associated with those steps:

1. Open your Web or create a new Web in FrontPage.
2. Select File | New | Page or Web from the menu bar. This brings up the New Page or Web sidebar, which allows you to open and create pages.
3. Select Page Templates from the sidebar. This brings up the Page Templates dialog box, which allows you to choose the page template from which to create your page.
4. From this dialog box, select Form Page Wizard and click OK. The wizard introduction appears, giving you basic information about the steps you are about to perform.
5. Click Next to begin the wizard process. You are now presented with the first step in the Form Page Wizard, as shown here:

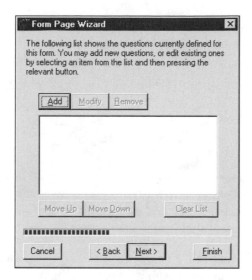

The first step of the wizard asks you to insert the questions you want for your form. If you are beginning with a new form, the field here will be blank. You will need to add questions to this field. To do so, continue with the next step.

6. Click the Add button to bring up the selection box for your questions, as shown here:

7. Select from the available entries. You will see that a sample question or statement appears in the question's prompt field at the bottom of the dialog box. This field may be edited to suit your form's requirements.

Many types of data can be collected in this section of the wizard. The choices you make here will affect the options in the next step of the wizard because it will ask you to customize the questions asked. The following list explains each of the fields associated with a selected response.

NOTE

When working with any of the secondary dialog boxes associated with the question types, be sure to enter a base name to be associated with the group you have selected. This name is used for the processing of this group of information within the form.

▶ **Contact information**   This type has fields associated with basic personal information input, such as the user's name, address, and phone number. You may select any or all of the fields for incorporation into your form.

▶ **Account information**   Use this type if you want a user to input user name and password information into the form. This is a basic screen, but it does have a couple of options that I want to mention:

   ▶ **Username**   You can select to have the user name as a single field or as first and last name fields. The selection of first and last name fields is necessary if you are working with the Registration Form handler. (See Chapter 6 for more on Registration Form handlers and their implementation limits.)

   ▶ **Password**   Here you have the option of having users confirm their passwords by retyping them. This is useful if the user is creating an account using your form but is unnecessary if the user will be accessing your pages by simply entering his or her password in your form. Password fields are one-line text boxes and display the user's input as asterisks (*******) instead of the actual text entered.

▶ **Product information**   This type allows you to ask for basic product information in your form. Once you complete the wizard, you can modify the fields in this form to fit your requirements.

▶ **Ordering information**   Use this type to obtain product-ordering information from your visitors. Once you complete the wizard, you can modify the options in this form to fit your requirements. Although the billing information options include the gathering of credit card information, you will not likely want to use this option unless the form and its output are within a secure environment (SSL), meaning that the information contained will be encrypted.

▶ **Personal information**   This question allows you to request personal information about your visitors. This contrasts with the contact information fields in that it asks for specific personal information about the visitor rather than simple contact information.

▶ **One of several options**   This allows you to ask a multiple-choice question of your visitors. Within the associated dialog box, you enter each choice on a separate line and then determine how you want those choices displayed.

NOTE

This option allows only one answer per question through the use of a drop-down menu, option buttons, or a list. If you want the user to supply multiple answers, use the Any of Several Options dialog box (discussed next) or select the List display option and later modify that list to allow multiple selections.

▶ **Any of several options**   This allows you to ask a multiple-choice question of your visitors. Within the associated dialog box, you enter each choice on a separate line. If you have several options for your users to select from, you can click the Multiple Columns box to display your options in multiple columns across the page.

NOTE

This option allows multiple answers per question through the use of check boxes. If you want the user to supply a single answer, use the One of Several Options dialog box.

▶ **Boolean**   With this option, you create a simple question for users to answer. This question can consist simply of a check box that your users can check or a yes/no or true/false question.

NOTE

Keep in mind that a form only submits a field's contents when it contains information. Yes/no and true/false questions that have a default selection will always return the user's answer, whereas single check box fields will only return a result when checked.

▶ **Date**   This option inserts a one-line text box into the form for the user to enter a date. The dialog box associated with this option simply tells how the date should be input into the form, with a descriptive label. The type of date formatting selected here does not limit or control the user's actual input other than to limit the maximum number of characters that may be entered.

▶ **Time**   This option inputs an area into the form for the user to enter a time value. The dialog box associated with this option tells how the time should be input into the form, similar to how the Date option does.

▶ **Range**   Use this option to incorporate a question with an answer based on a scale. The options associated with this selection let you determine how you want the range displayed (for example, a scale of 1–5). Of course, you may later modify this selection criterion within the FrontPage editor.

▶ **Number**   This option is associated with a question asking users to input a numeric value. The only option associated with Number is the length of the text box in which users will be entering the value.

▶ **String**   This option is associated with a question asking users to input a character string value. The only option associated with String, as in the Number option, is the length of the text box. (For nonprogrammers, a *string* is a data type, or way of referring to one or more text characters as a group.)

▶ **Paragraph**   This option inserts a multiline scrolling text box into your form for the collection of items such as comments. There are no options associated with this value. All you need to enter is the name of the variable.

8. Once you have added all your questions, click the Next button to be taken to the Presentation Options dialog box, shown here:

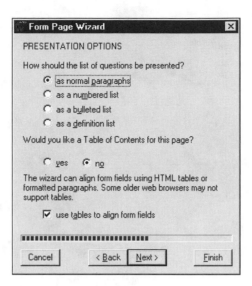

9. Select the presentation options you want for your form. Some notable options here include the auto-creation of a form-field table of contents (a nice feature if the form will be extremely long or the page will contain multiple forms) and the option to use tables to align forms. Although it's totally at your discretion as the developer, you will usually want to select this feature.

10. Click Next to proceed to the final phase of the wizard—what to do with all the data you collect.

    We have now reached the point in the wizard where all your elements are ready to be put into the form. All that is left is to decide what to do with the data that is collected in the form. You accomplish this by choosing from the options in the next dialog box, shown here:

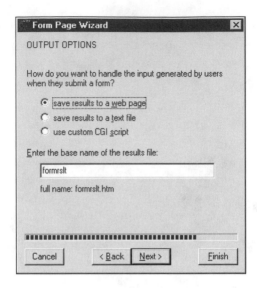

With the wizard and the FrontPage extensions on your server, you can select to save the results to a Web page or send them to a formatted text file. FrontPage also enables you to hook your form up to a custom script. The following information pertains to each of these three options; the one you choose will be based on your preference and requirements:

NOTE

Although FrontPage 2002 can send form results to a database (if you have configured database access within your Web), this feature has not been incorporated into this wizard. We'll cover database integration features in detail in Chapter 12.

▶ **Save results to a Web page**   You will be prompted to type the name of the Web page where you want the results saved. When your users input information into this form and submit it, the results will be posted on the page you have entered. If this page does not already exist, it will be created the first time a user submits the form. Use of this option requires the destination server to be running FrontPage server extensions.

NOTE

If this is to be a private page, you should place it in the _private subdirectory (or other restricted access subdirectory), because the destination page name will be visible in the form page's HTML source.

▶ **Save results to a text file**   You will be prompted to type the name of the text file where you want the results saved. When your users input information into this form and submit it, the results will be posted to the text file on your server. If this file does not already exist, it will be created the first time a user submits the form. Use of this option requires the destination server to be running FrontPage server extensions.

NOTE

Just as with the Save Results to a Web Page option, you may want to place this page in a restricted access subdirectory.

▶ **Use custom CGI script**   This option instructs FrontPage to create all the form elements and puts a placeholder in for you to change in the form's Action field. Custom scripts cannot be specified here, just the fact that you will be using one.

NOTE

This is the only option that does not require the destination server to be running FrontPage server extensions. This is also the option you would choose if you are planning on submitting your form to a database (see Chapters 11 and 12).

11. Once you have selected how your form will be processed, all that's left is to click Finish. FrontPage configures and creates your form and places it into a new page within your Web.

You can now work within your form to further customize it to meet your requirements.

NOTE

Once your form is created, you can build the page around it, or you can cut and paste the form into a page you have already created. You cannot reenter this wizard, but you may further customize each of the wizard's options at any time within the FrontPage editor.

Customizing Your FrontPage Forms

Creating a form in FrontPage is a simple task, as you saw in the previous section about the Form Wizard. You may find, however, that the form created by the wizard, or by entering your own information via the toolbar, is not quite what you need. This part of the chapter takes the creation of your form to the next level. It shows you how to customize your form to get the most out of it. Whether it is the replacement of those wonderful gray buttons with the new advanced buttons, the use of custom images, or more complex issues, such as creating forms with hidden fields for use with your custom scripts, you will find the answers here.

Customizing Your Buttons

One of the biggest complaints I hear from clients is that the standard gray buttons associated with forms take away from the look and feel of the entire Web site. There is nothing worse than creating a great looking Web site and then having to incorporate those ugly gray buttons into it when you want to gather information. For this reason, many developers have taken to using custom images in their forms. These images replace the standard Submit and Reset buttons found on many forms in use today.

Another way developers are creating more attractive buttons is through the use of the styles available in the newer versions of Internet Explorer, as discussed in Chapter 4. With these styles, you can customize the way the text within a button displays in the browser. This is a fairly simple process that is achieved by following these steps:

1. Create a form in FrontPage.

2. Select the button you want to assign a style to by clicking it.

3. Right-click and select Form Field Properties from the drop-down menu. This brings up the Push Button Properties dialog box.

4. Click the Style button to bring up the Modify Style dialog box.

5. Click the Format button and select Font from the drop-down menu. This brings up the Font dialog box, which allows you to select the font and style.

6. Click OK on each dialog box to close it. Your style is now embedded into the button's properties, as shown in the following code.

```
<INPUT TYPE=SUBMIT VALUE="Submit Form"
style="font-family: Arial Black;
font-style: italic; font-weight: bold">
```

As you can see, we have chosen Arial Black for our font, with an italic style and a bold font weight.

7. To preview the button font, click the Preview tab in your editor.

Incorporating an Advanced Button into Your Form

Just when you think everything is alright with the world and the browser wars are over, Microsoft goes and incorporates a new way of doing things that, while making your life easier, can also make it more difficult. This is the situation you're faced with when using the advanced buttons in your Webs. If you are creating for an IE-specific audience, this is a great solution that allows you to add one more level of customization to the look and feel of your forms. However, if you are wanting to have the widest audience possible see your sites, you can't use this technology. With that said, those of you in the first group will the Advanced buttons to be a great addition to your toolkit. Here's how you can easily add a custom look and feel to your buttons with the new custom button feature:

1. Create a form in your Web.
2. Position your cursor where you want your custom button to appear.
3. Select Insert | Form | Advanced Button. You will see a gray button appear with its text highlighted. This highlighted text can be modified to display whatever you want.

Now, this is where the customization of the Advanced button comes in. There are two ways you can modify this button. The first is by right-clicking the button and selecting the Advanced Button Properties dialog box, shown here:

From this dialog box, you can specify the following information to determine how the button displays on the page and its function within the form:

▶ **Name**   This is the name the form uses to identify the button.

▶ **Value**   This is the value associated with the button.

▶ **Button Type**   This determines what function the button performs in the form. As you saw earlier in the chapter, you can specify a button as Submit, Reset, or Normal, with the last option needing custom code to determine the button's function.

▶ **Tab Order**   This is the order in which the button will be highlighted within the form as a user moves through the form using the Tab key.

▶ **Width**   This lets you give the button a specific width on the page.

▶ **Height**   This lets you give the button a specific height on the page.

▶ **Style**   This brings up the standard Modify Style dialog box. From here, you can modify the look and feel of the text within the button.

The second way to modify the button is to add specific code to the button's HTML. The following example shows how to add an image to the button:

1. Click the button and then select HTML from the view options at the bottom of your screen. You will see the code within the button brackets highlighted.

2. Add the following code in place of the text that is currently there:

```
<img src="yourimagefile.gif" height="x" width="x" alt="the alt
text for your image">
```

Now when you preview this button, you will see an image in place of the text.

Incorporating a Custom Submit Button into Your Form

Custom images can add a great deal to the look and feel of a form. The images you incorporate will replace the standard gray buttons associated with forms in HTML. From the following example, you will learn how to incorporate a custom image into your forms that will work the same way as a standard button. For this example, we will be using the page titled feedback.htm in the Dogs by the Bay Web on the CD-ROM. Here are the steps to follow:

1. Create a form in your Web or open the feedback.htm page.

2. If your form currently contains a standard Submit button, select the button and delete it.

3. Position your cursor where you want your image to appear.

4. Select Insert | Form | Picture from the menu bar. This brings up the Picture dialog box, which allows you to select an image.

5. Select the image you want to use for your form submission and click OK. The image now appears where you placed it on your page, as shown in Figure 7-3.

6. Now that your image is in place, you will want to give it an identifying name. To do so, select the image and choose Format | Properties from the menu bar. This brings up the Picture Properties dialog box.

NOTE

You will notice that this version of the Picture Properties dialog box is slightly different from the standard version. This is due to FrontPage understanding that you want to use this image within your form rather than as just a standard image. For this reason, FrontPage adds the extra Form Field tab to the standard dialog box.

7. In the Form Field tab, enter a name for the submission button and click OK.

FrontPage now creates the final code associated with the submission button. When you have completed the steps, your HTML code should look similar to the code listed here:

```
<input border="0" src="images/submit.gif"
name="submit" align="right" width="68" height="63"
type="image">
```

Now we have an image that complements the overall look of our site and replaces the standard gray button. Unfortunately, you can only create a custom image button in this manner for use as your Submit button. It will not work with the Reset button. To use a custom image for a Reset button, you need to use a slightly different technique, which we discuss in the Hands On box.

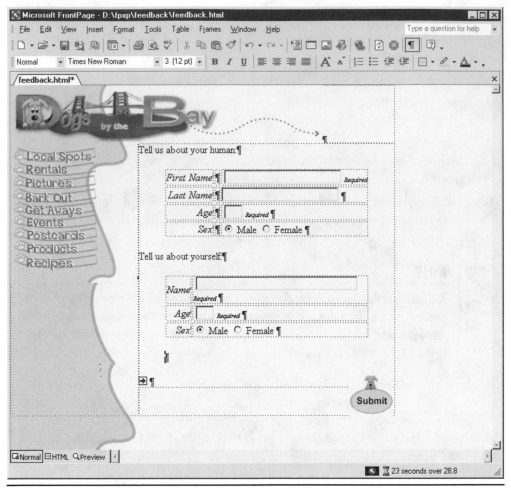

Figure 7-3 *Feedback page with a custom Submit button*

Using Scripts with Forms

As you will see in the Hands On exercise, scripts written in JavaScript or VBScript are often used in association with forms and form fields. It may be that you are working with a particular form and want to add some functionality that is not currently available, or you simply need to use the form elements within your script to perform a function. Whatever the case, forms and scripts can go hand in hand, and FrontPage makes the marriage between the two even easier with its form capabilities.

Hands On: Bypassing a Form's Limitations with Image Buttons

As we just discussed, HTML forms treat any named image within the form as a Submit button. Although this implementation makes adding an image-based Submit button quite easy, it also places unwanted limits on your creativity. To work around this limitation, we must tap into the form object model and make a call to it using a little JavaScript. As you'll see, this is quite easily accomplished:

1. Remove the existing Submit and Reset buttons from your form.

2. Open the Form Properties dialog box and make sure the form has a name. For this example, we'll use the name "myform."

3. Move to a position on the page immediately following the form.

4. Insert the images you want to use as your graphical Submit and Reset buttons.

5. Switching to the editor's HTML view, locate the image tags. Your code will look something like this:

```
</form>

<img border="0" src="images/submit.gif"
width="76" height="79">
<img border="0" src="images/reset.gif"
width="76" height="79">
```

6. Now add the following code in front of each of your <img> tags. In front of the Submit button image, add this:

```
<a language="JavaScript" onclick=myform.submit();>
```

In front of the Reset button image tag, add this:

```
<a language="JavaScript" onclick=myform.reset();>
```

7. Finally, at the end of each image tag, add the anchor end tag (</a>). Your code should now look something like this:

```
</form>

<a language="JavaScript" onclick=myform.submit()>
<img border="0" src="images/submit.gif" width="76"
height="79"></a>
```

```
<a language="JavaScript" onclick=myform.reset()>
<img border="0" src="images/reset.gif" width="76"
height="79"></a>
```

8. Save your page and preview it in a browser. (Reset works in the FrontPage preview view, but Submit does not because it requires interaction with a server.)

That's all there is to it. You now have custom images controlling your form actions from outside the form.

So how does it work? Quite simply, we're accessing two of the intrinsic form methods exposed by the browser. When you click an image, the associated function is called, triggering an action within the form. We enclose it in an anchor (<a>) tag because the standard image tag (<img>) does not have an onclick event.

NOTE

Keep in mind that this method does not work in non-Java-compatible browsers. To avoid incompatibility, you may want to check the users' browser versions and either warn users with outdated browsers that they must use a newer browser or simply redirect them to another page with standard gray buttons. See "Integrating Cross-Browser-Compatible DHTML" in Chapter 4 for an example of a script that detects a browser's make and version.

Removing the Automatic Form Element Insertion in FrontPage

If you are attempting to add form field elements to your pages and find that FrontPage always inserts the form tags around them, have no fear. This is the default setting in FrontPage and can easily be changed by following these steps:

1. Select Tools | Page Options from the menu bar. This brings up the Page Options dialog box.
2. Select the General tab and uncheck the Automatically Enclose Form Fields within a Form option.
3. Click OK.

Once you have unchecked this box, you will be able to insert form elements anywhere within your documents without having the form tag inserted with them.

The other method of accomplishing this is simply to remove the inserted <FORM></FORM> tags from the editor's HTML view. Your choice here will depend on what you do most. You can also turn the automated form insertion feature on and off as needed.

FrontPage Form Validation Scripts

When you set up validation for the forms within your Web, FrontPage will create scripts to check the form fields and also notify visitors of any problems. These scripts are written in JavaScript or VBScript, depending on the settings you have chosen in the Web Settings dialog box. Later in this chapter, we will take a close look at how these scripts are created as well as their functions. This topic is mentioned here because we are talking about using scripts with forms. For more information on this aspect of FrontPage, take a look at the "Form Validation" section, later in this chapter.

Hands On: Using a JavaScript to Change the Elements in Your Form

Many times I have developed forms that require input based on individuals' geographic locations. In these cases, I have been forced to create simple text boxes that allow free-form entry of data, such as state versus province for individuals coming from the United States or Canada. This has proven to be a drawback because I cannot control the user input, and many times the data cannot be processed the way it is meant to be.

The following example is designed to show you how you can control the elements of your form based on an entry made by your user. For example, if a user is from the United States, he or she will enter that in the form, and then a corresponding drop-down menu will display all the state names from which the user can choose. If the user selects Canada, he or she is presented with the names of the Canadian provinces. This allows you to dynamically regulate the information displayed by and obtained through your form. To see how to do this, follow these steps:

1. Create a form in FrontPage. Here's an example of the type of form we are creating in the next exercise.

2. Input the fields you want for your form. For this example, you will need to include one drop-down menu that contains the country information and another drop-down menu that contains the state or province information.

3. In the Select a Country drop-down menu, right-click and select Properties from the drop-down menu. This brings up the Drop-Down Menu Properties dialog box shown here:

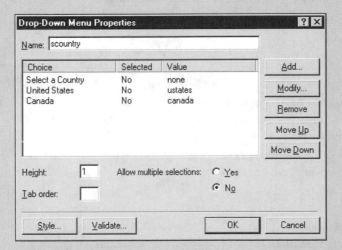

4. Give this drop-down menu the name "scountry" by typing it in the Name field.

5. Click the Add button and add the following choices by typing them in the Choice box, checking the Specify Value box, and entering the corresponding values:

Choice	Value
Select a Country	None{cell}
United States	Ustates
Canada	Canada

6. Click OK to close the dialog box.

7. Select the second dialog box (the one we will be using to display states and provinces) and right-click to select its Properties dialog box.

8. Give this drop-down menu the name "fields" by typing it in the Name field and then clicking OK.

NOTE

You will notice that we are leaving the choices and values for this drop-down menu blank because we will be filling in these choices with the JavaScript.

We now need to switch to the HTML view so we can implement the JavaScript necessary to make this function of the form work.

9. Click the HTML tab in your editor.

10. Within the <HEAD> tag, enter the following script.

NOTE

This script is available on the CD-ROM.

```
<SCRIPT LANGUAGE="JavaScript">
<!-- Begin
var noneArray = new Array("('----------','',true,true)",
"('Please select a Country')");
var ustatesArray =  new Array
("('Choose a State','',true,true)",
"('Alabama')",
"('Alaska')",
"('Arizona')",
"('Arkansas')",
"('California')",
"('Colorado')",
```

```
"('Connecticut')",
"('Delaware')",
"('Columbia')",
"('Florida')",
"('Georgia')",
"('Hawaii')",
"('Idaho')",
"('Illinois')",
"('Indiana')",
"('Iowa')",
"('Kansas')",
"('Kentucky')",
"('Louisiana')",
"('Maine')",
"('Maryland')",
"('Massachusetts')",
"('Michigan')",
"('Minnesota')",
"('Mississippi')",
"('Missouri')",
"('Montana')",
"('Nebraska')",
"('Nevada')",
"('New Hampshire')",
"('New Jersey')",
"('New Mexico')",
"('New York')",
"('North Carolina')",
"('North Dakota')",
"('Ohio')",
"('Oklahoma')",
"('Oregon')",
"('Pennsylvania')",
"('Rhode Island')",
"('South Carolina')",
"('South Dakota')",
"('Tennessee')",
"('Texas')",
"('Utah')",
"('Vermont')",
"('Virginia')",
"('Washington')",
"('West Virginia')",
"('Wisconsin')",
"('Wyoming')");
```

```
var canadaArray = new Array
("('Choose a Province','',true,true)",
"('Province 1')",
"('Province 2')");
function populateFields(inForm,selected) {
var chosenArray = eval(selected + "Array");
while (chosenArray.length < inForm.fields.options.length) {
inForm.fields.options[(inForm.fields.options.length - 1)]
 = null;
}
for (var i=0; i < chosenArray.length; i++) {
eval("inForm.fields.options[i]=
" + "new Option" + chosenArray[i]);
}
}

// End -->
</script>
```

As you can see, we have included all the states and a representation of all the Canadian provinces within this script. This way, the script can call up the associated arrays and display the information in the drop-down menu.

We now need to do some work with the drop-down menus themselves so that they can use this script.

11. Move your cursor to the first drop-down menu, where we set up our country options.

12. Add the following code to the <SELECT> tag in this drop-down menu:

```
onChange="populateFields
(document.globe,document.globe.scountry.options
[document.globe.scountry.selectedIndex].value)"
```

Your code should look like this when you are done:

```
<select name="scountry" onChange="populateFields
(document.globe,document.globe.scountry.options
[document.globe.scountry.selectedIndex].value)">
<option value='none'>Select a Country</option>
<option value='ustates'>United States</option>
<option value='canada'>Canada</option>
</select>
```

13. Finally, we need to give this form a name that the JavaScript will recognize. To do so, switch back to normal view.

14. Right-click anywhere within the form and select Form Properties from the pop-up menu. This brings up the Form Properties dialog box shown earlier in Figure 7-2.

15. In the Form Name field, enter the name **globe**.

16. Click OK and save your page.

Now when a user selects a country from the drop-down menu, the next menu will change to represent the options available for that country. When the user submits the form, the proper selection will be processed.

Setting the Tab Order in Your Form

Traditionally, when you create a form for use within a page, each time users press the TAB key, they are automatically taken to the next field in the form. This standard works for many forms, but you may find that you want to change the order in which fields are accessed using the TAB key. There could be any number of reasons you want this to happen; for our example, we are implementing the tab order to tab to those fields that are required prior to the submission of the form. This way, a visitor can simply tab to the information we require and skip the rest.

FrontPage makes creating a tab order a simple task through the use of the various form field properties dialog boxes. The Text Box Properties dialog box is shown here:

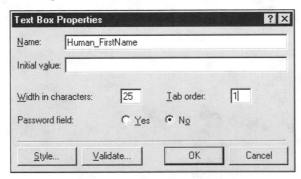

To set your tab order, follow these steps:

1. Open or create a form in your Web. For this example, we will be working with the feedback.htm file found in the Dogs by the Bay Web on the CD-ROM.

2. Create the form fields you want for your form.

3. Once you have inserted your form fields, select a text field you want to set the tab order for and then double-click it. This brings up the Text Box Properties dialog box.

4. In the Tab Order field, enter a numeric value representing the order in which you want this field to be selected when the user presses the TAB key. Then click OK.

5. Repeat steps 3 and 4 for each field you want within the tab order.

When you add this information in a properties dialog box, FrontPage inserts code into your form field's tag. This code—the tabindex attribute—instructs the browser that this field should be associated with the tab order you have specified. The tabindex attribute appears in your field tags as follows:

```
<INPUT NAME-"Human_FirstName" SIZE=25 tabindex="1">
```

CAUTION

The tab ordering will only work in Internet Explorer 4.0 and above. This ordering does not work in Netscape browsers. Users working in Netscape browsers will simply tab in the standard order (left to right, top to bottom).

Adding Labels to Form Fields

Microsoft has added an element to HTML that allows you to create labels that are associated with your form fields. You can select the form fields by clicking their corresponding labels, which makes selection a much easier process. Here are the steps to follow.

CAUTION

This functionality only works in Dynamic HTML-capable browsers such as Internet Explorer 4.0 and above.

1. Create a form field and add description text next to the field.

2. Select the form field and the description text.

3. Select Insert | Form | Label from the menu bar. You will see that the description text now appears with a dotted line around it, designating it as a label.

Now when a user clicks the description text, the associated form field will automatically be selected. This association is accomplished by placing the text within a tag that Microsoft has added to its browsers' HTML interpreters: the <label> tag. Within the label tag is a single attribute, the for="id" attribute (where "id" is the ID of the form field associated with the label). Unless you have already assigned an ID attribute to the form field, FrontPage automatically adds one when you create a label for the field. Labels are not limited to text, either. You can make an image a label or a combination of images and text.

WARNING

Once a label has been created for a form field, changing the field's ID will break its relationship with the label. To prevent this, make sure you change the label's "for" attribute value to match the new ID of the associated field.

Working with the Confirmation Page

Anytime users successfully submit a form, they are presented with a confirmation page that displays the information they have sent. When you create a form in FrontPage, the default option is for FrontPage to automatically generate a confirmation page for users to see. This page, however, leaves much to be desired in the way of appeal— it is a fairly basic page. The default confirmation page is also created on-the-fly by the FrontPage server extensions whenever a user submits a form, so you can't modify its formatting.

FrontPage also gives you the ability to create a confirmation page that functions with the layout and design you have worked so hard to achieve in your Web. This way, you do not lose that look and feel when a user submits a form. The following section takes a look at setting up a confirmation page, along with what goes into the creation of the page behind the scenes.

Setting Up a Confirmation Page

FrontPage creates a default confirmation page that displays the data users have entered when they submit a form. As mentioned earlier, this page leaves quite a bit to be desired in the viewing department. That's where your custom confirmation page comes in. Setting up a custom page is quite simple and can be accomplished by following the steps listed next.

NOTE

You can see an example of a custom confirmation page in the Dogs by the Bay Web on the CD-ROM. The page is titled submit.html.

1. Create a form in your Web. You will need to use the form fields in this form to create your custom confirmation page.

2. Create a new page in your Web to contain your confirmation information.

3. Position your cursor where you want a confirmation field to appear on the page.

4. Select Insert | Web Component from the menu bar. This brings up the Insert Web Component dialog box. Contained within this dialog box are two lists: Component Type and Choose an Effect.

5. In the Component Type list, scroll down to the next-to-last item, Advanced Controls, and select it.

6. In the Choose an Effect list, select Confirmation Field.

7. Click the Finish button to insert the confirmation field into your page and close this dialog box. This brings up the Confirmation Field Properties dialog box.

8. Type the name of the form field you want to appear on the page and then click OK. You will now see the form field appear on the page. This form field will be replaced with the text the user enters in the form.

9. Repeat these steps for each field you want confirmed in the confirmation page.

10. Save your page.

You now need to instruct the form that you want to use this page for confirmation. Here are the steps to follow:

1. Open the page containing your form.

2. Position the cursor inside the form and right-click to display the pop-up menu.

3. Select the Form Properties option on the menu. This brings up the Form Properties dialog box.

4. Click the Options button to bring up the Saving Results dialog box.

5. Click the Confirmation Page tab to bring up the Confirmation Page options.

6. Type the path for the file you have just created or click the Browse button to select the file from the file list.

7. Click OK to close the dialog boxes.

That's all there is to it. Now when a user enters data into your form and submits it, he or she will be presented with your custom confirmation page. Although you cannot use this page as a preview before saving the submitted information, you can always instruct your users that they may click the browser's Back button, make any needed corrections, and then resubmit the information. The only downside to this is that you will have duplicate information saved to your form destination and will have to manually sort through and remove incorrect information. The upside is that you will end up with more accurate information. When dealing with fully automated systems, you should consider using an Active Server Page (ASP) or other CGI script to allow users to preview and correct their information before actually submitting it; however, this topic goes beyond the scope of this book.

NOTE

Be sure to test the confirmation page in your browser before publishing it.

Confirmation Pages: Behind the Scenes

The previous section showed you how to set up your confirmation page in FrontPage. This is a fairly simple task to perform, but you may be wondering what goes into the actual creation of this setup. We will discuss two aspects of the creation of the confirmation interface in this section. The first involves what is inserted into the form to instruct it to use the confirmation page, and the second involves what is actually happening inside the confirmation page to allow it to display the information.

When you set up a confirmation page for your form, the following code is inserted into the WebBot associated with the form:

```
U-Confirmation-Url="submit.html"
```

This code instructs the WebBot to use the specified HTML file as the confirmation page.

Once the form is submitted, the WebBot brings up the specified confirmation page and takes a look at the confirmation fields you have inserted into the page. This is done via a WebBot inserted into the confirmation page. Here's an example of what the code for your WebBot might look like:

```
<!--WebBot bot="ConfirmationField"
S-Field="Human_FirstName" -->
```

The system reads the information in the WebBot and then maps the field names to the information the user has entered into the form fields. Once the mapping is complete, the confirmation fields are replaced with the form information entered by the user.

Data Collection

The primary function of a standard form is to collect data for later use. This data may be collected in several ways, and FrontPage gives you easy access to the setup functions for the collection of data.

When you set up your forms in FrontPage, you will be performing many functions through the use of the Saving Results dialog box, shown in Figure 7-4. I discussed the options on the Confirmation Page tab previously; other aspects of this dialog box are discussed in the following section, with the exception of the Saved Fields tab (shown in the figure), which I'll cover here.

This tab allows you to specify what aspects of your form you want saved when the form is processed. You may be wondering why you would not want all the fields saved, and we will discuss that here. There could be any number of reasons why you would want to collect data in a form but not have it saved to your output destination. One example would be if you are having the file sent via e-mail and want to use the user's e-mail address in the Reply-to field but have no other use for the e-mail address. If this were the case, you would specify that form field in the Reply-to field in the E-mail Results tab but remove the field from the Saved Fields tab. With this in

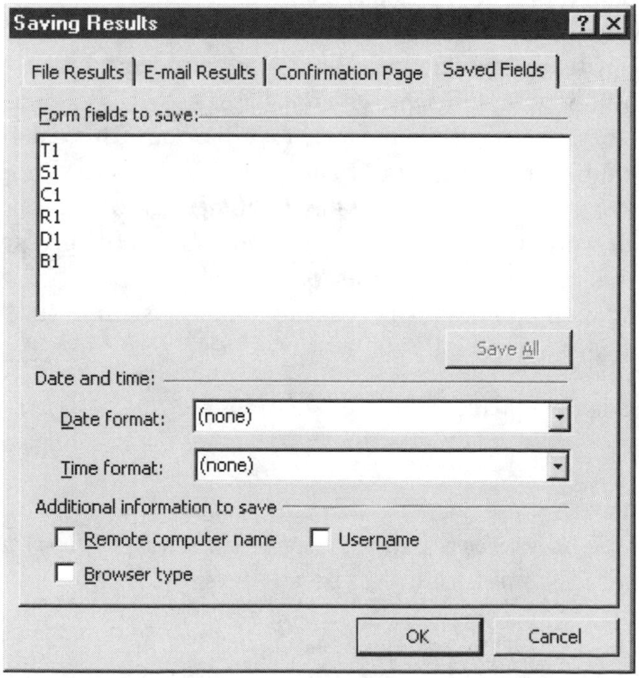

Figure 7-4   *The Saved Fields tab of the Saving Results dialog box*

mind, we will now take a look at what you can do in FrontPage when it comes to processing your forms.

Saving Forms to Files

One of the simplest and most common ways of retrieving useful data via forms is to have the information saved directly to a file on the server. Once the data is collected in the file, you can then take the data and import it into a program for the purposes of sorting, counting, and so on. One popular text file format is the CSV (comma-separated values) file. When you open a CSV file with Internet Explorer and have Microsoft Excel installed, IE automatically opens Excel and turns this comma-separated text into a spreadsheet.

This style of obtaining data comes in between having the information sent as e-mail and having it sent to a database. It allows you to collect and save the information in a file, which is more useful than an e-mail, but it stops short of connecting directly to a database. You see, when you send information via e-mail, you lose the ability to work with it. Time and time again I have heard people say, "Well, it's great to get the information, but I have to cut and paste each e-mail into another program to use it." This problem generally occurs when you are using a form to collect data for purposes such as marketing.

In contrast, you have the other extreme, which is to send the information to a database. This is actually quite a nice solution for your data storage, but to use it, you need the know-how for working with databases as well as access to a database on your server where you can send the data. (We'll discuss this database setup and integration in detail later in Chapters 11 and 12.) This is where saving to a file comes in. It can be used on any server running the FrontPage server extensions, and just about anyone can work with it. Also, saving your data to a file gives you the ability to create pages that can be updated by users.

When working with FrontPage, it is easy to tell the system to save to a file. To do so, simply follow these steps:

1. Create a form in your Web.

NOTE

This example assumes you have created your own form because the Form Wizard prompts you for the form-processing information during the setup process.

2. Once you have completed the form, position the cursor inside it and right-click.

NOTE

The form is represented by a dotted box that surrounds all your form elements.

3. Select Form Properties from the pop-up menu. This brings up the Form Properties dialog box (shown earlier in Figure 7-2).

4. Click the Send To radio button and then click the Options button to bring up the Saving Results dialog box.

5. In the File Results tab, shown in Figure 7-5, make your selection under File Format for your results file. You have the option to save the information in a text or HTML format, with further options as to how the data will be stored.

6. In the File Name field, enter a name for the file where you want your results saved.

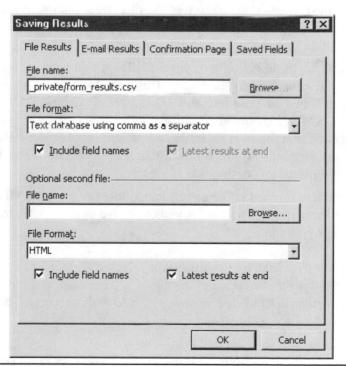

Figure 7-5   *The File Results tab of the Saving Results dialog box*

TIP

If you do not know the path and filename for the file you want, click the Browse button to select a file on your system. If the file does not already exist, it will be created when you save the page. It will also be re-created each time a user submits the form if it does not already exist. This is a nice self-repairing feature offered by FrontPage.

7. If you want the field names to be included with your results, check the Include Field Names box.

TIP

When working with CSV files, do not include the field names. Instead, manually create the destination file and enter the first record by hand, using the field names as the data. This first record will then become the column headers when the file is opened in Excel.

8. FrontPage lets you choose where the latest results are posted on the page. To post the latest results at the bottom of the file, check the Latest Results at End check box; if you want your latest results to appear at the top of the page, be sure that this check box is unchecked.

9. Within this tab of the dialog box, you will also see an option for listing a secondary file for saving your results. This is useful if you want a second copy of the results in a different format. For example, if you are posting the results directly to a Web page but also want a copy to drop into a spreadsheet, you can make the first file an HTML file and the second file a database file with comma-separated text. If this is the case, repeat steps 5 through 7 for these fields and give the text destination file a .csv extension.

10. Once you have finished making your selections, you can click OK to close the Form Properties dialog box, or you can move to another tab to continue configuring your form.

FrontPage will now send your results to the selected file(s) when a user submits the form. It accomplishes this through the use of a WebBot, which requires the FrontPage extensions to be loaded on your server to work properly. The text of a sample WebBot function is shown here:

```
<FORM METHOD="POST" action="--WEBBOT-SELF--">
<!--WebBot bot="SaveResults" startspan U-File="formrslt.txt"
 S-Format="TEXT/TSV" B-Label-Fields="TRUE" -->
<input TYPE="hidden" NAME="VTI-GROUP" VALUE="0">
<!—WebBot bot="SaveResults" endspan -->
```

Sending Form Results via an E-mail Message

As I mentioned earlier in this chapter when discussing data collection through the use of a file, sending form results via an e-mail message is the least useful way of collecting data when you are planning on using that data to track information. There are exceptions to this rule, however. At times, an e-mail message is the perfect function to associate with a form.

An e-mail message is useful, for example, when you are simply attempting to collect real-time feedback on your site. Through the use of an e-mail form, you can be notified right away of problems with the site or changes that your users want to see. Another useful application of e-mail settings is having e-mail sent to you in conjunction with the form being sent to a file. This allows you to keep up-to-date on the information being submitted via your forms.

Setting Up the E-mail Options

When creating a form, you can specify the way that form is processed, as discussed extensively throughout this chapter. One function you can specify is that the form be sent to an e-mail address when processed by the browser. This is a rather simple setting that is taken care of through the use of the Saving Results dialog box. The following steps take you through the process of setting up your form to be sent via e-mail:

1. Create a form in FrontPage.

2. Position your cursor within the form boundaries and select Insert | Form | Form Properties from the menu bar. This brings up the Form Properties dialog box. As you can see, this dialog box has a field for entering an e-mail address. You can simply enter an e-mail address and click OK in this dialog box if you have your settings already in place, but for this example we want to take it one step further.

3. Click the Options button in the dialog box, and you will be presented with the Saving Results dialog box.

4. Click the E-mail Results tab to bring up your e-mail options, as shown in Figure 7-6.

5. Enter an e-mail address where you want the form results sent.

6. From the E-mail Format drop-down menu, select the style in which you want your results presented.

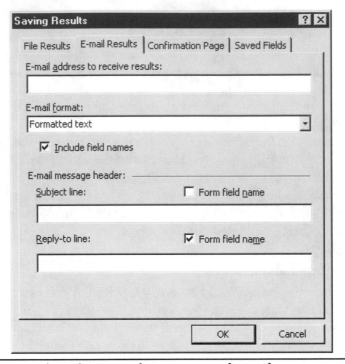

Figure 7-6 *The E-mail Results options for saving your form information*

7. If you want the field names to be presented in the e-mail, along with the responses, check Include Field Names.

TIP

It is almost always best to include the field names when dealing with an e-mail form handler because they quickly give you information related to the question asked of your user and make deciphering the information in the e-mail much easier.

You now want to configure the headers that will appear within the e-mail message. When you configure your Subject and Reply-to lines, you have the option of including text for each or specifying that fields within the form be used.

For example, you may have a form on your site for submitting information. Within this form, you may ask users to specify the type of information they are submitting. If you look at our submission form in the Dogs by the Bay Web (submit.html on the CD-ROM), you will see that we ask users to choose what they are submitting (article, picture, or story). We then have the form configured to place that field name in the subject line so that we know what is being submitted.

8. Enter a subject for your message or check the Form Field Name box to have the subject automatically inserted from a field name.

9. Enter a reply-to address or check the Form Field Name box to have a reply-to address inserted automatically from a field name. This is similar to the subject information discussed previously. Once again, if you look at the submit.html page, you will see that the user's e-mail address is used for the Reply-to field.

10. Click OK to close the dialog box and save your settings.

You will now have your messages e-mailed to you when users submit the form.

CAUTION

You must have your server set up to process and send e-mail messages before this functionality will work. Setting up your server is discussed as the next topic in this chapter.

Configuring Your Server to Send E-mail Messages

If you are planning to have your forms sent to you via e-mail, you must first set up your server to handle the sending of forms. If you do not set up your server, your forms will not be sent via e-mail, and you will be presented with error messages in FrontPage when you attempt to set up an e-mail address for your form processing.

   If you are using an ISP to host your site, you will need to contact your ISP to make sure its server is set up to handle FrontPage e-mail processing. However, it is preferable that you also set up your local server, if you have one, so that you can test your forms before posting them on the Web. Here are the steps to follow.

TIP

Before setting up your server, be sure you know the name of your SMTP (Simple Mail Transfer Protocol) server, because you will need to enter it in the setup process. If you do not know the name of your SMTP server, ask your system administrator or your ISP.

1. From the Start menu, select Programs | Administrative Tools | Server Extensions Administrator. This will launch the Microsoft Management Console, which allows you to make changes to your server settings. The Management Console is shown in Figure 7-7.

NOTE

For this setup, it is assumed that you have installed the FrontPage 2002 server extensions on your server.

2. Expand the list in the tree to display your Web server (your computer's name by default). Right-click the server name to display the pop-up menu.

3. Select Properties from the menu to bring up the Properties dialog box, shown here:

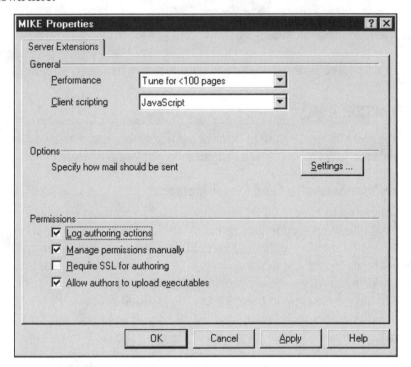

4. Click the Settings button under the Options section of the dialog box. This brings up the E-mail Settings dialog box, shown here:

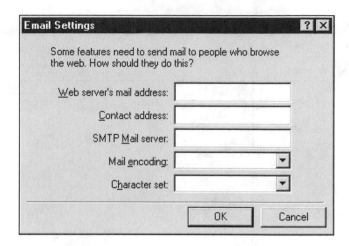

5. Enter your address information, making sure you include the SMTP server address.

6. Select the encoding and character set to be used when sending mail via your system.

NOTE

The encoding you will use depends on your system. If the encoding is not set properly, your mail will be corrupted. Normally, you should leave it set to the Use Default Encoding setting.

7. Click OK to close the dialog boxes and exit the Microsoft Management Console.

Your server is now set up to send mail from your FrontPage forms.

TIP

Even though your server is set up to send e-mail, you still need to be connected to your SMTP server for it to work properly. If you have a dedicated connection, this will not be a problem, but if you do not have a dedicated connection, you need to make sure you are connected to the Internet, or your network, for this functionality to work properly.

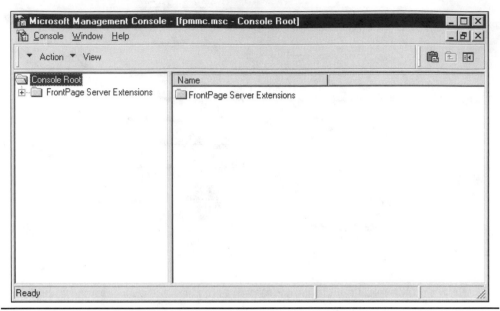

Figure 7-7   *Microsoft Management Console*

Form Validation

Form validation is the process of specifying certain requirements prior to the acceptance of a form. This functionality is useful because it lets you have some control over the information submitted via your forms. You can specify that only certain types of data are entered into text fields, that specific fields are required for processing, and many other functions. The following topics take a look at the form-validation functionality available to you through FrontPage.

Form validation is handled by client-side scripts. Depending on your settings in the Web Settings dialog box, you will use either JavaScript or VBScript for your validation. Because only Microsoft browsers support VBScript by default, you should normally use JavaScript on all public Internet sites.

CAUTION

Form validation will only work in script-capable browsers. This should not be much of a problem, however, because most Internet users now have script-capable browsers. This is necessary to mention, though, because there are still people out there using non-script-capable browsers such as WebTV and older browsers, and others who have scripting deactivated on their browsers. That being the case, non-script-enabled browsers will submit forms "as is," without processing any validation rules.

Validating Forms in FrontPage

FrontPage offers many validation options to use with your forms. When working in FrontPage, you configure validation settings by following these steps:

1. Create the form fields for your form.
2. Double-click the form field for which you want to set up validation. This will bring up the corresponding properties dialog box for the form field you have selected.
3. Click Validate to bring up the corresponding validation dialog box (these dialog boxes are described in the following sections).

TIP

You will notice that many of the validation dialog boxes ask for a display name. This name is associated with the form field and will display if an error occurs in the processing of that field. This is useful for telling users which field contains the error, without forcing you to use the often less user-friendly field names.

Text Box Validation

The most complex of the validation offerings is for text boxes. This type of validation may be for one-line text boxes or for scrolling text boxes, and it gives you quite a bit of control over what is entered by the user. When configuring text box validation, you work in the Text Box Validation dialog box, shown in Figure 7-8.

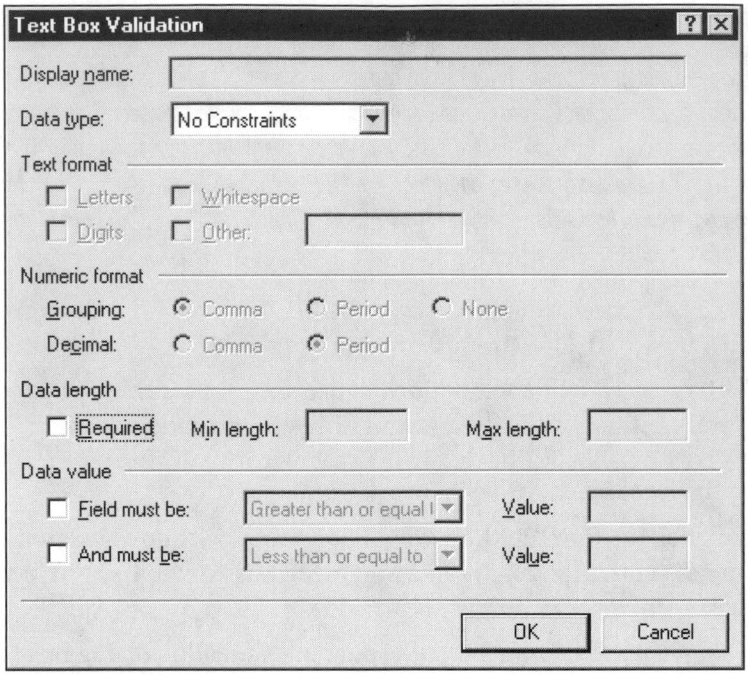

Text Box Validation [?] [X]

Display name: [_____]

Data type: [No Constraints ▼]

Text format
  ☐ Letters   ☐ Whitespace
  ☐ Digits   ☐ Other: [_____]

Numeric format
  Grouping: ⦿ Comma   ○ Period   ○ None
  Decimal: ○ Comma   ⦿ Period

Data length
  ☐ Required   Min length: [_____]   Max length: [_____]

Data value
  ☐ Field must be: [Greater than or equal ▼] Value: [_____]
  ☐ And must be: [Less than or equal to ▼] Value: [_____]

  [OK]   [Cancel]

Figure 7-8   *The Text Box Validation dialog box lets you control what is entered by the user.*

When working with a text box, you first need to specify a data type, which can be text, an integer (no decimal point), or a number (decimal point allowed). Once you have specified that option, the corresponding validation options will become active within the dialog box based on your selection. The following subsections outline each of these options and their corresponding choices within the dialog box.

NOTE

Once you have specified the option, be sure to enter a value to associate with it; otherwise, your selected option will be ignored.

Text   Selecting the Text option specifies that you want users to input some form of text into the text box. When this option is selected, the following actions can be specified as requirements:

Text format	Select the type of text you want input into the box. You can specify that the user must enter letters, whitespace, digits, or "other." When "other" is specified, you must enter the text that is required.
Data length	Specify a minimum and/or maximum length for the data entered into the field.
Data value	Select Greater Than/Less Than or Equal To/Not Equal To values for your field.

Integer   Selecting the Integer option instructs the validation to require some type of integer within the field. Once this option is selected, you can specify the following parameters:

Numeric format– Grouping	Specify the grouping format in which the data must be entered. For example, if you select comma, a user who wished to specify one thousand would need to enter the integer as 1,000 (being sure to include the comma). If the data is not entered in this format, it will be rejected.
Data length	Specify a minimum and/or maximum length for the data entered into the field.
Data value	Select Greater Than/Less Than or Equal To/Not Equal To values for your field.

Number   Selecting the Number option specifies that the user must enter a number into the field. Once this option is selected, you can set the following parameters:

Numeric format– Grouping	Specify the grouping format in which the data must be entered. For example, if you select comma, a user who wished to specify one thousand would need to enter the integer as 1,000 (being sure to include the comma). If the data is not entered in this format, it will be rejected.
Numeric format– Decimal	Specify the decimal settings for the number. An example is shown in Figure 7-8.
Data length	Specify a minimum and/or maximum length for the data entered into the field.
Data value	Select Greater Than/Less Than or Equal To/Not Equal To values for your field.

Drop-Down Box Validation

When you include a drop-down box in your form, you can incorporate basic validation through the use of the Drop-Down Box Validation dialog box, shown here:

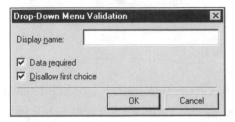

When this dialog box is opened, you can specify two options. The first option indicates that some sort of data must be selected within the drop-down menu, and the other option disallows the first choice in the menu. The reason for disallowing the first choice is to allow you to incorporate some meaningful text as the first selection in the box to tell users what they are looking at. For example, you may be asking users to select from a list of product names. In this case, you could specify "Select Product" as the first selection in the drop-down menu and then specify the product names as the remaining options in the menu. Obviously, you would not want users to select "Select Product" as their entry, so you would want to disallow this as a valid selection.

Option Button Validation

Option buttons allow users to specify one or more choices within a group in your form. When you set up validation for this form element, you are presented with the Option Button Validation dialog box, shown here:

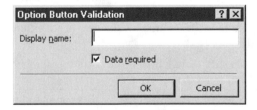

This dialog box covers validation for all the option buttons found within a specific group. Once an option is selected, you can specify that one or more choices must be made by checking the Data Required box in the dialog box. If this box is checked, be sure to enter a display name to associate with this group.

Validating Forms: Behind the Scenes

As you have seen, FrontPage makes form validation a simple-to-implement process that will make your life much easier in the long run. The question still remaining, however, is what exactly FrontPage is doing when a user enters information into your form and then submits the form. The answer to this is simple: FrontPage incorporates various scripts to perform the validation on your forms, and these scripts are based on the settings you have specified in the Web Settings dialog box—they can be either JavaScript or VBScript.

TIP

I suggest you use JavaScript for your development projects unless you are sure all your users will be working with the Internet Explorer browser. Internet Explorer is the only browser that supports VBScript without the use of special plug-ins.

If you take a look at the sample feedback form for Dogs by the Bay, you will see that we have incorporated validation on many of the fields. The following is an example of one of the WebBots set up for this validation.

```
<!--WebBot bot="Validation" startspan S-Data-Type="Number"
S-Number-Separators="," B-Value-Required="TRUE"
I-Minimum-Length="1" I-Maximum-Length="3" -->
<!--WebBot bot="Validation" endspan -->
```

This validation WebBot was set up for our Human's Age field, and it requires that a numeric entry be made that has a minimum length of one character and a maximum length of three characters. This is what you will see if you take a look at the page in your HTML view. However, when the page is saved and then viewed in a browser, the following script will appear in place of the WebBot:

```
<script Language="JavaScript"><!--
function FrontPage_Form1_Validator(theForm)
{
if (theForm.Human_Age.value == "")
{
  alert("Please enter a value for the \"Human_Age\" field.");
  theForm.Human_Age.focus();
  return (false);
}
```

```
if (theForm.Human_Age.value.length < 1)
{
  alert("Please enter at least 1
  characters in the \"Human_Age\" field.");
  theForm.Human_Age.focus();
  return (false);
}
if (theForm.Human_Age.value.length > 3)
{
  alert("Please enter at most 3 characters
  in the \"Human_Age\" field.");
  theForm.Human_Age.focus();
  return (false);
}
var checkOK = "0123456789-.,";
var checkStr = theForm.Human_Age.value;
var allValid = true;
var decPoints = 0;
var allNum = "";
for (i = 0;  i < checkStr.length;  i++)
{
  ch = checkStr.charAt(i);
  for (j = 0;  j < checkOK.length;  j++)
    if (ch == checkOK.charAt(j))
      break;
  if (j == checkOK.length)
  {
    allValid = false;
    break;
  }
  if (ch == ".")
  {
    allNum += ".";
    decPoints++;
  }
  else if (ch != ",")
    allNum += ch;
}
if (!allValid)
{
  alert("Please enter only digit characters
  in the \"Human_Age\" field.");
  theForm.Human_Age.focus();
```

```
    return (false);
  }
  if (decPoints > 1)
  {
    alert("Please enter a valid number
    in the \"Human_Age\" field.");
    theForm.Human_Age.focus();
    return (false);
  }
  return (true);
}
//--></script>
```

As you can see, this is a rather long script that would take a fair amount of programming to implement. This JavaScript checks for the various aspects of the validation we have required of the field. If it finds those requirements to be met, it allows the form to be processed. If it finds that those requirements have not been met, it opens a dialog box that informs users of the problem, and it takes them to the field with errors once they click OK in the dialog box.

Summary

This chapter covers the many features of form creation available to you when working with FrontPage. After viewing the examples in this chapter, you should have a good grasp of how to create and customize a form in FrontPage. We have touched on many aspects of basic form creation in this chapter, and this should get you started in advanced creation. Along with the basics, we have also taken a look at extending your forms to add functionality beyond that of the standard form. We have discussed how FrontPage processes and validates forms, and you have learned some advanced techniques involving the integration of scripting into your forms.

As mentioned throughout the chapter, FrontPage 2002's new database integration features were intentionally not covered here but will be discussed in detail later in Chapters 11 and 12. At that point, you will gather a great deal more information about this technology, and it will give you a better grasp of the topics we have described in this chapter.

Creating Dynamically Driven Web Sites

Integrating Office Elements into Your Webs

IN THIS CHAPTER:

How Office Works with the Web

Work with Web-Enabled Office Features

Integrate Spreadsheet Components
into Your Web

With the release of Office XP, Microsoft continues its integration of Office and the Web. Many of the features found in Office XP were available in Office 2000, but they have added to the Office 2000 list with new features and enhanced previous features. This version takes the integration one step further by making many of the previous features more "user friendly," especially when it comes to the Spreadsheet Web Component.

This chapter takes a look at the integration of Office and the Web. We will look at the options available to you within the Office suite, along with some applications that mimic Office functionality within FrontPage. Although this chapter by no means covers every aspect of Office's integration with the Web, it will give you a good understanding of the changes that have taken place within this release of the product.

Developing with Word

Although the HTML editing capabilities of Word have significantly improved with the release of Office XP, you will very likely still want to use FrontPage as your primary HTML editor. As an Internet developer, you will find Word's improved features primarily of use when working with existing Word documents that need to be ported to HTML.

In previous releases of FrontPage, you had the ability to open Word documents within the editor view of FrontPage. Starting with FrontPage 2000, a Word document opened from FrontPage causes the Word application to launch and display the document. Once the document is open in Word, you can perform various tasks to turn it into an HTML-formatted document. This part of the chapter outlines and describes the tasks associated with this process.

Saving Word Files to HTML

When you open a document in Microsoft Word, it is displayed in a specific format designed so that Word can view the document and its formatting. This format is obviously not compatible with the Web. However, since the release of Office 2000, HTML has become a native file format. With the exceptions of document versioning and password protection, all of Word's advanced formatting can be saved within HTML documents using XML (Extensible Markup Language) and styles. Previously, this level of compatibility was only available with Word's binary DOC format.

As you export your documents, Word converts any images and formatting so that it will display properly within your browser window. This is done through the Save As Web Page option found on the File menu.

To save your Word document in HTML, follow these steps:

1. Open a document in Word.

2. Select File | Save As Web Page from the menu bar. This brings up the Save As dialog box shown in Figure 8-1.

3. Select the directory where you want to save your document.

TIP

If you are planning on incorporating this document into one of your Webs, click the Web Folders button (My Network Places in Windows 2000), move to the desired Web and directory, and save it there. Once you move back into FrontPage, recalculate your hyperlinks, if necessary, and the document will appear.

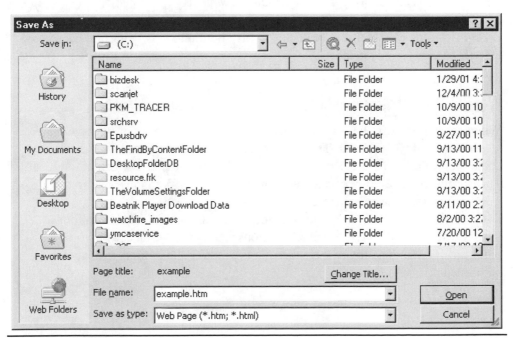

Figure 8-1   *Word's Save As dialog box*

4. Click the Change Title button to bring up the Set Page Title dialog box, shown here:

5. Type the title you want for your page and click OK.

6. Enter a filename in the File Name field of the Save As dialog box.

NOTE

Check to ensure that the Save As Type drop-down menu displays the Web Page (*.htm; *.html) option. If it does not, select that option from the menu.

At this point, you can simply click the Save button to save your newly created HTML file on your system.

Word's Web Options

When saving a file in the HTML format, Word gives you a set of options that affect how that file is saved. This is a great little feature of Word that gives you some control over the process of converting files from the DOC format to HTML. The options themselves are accessed from the Save As Web Page dialog box's Tools | Web Options menu (refer to Figure 8-1).

Once you open the Web Options dialog box, you are presented with four tabs. These tabs allow you to specify various settings associated with your output to HTML. The following subsections describe the options available to you in each tab.

Setting Word's Options in the Browsers Tab

The Browsers tab of the Web Options dialog box, shown here, allows you to set up the features that will be available to you when viewing the document in HTML:

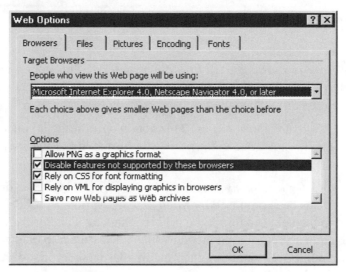

Depending on the options you select here, some features of your page might not be enabled when converted to an HTML page. Within this tab, you have the option of setting several parameters, which are explained in the following list:

▶ *People who view this Web page will be using*   This option allows you to specify which browsers you want your document, when converted, to be compatible with. If you know your targeted audience, the choice here is simple; however, if you are creating for the Web, you will want to choose a browser option that you believe will be compatible with the majority of viewers coming to see this page. The reason for this is that many features that will be used are not supported by older browsers and will cause your pages to display incorrectly.

▶ *Allow PNG as a graphics format*   PNG (Portable Network Graphics) is another format that is being recommended for inclusion in the next HTML specification. This format, if accepted, will replace the JPG format due to its higher-quality, lossless compression. Check this setting if you want to allow for the PNG format when saving your images.

NOTE

The PNG file format is not directly supported by older browsers.

▶ *Disable features not supported by these browsers*   This option will disable all features in the document that are not supported by the browsers you have selected in the drop-down menu.

▶ *Rely on CSS for font formatting*   This option specifies that you want to use cascading style sheets (CSS) to specify the formatting of fonts within your document.

▶ *Rely on VML for displaying graphics in browsers*   VML (Vector Markup Language) has been proposed by Microsoft and various other companies to be included in the next version of the HTML standard. This format allows images to be saved in a vector-based layout, which allows them to be manipulated by other programs while retaining their quality. Use this setting to save your images with the VML format.

CAUTION

This format is still in the preliminary stages and is not supported by most browsers. At the time of this writing, it is only supported by IE 5.0 and above.

▶ *Save new Web pages as Web archives*   This option packages your entire page in a single file, including all your image work. This option is useful when you are sending your page to other people.

NOTE

If you have features that are not supported in any of the latest browsers, Word will prompt you with a warning message. You will then have the option to cancel the save operation and change your document or to continue with saving your document.

Setting Word's Options in the Files Tab

The options on the Files tab, shown here, allow you to specify how your files are saved when your Word document is converted to HTML:

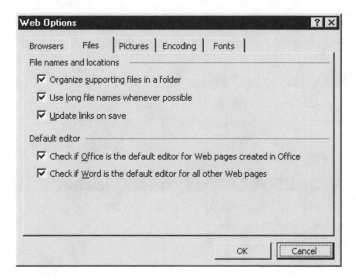

This mainly deals with your supporting files, such as associated images or any frame-embedded pages in your document layout. Along with the way in which your supporting files are saved, you have the option of checking your system to find out what the default editing settings are. When working in this tab, you have the following options:

▶ *Organize supporting files in a folder*   This option specifies that any files created in conjunction with your document (for example, associated images) be placed in a folder on the system. This folder will be created in the directory where you save your file with the name "*xxxx*_files" (where *xxxx* is your filename), provided you select the following option.

▶ *Use long file names whenever possible*   This option instructs Word to use long filenames that describe the contents of the actual supporting files.

▶ *Update links on save*   This option specifies that any links within the document should be updated when you save the file.

▶ *Check if Office is the default editor for Web pages created in Office*   This option instructs Word to automatically check whether Office is the default editor for Web pages created in Office. When this option is selected and Office is not the default, a message appears asking if you would like to make it the default.

▶ *Check if Word is the default editor for all other Web pages*   This option instructs the system to automatically check whether Word is the default editor for pages created outside of Office. When this option is selected and Word is not the default, a message appears asking if you would like to make it the default.

Setting Word's Options in the Pictures Tab

When your document contains pictures, you will want to optimize your settings for the browser environment in which your pictures will be viewed. The following settings on the Pictures tab, shown here, allow you to specify how your images will be saved for viewing in a browser:

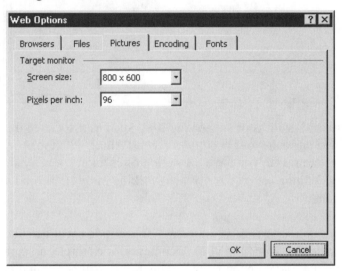

► *Screen size* Use this setting to specify the screen size you are targeting when saving your images. This will determine the sizing set forth when your images are saved.

TIP

Although many individuals work with monitors that have a setting above 800×600, I recommend that you specify the 800×600 setting because it ensures that all viewers will be able to see your images without needing to scroll left to right.

▶ *Pixels per inch*   Use this setting to specify the resolution associated with the images when they are saved.

NOTE

The actual resolution for PCs is 96 ppi, and for Macintoshes it's 72 ppi. As such, Office XP's default resolution is 96 ppi. Because the resolution of images is only important when you're specifying an altered display size, 72 ppi is generally accepted as the standard for image resolution as viewed on a monitor.

Setting Word's Options in the Encoding Tab

The options on the Encoding tab, shown here, determine what international text encoding will be used when you save your documents to HTML:

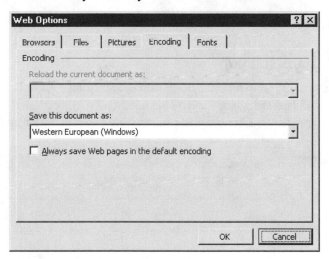

Setting Word's Options in the Fonts Tab

The options on the Fonts tab, shown here, determine what the default fonts associated with this file should be; from here, you can select both the proportional font and fixed-width font that will be the defaults for your document, as shown next.

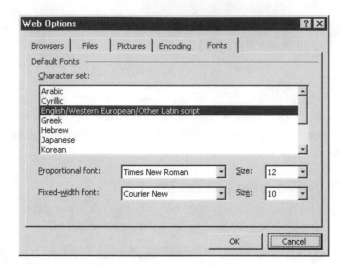

Word's Web Tools Toolbar

The Web Tools toolbar, shown here, allows you to incorporate various features into your documents that will be used when they are viewed in a browser (these features include the incorporation of many of the same items available when using FrontPage):

Button	Name	Description
	Design Mode	Switches you to form design mode, allowing you to create and edit a form using the tools in the Control toolbox. Once this mode is activated, clicking the button again deactivates it.
	Properties	Brings up a properties box that allows you to view and modify the properties for the selected item. This option is only available in design mode.
	Microsoft Script Editor	Launches the Microsoft Script Editor.

Table 8-1   *Tools Available on Word's Web Tools Toolbar*

Button	Name	Description
	Check Box	Inserts an HTML check box into your document.
	Option Button	Inserts an HTML option button into your document.
	Drop-down Box	Inserts an HTML drop-down box into your document.
	List Box	Inserts an HTML list box into your document.
	Text Box	Inserts an HTML single-line text box into your document.
	Text Area	Inserts an HTML text area (multiline scrolling text box) into your document.
	Submit	Inserts an HTML Submit button into your document.
	Submit with Image	Brings up the Insert Picture dialog box, allowing you to select an image to use as an HTML Submit button.
	Reset	Inserts an HTML Reset button into your document.
	Hidden	Inserts an HTML hidden form field into your document.
	Password	Inserts an HTML password field into your document.
	Movie	Brings up the Insert Movie Clip dialog box, allowing you to incorporate and configure a movie for your document.

Table 8-1   *Tools Available on Word's Web Tools Toolbar* (continued)

Button	Name	Description
	Sound	Brings up the Background Sound dialog box, allowing you to incorporate and configure a background sound for your document.
	Scrolling Text	Brings up the Scrolling Text dialog box, allowing you to incorporate and configure a marquee for your document.

Table 8-1   *Tools Available on Word's Web Tools Toolbar* (continued)

Table 8-1 describes the options available to you from the Web Tools toolbar.

As previously mentioned, Word's strength as an HTML editor particularly comes into play when you're exporting existing binary Word documents to documents in HTML format. An important topic we haven't talked much about thus far is Word's ability to open and accurately depict HTML documents created in other editors. You may edit documents with little fear of Word breaking HTML that it doesn't understand, and you may even choose to save your HTML documents in Word's binary DOC file format. You've likely run into this situation when developing content that you want to be viewable within a Web site and also downloadable as a Word document. Now having two versions of your document is as easy as using Word's Open and Save As features.

NOTE

These features are not suitable for dynamically generated HTML documents, such as Active Server Pages.

Integration of PowerPoint Presentations

PowerPoint has become the de facto tool used by marketing departments in just about every major company today. The product allows for the easy creation of animated presentations for a wide variety of purposes.

The release of PowerPoint 2000 greatly increased your ability to deliver PowerPoint presentations over the Web, but PowerPoint 2000 had some notable drawbacks that have now been rectified with the release of PowerPoint 2002. For example, with PowerPoint 2002, you now have the ability to carry over your animations and sounds from your presentation to the Web. This adds a whole new level of interactivity that was missing in the previous version.

Saving PowerPoint Presentations to HTML

PowerPoint gives you the ability to save your presentations to HTML while retaining their quality and formatting. This is accomplished by exporting your presentations into an HTML format. When you export a presentation, PowerPoint keeps all your settings intact based on the options you specify in the Web Options dialog box. Just as in Word, this is accomplished through the use of XML, styles, and, in this case, JavaScript. Creating an online presentation is accomplished by following these steps:

1. Create or open your presentation.

2. Select File | Save As Web Page from the menu bar. This brings up the Save As dialog box, which is almost identical to the one shown previously in Figure 8-1.

3. Select the directory where you want to save your presentation.

TIP

If you are planning on incorporating this presentation into one of your Webs, click the Web Folders button (My Network Places in Windows 2000), move to the desired Web and directory, and save it there. Once you move back into FrontPage, recalculate your hyperlinks, if necessary, and the presentation will appear.

4. Click the Change Title button to bring up the Set Page Title dialog box. (This is the same dialog box you saw earlier when working with Word.)

5. Type the title you want for your page and click OK.

6. Enter a filename in the File Name field.

NOTE

Check to ensure that the Save As Type drop-down menu displays the Web Page (.htm; *.html) option. If it does not, select this option from the menu.*

At this point, you can simply click the Save button to save your newly created HTML file on your system or click the Publish button for additional options that will not affect the copy of the file open in PowerPoint. (See "Publishing a PowerPoint Presentation as a Web," later in this chapter, for more information on the Publish option.)

PowerPoint's Web Options

When saving your files as HTML, PowerPoint gives you a set of options that affect how these files are saved. These options are similar to the Word Web options, and they give you some control over the process of converting your files from the binary PPT format to HTML. The options themselves are accessed from the Tools | Web Options menu of the Save As dialog box (refer back to Figure 8-1).

Once you open the Web Options dialog box, you are presented with four tabs. These tabs allow you to specify various settings associated with your output to HTML. The following subsections describe the options available to you in each tab.

Setting PowerPoint's Options in the General Tab

The General tab of the Web Options dialog box, shown here, allows you to specify how viewers will see your presentation in their browsers:

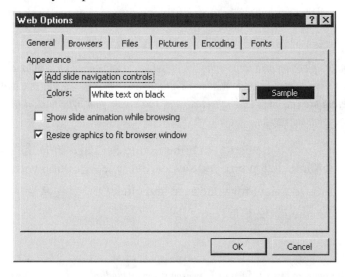

This tab comes with the following set of configurable options for you to set when saving your file to HTML:

▶ *Add slide navigation controls* This option specifies that you want PowerPoint to add a navigation frame and contents frame to the presentation's frameset. These controls allow users to move throughout the presentation by selecting a particular slide or by clicking Previous/Next buttons. The controls also add buttons that allow viewers to expand the contents page to include the related slide's text in the form of notes, and they add a Full Screen Slide Show button. You may set the color scheme for the contents frame page using the Colors drop-down menu.

TIP

When you select a color for your navigation controls, a sample of that color scheme appears in the sample box.

▶ *Show slide animation while browsing*   This option specifies that you want the animation settings you created for your presentation to be retained in the Web version. Keep in mind that the HTML representation of these effects is implemented using DHTML and might not be visible in older browsers. Because DHTML degrades gracefully, this is a browser-safe feature that will simply not show up in nonsupporting browsers.

▶ *Resize graphics to fit browser window*   This option specifies that you want the graphics in your presentation to resize based on the size of the browser window viewing the presentation.

Setting PowerPoint's Options in the Browsers Tab

The Browsers tab, shown here, is a new addition to the options you have available when saving your PowerPoint presentations for the Web:

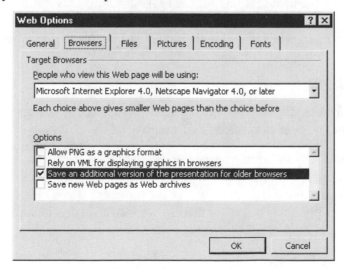

This tab allows you to target specific browsers for your pages so that the features you include will work for the majority of your audience. Here are the options found on this tab:

► *People who view this Web page will be using*   This option allows you to specify which browser you want your presentation, when converted, to be compatible with. If you know your targeted audience, the choice here is simple; however, if you are creating for the Web, you will want to choose a browser that you believe will be compatible with the majority of viewers coming to see this page. The reason for this is that many features that will be used are not supported by older browsers and will cause your pages to display incorrectly.

► *Allow PNG as a graphics format*   PNG (Portable Network Graphics) is another format that is being recommended for inclusion in the next HTML specification. This format, if accepted, will replace the JPG format due to its higher-quality, lossless compression. Check this setting if you want to allow for the PNG format when saving your images.

NOTE

The PNG file format is not directly supported by older browsers.

► *Rely on VML for displaying graphics in browsers*   VML (Vector Markup Language) has been proposed by Microsoft and various other companies to be included in the next version of the HTML standard. This format allows images to be saved in a vector-based layout, which allows them to be manipulated by other programs while retaining their quality. Use this setting to save your images with the VML format.

CAUTION

This format is still in the preliminary stages and is not supported by most browsers. At the time of this writing, it is only supported by IE 5.0 and above.

► *Save an additional version of the presentation for older browsers*   This option informs PowerPoint that you want to save two versions of your presentation: One that has all the latest features for the browser set you have selected, and another stripped-down version that allows viewers with older browsers to view your presentation.

▶ *Save new Web pages as Web archives*   This option packages your entire page in a single file, including all your image work. This option is useful when you are sending your page to other people.

Setting PowerPoint's Options in the Files Tab

The options on the Files tab, shown here, allow you to specify how your files are saved when your presentation is converted to HTML:

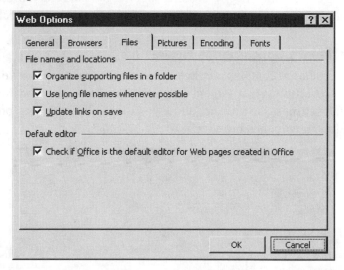

This mainly deals with your supporting files, such as associated images or any frame-embedded pages in your presentation layout. Along with the way in which your supporting files are saved, you have the option of checking your system to find out what the default editing settings are. When working in this tab, you have the following options to work with:

▶ *Organize supporting files in a folder*   This option specifies that any files created in conjunction with your presentation (for example, video clips) be placed in a folder on the system. Because multislide PowerPoint presentations will generate separate pages for each slide, along with image files and other associated files, you should always utilize this feature unless your presentation will be the only thing in the Web.

▶ *Use long file names whenever possible*   This option instructs PowerPoint to use long filenames that describe the contents of the actual supporting file.

Because spaces are not supported in HTTP addresses, underscores are used to separate words in long HTML filenames.

▶ *Update links on save*   This option specifies that any links within the presentations should be updated when you save the file.

▶ *Check if Office is the default editor for Web pages created in Office*   This option instructs PowerPoint to automatically check whether Office is the default editor for Web pages created in Office. When this option is selected and Office is not the default, a message appears asking if you would like to make it the default.

Setting PowerPoint's Options in the Pictures Tab

When your presentation contains pictures, you will want to optimize your settings for the monitor resolution environment in which your presentation will be viewed. The Pictures tab settings, shown here, allow you to specify how your presentation will be saved for viewing in a browser:

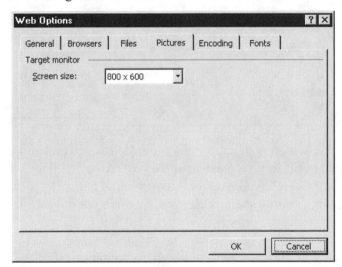

Use the Screen size setting to specify the screen size you are targeting when saving your images. This will determine the sizing set forth when your images are saved.

TIP

Although many individuals work with monitors that have a setting above 800×600, I recommend that you specify the 800×600 setting, because it will ensure that all viewers will be able to see your images without needing to scroll left to right.

Setting PowerPoint's Options in the Encoding Tab

The options on the Encoding tab, shown here, determine what international text encoding will be used when you save your presentation to HTML:

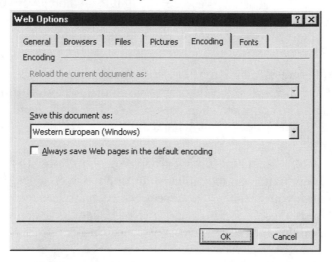

Setting PowerPoint's Options in the Fonts tab

The options on the Fonts tab, shown here, determine the default fonts associated with this file; from here, you can select both the proportional font and fixed-width font to be the defaults for your presentation.

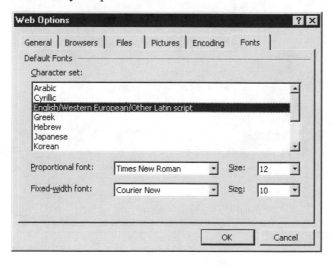

Publishing a PowerPoint Presentation as a Web

In addition to saving your presentation to a folder as HTML, PowerPoint gives you the opportunity to publish it as a Web. Using this method gives you additional options on how your presentation will be saved and makes a complete copy of your presentation without changing the source code of the version currently displayed in PowerPoint.

As shown in Figure 8-2, the Publish as Web Page dialog box gives you much greater control over how your presentation is saved than when you simply save it as HTML. This dialog box appears when you click Publish in the Save As dialog box. The options are explained in the following list:

▶ *Publish what?* Within this option group, you may choose to publish your complete presentation, an individual slide, or a range of slides. To allow viewers to see your speaker notes, check the Display Speaker Notes option. Within this area, you may also access the Web Options dialog box by clicking the corresponding button.

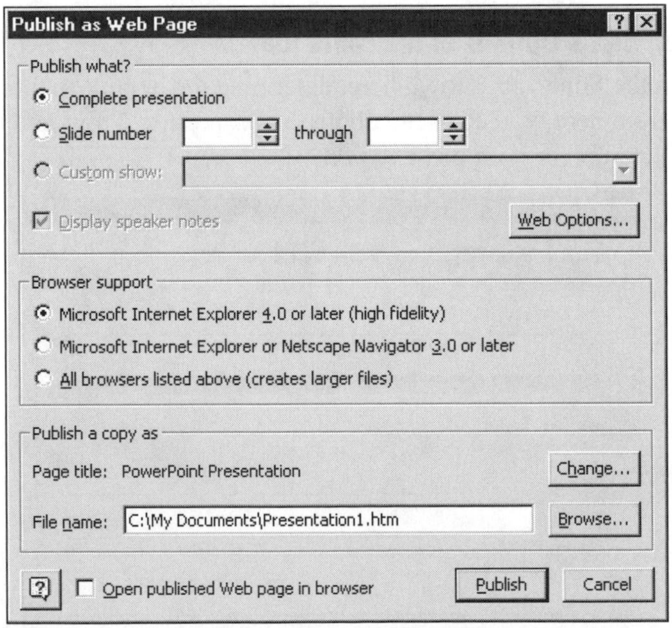

Figure 8-2 *PowerPoint's Publish as Web Page dialog box*

▶ *Browser support*   PowerPoint 2002 can reduce the resulting file sizes by fine-tuning your presentation for a particular browser or set of browsers. To take advantage of DHTML animation and sound effects, select the Microsoft Internet Explorer 4.0 or Later (High Fidelity) option. To improve compatibility with older/other browsers, you may want to select the Microsoft Internet Explorer or Netscape 3.0 or Later option. By doing so, you'll lose some functionality but guarantee that your presentation is available to a wider audience on the public Internet. Although the All Browsers Listed Above option gives you the best of both worlds, it also significantly increases the overall file sizes by providing multibrowser support options within each page. If you select this option and find that your presentation takes too long to load, you may want to actually create separate versions using the first two options and then direct the viewer's browser to the correct presentation based on the browser type and version.

▶ *Publish a copy as*   The final option group within this dialog box lets you specify the title of your published presentation and where you want to publish it. This may be to a folder on your local hard drive or network or directly to your Web server. You may also choose to immediately open the published files in your browser by selecting the corresponding check box.

▶ *Publish button*   Once you've completed your option settings, just click the Publish button to send your presentation on its way to the selected destination.

TIP

When using PowerPoint presentations on the public Internet, it's important to keep in mind the size of your image files. For this reason, you should always check for large files and reduce their size whenever possible through the use of compression, color palette reduction, forced image sizing, and other similar methods. For example, a shaded PowerPoint background image can often be cropped to a narrow horizontal line and then stretched within the page to fill the desired area. This method does not work with starburst and other non-vertically consistent images, but it can be effectively utilized in many cases with a little planning. Of course, another option is to use only solid background colors in Web-based presentations.

HTML-based PowerPoint presentations provide a great way to add spark to ordinary information. With PowerPoint 2002's improved publishing features, you may efficiently port most presentations to the Web without creating undue delays for your viewers.

Creating Excel Spreadsheets for Distribution

Microsoft Excel allows you to create and distribute spreadsheets for use with a multitude of real-world applications. With the onset of recent browser technology, you can incorporate these spreadsheets into your Web pages with all your calculations intact. This capability allows users to perform calculations on the Web, just as they would if they were using the Excel program.

Microsoft has greatly expanded its approach to the incorporation of spreadsheets into the Web environment, especially when it comes to integrating XML capabilities. However, there is much more information about this and the many other features than can be (or should be) covered within the context of this book. For the purposes of our discussion, we will focus on the incorporation of spreadsheet technology into FrontPage through the use of the Office Spreadsheet Web Component. This ActiveX control allows FrontPage users to develop and distribute spreadsheets even if they do not currently have Excel on their system.

CAUTION

Office Web Components are subject to the Office licensing agreement. This means that they can be distributed in any Web page, but only viewers with a valid Office XP license can interact with the components. Those viewers without a valid license may still view and print the information but cannot interact with it; for instance, they cannot change the data or manipulate a component.

Saving Excel Spreadsheets for Use on the Web

Consistent with Office XP's Web integration goals, Excel 2002 allows you to develop a spreadsheet and save it for viewing and manipulation within a browser, or you can simply create your spreadsheet and save it as an HTML file for viewing.

To save a spreadsheet for use on a Web page, follow these steps:

1. Create or open an Excel spreadsheet.
2. Select File | Save As Web Page from the menu bar. This brings up the Save As dialog box, similar to the one shown previously in Figure 8-1.
3. Select the directory where you want to save your spreadsheet.

TIP

If you are planning on incorporating this spreadsheet into one of your Webs, click the Web Folders button (My Network Places in Windows 2000), move to the desired Web and directory, and save it there. Once you move back into FrontPage, recalculate your hyperlinks, if necessary, and the spreadsheet will appear.

4. Click the Change Title button to bring up the Set Page Title dialog box. Type the title you want for your page and click OK.

5. Determine whether you want to save the entire workbook or the selected sheet.

TIP

You can use the Add Interactivity option with single spreadsheets or entire workbooks. If you choose to save an entire workbook without the Add Interactivity option, you get a frameset with a navigation bar to the other pages at the bottom. If you choose to save the entire workbook with the Add Interactivity option, you get the same ActiveX control, with the ability to choose the sheet to view by clicking the sheet's tab at the bottom of your screen.

6. Enter a filename in the File Name field.

NOTE

If you have selected the Sheet option, the Save As Type box is grayed out.

At this point, you can simply click the Save button to save your newly created HTML file(s) on your system, or you can click the Publish button for additional options that will not affect the copy of the file open in Excel. (See "Publishing Excel Spreadsheets," later in this chapter, for more information on the Publish option.)

Excel's Web Options

When you save your Excel files to a Web page, you will want to use the Web Options dialog box to specify how Excel handles the files when it saves them. The Web Options dialog box is available to you by selecting Tools | Web Options in the Save As dialog box.

Once you open the Web Options dialog box, you are presented with six tabs, similar to those for Word and PowerPoint. These tabs allow you to specify various settings associated with your output. The following subsections describe the options available to you in each tab.

Setting Excel's Options in the General Tab

The General tab of the Web Options dialog box, shown here, allows you to configure the appearance and compatibility options associated with your spreadsheet files:

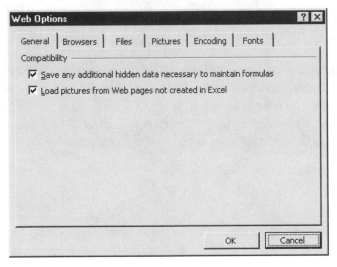

This tab comes with the following set of configurable options:

▶ *Save any additional hidden data necessary to maintain formulas*   This option instructs Excel to save all information required to perform the calculations you have set up in the spreadsheet. If you select this option, all your formulas will be saved in the HTML file(s) and will be visible to anyone viewing the page's source code or opening the page in Excel. This is necessary to maintain future (reentrant) functionality within Excel, but it may also expose more, possibly sensitive, information to the viewer than you intended. You should always consider your future use and security requirements when making your selection here.

▶ *Load pictures from Web pages not created in Excel*   This option instructs Excel to copy pictures that have been inserted into the spreadsheet when saving the HTML file. If this option is unchecked, all images that were not created directly in Excel will be linked to in their current locations and not published with the spreadsheet.

Setting Excel's Options in the Browsers Tab

The Browsers tab, shown here, is a new addition to the options you have available while saving your Excel spreadsheets for the Web:

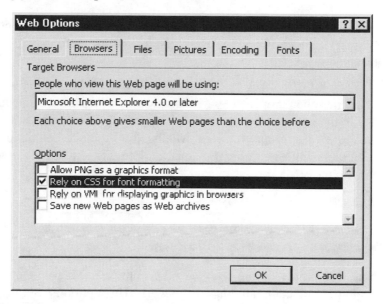

This tab allows you to target specific browsers for your pages so that the features you include will work for the majority of your audience. Here are the options available:

▶ *People who view this Web page will be using*   This option allows you to specify which browsers you want your spreadsheet, when converted, to be compatible with. If you know your targeted audience, the choice here is simple; however, if you are creating for the Web, you will want to choose a browser option that you believe will be compatible with the majority of viewers coming to see this page. The reason for this is that many features that will be used are not supported by older browsers and will cause your pages to display incorrectly.

▶ *Allow PNG as a graphics format*   PNG (Portable Network Graphics) is another format that is being recommended for inclusion in the next HTML specification. This format, if accepted, will replace the JPG format due to its higher-quality, lossless compression. Check this setting if you want to allow for the PNG format when saving your images.

▶ *Rely on CSS for font formatting*   This option specifies that you want to use cascading style sheets (CSS) to specify the formatting of fonts within your spreadsheet.

▶ *Rely on VML for displaying graphics in browsers*   VML (Vector Markup Language) has been proposed by Microsoft and various other companies to be included in the next version of the HTML standard. This format allows images to be saved in a vector-based layout, which allows them to be manipulated by other programs while retaining their quality. Use this setting to save your images with the VML format.

▶ *Save new Web pages as Web archives*   This option packages your entire page in a single file, including all your image work. This option is useful when you are sending your page to other people.

Setting Excel's Options in the Files Tab

The Files tab options, shown here, allow you to specify how your files are saved when you save your spreadsheet to a Web page:

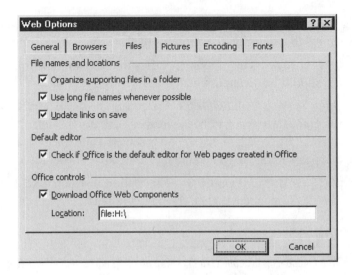

These options mainly deal with your supporting files, such as associated images or any frame-embedded pages in your spreadsheet. Along with the way in which your supporting files are saved, you have the option of checking your system to find out what the default editing settings are, and you can download the Office Web Components. Here are the options:

▶ *Organize supporting files in a folder*   This option specifies that any files created in conjunction with your spreadsheet (for example, associated images) be placed in a folder on the system. If this option is selected, the folder will be created in the same location you've chosen to save the file and will use a *xxxx*_files naming convention, where *xxxx* is the HTML page's selected filename.

▶ *Use long file names whenever possible*   This option instructs Excel to use long filenames that describe the contents of the actual supporting files.

▶ *Update links on save*   This option specifies that any links within the spreadsheet should be updated when you save the file.

▶ *Check if Office is the default editor for Web pages created in Office*   This option instructs Excel to automatically check whether Office is the default editor for Web pages created in Office. When this option is selected and Office is not the default, a message appears asking if you would like to make it the default.

▶ *Download Office Web Components*   This option instructs Excel to download the Office Web Components when the page is saved.

CAUTION

Office Web Components are subject to the Office licensing agreement. This means that they can be distributed in any Web page, but only viewers with a valid Office XP license can interact with the components. Those viewers without a valid license may still view and print the information, but cannot interact with it; for instance, they cannot change data or manipulate a component.

Setting Excel's Options in the Pictures Tab

When your spreadsheets contain pictures, you will want to optimize your settings for the browser environment in which your pictures will be viewed. The following settings on the Pictures tab, shown here, allow you to specify how your images will be saved for viewing in a browser:

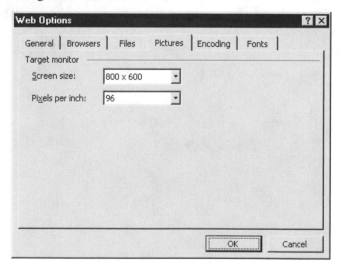

▶ *Screen size*   Use this setting to specify the screen size you are targeting when saving your images. This will determine the sizing set forth when your images are saved.

TIP

Although many individuals work with monitors that have a setting of 800×600 or above, I recommend that you specify the 800×600 setting because it will ensure that the vast majority of viewers will be able to see your images without needing to scroll left to right.

▶ *Pixels per inch*   Specifies the resolution associated with the images when they are saved.

NOTE

The actual resolution for PCs is 96 ppi, and for Macintoshes it's 72 ppi. As such, Office XP's default resolution is 96 ppi. Because the resolution of images is only important when you're specifying an altered display size, 72 ppi is generally accepted as the standard for image resolution as viewed on a monitor.

Setting Excel's Options in the Encoding Tab

The options on the Encoding tab, shown here, will determine what international text encoding will be used when you save your spreadsheets to HTML:

Web Options

General | Browsers | Files | Pictures | Encoding | Fonts

Encoding

Reload the current document as:

Save this document as:

Western European (Windows)

☐ Always save Web pages in the default encoding

OK   Cancel

Setting Excel's Options in the Fonts Tab

The options on the Fonts tab, shown here, will determine the default fonts associated with this file; from here, you can select both the proportional font and the fixed-width font that will be the defaults for your spreadsheet:

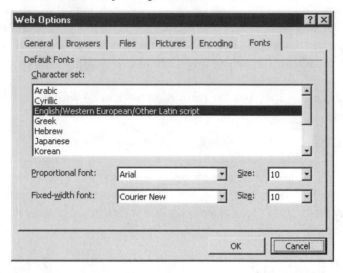

Publishing Excel Spreadsheets

Although Excel allows you to save a spreadsheet in its improved native HTML format, you will usually want to publish (copy) your spreadsheet to its destination instead of changing the original file's format. Publishing a spreadsheet instead of saving it also gives you additional options for exporting the spreadsheet and its associated files.

As discussed previously in "Saving Excel Spreadsheets for Use on the Web," you initiate the process of publishing your spreadsheet(s) in HTML format by selecting the File | Save As Web Page menu option. From the displayed Save As dialog box, click the Publish button to display the Publish as Web Page dialog box, as shown in Figure 8-3. From this dialog box, you may set your publishing options by following these steps:

1. Make your selection under Item to Publish. The Options here include the following:

   ▶ **Previously Published Items** Displays a list of items within the spreadsheet that you have published in the past. This is particularly useful when you're updating data in existing pages created in Excel.

- ▶ **Entire Workbook**   Allows you to publish the entire workbook, including all spreadsheets. This option automatically sets the Add Interactivity With option to Spreadsheet Functionality and disables that option from being changed.

- ▶ **Range of Cells**   Allows you to enter a range of cells within the current spreadsheet, along with a range selection button that lets you return to the spreadsheet and highlight the desired range. Once you're finished, click the corresponding button in the selection dialog box to accept your selected range.

- ▶ **Items on *xxxx*** (where *xxxx* is the name of your spreadsheet)   Allows you to choose items in a spreadsheet that you want to publish, including the entire spreadsheet. There will be an Items On *xxxx* option for each sheet in your workbook.

2. Make your selections under Viewing Options. This area includes the Add Interactivity With check box. By checking this box, you enable a drop-down menu that requires you to select either Spreadsheet Functionality or PivotTable Functionality. Each of these options instructs Excel to publish your data using the corresponding Office Web Component.

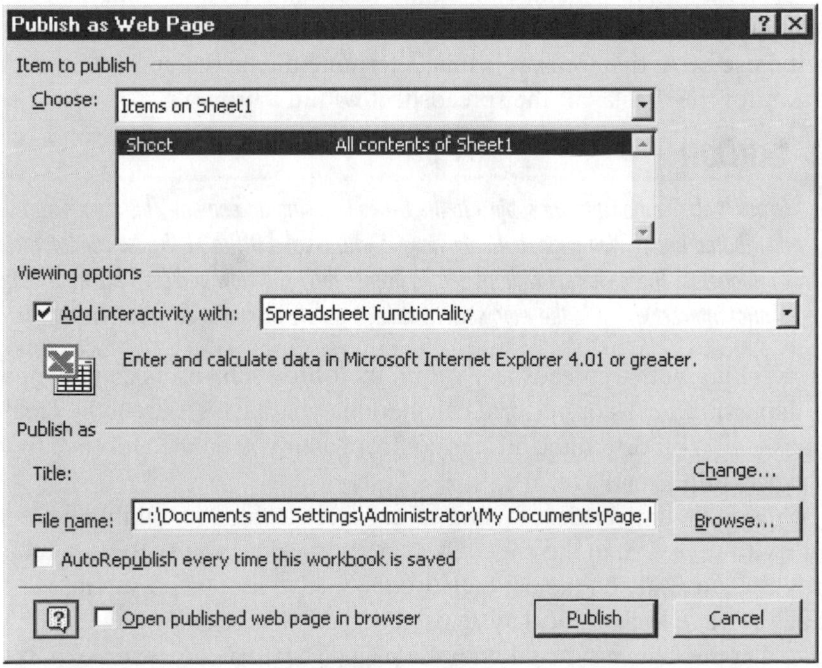

Figure 8-3   *Excel's Publish as Web Page dialog box*

3. Select the location where you want to publish your HTML spreadsheet. You may publish to a folder on your local drive or network or directly to your Web server.

TIP

Microsoft has added a new feature to its publishing capabilities that allows you to update your Web page every time you update your spreadsheet in Excel. You will see the check box AutoRepublish Every Time This Workbook Is Saved. This is a great new feature that allows you to always have an up-to-date Web page without having to resave as a Web page each time.

4. If you want to view your published page in your default browser after publishing, select the Open Published Web Page in Browser option as well.

5. After you've set your publishing configuration, click the Publish button to complete the process.

Using the Office XP Spreadsheet Web Component

On a private intranet, spreadsheets can easily be incorporated into your FrontPage documents so that users can edit and manipulate data directly within their browsers, even if they do not have Excel on your system. This application is made possible through the use of ActiveX controls that determine the layout and data source information for the display of the spreadsheet within a browser.

CAUTION

Office Web Components are subject to the Office licensing agreement. This means that they can be distributed in any Web page, but only viewers with a valid Office XP license can interact with the components. Those viewers without a valid license may still view and print the information but cannot interact with it in the way, such as changing data or manipulating a component.

When working with a spreadsheet within their browsers, users can manipulate and edit data within cells or perform calculations you have set up in the creation of the spreadsheet. You determine all this control when you create and save the spreadsheet within FrontPage.

One of the main drawbacks of using spreadsheet technology within a browser is the inability to save data to the page. Users only have the ability to view and print the data while currently on the page; they cannot save it to their systems. Even if users save the page to their local systems, any data changes they have made within the ActiveX control are not saved with the page. They can, however, export the data to Excel in a spreadsheet if you give them that capability when setting up the spreadsheet you will be placing within your page.

NOTE

The use of interactive spreadsheets within a browser is limited to Internet Explorer 4.01 and above.

Inserting a New Spreadsheet

Incorporating a spreadsheet into your Web is as easy as following these steps.

NOTE

These steps are intended to give you an example of inserting a new spreadsheet. The incorporation of existing spreadsheets is discussed later in this chapter.

1. Open a Web in FrontPage.

2. Position your cursor where you want the spreadsheet to appear within your document.

3. Select Insert | Web Component from the menu bar. This brings up the Insert Web Component dialog box.

4. Select Spreadsheets and Charts from the Component Type pane. Then select Office Spreadsheet from the Choose a Control pane, as shown here:

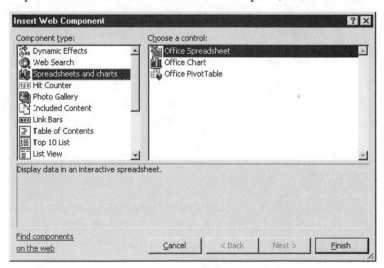

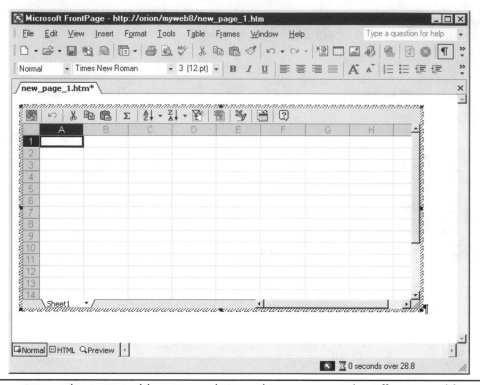

Figure 8-4   *A basic spreadsheet inserted into a document using the Office Spreadsheet Web Component*

5. Click Finish. FrontPage now inserts an Office Spreadsheet Web Component into your document, as shown in Figure 8-4.

You will notice that the Spreadsheet Web Component inserted into your document looks much like a standard Excel spreadsheet and comes complete with a toolbar, rows, and columns. The Spreadsheet Web Component is an ActiveX control and is fully configurable.

Spreadsheet Toolbar

If you take a look at Figure 8-4, you will see that the spreadsheet contains a standard toolbar. This toolbar allows you to perform basic functions within the spreadsheet. The toolbar, itself, is shown here, and each icon is explained in Table 8-2:

Button	Name	Description
	About	Displays the About Microsoft Office Web Components dialog box, which includes version, licensed user, and licensing information
	Undo	Reverts to the previous entry
	Cut	Cuts the selected data to the clipboard
	Copy	Copies the selected data to the clipboard
	Paste	Pastes data from the clipboard
	AutoSum	Totals the selected data through the use of addition
	Sort Ascending	Sorts the selected data in ascending order
	Sort Descending	Sorts the selected data in descending order
	AutoFilter	Allows you to specify the display of data that meets your required values
	RefreshAll	Allows you to refresh data in a PivotTable
	Export to Excel	Exports the spreadsheet to Microsoft Excel, where you can perform more complex calculations and save your data
	Commands and Options	Displays the Commands and Options dialog box, containing basic Excel commands and options
	Help	Displays the help files associated with the Spreadsheet Web Component

Table 8-2 *Tools on the Spreadsheet Toolbar*

ActiveX Control Properties

The ActiveX Control Properties dialog box determines the layout and internal information associated with your spreadsheet. This dialog box appears when you select your spreadsheet and then select Format | Properties from the menu bar. The nine tabs in the dialog box are discussed in the following subsections.

Format Options

The Format tab, shown here, is where you will set up the look and feel of the text, columns, and rows in your spreadsheet. This tab contains basic text-formatting options, along with settings for the alignment, height, and width of your rows and columns; it also contains the settings associated with the standard display of information within your cells:

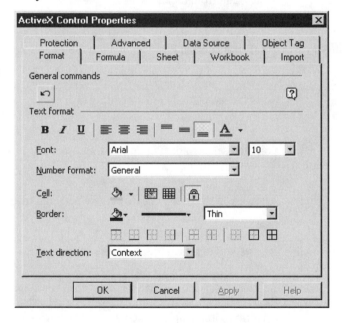

Formula Options

The Formula tab, shown here, allows you to manipulate various formulas within your spreadsheet:

Sheet Options

The Sheet tab, shown here, allows you to search for various items in your
spreadsheet as well as determine how the spreadsheet will appear in the browser:

The Sheet tab consists of the following options:

▶ **Find what**   This option invokes a standard dialog box that allows you to search through your data for specific information.

▶ **Show/Hide**   This option contains the settings of how the actual spreadsheet will appear on your screen. Within this section, you can specify what is displayed to the user in the way of row and column headers and gridlines within the sheet. When working in FrontPage, you will probably want to keep all these items displayed on your screen—this will make the creation and layout of your design easier to configure. You may find, though, that you do not want your users to see this information when the sheet is displayed in their browsers. If this is the case, you can change these settings prior to saving your spreadsheets. Additional options within the Sheet tab include the ability to reverse the column display order to right to left, specify a viewable range, and to freeze specified panes by setting the frozen pane divider location to the upper-left corner of the currently selected cell.

Workbook Options

The Workbook tab, shown here, allows you to specify how calculations are performed within a workbook, along with what will be displayed and the order in which your worksheets are shown:

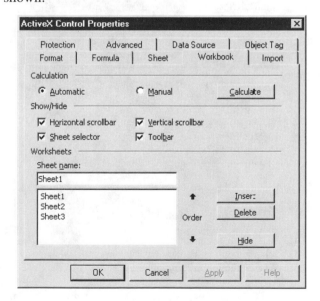

The Workbook tab consists of the following options:

▶ **Automatic Calculation**   Specifies that the calculation in the selected field should be performed automatically when data is entered.

▶ **Manual Calculation**   Specifies that the calculation in the selected field should only be performed when the Calculate button is clicked.

▶ **Calculate button**   Performs the calculation displayed if Manual is the selected Calculation option.

▶ **Show/Hide**   Contains the settings for how the actual spreadsheet will appear on your screen. Within this section, you can specify what is displayed to the user in the way of horizontal and vertical scroll bars, the sheet selector, and the toolbar. When working in FrontPage, you will probably want to keep all these items showing on your screen—this will make the creation and layout of your design easier to configure. You may find, though, that you do not want your users to see this information when the sheet is displayed in the browser. If this is the case, you can change these settings prior to saving your spreadsheets.

▶ **Sheet Name**   Allows you to specify sheet names and the order in which they are displayed. You can also insert, delete, and hide sheets.

Import Options

The Import tab, shown next, allows you to specify a data type and URL for data you want to import into your spreadsheet.

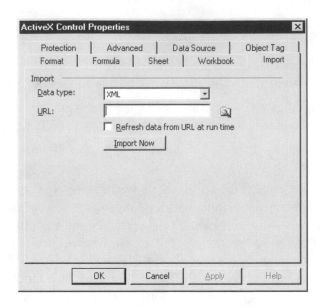

Within this tab, you can specify that the information imported be updated at runtime. This means that the imported data will be updated each time the page is loaded in a browser rather than being imbedded in the page.

NOTE

The data you import should be in tabular format and must reside on the same server as the page you are working with. Also, any existing data in the spreadsheet will be overwritten. When using an XML data source, the source document must be in XML-Spreadsheet format. See Excel's documentation for more information on the XML-Spreadsheet format.

Protection Options

The Protection tab, shown here, allows you to specify what can and cannot be operated on or edited within the spreadsheet (in other words, you can set the Protection tab's options so users will not be able to manipulate various aspects of your spreadsheet when working with it in their browsers):

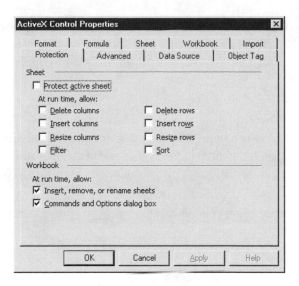

Various settings are available in this tab, but they are all controlled by one basic element—the Protect Active Sheet check box. If this box is not checked, protection will not be implemented.

Advanced Options

The Advanced tab, shown here, allows you to specify how your spreadsheet will actually appear in the browser window:

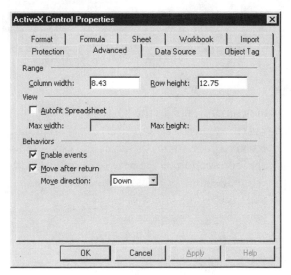

These settings determine how users will see your spreadsheet information. Along with the display settings, you can also specify how users will move through the spreadsheet and whether external scripts will be able to operate in your spreadsheet.

Data Source Options

The Data Source tab, shown here, allows you to specify a database or other ODBC data source connection to retrieve data for the spreadsheet. Within this tab, you can configure a data connection, along with command or SQL text to be associated with the connection:

Object Tag Options

The Object Tag tab, shown here, sets up the basic layout of your spreadsheet within the browser. Within this tab, you can specify the name, alignment, size, and spacing layout options; an alternative page to be displayed in browsers that do not support this technology; and data connection to the network containing your data if you are obtaining data from an outside source:

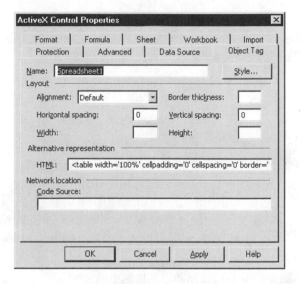

Hands On: Creating an Online Expense Report

One great aspect of the spreadsheet capability is that you can create a spreadsheet form in which users can insert data. The data they insert will be based on the format and calculations you have set up when designing the spreadsheet.

This example takes a look at an implementation of this capability through the creation of an online expense report. The report we will be using in this example can be found on the CD-ROM and is entitled expense_report.html. An example of the report is shown in Figure 8-5.

To create an online expense report, follow these steps:

1. Open a page in your Web. For this example, we will be working with the page titled expense.html.

2. Position your cursor where you want the spreadsheet to appear within your document.

3. Select Insert | Web Component from the menu bar. This brings up the Insert Web Component dialog box.

4. Select Spreadsheets and Charts from the Component Type pane and select Office Spreadsheet from the Choose a Control pane.

5. Click Finish. FrontPage now inserts a spreadsheet into your document, as shown previously in Figure 8-4.

6. Click inside the spreadsheet you have just inserted.

   For our expense report, you want to enter a title for the report. You also want to request that the users input their name, phone number, and manager into the spreadsheet. The following steps will complete this operation. Once you have added these fields, you will configure their font settings.

7. Type a title for the report in cell A1, as follows:
   Online Expense Report

8. Move to cell A2 and type the following text:
   Use this report to determine your reimbursable expenses. Print this report when complete.

9. Move to cell A3 and type **Name:**. Then move down one more cell, to A4, and type **Phone:**. For the final entry, you will want to move to cell A5 and type **Manager:**. These are the fields we will use to have users enter their basic information.

   Now create a header row for the expense report calculation form.

10. Enter the following headings in cells A7 through I7:
    Date, **Account**, **Transport**, **Fuel**, **Meals**, **Accommodation**, **Phone**, **Entertain**, **Total**

    Next, create the actual expense report calculation form. For this example, you will allow the user to enter a maximum of five dates, and then show the totals. You really don't want to total the Date and Account columns, so start with the Transport column and work your way across the other columns.

11. Move to cell C13 and enter the following calculation:
    =SUM(C8:C12)

This calculation instructs the spreadsheet to add all the expenses that appear in column C, rows 8 through 12.

NOTE

Your calculation will vary depending on the number of rows and columns you use for your expense report.

12. Moving to the right, repeat step 11 for each of the remaining fields you would like to enter a calculation for in the spreadsheet (except the Total column), changing the column letter to match the current column. After completing this step, you should have formulas entered in cells C8 through H8.

13. In the first row of the Total column (cell I8), enter the following equation: **=SUM(C8:H8)**

    This calculation instructs the spreadsheet to add all the expenses found in row 8 of our spreadsheet in a horizontal manner.

14. Moving down column I, repeat step 13, entering the row total calculations in each of the remaining four rows, until you reach the Grand Total cell (13I).

    You now want to enter a grand total for the spreadsheet. To do so, continue with the steps.

15. Click the cell where you want your total to appear and enter the following calculation:
    =SUM(I8:I12)

    You have now completed the calculation portion of our spreadsheet. At this point, you can click the Preview tab to preview the spreadsheet in your browser. Next, you are going to configure the font style for the title of the spreadsheet. This process can be repeated to set up all the formatting for the spreadsheet.

16. Back in the FrontPage Normal view, position your cursor in the cell containing the spreadsheet's title. For this example, this is cell A1.

17. Open the ActiveX Control Properties dialog box by clicking Format | Properties from the FrontPage menu bar.

18. Click the Format tab to bring up the formatting properties.

19. Set your text formatting properties any way you wish. For our title, we have set the properties to Arial, 16 point, bold. Your settings will appear on the screen once you enter them.

NOTE

I won't walk you though formatting the text in the rest of the spreadsheet. If desired, you can easily make your page look like the example in Figure 8-5.

Now that we have set up the look and feel of our spreadsheet, we want to determine how it will appear within the browser. We do not want any options available to the user, except the ability to enter data into the spreadsheet. To accomplish this, we will modify the various settings, as outlined in the remaining steps.

20. In the ActiveX Control Properties dialog box, click the Sheet tab.

21. In the Show/Hide section of the Sheet tab, uncheck the Row Headers and Column Headers check boxes. You will see that these items disappear from your spreadsheet.

22. Click the Workbook tab and uncheck the Sheet Selector and Toolbar check boxes. Once again, you will see these items disappear from the spreadsheet.

23. Click OK to close the dialog box and save your page.

View the page in your browser to ensure that all your calculations work properly. When users enter data into this spreadsheet, the calculations will take place. Once users have completed their expense reports, they can print the page.

NOTE

Users cannot save the data in this spreadsheet. If you want to give users the ability to save their data, you will need to activate the toolbar on your spreadsheet. From the toolbar, users can click the Export to Excel button, which opens Excel and allows them to save their data in a spreadsheet.

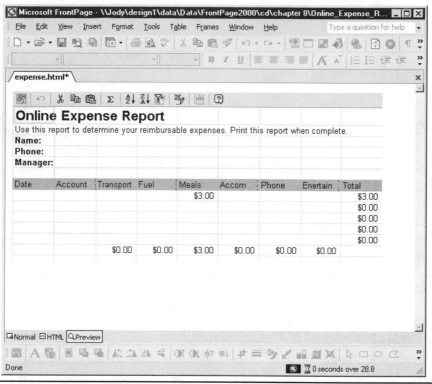

Figure 8-5   *The expense report spreadsheet inserted into FrontPage*

Exporting Spreadsheets to Excel

One problem associated with users inserting data into spreadsheets online is that they cannot save the spreadsheet once they add their data. For this reason, among others, the Office Spreadsheet Web Component allows you to incorporate the ability to export data entered in the Spreadsheet Web Component into Excel. Doing so will allow users to save the data to their local computers or even send it as an e-mail attachment using Excel's Send To command.

To enable this export capability, follow these steps when you create your spreadsheet:

1. Create a new HTML page in FrontPage and insert an Office Spreadsheet Web Component.

2. Click the Spreadsheet Web Component, and select Format | Properties from the menu bar. This brings up the ActiveX Control Properties dialog box.

3. Click the Workbook tab and make sure Toolbar is checked under the Show/Hide settings.

4. Click OK and save the spreadsheet.

Users will now have the toolbar available to them when working within your spreadsheet. From the toolbar, they can click the Export to Excel button to open the current spreadsheet in Microsoft Excel. Of course, they'll need to have Excel installed on their computers to use this option. From there, they can save the data to their computers.

Importing Data into Your Spreadsheet

If you have information that you would like to import into your spreadsheet, you can easily accomplish this with FrontPage. The following steps show you the process involved in importing data into a Spreadsheet Web Component incorporated into a FrontPage Web:

1. Create a new HTML page in FrontPage and insert an Office Spreadsheet Web Component.

2. Click the Spreadsheet Web Component and select Format | Properties from the menu bar. This brings up the ActiveX Control Properties dialog box.

3. Click the Import tab to display the import options.

4. Select the data type you want to import and type the URL where the data resides. For example, an HTML data source might be
    http://localhost/spreadsheets/import.html
    or
    C:/data/spreadsheet/import.html

5. Check the Import Data from URL at Run Time box.

6. Click the Import Now button to import the data into your spreadsheet while working in FrontPage.

7. Click OK and save the document.

This page will now import the specified data each time a user opens the page. You can modify this data to display new information by editing the source document.

NOTE

When you're importing data from an external source, existing data will be overwritten without warning, starting with cell A1.

Outlook and the Web

Outlook is not only a great tool for keeping track of all your day-to-day operations, it also has many features that provide Web capabilities. These features allow you to share information with others, mainly through the use of a shared folder system. Outlook also comes with a very capable e-mail component. All in all, Outlook helps you get organized, share information, and become more productive.

Because Outlook is designed to be used in conjunction with a network, it has its own setup for the sharing of information. Because of this, the capabilities for saving your information to HTML are rather limited. This is not to say that this limits the program—it's just that the types of features we are talking about in this book are not the same as the features Outlook uses when working on the Web. However, Outlook docs have some nice Web features when it comes to the calendar portion of the program, and that is what we'll look at here.

Saving Your Calendar as a Web Page

Unlike the other Office programs, which bring up a standard Save As dialog box and allow you to configure your output through the use of Web options, the Outlook Calendar contains its own Save as Web Page dialog box, shown in Figure 8-6. This dialog box allows you to specify all your output options. We'll start with a brief rundown of the options and then go through the steps of saving your calendar as a Web page.

▶ **Duration**   Specifies the range of dates you want to be saved in your Web page.

▶ **Include appointment details**   Instructs Outlook to include the details of your appointments in hyperlinked files.

▶ **Use background graphic**   Allows you to incorporate a background image to be used with the Web page.

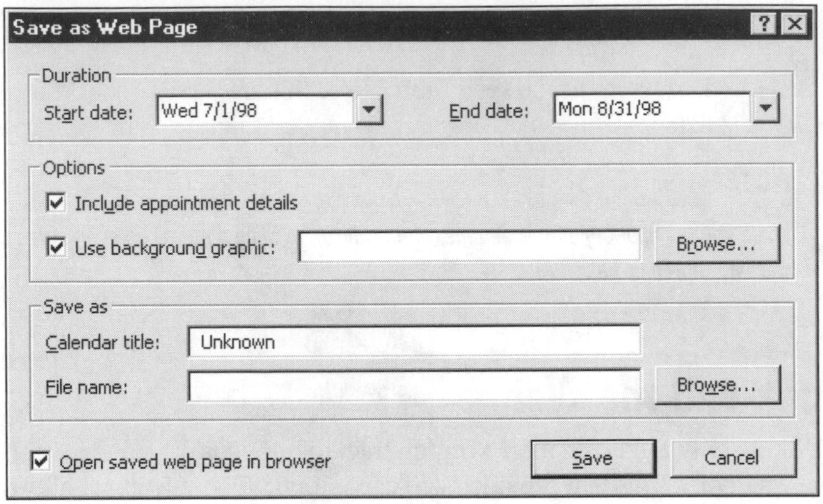

Figure 8-6   *Outlook's Save as Web Page dialog box*

▶ **Calendar title**   Gives a name to the HTML document containing your calendar.

▶ **File name**   Assigns a filename to the main calendar document.

▶ **Open saved Web page in browser**   Instructs Outlook to launch your default browser with the calendar page when the file is saved.

To save your calendar as a Web page, follow these steps:

1. Open your calendar in Outlook.
2. Select File | Save As Web Page from the menu bar. This brings up the Save as Web Page dialog box.
3. Select the dates you want to appear in your calendar page.
4. If you want your appointment details to appear in the calendar, check the Include Appointment Details option.
5. If you want to add a little flare to your calendar, you can do so by incorporating a background image. Simply check the Use Background Graphic check box and enter the name of the image or click the Browse button to select one.
6. Give your calendar page a title by entering it in the Calendar Title text box.
7. Type a filename in the File Name text box. If you want to specify the directory for your pages, click the Browse button and select a directory.
8. Enter the remaining settings you want for your calendar and then click Save.

TIP

If you want to see the output immediately, check the Open Saved Web Page in Browser option in the dialog box.

Your page is now saved on the system. If you have the Open Saved Web Page in Browser check box marked, your browser will automatically display the page.

Summary

Although much of the information in this chapter does not relate directly to using FrontPage 2002, it will come in handy with FrontPage's integration into the Office XP suite. After reading this chapter, you should have a good grasp of the basics associated with taking documents from other Office applications and porting them for use on the Web.

By no means is this a complete look at the features and capabilities of the Office suite when it comes to integration with the Web. It is, however, a quick look into how Microsoft has integrated its products for use on the Web today.

Along with the basics of using the Office suite applications for creating Web pages, we have discussed how some of the applications have been incorporated into the FrontPage development environment, as demonstrated by the Office Spreadsheet Web Component.

You've probably noticed that a discussion of Access is not included in this chapter, even though Access is part of the Office suite. We will be covering the integration of database technology extensively later in this book, so we will tackle Access separately.

Preparing for Database-Driven Webs

IN THIS CHAPTER:

Understand Databases

Set Up FrontPage for Databases

oday, more than ever, designers are using databases to drive their Web sites. Traditionally, the use of databases was limited to those with large-scale budgets and high-traffic sites, but now every site can come equipped with database technology without the large price tag. This availability has caused a great surge in the use of databases with Web sites for the creation of everything from page layouts to secure shopping cart systems. The variety of databases, such as SQL 2000 from Microsoft, that allow this dynamic deployment of content and user interaction vary almost as much as the implementations you are seeing today.

In this chapter you take a look at the requirements for implementing a database-driven site. Although the chapter covers a lot of the available technology, you are going to focus on the setup and requirements associated with Microsoft Access. This application is part of the Microsoft Office suite and integrates very nicely with FrontPage XP. Using Access databases, you can quickly and easily develop dynamic sites without a lot of programming or cost.

Working with Databases

Databases are used to store and sort information (in this case, you will be looking at how databases store and sort information in relation to a Web site). This is the basic fact behind the database system. What you do with that information is something entirely different. As mentioned earlier, you can use a database for a multitude of implementations. However, some basic aspects of the database hold true no matter what you are using it for.

If you look at a simple flat-file database, you will see that it is made up of a single table (hence the name, *flat file*) that contains a set of rows and columns. Within these rows and columns are records that make up the information within the database. For example, you may have a client database that contains all the information about your clients. Each client within that database makes up a single record. The record for each client is then stored in a row within the database, with each column representing one aspect of that client, as shown here:

	First Name	Last Name	Address	City	State/Province	Postal Code
+	Bob	Smith	59499 Street Dr	San Jose	CA	99320-3845
+	Jim	Rogers	883 My Drive	Berkeley	CA	99934-3334
+	Nancy	Jones	1064 The Alame	San Jose	CA	95124-3993

Contacts : Table

Record: 4 of 4

This style of database is useful, but it is limited because the only information it can contain is the information relating to your clients. What if you want a database that lists all the contact information relating to your clients and also contains billing information, project information, and other items pertinent to working with them? Well, this is where it gets more complicated. You see, to incorporate all this information efficiently, you need multiple tables. You would use key fields within these tables which would then interact with one another to obtain the information you want on your clients. This is what is called a *relational* database, because the various tables interrelate with each other. Relational databases are much more versatile than flat-file databases because they allow you to gather and compare vast amounts of information. Microsoft Access is an example of a relational database program.

Access is an outstanding relational database program that's easy to use because of the integration of wizards into the program, along with the various views which allow you to see the data in your database visually. You will take a close look at Access, its strengths, its weaknesses, and how it works with FrontPage later in this chapter and again in Chapter 10.

Client-Server Interaction

When working with a database used for a Web site, you need to understand that you are working with both the client (browser) and the server. The interaction between the two is what allows you to obtain, view, and update information found within the database. The basic principle behind client-server interaction is that the client initiates an action by sending a message to the server, and the server then performs the action and sends a response to the client.

For the purposes of this chapter, you will be looking at the client-server architecture using a Web browser as the client on either your computer or your user's computer. The server will be your Web server and will house the database. When a user enters a page that is linked in some way to a database, the browser makes a call to the server, asking for the information contained within the database. The server then retrieves the requested information from the database, returning it to the client browser for display or further processing.

Tiered Architectures in Data-Driven Application Design

With single-user systems, databases and the applications that use them are often stored on the user's system. Although the application and database are separate files, all the processing (computing) takes place on a single computer. This is known as *single-tier architecture.* When you install Microsoft Access on your computer and then build and use databases, you are implementing single-tier design. Even if you store your Access database on another computer, such as a file server, and allow several people to access it simultaneously, all the processing is still being performed on each user's personal computer, making it a single-tier architecture system.

The upside to the single-tier design is that it is easy to implement and maintain in addition to being cost effective. If you're planning on using a database only to accept and store information from your users, without the worry of many users trying to access that information at the same time, a single-tier system will likely suffice for your needs. The downside to single-tier systems is their lack of performance and scalability. When multiple users interact (read and write) with a database at the same time, you'll encounter record locking and performance problems in a single-tier system. To resolve these types of problems, you should consider another approach, such as a multitier system, which allows you to use multiple computers to handle different programs for your system.

The term *client-server* is often misunderstood. When you just store files on a central computer and allow access to those files by other computers on the network, you are not using client-server architecture. Of course, the same goes for sharing printers on a network. Although file and printer sharing are extremely important and useful aspects of networking, true client-server systems take things a step further. With the advent of the client-server architecture, servers can now run true *server applications*, which handle varying amounts of the processing required by today's multiuser applications. Not very surprisingly, server-based database-management systems have led the way in this arena. Examples of these systems include Microsoft's SQL Server, Oracle, Sybase's Adaptive Server (formerly SQL Server), and Informix's Dynamic Server.

Although these database servers differ considerably, they share the ability to perform complex queries and other tasks on the computer they run on, resulting in better management of database access, reduced bandwidth usage, and improved client performance. By taking on these tasks that had previously been left to the client computer, true client-server architecture—also known as *two-tier architecture*—is achieved.

NOTE

To avoid confusion, it should be noted that the term database server commonly refers to both the database management software and the computer upon which it runs. Although not always the case, database servers are normally high-performance systems, serving that single role.

With the pervasiveness of the public Internet and private corporate intranets, the Web browser is quickly becoming the client application of choice. Although the reasons for this are many, one of the most compelling is the fact that HTML and HTTP, the primary language and protocol of the Web, have been accepted by all major platforms. Using a Web browser as your client, you can now deploy an application on the Internet or your private intranet and immediately have users access the application, whether they're using PCs running Windows, PCs running OS/2, Macintoshes, or UNIX boxes. Of course, with the limitations of browsers, you'll likely want to do most of your processing on the server. Also, because your Web server and database server are already overtaxed, you now need an application server to handle the processing of your application logic and business rules. The software that handles this type of processing is known as *middleware*, because it makes up the second tier in what is now a three-tier architecture system.

So here's your new structure: Tier one is the client, often a Web browser. The client makes a request to the second tier, the application server running middleware. The application server retrieves information from the third tier, the database server, and also handles any necessary processing of the client's request or the information retrieved from the database server. Finally, the application server sends the appropriate information back to the client. If the client is a Web browser, the server will likely create a new HTML page that is returned to the client browser. This is a slightly simplified example, but it should give you a basic understanding of the flow within a multitier system.

A simple Web server is pretty much just a file server. Different Web servers implement technologies such as JavaScript and Perl interpreters. These technologies add intelligence to the Web servers, making them more like application servers. Microsoft's intelligent Web server implementation in Internet Information Server (IIS) includes Active Server Page (ASP) server extensions and FrontPage server extensions. When you use a FrontPage WebBot or an Active Server Page in your Web, you're using client-server architecture. FrontPage makes use of both technologies to greatly simplify adding database access to your Web site.

This interaction needs a lot to take place behind the scenes for it to be able to work properly, but the main aspects of the interaction you want to focus on involve SQL (Structured Query Language), ODBC (Open Database Connectivity), and ADO (ActiveX Data Objects), which are explained in the following sections. For simplicity, you'll also be focusing on the Access database.

SQL

Structured Query Language (SQL) is the language you use to make requests of a database. The language itself is quite easy to read and implement, on the surface, because it consists of only a small number of commands. The commands used in SQL read much like simple English. However, SQL statements can be combined to create powerful queries. SQL is used to perform maintenance on the database, request information from the database, and add information to the database.

We will not go into a complete discussion of SQL in this book. There are, deservedly, entire books covering individual *flavors* (implementations) of SQL. If you're serious about learning SQL, you'll want to consult more detailed, specific references. Still, it is important to be aware of some of the capabilities of the language. The basic instructions within SQL are SELECT, UPDATE, INSERT, and DELETE. They are defined in the following sections.

TIP

Although SQL statements are not case sensitive, it is general practice to enter SQL instructions in uppercase and database references in mixed case.

SELECT

The SELECT instruction is used to fetch a record or set of records from a database. The returned information is known as a *recordset*. This is the most commonly used instruction in SQL. When working with this instruction, you may also associate specific criteria for the selection you want to make. For example, if you are working with a database that contains all your contacts in a table called ContactList and want to query that database, you could create an SQL statement such as this:

```
SELECT FirstName, LastName, PhoneNumber FROM ContactList
```

In this example, you are looking up the first name, last name, and phone number of all individuals who are stored in the ContactList table in your database.

To find a particular contact, you'll need to add another SQL statement: a WHERE clause. The WHERE clause allows us to specify certain conditions that data must meet in order for it to be returned in your recordset. The syntax of a simple WHERE clause is <field> <operator> <value>, where <field> is the name of a column in the table you're working with, <operator> is a comparative statement, and <value> is what you're searching for. You'll see some examples of WHERE clauses in a moment.

SQL's variety of operators gives you great flexibility when setting criteria. These operators include

<	Less than.
>	Greater than.
=	Equals.
<>	Not equal to.
<=	Less than or equal to.
>=	Greater than or equal to.
LIKE	Use this operator to search for partial matches and sliding searches, such as all last names beginning with the letter *G* or all company names containing "Inc."

So, armed with the WHERE clause, you can now limit your returned recordset to a particular record or records, as shown here:

```
SELECT FirstName, LastName, PhoneNumber FROM ContactList WHERE
LastName = 'Smith'
```

This query returns the first name, last name, and phone number of all records in the table ContactList with the last name of Smith.

If you are not sure of the entire query, you can use a wildcard symbol, e.g.,

```
SELECT FirstName, LastName, PhoneNumber FROM ContactList WHERE
LastName LIKE 'S*'
```

This query returns the first name, last name, and phone number of all records in the table ContactList with a last name that begins with the letter *S* (* is used as a wildcard symbol).

To go one step further, you can use wildcard characters on both sides of your query to find anything containing that text, e.g.,

```
SELECT CompanyName, PhoneNumber FROM ContactList WHERE CompanyName
LIKE '*Inc*'
```

This query returns the company name and phone number of all records in the table ContactList with a company name that contains "Inc" anywhere within the company name.

NOTE

The exact syntax of wildcard symbols varies from database to database. With an Access MDB file, * is used. With SQL Server, % is used. You should consult your database documentation and instruct your users on which symbol to use, or you can just append the proper symbol through your code if you want all searches to be open ended.

UPDATE

The UPDATE instruction makes changes to existing data within a database table. When working with this instruction, you specify the instruction and the name of the table(s) containing the data you wish to modify, and then you attach the criteria for the update to it. For example, if you are working with a database that contains all your contacts and want to change a single contact's phone number, you could create an SQL statement such as this:

```
UPDATE ContactList SET PhoneNumber = '555-1212'
WHERE ContactID = 3
```

This example updates the phone number of any contacts in your ContactList table with a ContactID value of 3 (a unique record in this case). The SET statement tells SQL that what follows is a list of fields to change, along with their new values. In this case, PhoneNumber is the field name and 555-1212 is the new value. To change multiple fields at once, simply separate the <field> = value statement with commas. You will also notice that you have used the WHERE clause in this statement to limit the effects in this way. Although its use is optional, leaving it out would result in changing the phone number of all the contacts within your table to 555-1212. Although you might occasionally want to do something similar to this, don't get caught accidentally making this kind of mistake. Once changes have been made to a database using an UPDATE query, there's no way to undo the damage.

INSERT

The INSERT instruction adds one or more new records to a table. This is commonly known as an *append query*. In contrast to the UPDATE instruction, where you simply change data that's already available, INSERT allows us to append new records to the table. For example, if you are working with a database that contains all your contacts and want to add a new contact to that database, you could create an SQL statement such as this:

```
INSERT INTO ContactList (FirstName, LastName, PhoneNumber)
VALUES ('John', 'Doe', '555-1212')
```

As you can see from this example, you are inserting John Doe and his phone number into your ContactList table. In the first line of the statement you determine the fields in which you want to enter data. In the second line, you associate values with those fields for entry into the table.

> ### NOTE
> *If this table contained other fields, such as Address and Department, they would be given NULL values, because you have not specifically entered them here. This means that no value has been entered for those fields, and they will be left blank. You could then go back at a later time and update these fields using the UPDATE command.*

DELETE

The DELETE instruction removes entire records from a database table. This instruction will remove all records that meet your specified criteria. When working with DELETE, you specify the table you want to remove information from and then append a search condition using the WHERE clause. For example, if you are working with a database that contains all your contacts and want to remove all contacts for a specific company you no longer work with, you could create an SQL statement such as this:

```
DELETE * FROM ContactList
WHERE CompanyName = 'Widgets'
```

For this example, you have specified that the DELETE operation is to take place in the ContactList table and have asked to search for and remove all contact records containing the name Widgets in the CompanyName field.

The features available within SQL go way beyond what you will be shown in this book, but this gives you an idea of the basic principles behind the language. As you can see, the basic layout of the language makes it rather easy to implement on the surface, but be aware that SQL syntax can get very complex as you move into more advanced levels of usage, such as multitable joins, unions, and subqueries.

ODBC

Open Database Connectivity (ODBC) is a standard that allows a variety of programs to use SQL statements to access information within a database, without the need to use the proprietary interface associated with the database. The use of ODBC allows you to create your database in whatever ODBC-compliant database format you want and have it accessed via a Web browser.

You can think of ODBC as a translation layer between the database and the application querying the database. This translation layer removes the proprietary aspects of the database, which then allows the application access to it. In essence, ODBC solves the "round peg in the square hole" problem, allowing you to access and control a variety of data sources without having to install the respective complete database-management application on each machine accessing the data. This is known as *heterogeneous database access* and is a primary feature of ODBC. The only downsides to ODBC are the complexity of its connection statements and the reduction in performance compared with proprietary access methods. For ODBC data access to work properly, you must set up a database-specific ODBC driver on the Web server that will be hosting the database. You may already have all the necessary drivers on your system, but if you do not, you can obtain them from Microsoft's Universal Data Access Web site (http://www.microsoft.com/data) or from the database manufacturer.

Once you have loaded the appropriate ODBC driver, you then register your database with the driver, creating a DSN (Data Source Name). DSNs, which are used to store information about how to connect to a particular data provider, come in three flavors:

▶ **User DSN** A user DSN is only visible to the single user and can only be used on that user's machine.

▶ **System DSN** A system DSN is visible to all users on a machine including Windows NT 2000 services. This is the typical DSN type used for Internet and intranet database connectivity.

▶ **File DSN** A file DSN may be shared by users (servers) who have the same ODBC drivers installed.

To configure a DSN on a Windows-based system, open the Control Panel and run the ODBC Data Source Administrator applet.

ActiveX Data Objects (ADO)

ActiveX Data Objects (ADO) is the next generation of data access for programming remote-access applications. This data-access model is a step up from the traditional programmatic models, such as DAO (Data Access Objects) and RDO (Remote Data Objects). Originally introduced by Microsoft in conjunction with its Visual InterDev tool, which is used to build ASP applications, ADO has spread like wildfire throughout the database-programming industry. ADO takes the best of DAO and RDO and is the common interface for OLE-DB, which is a set of APIs (Application Programming Interface functions) that standardize access to disparate data sources, with each data source needing its own OLE-DB provider. ADO gives high-level access to the common interfaces that all OLE-DB providers share.

What all this means is that ADO allows you to create an application that accesses a database (for example, an ASP page). Using ADO also simplifies the process of porting your application to a different tier level, thus greatly improving scalability. This technology is beneficial because it is easy to work with and requires very little in the way of memory to function properly on a system. We take a quick look at this technology in the next few paragraphs and will discuss it in depth in Chapter 11.

ADO is implemented within ASP pages through the use of either JavaScript or VBScript. Because the implementation takes place on the server, you don't even have to worry about compatibility with the client browser. When working with ADO, you will find that the components are much simpler than those of DAO and RDO. The main components within ADO are explained in the following list.

TIP

For more information on ADO, check out http://www.microsoft.com/data/ado.

▶ **Connection object**   Makes a connection to a data provider. This connection is similar to those found in the rdoConnection object and the database object in RDO and DAO, respectively. This is the primary function necessary to connect the application and the data source, and it must be set for the interaction of the two to perform properly.

▶ **Recordset object**   Works with and manipulates the records within your database. This object is the main connection for your data manipulation. It can be compared to the DAO Recordset object and the RDO rdoResultset object.

▶ **Command object**   Points to SQL strings within your system. This object is your command layer, where you connect to items that can be executed. It can be compared to rdoPreparedStatement in RDO and QueryDef in DAO.

▶ **Errors collection**   Defines a collection of errors so that you can perform checks. This is due to multiple errors being possible through one data-access statement. The collection allows you to check each error.

Preparing to Use Active Server Pages

Active Server Pages (ASP) is a Microsoft technology that allows you to display dynamic information on your Web pages. Basically, an Active Server Page is an HTML page that also contains some server-side scripting, which is used to perform certain functions, such as retrieving information from a database. FrontPage XP allows you to incorporate this technology into your Webs quickly and easily, and you will be discussing its uses and the integration of Active Server Pages into your Web in depth in Chapters 11 and 12.

NOTE

Many of the functions explained in the following chapters won't work properly unless ASP is installed on your server. FrontPage relies extensively on ASP for the display of active data within your Web.

Using Microsoft Access as Your Database

With the inclusion of FrontPage 10 in the Microsoft Office suite of products, you now have an even better integration of Access with FrontPage. This integration makes creating and implementing a database using Access a task that can be accomplished by anyone, from the most advanced developer to the new user just getting started. This part of the chapter takes an in-depth look at the tools available to you when working with Access as your Web database system. You will look at how to best set up Access to work as your database, along with the tools available within the product for implementing your database.

This discussion is meant as a precursor to Chapter 10, which will take an in-depth look at actually implementing database content within your Webs.

Setting Up FrontPage to Work with Your Database

FrontPage comes with an extensive set of tools that allows you to easily connect Access databases to the pages within your Web. You can create pages that simply display information from an Access database as well as pages that send information to the database. FrontPage can even create Access databases for you (we'll cover this further in Chapter 10). Before you begin working with a database, however, some things need to be set up within FrontPage to allow your pages to interoperate with the database.

Setting Up an ODBC Data Source on the Server

One method of setting up a database for use with FrontPage is to set up the database on your current server. This is accomplished by creating an ODBC DSN for the database you want to use. Setting up a DSN allows users to access the database from your network. When working with DSNs, you need to remember that there are three types: user DSN, system DSN, and file DSN.

Recall that the user DSN allows the data source to be viewed by the current user on the current computer only. This setup will not allow other individuals accessing the computer via a network to view the information associated with the DSN and is therefore not applicable to your needs. The system DSN, which allows the data source to be viewed by individuals with access to the current computer, is the DSN you will be using, because it allows individuals with access to the Web server to access the information you set up.

The file DSN allows only those users with the same ODBC drivers to access the information. Although similar to the system DSN, the file DSN stores its information in a simple text file that can easily be copied to other machines. In addition, after you've added a data connection to your Web project, the necessary information is copied to the Web's global.asa file, eliminating the need for the DSN and creating what is called a "DSN-less connection."

The following steps show you how to set up a DSN for your database:

1. Click Start | Settings | Control Panel.

2. In the Control Panel, double-click the ODBC icon. This brings up the ODBC Data Source Administrator.

NOTE

In Windows 2000, this icon has been moved to the Administrative Tools area and is called Data Sources (ODBC).

3. Click the System DSN tab to bring up the System DSN display, as shown in Figure 9-1.

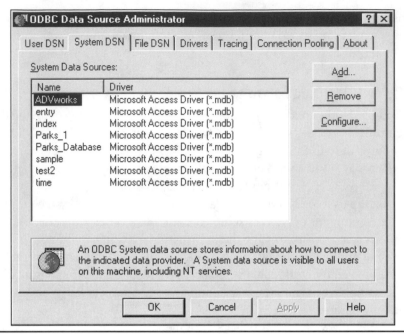

Figure 9-1   *The System DSN tab in the ODBC Data Source Administrator*

4. Click the Add button. This will bring up the Create New Data Source dialog box shown here:

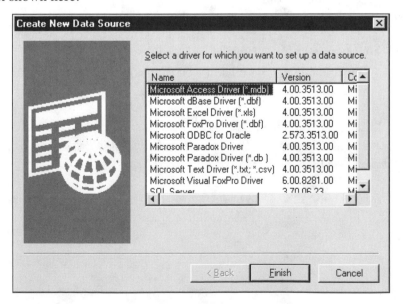

5. Select the Microsoft Access driver and click Finish. The ODBC Microsoft
   Access Setup dialog box, shown here, will open:

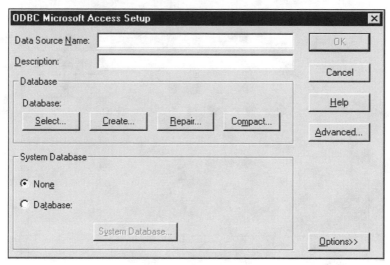

6. Enter a name and description for your DSN and click Select. You are
   given a standard Windows dialog box, allowing you to select the path for
   your database.

7. Select the path for your database and click OK.

8. Click OK once more to close the setup dialog box. You will see the source
   name you entered in the Administrator.

9. Click OK one more time to close the Administrator. Your DSN is now
   registered, and you can begin working with the database within FrontPage.

Working with the Database Web Settings

Within FrontPage, you have the ability to set up various data sources for use with
your Web. This is accomplished by adding databases within the Database tab of the
Web Settings dialog box shown in Figure 9-2.

   To add a database connection to your Web, follow these steps:

1. Open a Web in FrontPage.

2. Select Tools | Web Settings from the menu bar. This brings up the Web
   Settings dialog box.

3. Click the Database tab in the dialog box to open the database options shown
   in Figure 9-2.

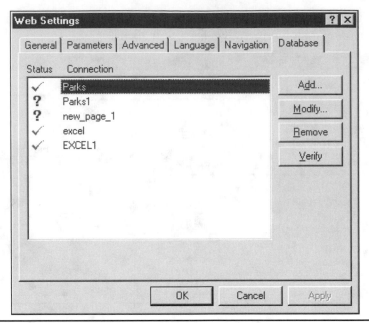

Figure 9-2 *The Database tab of the Web Settings dialog box*

4. Click the Add button to bring up the New Database Connection dialog box shown here:

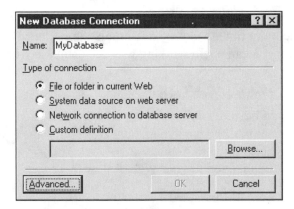

5. Type a meaningful name for your new database connection.

6. Select the location where your database resides and click the Browse button
to bring up the corresponding dialog box. Here, you have four options:

▶ **File or folder in current Web**   Selecting this option instructs FrontPage
to search for a database within the current Web. When you click the
Browse button, the Database Files In Current Web dialog box appears
(shown here), allowing you to select a database. Select the database you
want to use and click OK. Although this is the proper method within these
options to create a data connection for a database that will be stored in your
Web, FrontPage automates this task for you when importing a database.
See "Importing an Access Database Directly into a FrontPage Web,"
later in this chapter, for further details.

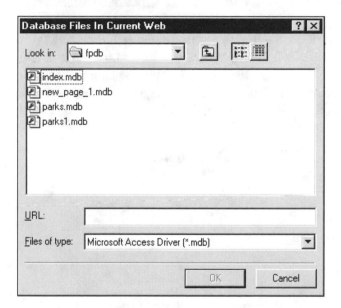

▶ **System data sources on Web server**   Selecting this option instructs
FrontPage to search for a database on the current Web server. When
you click the Browse button, the System Data Sources On Web
Server dialog box, shown next, appears, allowing you to select a
database that was previously set up on the server. Select the database
and click OK.

▶ **Network connection to database server**   Selecting this option instructs FrontPage to search for a database server on the network. When you click the Browse button, the Network Database Connection dialog box, shown here, appears, allowing you to select a database server from your network. Select the type of database, the server name, and the database name and then click OK.

▶ **Custom definition**   Selecting this option instructs FrontPage that you want to use a file DSN. In order to use this option, you must have already imported a file DSN definition file (*.dsn) into your Web. Although file DSNs may be used when accessing data sources from Web servers, you shouldn't use them for databases located within your Web. See "Importing an Access Database Directly into a FrontPage Web," later in this chapter, for more information.

7. Select the database you want to use and click OK. Your database name will now appear in the New Database Connection dialog box (shown earlier in step 4).

8. Click the Advanced button to bring up the Advanced Connection Properties dialog box, shown here:

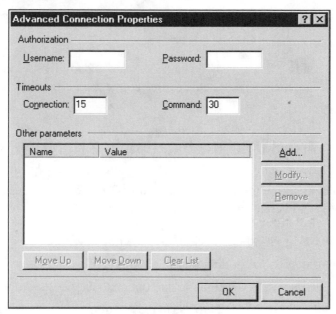

9. Enter a username and password that users will need to enter to access your database.

NOTE

These advanced options do not have to be set for you to add the new database connection.

10. Set your options under Timeouts. These options will instruct the system when to disconnect the database connection.

11. Add any other parameters you want for your database and click OK.

12. Click OK again to close the Database Connection dialog box. You will now see the Database tab of the Web Settings dialog box with your new database connection.

    You now want to verify the database connection you have just created. To do so, continue to the next step.

13. In the Database tab, select the database you have just created.

14. Click the Verify button. FrontPage will now check to ensure your database connection is working properly. If the connection is functioning properly, a check mark will appear next to your database once it is verified.

15. Click OK to close the Web Settings dialog box. Your database connection is now set.

If it did not already exist, a new file has now been added to your Web—the global.asa file—which contains all data source connection information for all your data connections.

Importing an Access Database Directly into a FrontPage Web

When working with Access databases, FrontPage greatly simplifies the task of creating a data connection through its Import utility. To add an Access database to a FrontPage Web (and create a data connection in the process), follow these steps:

1. Open an existing FrontPage Web or create a new one.

2. Make sure the Web's root directory is highlighted in the Folder List.

3. Click the File menu and select the Import option to display the Import dialog box.

4. Click the Add File button and browse to the location of your existing Access database. Select the file by double-clicking it, adding it to the list of files to import.

5. Click the Import dialog box's OK button to begin the process.

6. When FrontPage recognizes the file you are importing as an Access database, it automatically opens the Add Database Connection dialog box. Within this dialog box, you have the single option of naming your data connection. Although not required, you'll likely want to change the default, Database1, to a more meaningful name.

7. After making any desired changes to the data connection name, click the OK button to continue the process. FrontPage reports that it is recommended that you store your databases in a special folder named "fpdb" and asks you if you would like to import your database into that location. Unless you are an advanced user with a good understanding of data connections, you should agree by clicking the Yes button.

8. FrontPage then imports the selected database file into the /fpdb folder, creating it if necessary, and adds a global.asa file (or appends to it if this file already exists within the Web).

Using this method, you do not need to create a separate DSN, because FrontPage, in effect, creates a DSN-less connection, storing the connection information within global.asa.

FrontPage Data Connections: Behind the Scenes

When creating a data connection, FrontPage adds a hidden directory to the Web called _fpclass. To display this hidden directory and its contents, open the Web Settings dialog box from the Tools menu, click the Advanced tab, and check the Show Documents In Hidden Directories option. After you click OK, FrontPage informs you that you must reload the current Web in order to display the hidden content, and it prompts you to do so.

Once the content is displayed, you'll see that the _fpclass folder contains three text files. These files contain server-side scripting, used by the ASP server extensions to handle database functions, as follows:

▶ **fpdblib.inc**   Contains a library of database functions used by the other files.

▶ **fpdbrgn1.inc**   Contains the ASP functions that create the ADO data connection and properly format and submit queries and the iteration of records within the returned recordset.

▶ **fpdbrgn2.inc**   Contains the ASP functions used to complete the record iteration loop started by fpdbrgn1.inc. It also contains the code that closes the database connection when finished.

In addition to these three files, fpdbform.inc is also added to this directory the first time a Save to Database form handler is used. This file contains the ASP code used to implement this feature.

NOTE

Although these files can be manually edited, doing so goes beyond the scope of this book and should not be attempted without extensive knowledge of ADO and ASP.

About Data Access Pages

Data Access Pages take the old style of developing forms within Access for updating, viewing, and editing information and port them to the Web. This implementation allows you to create expansive database interfaces that work both within a browser and in conjunction with a database you have created in Access. This is a great feature that lets you quickly and easily create Web applications based on databases without the need for extensive programming and designing, and it all comes to you in native HTML format.

NOTE

Unfortunately, Access's Data Access Pages only work with Microsoft's IE 4.0 and above and therefore should normally only be used in intranet environments.

Data Access Pages can be created within Microsoft Access, or you can link them to an existing HTML document. This is where the integration of FrontPage and Access really shines. Through this integration, you can use Access to create an extensive form around your database, yet based on your layout needs within FrontPage, and then port that form to FrontPage, maintaining its functionality with the Access database. Although you can create a similar functionality using functions within FrontPage, this option gives you much more control and flexibility when creating your layout and integration. This type of interface gives you quite a bit in the way of functionality when developing your pages. The following list outlines the capabilities you have within Data Access Pages for creating live, interactive database Web pages:

▶ **Reporting** Allows you to display real-time reports right in your users' browsers. These reports allow for complete sorting and filtering to give users the information they need when they need it. This style of page is similar to a standard report you might see printed out for review, but it gives you the interactive features that just would not be available in print.

▶ **Data entry** Enables you to create interactive forms that connect directly to your database. This gives you and your users the ability to update and edit database information right from the browser window.

CAUTION

Office Web Components are subject to the Office 2000 licensing agreement and may not be redistributed. For this reason, never publish Office Web Components on the public Internet or make them available to other non-licensed users.

▶ **Data analysis** Gives you the ability to create interactive forms or charts that can be manipulated to analyze data from different viewpoints. Using this technique, you can add formulas, change layouts, and perform calculations for analyzing your data.

When you are working with a Data Access Page, you can develop your pages using four different methods, which are described here:

▶ **AutoPage**   Creates a Data Access Page based on a source database you choose on the system. Once you choose the database, AutoPage will create a page that contains all the fields found in your data source.

▶ **Data Access Wizard**   Creates your page by asking you specific questions in relation to the data source, the fields, and the layout you require for your page. The page is created for you based on the information you supply.

▶ **Converting an existing Web page**   Creates a Data Access Page from an existing HTML page. This allows you to create a page containing the layout and design elements you want in FrontPage and then have Access bring that page in and create the Data Access Page based on it.

▶ **Creating your own**   Gives you the ability to create a page directly in Access based on all your own specifications.

As you can see, Data Access Pages are a great feature of the integration of FrontPage and Access. Through the use of these pages, you have the ability to create truly interactive interfaces. For information on implementing Data Access Pages, see Chapter 10.

Summary

The information in this chapter should give you a good understanding of the basics associated with setting up a database system to work with your Web. It should also give you a core understanding of what is necessary to analyze and accomplish the tasks set out in the next chapter. You've learned about multitiered architecture, DSNs, data connections, and even how to add an Access database directly to a FrontPage Web.

Within this chapter you have looked at the underlying structure associated with incorporating a database system into your Webs. You should now have a basic understanding of SQL and ODBC, along with some background knowledge of ASP and ADO, which will be necessary when you're working with databases in Chapters 11 and 12.

As you continue through the next few chapters, you may want to refer back to the information in this chapter to help you with your understanding of the setup of your database.

CHAPTER 10

Adding Database Access
to Your Webs

IN THIS CHAPTER:

Create New Web Sites with Database Access

Add Database Access to Your Web Sites

Modify Pages with Database Interfaces

I n the past few years, databases have worked as the backbone of the new Internet economy, allowing developers to create dynamic Web sites chocked full of features such as commerce capabilities, user tracking, visitor preferences, and just about any other information deemed useful for buying and selling products and information. Although databases are not a necessity when it comes to developing a Web site, they can be a useful addition to any site.

In this chapter, we are going to take a look at how to create database-driven sites using FrontPage and Access. In my opinion, this version of FrontPage is leaps and bounds ahead of previous versions in integrating databases into webs. We now have the ability to develop truly interactive sites along with the ability to manage those sites through the use of Web-based interfaces. This chapter will give you a good understanding of how to implement these features in your Web and make FrontPage an even more powerful tool for your development needs.

Working with the Database Interface Wizard

With the release of FrontPage 2002, a new feature has been added to the program that makes creating database-augmented Web sites easier than ever. Microsoft has included the Database Interface Wizard, which allows you to create a new Web site complete with a built-in database, entry forms, display pages, and online editing capabilities. One of the great aspects of this new wizard is that you can create the basic framework of your database and then customize it to your needs as you develop, adding new pages, search capabilities, and other features.

To begin using the Database Interface Wizard, follow these steps:

1. Select File | New | Page or Web from the menu bar. This activates the New Page or Web pane on your screen.

2. Select Web Site Templates from the New from Template section of the pane. This brings up the Web Site Templates dialog box, shown in Figure 10-1.

3. Type the location where you want to create your Web site in the Specify the Location of the New Web text box.

4. Select Database Interface Wizard from the available templates and click OK to begin setting up your Web site.

   A dialog box will appear on your screen informing you that FrontPage is setting up your new Web site. Once the setup is complete, you will be presented with the Database Interface Wizard's first dialog box, shown here:

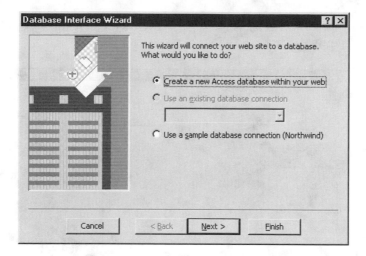

5. Select the type of connection you want for your database. For this example, I will assume that you are starting from scratch. You can have FrontPage create

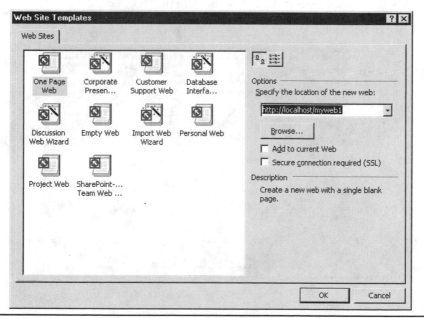

Figure 10-1   *The Web Site Templates dialog box, displaying available templates and options for Web site location*

a new database for you by leaving the default selection. Click Next to bring up the next step in the wizard, shown here:

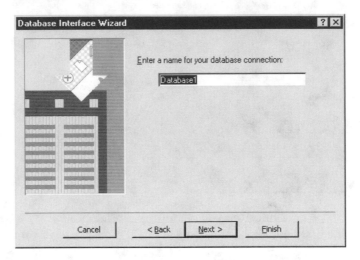

6. Type a name you want to associate with your new database. This name should have a meaning that is in line with the data that will be stored in the database. Click Next to bring up the next step of the wizard, shown here:

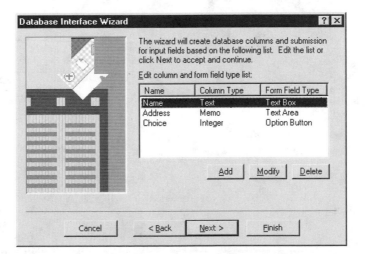

TIP

This next step in the process is where you can do a lot of customization to create all the elements you want for your forms. If you don't enter everything you want in this step, don't worry—you can always come back and make additions and modifications, which I'll show you in later steps.

7. In this step, we want to determine the columns and field types that will appear in our database and on our resulting Web pages. You can see that FrontPage already has examples in the dialog box you can use, but, for the purpose of this example, we'll go ahead and make a modification so that you can see how this works.

8. Click the Add button. You are now presented with a dialog box that allows you to add a new column to your database, as shown here:

When adding a new column, you have the following fields you need to complete in the dialog box:

▶ **Column name**   The name that will be assigned to the new column (field) you are creating in the database.

▶ **Column type**   The type of column you will be creating in the database. For example, if this column is going to contain text, you will want to select Text from the drop-down menu.

▶ **Form field input type**   The type of input field you want displayed on your Web page. Here, you can select from Text Box, Drop-Down Box, and Option Box. If you select Drop-Down Box or Option Box, you are then presented with the Number of Options box, which allows you to specify the number of options that will be available for those types of boxes on your Web page.

9. Click OK when you are finished adding your new column. You can repeat step 8 any number of times to add more columns to the database.

10. We now want to modify an item in the list of available columns. To do so, click Modify. You will see that you are presented with the same dialog box used for adding new columns. Make your modifications and click OK.

11. Click Next to move to the next step. The wizard now presents you with a dialog box showing that it is creating and connecting to your new database. Once this is complete, you are asked to click Next again.

12. You are now asked to specify the pages you want displayed in your new Web site that will work in conjunction with the database you have just created, as shown here:

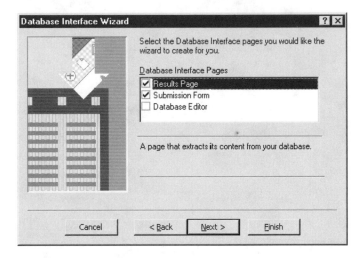

Within this dialog box, you are given three options for pages to display on the Web site:

▶ **Results Page**   The Results page will display all the contents of your current database on a page.

▶ **Submission Form**   The Submission form allows your users to submit information to your database from a Web page.

▶ **Database Editor**   The Database Editor allows you to have a set of pages created so that you can edit entries in the database from a Web browser.

13. For this example, we will select all three page options. Click Next.

14. You are now presented with the next step in the wizard, where you are asked to enter a username and password to protect the Database Editor, as shown here:

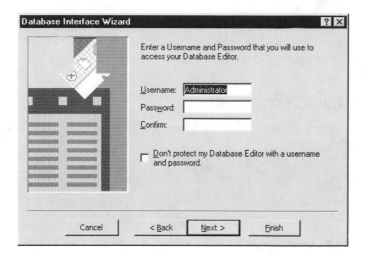

NOTE

*If you do not request the wizard to create a Database Editor, this step of the wizard will
be skipped.*

You have the choice of entering a username and password or checking that you
do not require the editor to be password protected. I recommend that you always
password-protect any type of editing capability for your database.

15. Click Next. You are now presented with a confirmation dialog showing the pages
the wizard will create, along with the location where these pages will be stored.
All that is left to do is to click Finish to have the wizard complete your setup.

Once the wizard has completed the setup of your new Web site, you will see
several pages open in the editor. From here, you can make modifications to any
section by right-clicking it and selecting its respective properties. If you want to
make modifications to the database result areas that are found in your new Web,
see the following sections of this chapter.

Working with the Database Results

FrontPage 2002 makes incorporating information directly from a database a simple
process through the use of the Database Results Wizard. This wizard takes you through
all the steps of setting up the fields on your page that will connect with the database.

Furthermore, this wizard asks you the questions necessary for the layout of your database fields on the page. This section takes a look at the wizard and gives you some inside tips for using it to create custom pages.

Using the Database Results Wizard

To incorporate database information into your page using the Database Results Wizard, follow these steps:

1. Create or open a Web in FrontPage.

2. Position your cursor where you want the database information to appear on your page.

3. Select Insert | Database | Results from the menu bar. This brings up the first screen of the Database Results Wizard, shown here:

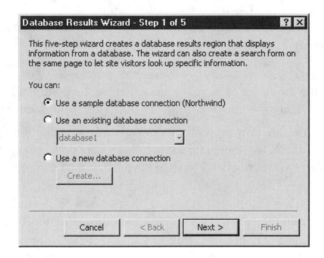

You will begin setting up the database connection for your page in this screen. As you can see, the screen contains three options for connecting to a database:

▶ **Use a sample database connection (Northwind)**   Allows you to connect to a sample database that comes with FrontPage. Using this database will give you a chance to get to know how the database setup works, but this database will not be used for a real Web implementation.

▶ **Use an existing database connection**   Allows you to connect to a
database that is already associated with the current Web. If there is
a database associated with the current Web, it will display in the
drop-down menu associated with this option.

▶ **Use a new database connection**   Allows you to create a new connection
to a database. This is accomplished by selecting the option and clicking
the Create button. Once you click the Create button, the Web Settings –
Database dialog box appears, allowing you to create a new connection.
For more information on creating new database connections, see
"Working with the Database Web Settings" in Chapter 9.

4. Select the option you want and click Next. For the purposes of this example,
we will be working with the sample Northwind database.

You are now presented with the next step in the wizard, which asks you to
select a source for your records or to enter a custom query for obtaining
records, as shown here:

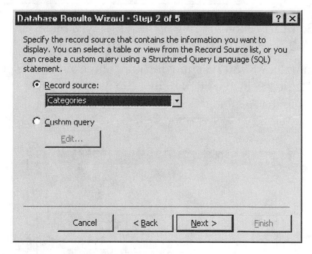

Because we are working with the sample database, we will not be
entering a custom query. For information on entering custom queries,
see "Entering Custom Queries in the Database Results Wizard," later
in this chapter.

5. Select Customers from the drop-down list and click Next. You are now presented with the next step of the wizard, shown here:

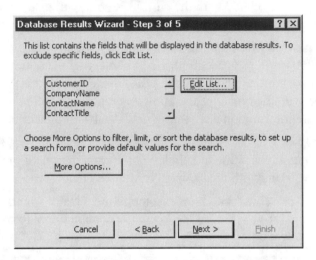

6. Click the Edit List button to bring up the Displayed Fields dialog box, shown in Figure 10-2.

7. For this example, we will be removing one field from the Displayed Fields list. Select the Region field and click Remove. You will see that the Region field now appears in the Available fields area of the dialog box.

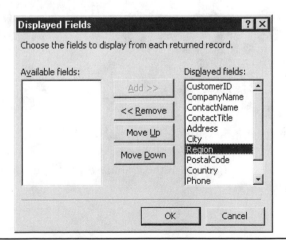

Figure 10-2   *The Displayed Fields dialog box, used to add and remove fields from a results database*

8. Click OK to close the dialog box. Now, if you scroll through the list of fields, you will see that Region no longer appears.

NOTE

Clicking More Options brings up the More Options dialog box. For information on these advanced options, see "Setting the Advanced Options in the Database Results Wizard," later in this chapter.

9. Click Next to move to the next step in the wizard. In this step, we will select the formatting options that control how our results will appear on the page.

When working in this step of the wizard, you have the option of selecting your results to be displayed in either a table or a list format. Depending on which format you choose, you will be presented with screen options for a table, a simple list, or a drop-down list.

If you select Table – One Record Per Row, you will be presented with the following options for your display layout:

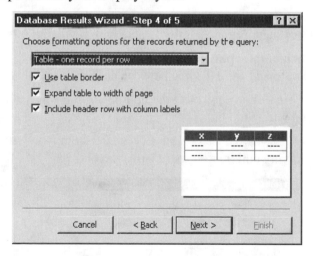

▶ **Use table border**   Checking this box instructs the wizard to place a border around your table when displayed within your page

▶ **Expand table to width of page**   Checking this box instructs the wizard to set the table width to 100 percent of the page in which you are displaying your results

▶ **Include header row with column labels**   Checking this box instructs the wizard to include a header row in your table that will display labels for each of the columns within the table

If you select List – One Field Per Item, you will be presented with the following options for your display layout:

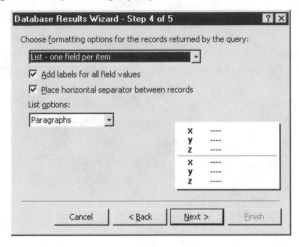

▶ **Add labels for all field values**   Checking this box instructs the wizard to add a label identifying each field value within your results.

▶ **Place horizontal separator between records**   Checking this box instructs the wizard to add an <HR> tag between each result displayed on the page.

▶ **List options**   You can select the options for the way your data is displayed within the list.

If you select Drop-Down List – One Record Per Item, you will be presented with the following options for your display layout:

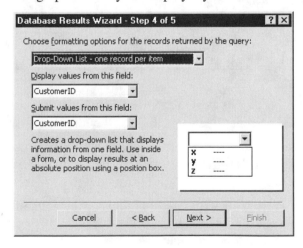

▶ **Display values from this field**   Allows you to select the field you want to display in a drop-down list on your page from the list of display fields you previously selected. When your page is viewed, this list will contain the selected field's content for each record in the recordset you previously chose to display.

▶ **Submit values from this field**   Allows you to select a field, the contents of which will be linked to the user-selected Display field value. For instance, you might choose to have the user select a company name from the Display list and then choose to submit a CompanyID field value to the database instead. This option is particularly useful when you're working with relational databases in which the CompanyID field would constitute a foreign key.

10. For this example, select Table – One Record Per Row and check all three options. Click Next.

   We now want to decide how the records are displayed. The next step in the wizard, shown here, allows you either to display all your records in a single table or to group them. If you group your tables, the system will add navigation buttons that allow users to move through the groups.

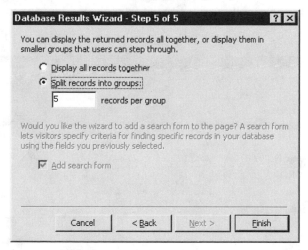

11. Select Split Records into Groups, enter **5** in the Records Per Group field, and click Finish. This option's true significance may not be apparent at first glance, but you'll soon learn that being able to limit the number of records displayed in each screen will greatly improve performance.

The wizard will now create a layout based on the options you have set. Once the wizard has completed the operation, it will display the results in your page, as shown in Figure 10-3.

CAUTION

You will need to save your script as an ASP (Active Server Page) file for the database connectivity to function properly.

12. Once the results information is inserted, select File | Save As from the menu bar to save your file with an .asp extension.

Once you have saved your database, you will want to test it in your browser to ensure that all aspects work correctly. To do so, open the page in your browser using a Web address. You will see the first five records displayed, and a number of arrow buttons. These buttons allow you to move through the records in the database, displaying a set of five records for each page.

Entering Custom Queries in the Database Results Wizard

Along with setting basic parameters in the Database Results Wizard, you can also insert custom SQL query statements into the wizard that override the default query

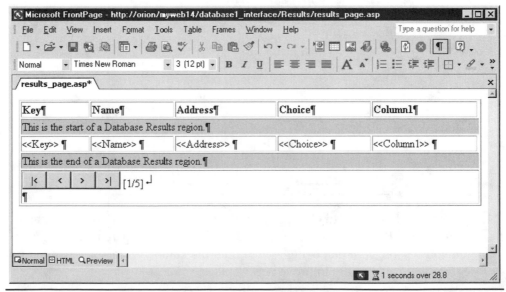

Figure 10-3   *An example of database results inserted via the Database Results Wizard*

settings. This capability is presented to you in step 2 of the Database Results Wizard by selecting the Custom Query radio button and clicking Edit. When you click Edit, you are presented with the Custom Query dialog box, shown in Figure 10-4.

From the Custom Query dialog box, you can simply type custom queries into the available text area, or you can work with options in the dialog box that make inserting statements a bit easier. These options are the Insert Parameter capability and the Paste from Clipboard capability, which are described here:

▶ **Insert Parameter**   Clicking this button brings up the Insert Form Field Parameter dialog box, where you can enter the name of a form field. When you click OK, the form field will be inserted into the text area with the proper formatting already set.

▶ **Paste from Clipboard**   Clicking this button pastes information from your Windows clipboard. This is useful if you have a query saved in another file or application because you can simply copy that query statement from the other file or application and past it here.

Once you have inserted your query into the text field, you can test the query to ensure it will function properly by clicking the Verify Query button. Clicking this

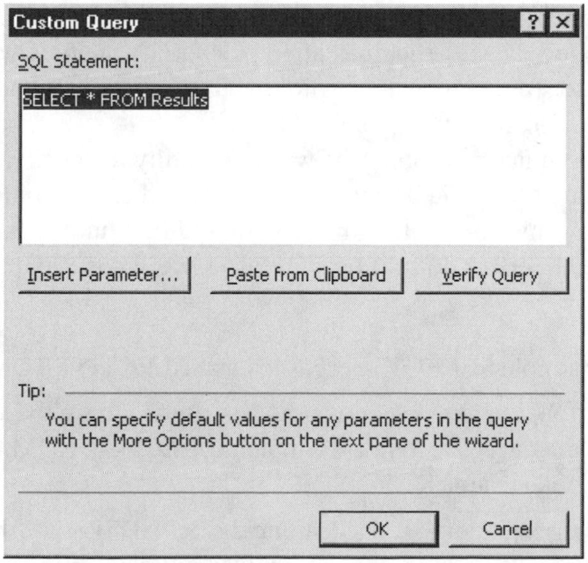

Figure 10-4   *The Custom Query dialog box appears when you click Edit in step 2 of the Database Results Wizard.*

button will cause the system to run the statement against the database and verify the syntax. If the syntax is incorrect, you will be informed with an error message. You can determine what the problem is by clicking the Details button in your error dialog box.

Custom Query Limitations and Parameterized Queries

Although SQL is quite capable of adding new information to your database and performing updates on existing data, the Database Results Wizard places some significant limitations on your queries. Because its sole purpose is to return and display data, you may only use SELECT queries (queries that begin with the SELECT statement). Custom queries, on the other hand, can take full advantage of the powerful SQL engine and can contain multiple joins, as in the following example, or even more advanced options such as unions:

```
SELECT Suppliers.CompanyName, Products.ProductName, Categories.CategoryName
FROM Categories
RIGHT JOIN
(Suppliers LEFT JOIN Products ON Suppliers.SupplierID = Products.SupplierID)
ON Categories.CategoryID = Products.CategoryID
ORDER BY Suppliers.CompanyName, Products.ProductName
```

You may also save your custom query within your data source as a stored procedure (query or view) and still access it as an existing record source. Queries stored in this manner are not only more secure, but they also may offer increased performance because database engines often precompile them. If you don't have the ability to create stored procedures within your database and you need to use parameterized queries, follow the steps detailed next.

Entering a custom query disables the wizard's ability to specify criteria and automatically create search fields based on the selected criteria fields. You can still manually enter this information, but you should first understand the syntax of a parameterized query to do so. For this reason, we'll cover the basics of this syntax now:

1. Start with a simple SELECT query, such as SELECT * FROM Customers.

2. In a standard SQL query, you might add a criteria clause to limit the recordset returned by the query, as in this example: SELECT * FROM Customers WHERE (ContactName = "Joe Smith").

   In a parameterized query, you substitute the actual criteria ("Joe Smith") for a parameter that tells the query to use another source of information. By doing so, you create a dynamic query that can be reused in a variety of situations, without needing to manually re-create it.

3. When you're working with an Access database, a parameter is specified in the following form: '::*FieldName*::', where *FieldName* represents the name of an HTML form field. Applying this to our sample query, we end up with SELECT * FROM Customers WHERE (ContactName = '::ContactName::').

4. Optionally, multiple criteria may be used within a single query to further limit or expand the resultant recordset. For example, the query SELECT * FROM Customers WHERE (ContactName LIKE '::ContactName::' OR CompanyName LIKE '::CompanyName::') allows the user to enter a portion of a contact name or company name to locate a record. By using the LIKE operator, we enable sliding searches: Users may enter a percent sign (%) or other wildcard character at the beginning or end of their search text to retrieve records only partially matching the specified text.

By entering a parameterized custom query in this manner, the Database Results Wizard knows that you want to use these parameters as search fields, and it will even create a search form for you if you enable that option in step 5 of the wizard. We'll cover search forms in more detail a little later in this chapter. These parameters may also be filled when the page is requested. We'll cover that topic in detail in Chapter 11.

Adding and Removing Displayed Fields in the Database Results Wizard

When working in the Database Results Wizard, you will see that the fields within your table or form are linked to matching fields in your database. But how do you handle adding new display fields to an existing page created with the Database Results Wizard or removing existing display fields? Although it is possible to manually edit the actual source code of your Active Server Page, the Database Results Wizard makes your life much easier by allowing you to reenter the wizard and update existing content. In most cases, you can also fix pages that you've broken by editing that code with the wizard as well. The Database Results Wizard makes it rather easy for you to add and remove links between your form fields and your database columns. All you have to do is follow the steps shown here:

1. Right-click over the Database Results region of your page, select Database Results Properties from the pop-up menu, and proceed to step 3 of the wizard. Of course, if you don't already have a Database Results region, you may follow steps 1 through 6 in "Using the Database Results Wizard," earlier in this chapter.

2. Click the Edit List button in step 3 (the "displayed fields" step) of the wizard. This brings up the Displayed Fields dialog box, shown previously in Figure 10-2.

3. Select the field(s) you want to add or remove and then simply click the Add or Remove button within the dialog box. Depending on the button you choose, you will see the field appearing in either the Available fields (Remove) area or the Displayed fields (Add) area.

4. Click OK when you have completed adding or removing your fields.

You now continue through the process of the Database Results Wizard and update your new or existing Database Results region upon completion. Once again, this may be done at any time while you're editing the page, so mistakes discovered in later testing are easily corrected.

Setting the Advanced Options in the Database Results Wizard

One of the great things about the Database Results Wizard is the ability to customize the way information is retrieved from the database. With the wizard, you can set ordering properties for your retrieved information, along with criteria for how the data is retrieved. The latter is discussed in depth in "Hands On: Integrating a Searchable Database."

When working with the advanced options, you have the following settings available to you:

▶ **Criteria**   Allows you to specify SQL statements that create queries based on specific criteria. As previously discussed, these criteria may be hard-coded or entered as parameters.

▶ **Ordering**   Allows you to set the order in which the records are returned.

▶ **Defaults**   Allows you to set default values for queries. This option only becomes available when you have specified criteria for querying the database.

▶ **Limit number of returned records to**   Allows you to specify the number of records that will be returned for a specific query.

▶ **Display Message**   Allows you to specify a message that will appear if no matching records are found in the database.

Specifying Criteria in the Database Results Wizard

The wizard gives you the ability to specify certain criteria for querying the database. To specify criteria in this manner, you must select an existing record source. If you choose to enter a custom query, you must enter your criteria within that query because the wizard's Criteria option will be disabled. Using the wizard to specify criteria for an existing record source is accomplished by following these steps:

1. Follow steps 1 through 8 in "Using the Database Results Wizard," earlier in this chapter.

2. Click the More Options button to bring up the More Options dialog box, shown in Figure 10-5.

3. Click Criteria to bring up the Criteria dialog box, shown here:

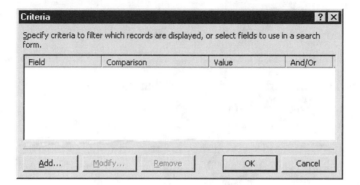

NOTE

If the Criteria button is disabled, you probably selected Custom Query earlier. To use the wizard's Criteria option, you must use an existing record source.

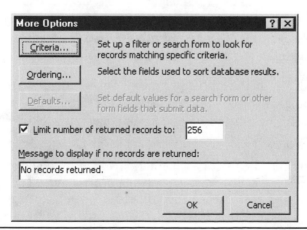

Figure 10-5   *The More Options dialog box, used for setting up advanced SQL statements*

4. Click Add to bring up the Add Criteria dialog box, shown here:

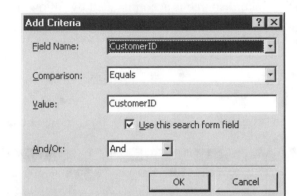

5. Select a field name from your database that you want to set criteria for.

6. Select a comparison option from the drop-down list. To make things simpler, the actual SQL operators are displayed in plain English within this list.

7. Specify the Value setting. You may either hard-code a value here or enter the name of a database/form field. You alert the wizard to the fact that a value is actually a field name in the following option.

8. If you entered a field name instead of an actual value in step 7, checking the Use This Search Form Field box instructs the wizard of this fact.

CAUTION

Be careful when setting this option. Checking the box without entering an actual form field will cause the existing form field to be renamed. Not checking the box when entering a form field name will cause the field name to be treated as the actual criteria text being filtered on.

9. Select And/Or from the drop-down menu. This setting specifies how this criteria setting will react with the other criteria settings in your query. If you only set a single criteria clause in your query, this setting is ignored.

10. Click OK. You will now see your criteria in the Criteria dialog box.

11. Repeat steps 4 through 9 for each criterion you want to add to your query options. Once you have completed all your criteria, click OK to continue.

NOTE

Although the Database Results Wizard does not allow nested logic in its criteria setup, you may later edit the actual query text within the page's source.

Setting the Ordering in the Database Results Wizard

If you have a large database that contains many entries, you may want to set up an ordering process that will determine how your records will be displayed. This can be especially useful if you have a database that is updated via forms. Records are simply appended wherever users enter data and then displayed based on the ordering you have determined in the wizard.

To set the ordering process, follow these steps:

1. Follow steps 1 through 8 in "Using the Database Results Wizard," earlier in this chapter.

2. Click the More Options button to bring up the More Options dialog box, shown previously in Figure 10-5.

3. Click Ordering to bring up the Ordering dialog box, shown here:

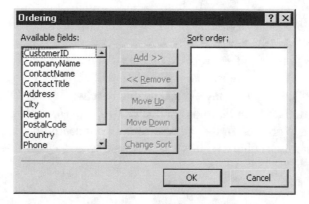

4. Select the fields you want your ordering based on and then click Add to move them into the Sort Order field. When setting up your ordering, you can use the following buttons to configure your sort order:

    ▶ **Add**   Select from the available fields and click this button to add the selected fields to your sort order.

    ▶ **Remove**   Select from the sort order fields and click this button to remove the selected fields from your sort order.

    ▶ **Move Up**   Select a single field in the sort order and click this button to move the field up in the order.

    ▶ **Move Down**   Select a single field in the sort order and click this button to move the field down in the order.

▶ **Change Sort**   Select a field in the sort order and click this button to change the way this column is sorted. An up arrow instructs the system to sort on the field in ascending order (A to Z), whereas a down arrow instructs the system to sort on the field in descending order (Z to A).

5. Click OK when you have completed setting up your ordering.

Hands On: Integrating a Searchable Database

Displaying data from a database is a great way of creating dynamic sites that keep information fresh and up-to-date. However, displaying this information limits the user's interaction with the site. For this reason, I want to show you how to take database information and set it up so that your users can retrieve the data that is relevant to them. This can be accomplished by creating a database interface that allows individuals to query the database rather than having the data just displayed for them onscreen.

Follow the steps in this exercise to create a database that allows users to pull information on demand. For our example, we will be working with the parks section of the Dogs by the Bay Web. The database we are working with is called parks.mdb and can be found on the CD-ROM. We will be creating two pages within a Web. The first page will contain our search form, and the second page will contain our query results.

NOTE

If you are using the database found on the CD-ROM, you will need to import it to your Web. When you import the database file, FrontPage will ask you to set up a new database connection. All you need to do is enter a name for the connection and click OK. FrontPage will do the rest.

1. Create a page in your Web titled parks.asp. This page will contain our search form used to query the database.

2. Select Insert | Database | Results from the menu bar. This brings up the Database Results Wizard discussed earlier in this chapter (see "Using the Database Results Wizard").

3. Move through the first two screens of the wizard, selecting your data source and your record source. For our example, choose the parks database for the connection and the Parks record source.

4. Once you reach the third screen, click More Options. This brings up the now-familiar More Options dialog box, shown earlier in Figure 10-5.

5. Click Criteria to bring up the Criteria dialog box. Then click Add to bring up the Add Criteria dialog box.

6. Select ParkName from the Field Name drop-down box. This is the database column that contains our park names.

7. Select Contains from the Comparison drop-down box. This instructs the query to look for any park name containing the characters the user types into the search box using the LIKE operator within the WHERE clause and also instructs the query to insert percent signs (%) on either side of the parameter (%::*FieldName*::%) to indicate a bidirectional sliding search.

8. Leave the rest of the items in this dialog at their defaults and click OK. Your Add Criteria dialog box should look like the one shown here:

9. Click OK twice. Then finish setting your wizard options the way you want them until you reach the last screen.

10. On the last screen, check Add Search Form. This causes the wizard to create a search form for you using the ParkName field as the search text field.

11. Click Finish to create the form on your page.

When you have finished with the wizard, your page will contain a form with a single text box, along with the database results. At this point, we are almost done creating our search page. You could simply save this page and be done with it, but we want to add some esthetics to our site by having the search box appear on a page separate from the results.

What we want to do now is remove the results from this page so we can display them somewhere else, but first we need to alter our form so that it will point to the proper page. To finish creating the initial search page, continue with the next steps.

12. Click within the form border and then right-click.

13. Select Form Properties from the pop-up menu and click Options in the Form Properties dialog box. This brings up the Options for Custom Form Handler dialog box, shown here:

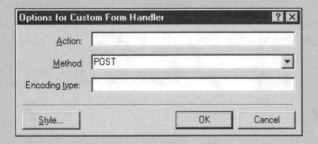

14. In the Action field, type **results.asp** and click OK twice to return to the document.

NOTE

Results.asp is the name of the file our database results will appear in.

15. Switch to HTML view and find the text that begins with the following:
    <form BOTID="0" METHOD="POST" ACTION="results.asp">
    This is the beginning of our search form, and it should appear right under the page's <BODY> tag.

16. Highlight all the text starting with the <form> tag and ending with the </form> tag, several lines below.

17. Cut this text from your page (don't just delete it) and switch back to the Normal view. Your page should now contain only the data display region created by the Database Results Wizard.

18. Save this page to your Web as results.asp.

NOTE

You must save your database-driven files with .asp extensions for them to work properly because they make use of Active Server Page scripting.

You now have your database information display page created. At this point, you should still have a search form stored on the clipboard from when you cut it earlier in step 17. We now want to make use of this information to create our search page. To accomplish this, we will create a new page and simply paste in the search form contained in the clipboard (memory). To finish creating your search page, continue with the next steps.

19. Create a new page and switch to the HTML view.

20. Locate the <body> tag and paste the previously cut search form code below it, within the body area of the page.

21. Switch back to the normal view.

22. Save this page with the name dbsearch.asp.

That completes all the steps necessary to create a searchable database within your Web. To see your query in action, preview your Web in Explorer.

Obviously, you can extend this concept to incorporate other query options, but this should give you the basics you need to create your query setups.

Adding New Column Fields to Your Results Database

Once you have created a database-driven page with the Database Results Wizard, you may find that you want to add new fields to your page—possibly to include information that was not available in your database when you first created the layout, or for some other reason. FrontPage makes adding columns to your layout a rather simple task. To add new fields, follow these steps:

1. Position your cursor within the database results region where you want to insert your new field.

2. Select Insert | Database | Column Value from the menu bar. This brings up the Database Column Value dialog box.

3. Select the field you want to add to your results from the drop-down list and click OK.

FrontPage now inserts the column value into your page.

NOTE

If your desired field does not appear in the list, you will have to reenter the Database Results Wizard and adjust your query or record source settings, along with your display field list, to include the additional column field.

Hands On: Incorporating Hyperlinks into Your Results

Say you have a database in which you want to display basic information and then let users link to detailed information about the records shown on the page. This functionality is important if you are working with a database that contains a good deal of information about specific topics, because displaying all the information on a single page would make the page very difficult to read. Using this technique, users can simply scan through titles and select the one that suits their needs.

This example takes a look at incorporating a results database containing a list of parks, with each park connecting to detailed information about the other parks in the database. For this to work, we need to create two database results pages. The first page will contain our list of parks, and the second will contain the detailed information about the parks that will be connected via a hyperlink on the first page. For this example, we will be working with the database parks.mdb on the CD-ROM.

1. Follow steps 1 through 5 in "Using the Database Results Wizard."

2. In step 3 of the wizard, click the More Options button to bring up the More Options dialog box, shown previously in Figure 10-5.

3. Click Edit List to bring up the Displayed Fields dialog box, shown previously in Figure 10-2. For this page, we want to display the detailed information about our parks. Ensure that the following fields appear in the Displayed Fields area of the dialog box if you are working with the parks example:

   ParkName
   Location
   City
   PhoneNumber
   Comments

4. Click OK to close the dialog box and then click Criteria to bring up the Criteria dialog box.

5. Click Add to bring up the Add Criteria dialog box and then select the criteria you want for your display results. For our database, we want to specify the following criteria:

Field Name	ParkName
Comparison	Equals
Value	ParkName
Use this search form field	(Checked)

This instructs the Database Results Wizard only to display parks that match the query entered based on the values found in the ParkName column of our database.

6. Click OK three times to return to the wizard.

7. Click Next and specify that you want the results displayed in a list format.

8. Click Next again to move to the final screen in the wizard.

In this step, we want to specify that the results are to be displayed together, but, more importantly, we want to specify that no form is generated on this page. This is because we will be creating a hyperlink that will perform our query for us.

9. Be sure the check box titled Add Search Form is unchecked and then click Finish.

Your detailed results page is now ready for use. Save the page with the name park_detail.asp and move on to the next steps to create the front-end interface that we will use to display our detailed results.

Now that we have created our detailed page, we want to create a front-end page that will display a list of parks based on a query entered into a form. This is the main search page of our interface. To develop it, follow the remaining steps.

10. Create another page within your Web.

11. Select Insert | Database | Results to begin the Database Results Wizard.

12. Select the Parks data connection and click Next.

13. Select the Parks record source and click Next.

14. We now want to determine which fields will be displayed in our initial results. For this example, select the following from the Displayed Fields dialog box:

    ParkName
    Location
    PhoneNumber

    These are the basic fields associated with our parks.

15. Click OK to close the Displayed Fields dialog box and then click Next to move on in the wizard.

16. For our formatting, we want to display the information as a list with line breaks. Make those selections and click Next.

17. Be sure that Display All Records Together is selected. Click Finish to insert your database region.

    We are going to adjust our formatting to display the park name, with the city directly below it and in italics. To do this, simply position your cursor after the ParkName field and press SHIFT-ENTER on your keyboard. Then select the City field and click the Italic icon on your Formatting toolbar. When you have finished, your page should look like the one shown here:

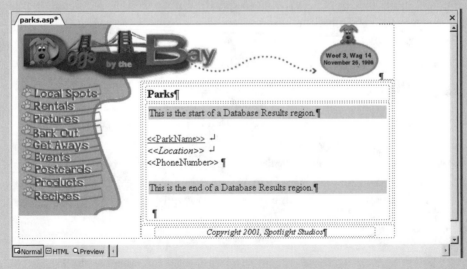

18. Save your page with the filename park_links.asp.

We have now completed the insertion of our two results regions, but we still have to link the two together. To do so, continue with the following steps.

19. In the parks.asp page you have just created, highlight the field name ParkName by clicking on it once.

20. Select Insert | Hyperlink from the menu bar. This brings up the Edit Hyperlink dialog box.

21. Type **park_details.asp** in the URL field of the dialog box.

22. Click Parameters to bring up the Hyperlink Parameters dialog box, shown here:

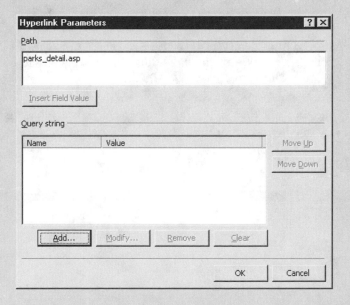

You will see that the URL you have just entered appears in the Path are a of the dialog box. Now we need to add the VBScript that will perform a specific query on our database so that only the information relating to the selected park displays on the details page.

23. Click Add to bring up the Add Parameter dialog box.

24. In the Name field, type **ParkName**. This tells the system that we will be looking at the ParkName column in our database.

25. In the Value field, type the following script and click OK:

```
<% If Not IsEmpty(fp_rs) And Not (fp_rs Is Nothing) Then Response.Write
CStr(fp_rs("ParkName")) %>
```

This script ensures that we have a valid park name before we send it to the park_details.asp page. If a record in our parks table had an empty or null ParkName field, an error would be generated were it not for this code.

NOTE

You may have noticed that we're using VBScript here. Fear not—this script will actually be processed on the server. For this reason, we're not concerned with browser compatibility with VBScript.

26. Click OK twice more to insert your new hyperlink in the page.

You have now completed all the necessary steps. Save your page and test it in your browser. When you view the page titled parks.asp, it should look like the one shown next. This is the page that contains our park names, along with the cities the parks are in. As you can see from the figure, each park is now a hyperlink. When you click the hyperlink, the park_details.asp page is called, and the query you entered earlier in the hyperlink parameters is passed to the results. Because of this, only the record matching that of the park name in the hyperlink is displayed.

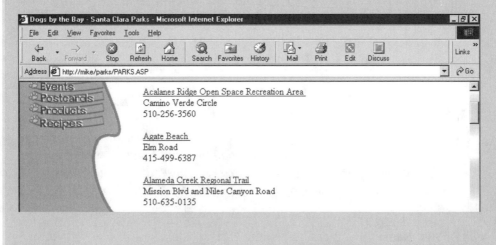

When working with the Database Results Wizard, all you have to do is make selections and answer questions to connect your page to a database. The wizard takes care of all the other aspects of creating the page. As a developer, though, it is always a good idea to know what the program is doing, in case you need to make some adjustments to get it to work just as you want it to. And even if you lay it out perfectly through the use of the wizard, it is still good to know what is going on, if only for the purposes of knowing how your pages are being created. Here, I will show you the basics of what the wizard does to create the database results on your pages when using the wizard.

NOTE

For the purposes of our discussion, I will assume you have inserted database results using the steps shown earlier in this chapter.

TIP

You can view all this information by selecting the HTML view.

When you click the Finish button within the Database Results Wizard, it creates an Active Server Page prototype and performs the following steps within your page:

1. The wizard creates a table with column headings (if selected) within the <thead> section of the table. To edit the column headings, either do so within the normal page editor view or within the <thead> tag of the HTML itself.

2. It enters the base wizard information within the <!--webbot bot="DatabaseRegionStart" tag. The attributes within this tag detail information that the server will use to gather and display the database information you have selected. Additionally, this information is used by FrontPage to make the Database Results Wizard reentrant. This means that after you've completed the wizard, you may later reenter it and alter your choices without having to start from scratch.

3. It inserts a small amount of server-side script within the <% and %> tags. This script doesn't perform any actions on its own, but it is used to set variable values that will be used by the server to build the returned page.

4. It fills out the table columns, each with its own <!--webbot bot="DatabaseResultColumn" tags. Similar in function to the DatabaseRegionStart WebBot, the DatabaseResultColumn WebBot is

used to store information that will be used by the server-based bot to populate each column with the correct record and field information.

5. If you have chosen to include search fields within your page, the search form is inserted at the top of the page. Looking at its code, you'll see that a search field is defined by a <%=Request(*database field name*)%> tag. When the user enters text into a search field and submits it back to your ASP, this information tells the server which field you have chosen to search on. This database field name corresponds to the s-criteria argument of the DatabaseRegionStart WebBot.

6. When the server receives a request for your page, two sets of Server Extensions are used to process the page. Because the page has an .asp extension, the server's ASP Extensions work on the page, looking for server-side scripts to process. Additionally, the FrontPage Extensions are used to handle the WebBots embedded in the page. The WebBots then create the appropriate server-side scripting and access additional static scripts contained within the .inc files of the hidden fpclass directory within your Web site. This differs from using straight ASP code, where you would normally do the work of the WebBot.

Sending Form Results to a Database

Up to this point, we've worked with displaying the data within Web pages created in FrontPage. However, with FrontPage 2002, you can take the results of a form you have created and have those results sent directly to a database. This capability is key to developing dynamic sites that make use of today's technology. Once you have sent your form results to a database, you can do any number of things with those results.

In my time as a developer, I have found that this type of interaction is one of the best ways of obtaining and using information from Web sites. Using database-capable forms allows you to create interactive functionality that gives the user real-time access to information. One example of this is using the information in a form to display the results of a survey or quiz—this gives viewers instant gratification because they can see their input right away. This type of interaction with your users can add that extra zing to your webs that keeps people coming back.

On a business level, this capability is equally useful. By sending information directly to a database, you can obtain data from your visitors and use many of the database's capabilities to sort and process that data.

To send your form information directly to a database, follow these steps:

1. Create or open a page in your Web.

2. Create a form on the page.

3. Position your cursor within the form and right-click.

4. Select Form Properties from the pop-up menu. This brings up the Form Properties dialog box, shown in Figure 10-6.

5. Click the Send to Database radio button.

6. Click the Options button. This brings up the Options for Saving Results to Database dialog box, shown in Figure 10-7.

   You will notice that this dialog box contains three tabs. Each of these tabs affects the way your information is sent to and saved within the database. As we proceed through these steps, we will take a look at each of the tabs and the settings that are associated with them.

   Our first step in sending our results to a database is to find a database to connect to that will house our information.

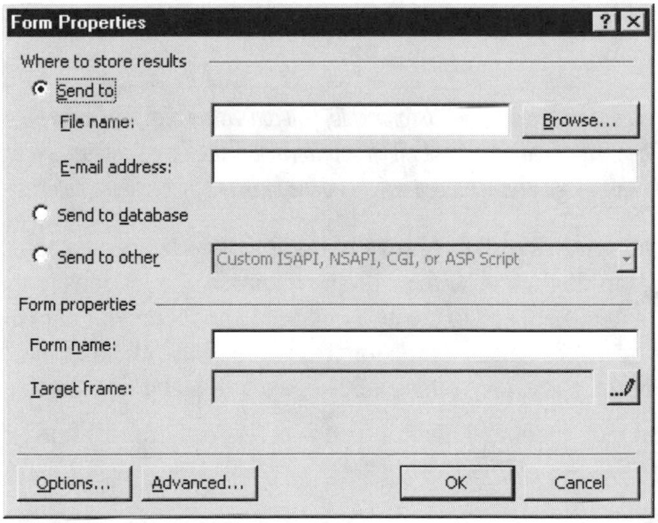

Figure 10-6   *The Form Properties dialog box*

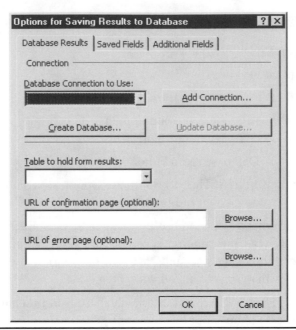

Figure 10-7   *The Database Results tab in the Options for Saving Results to Database dialog box*

TIP

If you do not have a database to connect to, you can simply click the Create Database button, and FrontPage will create a database within your current Web. The database will contain columns for each of the fields within your form and will set up the form to connect to the database automatically.

7. In the Database Results tab, shown in Figure 10-7, select a database connection from the drop-down box. If there are no database connections in the drop-down box, you will either need to create a database connection by clicking the Create Database button or add a connection to a database by clicking the Add Connection button. For the purposes of this exercise, we will add a new database connection.

8. Click Add Connection. This brings up the Web Settings dialog box shown in Figure 10-8.

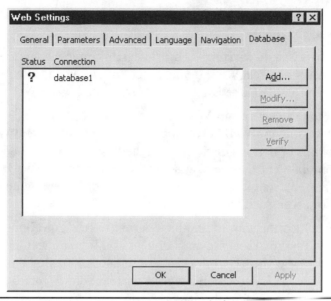

Figure 10-8   *The Database tab of the Web Settings dialog box*

9. Click the Add button to bring up the New Database Connection dialog box, shown here:

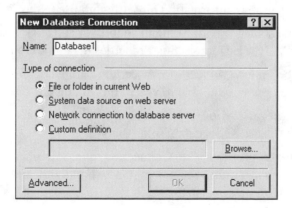

10. Type a name for your new connection and select a location. The following locations are available:

   ▶ **File or folder in current Web**   Select this option if you have a database within your current Web. If you select this option and click Browse, you will be prompted to select a database from the current Web.

   ▶ **System data source on Web server**   Select this option if you have a database on your Web Server that is not within the current Web. If you select this option and click Browse, the System Data Sources on Web Server dialog box appears, and you are prompted to select from previously configured data sources (for more information on setting up data sources on the server, see Chapter 9).

   ▶ **Network connection to database server**   Select this option to send your information to a database on your network. If you select this option and click Browse, the Network Database Connection dialog box appears, and you are prompted to select a type of database driver and to enter the server name and the name of the database you are connecting to.

   ▶ **Custom definition**   Select this option to connect to a file DSN. A connection to a file DSN is made here by selecting a previously created *.dsn file within your current Web or manually entering a fully qualified URL to the *.dsn file outside your Web. A file DSN has the advantage that its information resides in an easily copied file instead of the system's registry (for more information on setting up file DSNs, see Chapter 9).

11. Select the data source you are going to connect to and click Advanced. This brings up the Advanced Connection Properties dialog box, shown in Figure 10-9.

   This dialog box allows you to specify certain parameters for connecting to the database. The options available to you in this dialog box are as follows:

   ▶ **Authorization**   Allows you to specify a username and password required for users to access this database on the system.

   ▶ **Timeouts**   Specifies when Connection, duration of a database connection, and Command, duration of a command, should time out.

   ▶ **Other parameters**   Allows you to manually edit your connection string and specify the data source's cursor location (where the current record pointer is maintained).

12. Set your advanced options and click OK. You are now returned to the New Database Connection dialog box.

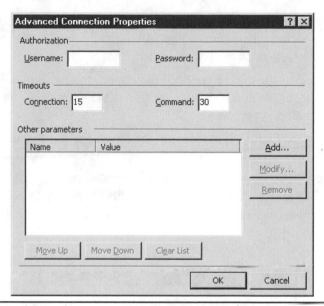

Figure 10-9   *The Advanced Connection Properties dialog box*

13. Click OK again to close this dialog box. You will now see the Database tab of the Web Settings dialog box (Figure 10-8), with your new connection appearing with a question mark next to it.

TIP

To ensure that your new connection works properly, click the Verify button in the Database tab. FrontPage will verify your connection. If the connection works properly, a check mark will appear next to your data source.

14. Click OK to close the Web Settings dialog box. You now return to the Database Results tab, and your data source will appear in the Database Connection to Use drop-down box.

    You will notice that the Table to Hold Form Results drop-down menu now contains text. These are the tables found within the data source you have connected to. Your selection here will be where the form you have created sends its information.

15. Select the Table to Hold Form Results information.

    The Database Results tab gives you the option of specifying a custom confirmation page and an error page for your form. If you want to include these items, enter the paths for these pages in the respective fields. If you do not want to include these, FrontPage will use the default forms, which are created by the server on the fly as needed.

We now need to specify the connection between the fields in our form and the fields within our database. This connection is the main determinant in how our form information is processed.

16. Click the Saved Fields tab to bring up the Saved Fields information, shown in Figure 10-10.

Each named field within your form will appear on the left side of the Form Fields to Save text area. We want to connect these form fields with the columns (fields) in our selected database table. To accomplish this, continue with the next step.

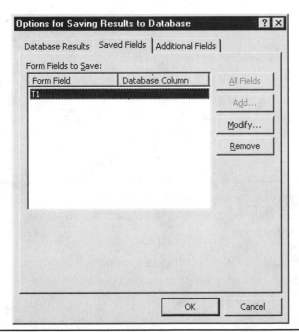

Figure 10-10   *The Saved Fields tab of the Options for Saving Results to Database dialog box*

17. Select one of your form fields and click the Modify button. FrontPage will connect to your database and bring up the Modify Field dialog box, shown here:

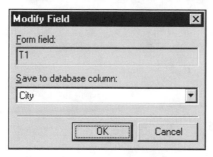

18. From the drop-down list, select the column within your database that you want this field to write to and then click OK.

19. Repeat steps 17 and 18 for each field within your form. You will notice that the Modify Field dialog box only shows you database fields that have not yet been connected to form fields.

20. When you have completed all your connections, click the Additional Fields tab to bring up the Additional Fields options, shown in Figure 10-11.

21. This tab allows you to specify additional fields you want saved to the database that do not appear within your form. Specify linkages for these fields or remove them by selecting each field and clicking the Remove button.

22. Click OK when you have finished with the Additional Fields tab. Click OK again to close the Form Properties dialog box.

That is all there is to it. Now when you enter information into this form, it will send your data to the database you specified and place the information in the columns you specified.

TIP

Using the form-to-database capability in conjunction with the database results capability allows you to create sites that can be updated in real time by your users. This is a great combination for use with community-based sites or when you are conducting surveys or quizzes.

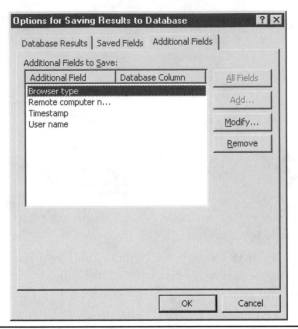

Figure 10-11 *The Additional Fields tab of the Options for Saving Results to Database dialog box*

Hands On: Using an Excel Spreadsheet as a Data Source

Although not as robust in data storage and retrieval as a typical database, an Excel spreadsheet can be used as your data source. Surprisingly, this can be handled almost identically to working with an Access database.

In order to use a spreadsheet as a database, you must first create a named range with the spreadsheet. As you will see, this named range then takes the place of a database table. Failing to create a named range within your spreadsheet will result in an error when attempting to specify the Table to Hold Form Results setting in the Options for Saving Results to Database dialog box.

Creating a named range in Excel can easily be accomplished as follows:

1. Open your spreadsheet within Excel.
2. Highlight the group (range) of cells that you wish to use as your virtual table.

3. Select Insert | Name | Define from the menu bar to open the Define Name dialog box.

4. Enter a name for your range and click the Add button to create the named range. You will note that the Refers To field at the bottom of this dialog box contains a range formula representing your cell selection.

5. Click OK to close the Define Name dialog box.

6. Save your spreadsheet, and you're done!

Now that you've created a named range within your spreadsheet, it's time to add it to your Web:

1. From FrontPage's File menu, select the Import option to display the Import dialog box.

2. Click the Add File button.

3. Browse to your spreadsheet and select it to add it to the import list.

4. Click the Import dialog box's Modify button.

5. In the Edit URL dialog box that is displayed, add "fpdb/" to the front of your spreadsheet's name, as shown in the following illustration. This tells FrontPage to create a subdirectory named fpdb and to import the spreadsheet to that location.

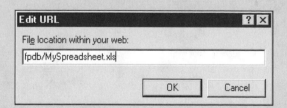

6. Click OK to accept your modification and OK again to import the spreadsheet into a newly created fpdb folder (or an existing fpdb folder, should it already exist).

Now we'll want to do a little additional maintenance to ensure the security of our new spreadsheet-based data source.

7. Right-click the fpdb folder and select Properties to display the Folder Properties dialog box.

8. Make sure the third option, Allow Files to Be Browsed, is unchecked, and click OK to save your changes. Failure to do this bit of security housekeeping might allow a savvy visitor to download your entire spreadsheet.

NOTE

When importing an Access database (.mdb file), FrontPage automatically creates the fpdb folder and removes its Allow Files to Be Browsed setting. With all other types of files, including our spreadsheet example here, you should always place the data file in a folder and make it nonbrowsable, as we have just done. Although the name fpdb is totally optional, it is FrontPage's default and therefore will always be easily recognizable to you as your data file location.

Now that we have our spreadsheet within our Web, we need to create a data connection to it so we'll be able to access its contents within our Web site. This is accomplished within the Database tab of the Web Settings dialog box, detailed as follows:

1. Open the Web Settings dialog box through the Tools | Web Settings menu.

2. Select the Database tab within the dialog box.

3. Click the Add button to display the New Database Connection dialog box.

4. Enter a meaningful name for your new spreadsheet data connection.

5. Click the Browse button and select your spreadsheet within the fpdb folder of your Web.

   If you will only be displaying information from your spreadsheet and not allowing users to add their own data (or automatically doing so yourself based on their actions), you may now skip to step 10. The following steps only apply to spreadsheet data sources that will be read/write capable.

6. Back in the New Database Connection dialog box, click the Advanced button to display the Advanced Connection Properties dialog box, shown previously in Figure 10-9.

7. Click the Add button in the Other Parameters area to display the Add Parameter dialog box.

8. In the dialog box's Name field, type **ReadOnly**, and in the Value field, enter **0**. This will instruct the server that the connection you are making to

this data source will *not* be read-only, which is the default for a spreadsheet data connection.

9. Click OK to add the parameter and OK again to close the Advanced Connection Properties dialog box.

TIP

If we didn't add this parameter, we would later have been presented with the following dialog box when binding our form fields to our spreadsheet columns. I'm showing you this dialog box so you'll know what it means if you ever encounter it.

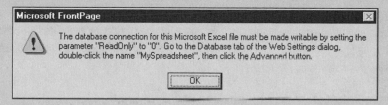

10. Click OK to save your newly created data connection.

11. Back in the Web Settings dialog box's Database tab, you should now see your newly created data connection with a question mark (?) in front of it. This indicates that the data connection has not been tested. Click the Verify button to make sure you have properly configured your new data connection. If this test is successful, the question mark will be replaced by a check mark. If there is a problem, you will be notified and should take the recommended steps to correct it.

Now that you've created a named range within your spreadsheet that will act as your database table, and have created a new data connection to the spreadsheet within your Web, you may go ahead and use your new data source just as you would an Access database. Instead of table fields, you'll see column names as data fields. Other than that, the differences will be rather transparent.

Creating a Database in the Form Options

So you say you do not have a database, do not want to set up a database, or do not know how to set up one to work with your Web. Well, then, this option is for you.

FrontPage has a great feature incorporated into the Database Results tab of the Options for Saving Results to Database dialog box, shown previously in Figure 10-7. This option automatically creates a database and inserts it into your Web.

Along with creating the database, it also creates all the column labels based on the fields you have created in your form. To have FrontPage automatically create your database for you, follow these steps:

1. Create a form within your Web.

TIP

When you create your form, be sure to give all your fields names that relate to the content you want entered into them. This way, when you create your database, all the columns in your database will have relevant names. Also, give your page a relevant name and pre-save it before having FrontPage create your results database, because FrontPage names the database after your page, changing the extension to .mdb.

2. Position your cursor within the form and right-click.

3. Select Form Properties from the menu. This brings up the Form Properties dialog box, shown previously in Figure 10-6.

4. Click the Send to Database option and then click the Options button. This brings up the Database Results tab of the Options for Saving Results to Database dialog box (refer to Figure 10-7).

5. Click Create Database. FrontPage will create a database with the same name as the current file you are working with. This database is then stored in the fpdb directory within your Web (this directory is created if it does not already exist).

When FrontPage finishes creating your database, you are given the following message:

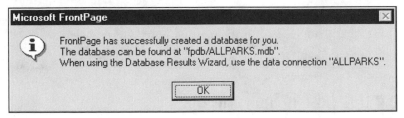

6. Click OK to close this dialog box.

You can now click OK to complete the operation, or you can set the other options as detailed in the earlier topic "Sending Form Results to a Database."

Connecting to an Existing Database in the Form Options

FrontPage does not force you to use a connection associated with the program when sending your results to the database. On the contrary, FrontPage gives you the option to connect to any database you have access to on your network. This gives you quite a bit of flexibility when working with forms.

The following steps take you through the process of connecting a form created in FrontPage to an existing database:

1. Create a form within your Web.

TIP

When you create your form, be sure to name all your fields with names that relate to the content you want entered into them. This way, when you create your database, all the columns in your database will have relevant names.

2. Position your cursor within the form and right-click.

3. Select Form Properties from the menu to bring up the Form Properties dialog box (refer to Figure 10-6).

4. Check the Send to Database option and click the Options button. This brings up the Database Results tab of the Options for Saving Results to Database dialog box (refer to Figure 10-7).

5. Click Add Connection, which will bring up the Database tab of the Web Settings dialog box (refer to Figure 10-8).

6. Click Add in this dialog box to bring up the New Database Connection dialog box. Then, type the name you want associated with your new connection.

TIP

It is a good idea to use a relevant name when creating your data connection. For example, if your data contains information relating to client contacts, you will want to give the connection a name such as Contacts.

7. From the Type of Connection options, specify where your database is stored or click Browse to retrieve the database location.

8. Click OK to close the New Database Connection dialog box. You will now see your database name in the Database tab.

9. Click OK again to return to the Options for Saving Results to Database dialog box. You will now see the database name appear in the Database Connection to Use field.

That is all there is to it. Your database connection is now ready to be hooked up to the form you are currently working with.

Summary

In this chapter, we have taken a close look at what you can do when it comes to developing database-driven webs with FrontPage. Upon completing this chapter, you should have a good grasp of the functionality built into FrontPage for the purposes of developing database-driven sites.

As we continue on to the next chapters, you will be able to take this knowledge to the next level by creating interactive pages using Active Server technology, which we have only touched the surface of in this chapter.

Inside Active Server Pages

IN THIS CHAPTER:

Learn How ASP Works

Create Interactive Pages with FrontPage

A ctive Server Page (ASP) technology allows you to create dynamic pages on-the-fly, giving you extended capabilities in the development of your Webs. Furthermore, FrontPage 2002 has complete support for ASP and was designed with ASP in mind. This chapter will give you a quick introduction to ASP, and then we'll jump right into working with the basics. Once you have completed this chapter, you'll have a good grasp of ASP and its uses, which you can take directly into Chapter 12, where you'll learn even more hands-on uses for ASP in your Webs.

About Active Server Pages

Active Server Pages (ASP) are an integration of HTML and common scripting languages used on the Web. This technology was originally developed exclusively for Microsoft's Internet Information Server (IIS), but third-party developers such as Chili!Soft have ported it to other Windows-based servers. In the summer of 1998, Chili!Soft also released a version for Netscape Enterprise Server running on Sun Solaris. Because the scripts used for Active Server Pages are embedded directly into your HTML code, you can create all your server actions within your page, rather than having the page connect to a technology such as CGI or an ISAPI application. This technology is quickly replacing older technologies such as CGI and Microsoft's IDC because it allows developers to implement their active content directly into their pages.

Another reason ASP has become so popular is that it works with intuitive scripting languages, offering powerful results. This is accomplished through the use of the ASP interpreter, which resides on your Web server. When you set up your Web server to work with ASP files, it simply associates any file that has the .asp extension with the interpreter.

When the server reads an ASP file, the interpreter looks through the code for any script that needs to run on the server. VBScript and JavaScript are the two primary scripting technologies used in ASP programming, but other scripting languages can be used once they have been configured on the server. When the server finds server-side script (script that has been specified to run on the server) within an ASP document, it runs the script through the interpreter and outputs the resulting information.

The great thing about working with ASP is that you mainly work with VBScript for your coding language. VBScript is a very easy scripting language to learn because it looks and reads much like English. Although only Microsoft's Internet Explorer version 3.0 and above directly supports VBScript, ASP makes your client's browser a non-issue by running the VBScript on the server. In fact, it's fairly common to see ASP using VBScript for server-side scripting and JavaScript for client-side scripting.

NOTE

Although you can use other scripting languages with ASP, we will focus on the use of VBScript in this chapter.

If you look at a page containing ASP code, you will see that it is fairly readable. It is also set off from the rest of the HTML code by one of two delimiters. These delimiters are the <%> and <SCRIPT RUNAT=SERVER> tags. RUNAT=SERVER is just a parameter added to the standard <SCRIPT> tag that tells the ASP interpreter that the script contained within it should be run on the server and not returned to the client. Looking at the example shown here, you will see that the code is set off with the <%> tag:

```
<input TYPE="TEXT" NAME="ParkName"
  VALUE="<%=Request.QueryString("ParkName")%>" size="20">
```

With this example, we have created a form field that uses VBScript to set the initial value of a single-line text box form field with information retrieved from the query string. We will get into the query string and implementation of ASP later in this chapter, but this gives you a quick glimpse of some code right off the bat.

CAUTION

If you are creating ASP code in multiple languages—that is, if you are mixing VBScript and JavaScript—be sure to use the <SCRIPT RUNAT=SERVER> delimiter tag and parameter within your code. This is because the ASP interpreter automatically assumes you will be working with VBScript in your scripting and will not process your scripts properly if you use the <%> tags.

ASP Objects

Active Server Pages come fully equipped with a variety of built-in objects that make working with the server a much easier task. In this section, we will take a look at the various ASP objects and their functions. The information you find here will give you a basic understanding of the ASP objects you will be using in your development projects.

Application Object

The Application object contains various collections, methods, and events that allow multiple users to share information within a specific application. The Application object, itself, is made up of all the files in its root directory and all the subdirectories within the root.

When you create an application using ASP, it works with a specific beginning and end in mind. The application begins when the first user opens an ASP file within the application, and it continues until the server shuts down. These two events, which make up the beginning and the end of the application, are known as the Application_OnStart event and the Application_OnEnd event, respectively.

ASP-based applications created in FrontPage have their OnStart and OnEnd event information stored in the Global.asa file. Along with the Application events, Global.asa can also contain your Session events, <OBJECT> declarations, and TypeLibrary declarations. Here's an example of a Global.asa file:

```
<SCRIPT LANGUAGE=VBScript RUNAT=Server>
Sub Application_OnStart
    '==FrontPage Generated - startspan==
    set fs = CreateObject("Scripting.FileSystemObject")
    sIniFilePath = "/var/opt/casp/chili.ini"
    If (fs.FileExists(sIniFilePath)) then
        Application("fp_sAspPlatform") = "CSASP"
    Else
        Application("fp_sAspPlatform") = "MSASP"
    End If
    set fs = Nothing
    '==FrontPage Generated - endspan==
End Sub
</SCRIPT>
```

The information in this file is automatically generated by FrontPage when you incorporate ASP-based information into your Webs. As you will see if you attempt to open this file, it is not configured to open in FrontPage. This is because it is a text file, and you really will not need to open it unless you are creating custom ASP files. If this is the case, you can open the Global.asa file by right-clicking it and selecting Open With from the drop-down list. This will bring up a dialog box listing the various editors you have configured on your system. I would suggest that you simply select TEXT EDITOR, which is the Windows Notepad utility, to view this file.

Request Object

The Request object is used to retrieve information from the server that the browser has previously passed to it. For example, if you have someone fill out an online form and submit it, you can use the Request object to display the information submitted in that form. The syntax associated with the Request object is as follows:

```
Request[.collection|property|method](variable)
```

As you see in this sample syntax, four items are associated with the Request object:

► Collection

► Property

► Method

► Variable

Collection   The Request object contains five collections that specify the basic function of the request. Each of those collections is outlined in the following list:

► **ClientCertificate**   Retrieves certification information. This collection is not used very much at this time because you must obtain a certificate from an issuing body such as Verisign. Where you may see this type of certificate in use is on some of the high-end software sites where individuals downloading information want to be sure of the origin of the information. The certificate itself is basically an identification that has been verified.

► **Cookies**   Retrieves cookie information on the server. Cookies allow you to store information about users viewing your site and can be a valuable tool for customizing features. Cookies are explained in detail in the section "Incorporating Cookies into Your Pages," later in the chapter.

► **Form**   Retrieves form information passed to the server using the POST method. This collection gives you an easy way to display information that was submitted by a user via a form. You can take the name of a form element and display it on the screen. For instance, if you want to give your users a custom experience, you can ask them to submit their name on the first page of your site. You can then use the Form collection to obtain that information and display it on your page. For more detailed information on the Form collection, take a look at the section "Form Data Collection," later in this chapter.

▶ **QueryString**   Retrieves the values associated with the variables within a string. This collection lets you pass variables directly into a URL. You may notice that many sites have hyperlinks that do not simply link to a basic HTML pages but rather link to a string such as this:

```
www.mysite.com/query.html?search=names
```

This is an example of the QueryString collection. It parses the information following the question mark and displays results based on the information in the string, along with any related scripts.

▶ **ServerVariables**   Retrieves a great amount of information relating to the server. This collection allows you to query the server for specific information using the following syntax:

```
Request.ServerVariables(environment variable)
```

The following table describes the variables available using the ServerVariables collection.

Variable	Description
ALL_HTTP	Retrieves all the HTTP headers sent by the client to the server.
ALL_RAW	Retrieves all the HTTP headers sent by the client to the server in raw format. Requesting the headers in raw format returns them exactly as they were sent by the client.
APPL_MD_PATH	Retrieves the metabase path.
APPL_PHYSICAL_PATH	Retrieves the physical path.
AUTH_PASSWORD	Retrieves the password value entered when basic authentication is used.
AUTH_TYPE	Retrieves the authentication method used to validate users.
AUTH_USER	Retrieves the authenticated username.
CONTENT_LENGTH	Retrieves the length of the content requested.
CONTENT_TYPE	Retrieves the type of content, such as GET or POST.
GATEWAY_INTERFACE	Retrieves the CGI version on the server.
HTTP_*HeaderName*	Retrieves a specific value associated with a header name.

Variable	Description
HTTPS	Retrieves information relating to whether the request came through a secure connection (such as SSL). If so, it returns ON; if not, it returns OFF.
LOGON_USER	Retrieves the NT account name used by the request.
PATH_INFO	Retrieves the virtual path information relating to a script.
PATH_TRANSLATED	Retrieves the physical path associated with the virtual path for a directory.
QUERY_STRING	Retrieves all information after the question mark (?) in a QueryString collection.
REMOTE_ADDR	Retrieves the IP address of the requesting machine.
REMOTE_HOST	Retrieves the hostname of the requesting machine.
REMOTE_USER	Retrieves the username sent by the user.
REQUEST_METHOD	Retrieves the request method used, such as GET or POST.
SCRIPT_NAME	Retrieves the virtual path to the script.
SERVER_NAME	Retrieves the Web server's name or IP address.
SERVER_PORT	Retrieves the port number handling the request.
SERVER_PORT_SECURE	Retrieves a flag representing whether the port is secure. If the port is secure, this will be 1; if not, it will be 0.
SERVER_PROTOCOL	Retrieves the name and revision of the protocol handling the request.
SERVER_SOFTWARE	Retrieves the name and version of the server answering the request.
URL	Retrieves the base portion of the URL.

Response Object

The Response object works in conjunction with the Request object—it sends the output of a request to the client. The syntax for the Response object is as follows:

```
Response.collection|property|method
```

The Response object consists of only one collection—the Cookies collection—but it consists of a variety of properties and methods, as outlined in the following tables.

(For more information on cookies, see "Incorporating Cookies into Your Pages," later in this chapter.)

Property	Description
Buffer	Specifies whether the ASP sends information to the client browser as it processes the page or stores all the output information until page processing is complete, the buffer is cleared and flushed, and a Response.End command is encountered. This property must be set to True if the Clear or Flush methods are used.
CacheControl	Tells proxy servers whether they may cache the output created by ASP.
Charset	Specifies the character set used within the document, appending its name to the content-type header.
ContentType	Specifies the HTTP content type being returned to the client browser. The browser then uses this information to launch the appropriate application to process the content.
Expires	Specifies the amount of time a page may be cached by a browser before the browser refetches the page.
ExpiresAbsolute	Specifies a specific date and time when a cached page expires and must be refetched by the browser.
IsClientConnected	Validates whether the client browser is still available and waiting. If the user closes the browser, disconnects from the Internet, clicks the Stop button, or navigates to another page while the page is loading, this property returns False.
Pics	Specifies the PICS rating tag for the page.
Status	Specifies the status value sent to the client browser. This property may be used to send custom status messages when a page is not found, unauthorized access is attempted, and so on.

Method	Description
AddHeader	Adds an HTML header with a specified value to your page. It is recommended that you not use this method if another Response method will do the same job.
AppendToLog	Adds a string to the Web server log for the current request.
BinaryWrite	Sends the associated data directly to the browser without any conversion. This method is useful if you are sending binary information, such as a graphic file.

Method	Description
Clear	Clears any buffered HTML. This is a useful tool if you have information being created dynamically, because it will clear any buffered HTML from the system and allow you to send new information without worrying about it crossing paths with the old information. *Note: If you are using the Clear method, you must first set Response.Buffer to True. If this is not set, you will receive an error message.*
End	Stops the current ASP file processing and displays the results immediately.
Flush	Sends out any buffered output immediately. *Note: If you are using the Flush method, you must first set Response.Buffer to True. If this is not set, you will receive an error message.*
Redirect	Instructs the browser to redirect to another page specified in the string.
Write	Writes out the specified text. This method allows you to dynamically add HTML and other information to your page, creating the HTML sent to the browser on-the-fly. The Response.Write method may also be abbreviated with a simple equals sign (=).

Server Object

The Server object provides utility functions for use with the server. The syntax for the Server object is as follows:

```
Server.method
```

The object consists of a single property and eight methods. The ScriptTimeout property specifies the amount of time a script is permitted to run before it is stopped, returning an error message. The Server object's eight associated methods are described in the following table.

Method	Description
CreateObject	Creates an instance of a server component. This method is used to reference a component that you want to initiate on the server. You will see in Chapter 12 that we use the CreateObject method to work with various standard components of ASP.

Method	Description
Execute	Runs another Active Server Page and then returns to the calling page, continuing its execution. This is useful when you place common functions in a separate page. You can execute the code in that separate page from any page within your site, thus providing a more modular approach to large and complex pages. Because the server caches commonly used pages, using the Execute method can also improve performance. *Note: This method is only available with IIS 5 running on Windows 2000.*
GetLastError	This method provides access to the ASPError object. This object contains information about the last error that occurred but can only be accessed if no information has been sent to the client browser. You should therefore always turn buffering on (Response.Buffer=True) when using the GetLastError method. *Note: This method is only available with IIS 5 running on Windows 2000.*
HTMLEncode	Encodes a text string so that it will display properly on a page. This handy utility allows you to convert strings so that reserved characters and spaces will be properly interpreted. For example, if you want to display the greater-than (>) and less-than (<) characters in your pages, use the HTMLEncode method to convert them to > and < (the HTML representations of the greater-than and less-than characters).
MapPath	Maps the specified path from a virtual path to a physical path.
Transfer	Transfers execution to another specified page. Unlike the Execute method, Transfer flushes the response buffer and does not return to the calling page. It is an improved replacement for the Response.Redirect method because it sends the client browser another page instead of telling the browser to request another page. This eliminates an extra roundtrip between the client and server. *Note: This method is only available with IIS 5 running on Windows 2000.*

Method	Description
URLEncode	Like the HTML Encode method, the URLEncode method replaces reserved characters in a query string with browser-safe encoded equivalents. For example, if you want to include a string that contains spaces within a query string, you need to convert the spaces because URLs cannot display spaces. To accomplish this, you would use the URLEncode method to convert the spaces to plus signs (+). *Warning: If this method is applied to an entire URL, it will also encode characters such as slashes and colons. It should therefore only be applied to a query string.*
URLPathEncode	The counterpart of the URLEncode method, URLPathEncode replaces reserved characters in the path of the URL, leaving the query string intact. Instead of replacing spaces with plus (+) signs, it uses the proper ANSI encoding, replacing spaces with %20. *Note: This method is only available with IIS 5 running on Windows 2000.*

Session Object

The Session object allows you to store information about users during their use of a specific application. The session begins when a user enters the application and ends when that user exits the application. The basic syntax of the Session object is as follows:

```
Session.property|method
```

WARNING

Active Server Pages use cookies to match users with sessions. If the user has cookies turned off on the browser, no Session object information will be available.

ADO Object Model

The ADO object model defines a collection of objects you can use with languages supporting COM to access a variety of data sources. Within the object model, you have various objects with which you can work. Here, we will take a look at some aspects of the following objects:

▶   Connection object

▶   Command object

▶   Recordset object

This section should in no way be considered a complete ADO reference but instead an introduction to the ADO object model that illustrates some of its capabilities. There are a variety of books whose sole topic is ADO, and I encourage you to seek them out and use them.

Connection Object

The Connection object is used to create the connection between your data and the server. Whenever you have a data source you want to make a connection to, you must first open it using the Connection object.

NOTE

Because opening a connection to the server uses resources on your system, you should always close your connection when access to the data is complete.

The Connection object consists of various methods, which are outlined next.

Open Method   The Open method makes the connection between the data source and the server. Along with creating the connection, this method also allows you to set the properties associated with the connection.

Transaction Methods (BeginTrans, CommitTrans, RollbackTrans)   The Transaction methods allow you to make multiple changes to a database, with the option of later canceling all those changes if an error occurs. For instance, when transferring funds from one bank account to another, you wouldn't want the bank to deduct the funds from one account and then encounter an error when adding the funds to the destination account. In this case, transactions allow the bank to roll back the first change to the database when the second change fails.

When working with the Transaction methods, you have the following capabilities:

▶   **BeginTrans**   Creates a new transaction with the data source.

▶ **CommitTrans**   Writes changes made to the data source since the BeginTrans command was issued and closes the transaction.

▶ **RollbackTrans**   Cancels any changes that have been made to the data source since the BeginTrans command was issued and closes the transaction.

Execute Method   The Execute method is where the actual queries or changes are entered to the data source.

Close Method   The Close method is used at the end of your connection when you want to close it. You should always include the Close method, because keeping the connection open will result in unnecessary resource usage.

Command Object

The Command object defines the various commands you will use in relation to your data source. An example of using the Command object would be when you have opened a connection to the data source and want to query it. You would use the methods and properties associated with the Command object to accomplish this.

When working with the Command object, you primarily work with the following two methods:

▶ **CreateParameter**   Creates a new parameter and assigns values to it.

▶ **Execute**   Processes the commands you have input.

Recordset Object   The Recordset object is used to manipulate data retrieved from a data source. This will be the main object you use when working with data in your data source. It allows you to update, add, edit, and delete data from the data source, along with various other actions.

Because this is the main object used when working with data sources, it contains a wide variety of methods and properties. The following table describes the various methods associated with the Recordset object.

Method	Description
AddNew	Adds a new record to your current recordset. This method needs to be used in connection with the Update method before it will write the record to the data source.
Clone	Makes a copy of the current Recordset object.
Delete	Removes a record from the recordset.

Method	Description
GetRows, GetString	These two methods transform the entire contents of a recordset into another format. GetRows returns a two-dimensional array. This is useful when you must perform additional processing on the information contained within the recordset. GetString accepts row and column delimiters and returns a single text string containing all the recordset's data with records and fields separated by the specified delimiters. For example, you can use the GetString method to turn your recordset into an HTML table.
Move	Moves the current record to a new spot in the recordset.
MoveFirst, MoveLast, MoveNext, MovePrevious	Moves the current record to the first, last, next, or previous position, respectively.
Open	Opens a cursor in your recordset.
Requery	Performs another query on the recordset to update it.
Update	Writes the current recordset to your data source.

As you can see, there are many methods associated with the Recordset object. Some of the more commonly used methods are listed, but we have not touched on the properties, events, and other fine-tuning aspects available. As we move into actually implementing Active Server Pages, you will see how some of these methods are used.

Active Server Pages and the Server

Active Server Pages truly show their power when viewed from the server's side. In this arena, they make the delivery of active content for your Web pages an increasingly easy proposal, allowing you to reach the bounds of what the Web is capable of today. There are, however, some things that need to be set up prior to working with ASP, and we will take a look at those here.

What Does ASP Run On?

To create ASP-enabled Webs, your system must be running either Windows NT/2000 with Internet Information Server (IIS) installed or Windows 95/98 with the Personal Web Server installed. Some of the latest ASP features are only available through IIS 5 on Windows 2000. If you're serious about writing ASP, I recommend you consider upgrading to Windows 2000 if you're not already running it. ASP can also be used on other Windows NT servers and non-Windows-based servers by installing Chili!ASP, which is an ASP clone developed by Chili!Soft (http://www.chilisoft.com).

NOTE

Although ASP is available for platforms outside of Windows, we will focus on the use of ASP in a Windows-based environment in this chapter.

Using Virtual Directories

ASP is a scripting language—that much has already been stated. Now, for a scripting language to work properly within your Web, you need to set up your Web to allow for the execution of scripts. This is performed through the use of *virtual directories*.

Virtual directories are aliases for directories on your Web server, and they are set up in the administration section of server software. In this section, we'll take a look at setting up a virtual directory using the Personal Web Server interface.

NOTE

If you do not set your virtual directory as executable, the server will not recognize your ASP files, and they will not function properly.

The following steps take you through the basic process of setting up a virtual directory so that it will process ASP files properly:

NOTE

If you are working with IIS 4.0 on Windows NT or IIS 5.0 on Windows 2000, you will want to use the Virtual Directory Wizard to create your new virtual directory. The wizard will take you through the steps of setting up the directory for use on your system.

1. Create a Web in FrontPage. You need to create a Web first so that you can set up the path for the ASP-based Web you want to create.

2. Launch the Personal Web Server by double-clicking its icon in the system tray of the Start menu bar in Windows. This brings up Personal Web Manager.

TIP

The Personal Web Server icon is next to the clock in the system tray.

3. Click the Advanced icon to bring up the Virtual Directories screen, shown in Figure 11-1.

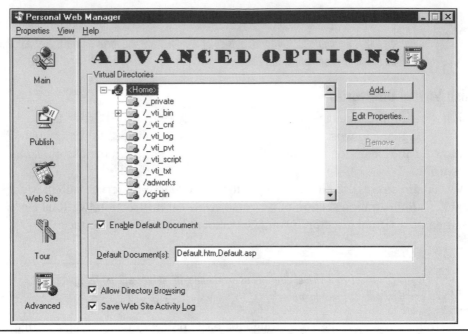

Figure 11-1   *Personal Web Manager displaying virtual directories on the Web server*

4. Click Add to bring up the Add Directory dialog box, shown here:

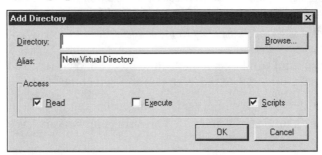

5. Enter the path for your new Web or click Browse to select the directory from your system.

6. Enter an alias you would like to use for your Web.

TIP

An alias should be a name that is easy to remember and relates to the Web. It should also be short, because the longer it is, the more characters your users will have to type if they are entering the path.

7. Now this is where we get to the important part in relation to ASP. In the Access section of the Add Directory dialog box, check the Execute box. This will allow your ASP scripts to run when viewed in a browser.

8. Click OK to close the dialog box and add your new directory.

You will now see your new virtual directory in the directory listing. That is all you need to do to set up your server (that is, if you already have ASP installed on your system).

Developing Active Server Pages

ASP not only allows you to create dynamic Web pages that can display personalized information, it also provides more advanced capabilities, such as form handling and database integration. In this part of the chapter, we will take a look at some of the features available to you when working with ASP.

Form Data Collection

ASP allows for a great number of ways to collect form data from users. Although FrontPage comes equipped with many options for form processing, ASP really gives you control over the processing, all with some simple scripting to implement it. The use of ASP in form handling can come in handy when you want to verify or display the input by a user. With ASP, you can easily redisplay the form with all the user's information inserted into the appropriate fields so that it can be edited or submitted.

In the following example, we will create a basic form that asks for personal and employment information from users. The information gathered in this form will then be posted to another page that formats it as a resume. First off, we will create the form. To do this, follow these steps:

1. Create a page within your Web or import resume.asp on the CD-ROM accompanying this book.

NOTE

Because ASPs require a Web server to interpret their code, you must place your ASPs in a Web and view them in your browser by referencing their location on the server, not the file location on your hard drive. Failure to do so will result in the page not being processed and all your server-side source code being passed to the browser as part of the page.

2. Create a form that includes entries for the user's information. Start with name, address, and phone number.

TIP

For this exercise, take a look at Figure 11-2 for one way of laying out the form. This will make it easier when you are creating yours.

The next items—company, dates employed, and responsibilities—should be placed within the form and then repeated to allow for entry of at least three jobs.

When you have finished adding to the form, your page should look something like the one shown in Figure 11-2.

Now that you have your form created, you need to set the attributes so you can later process them on the resume-formatting page. Continue with the steps.

TIP

FrontPage allows you to make changes to fields in the normal view by selecting the field and then selecting Format | Properties from the menu bar. This method is fine if you are editing one or two fields, but it can become tiresome if you have several fields to edit, as in this example. For that reason, I suggest working in the HTML view to make your changes.

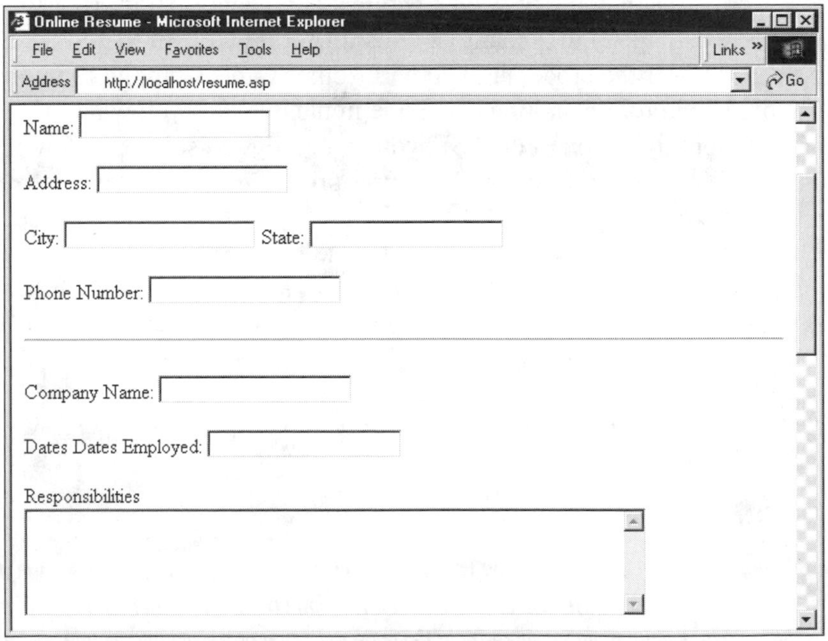

Figure 11-2   *Example of the resume form containing basic fields*

3. Switch to the HTML view and move your cursor to the beginning <FORM> tag. Within this tag, change the attributes to the following:

```
<form method="POST" action="resume_format.asp">
```

As you can see, the method is set to POST because you will be posting this information to another page. Also, the action is set to the file resume_format.asp. This is the file you will be working with next for the purposes of processing the form.

4. Move your cursor to the Name text box and change the name attribute from T1 to resume_name. The name attribute is what you will use to specify the displays in your display page.

5. Repeat step 4 for each form field in your form.

TIP

To make it easy to remember, give each field a name that relates to that field, as in step 4. This way, you will not have to keep coming back to see what the name is when you move to the next steps.

6. Once you have named all your fields, save the file with an .asp extension.

You are now ready to create the display page. This page will take all the information supplied within the form and display it in a traditional resume format. To create the display page, continue on with the next steps.

7. Create a new page in your Web and type in placeholders for each element of the form you have just created. You use placeholders so that you can set up your formatting prior to setting up the calls to the form.

TIP

You can also save your form page with the name resume_results.asp and simply remove the form tags and the form fields. This will save you the time of retyping all the elements you want to display on this page.

8. Take the name, address, and phone placeholders and center them on the page.

9. Change your font settings for the placeholders as follows: For the name placeholder, use 14-point, bold font; for the address and phone placeholders, use 12-point, italic font.

Now you will set up the employment history display.

10. Left-justify your paragraph and type **Employment History**.

11. Set this title to a Heading 3 style.

12. Change your font settings for the placeholders as follows: For the company name placeholder, use bold; for the dates employed placeholder, use italic.

    That does it for the formatting. Of course, you can format your page in any way you see fit, but this is the example we will be using. Now it is time to insert the calls for the form information so that it can be formatted on this page.

    This is where it gets a bit tricky, and you'll once again want to move into the HTML view of your page. In steps 7 through 12, you created placeholders for your information. It is now time to replace those placeholders with the calls for your data. To do so, follow the next steps.

NOTE

You may be wondering why you went through the trouble of setting up these placeholders if you are just going to write over them. In FrontPage, the calls you put in show up only as Microsoft Script Editor icons when Reveal Tags is turned on, and they are invisible if Reveal Tags is turned off. It would be rather difficult to try to set up your formatting without any reference to what you are setting your formatting for!

13. If you have not done so already, switch to HTML view and move to the name placeholder.

14. Highlight the word only and replace it with the following scripting:

```
<%=Request.Form("resume_name")%>
```

As you can see from this code, you are simply using the Form collection of the Request object to request the name attribute you have in your form. Because you are posting the form to this page, it will pass on the attribute to the script and display the result here.

15. Repeat step 14 for each of your placeholders, replacing them with the same script but substituting the name attribute from your form for each one. When you have finished, your code should look something like this:

```
<p align="center"><b><font size="5">
<%=Request.Form("resume_name")%><br></font></b>
<i><font size="4"><%=Request.Form("address")%><br>
 <%=Request.Form("city")%>, <%=Request.Form("state")%><br>
 <%=Request.Form("phone")%></font></i></p>
```

```
<h3>Employment History</h3>
<p><b><%=Request.Form("company1")%><br>
</b><i><%=Request.Form("date1")%><br>
</i><%=Request.Form("response1")%><br>
</p>
<p><b><%=Request.Form("company2")%><br>
</b><i><%=Request.Form("date2")%><br>
</i><%=Request.Form("response2")%><br>
</p>
<p><b><%=Request.Form("company3")%><br>
</b><i><%=Request.Form("date3")%><br>
</i><%=Request.Form("response3")%><br>
</p>
```

As you can see, you have replaced each element of the page with a request to the form. If you were to view this page in the normal view of your editor, it would look like what is shown in Figure 11-3. As you can see from this figure, it would be rather difficult to visualize your formatting if you did not use the placeholders.

16. Save your pages and test them in your browser.

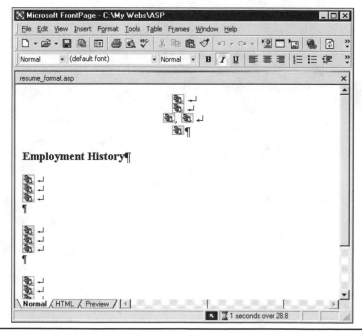

Figure 11-3 *Normal view of the resume response page after scripting is inserted*

Hands On: Creating a Validated Survey with ASP

The preceding form example showed you how to create a form that displays information on the resulting page, which we formatted to look like a resume. In this example, we want to take a look at creating a form that will validate the input information prior to the information being submitted. If information is missing from the form, the user will be prompted to enter the information again. Once all the proper information has been entered, the form will be written to a text file.

For this example, we will be using the files survey.asp and survey_res.asp on the CD-ROM. Here are the steps to follow:

1. Create a form in your Web that contains the following text fields:

   ► Name

   ► Age

   ► Location

   ► Number of dogs in house

   Your form should look similar to the one shown here:

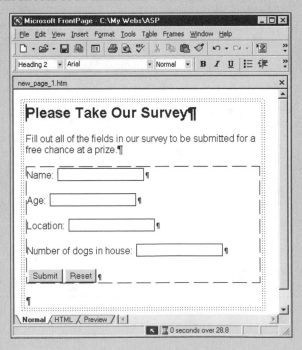

2. Position your cursor within the form, right-click, and select Form Properties from the pop-up menu. This brings up the Form Properties dialog box, shown here:

```
Form Properties                                          ? X
  Where to store results
    C  Send to
       File name:        [                    ]  [ Browse... ]
       E-mail address:   [                              ]
    C  Send to database
    (•) Send to other    [ Custom ISAPI, NSAPI, CGI, or ASP Script  ▼ ]
  Form properties
    Form name:          [                              ]
    Target frame:       [                          ]  [ ...✎ ]

  [ Options... ] [ Advanced... ]        [ OK ]  [ Cancel ]
```

3. Select Send to Other and click Options. This brings up the Options for Custom Form Handler dialog box, shown here:

```
Options for Custom Form Handler                         ? X
        Action:  [ survey_res.asp                       ]
        Method:  [ POST                              ▼ ]
  Encoding type: [                                     ]

  [ Style... ]                          [ OK ]  [ Cancel ]
```

4. In the Action field, type **survey_res.asp**. This is the file that will process your errors and write to the file.

5. Ensure that Method is set to POST and then click OK.

6. Click OK to close the Form Properties dialog box.

7. Select the Name text box and then select Format | Properties from the menu bar. This brings up the Text Box Properties dialog box, shown here:

```
Text Box Properties                                     ? X
  Name:          [ Name                               ]
  Initial value: [                                     ]

  Width in characters: [ 20 ]   Tab order:  [      ]
  Password field:       C Yes   (•) No

  [ Style... ] [ Validate... ]          [ OK ]  [ Cancel ]
```

8. In the Name field, type **Name** and click OK.

9. Repeat steps 7 and 8 for each text box, assigning unique names to each box.

TIP

It is a good idea to give your text boxes names that relate to their tags. This way, you will easily be able to reference them when you need to.

10. Save the file in your Web site with the name survey.asp.

   You are now ready to create your response page. This page will display the posted information, along with writing it to a file and displaying an error message if any information is missing. Because you will be working with possible omissions from the form, you are simply going to be saving the survey.asp file with another name. This way, you can edit the page to fit the requirements for the response.

11. Be sure you have saved your survey.asp file and then select File | Save As from the menu bar.

12. Save this file as survey_res.asp in the same directory as survey.asp.

13. Highlight any introduction text you added to the survey page and replace it with the following:
   "Thank you for filling out our survey. It appears that you have not completed all of the fields. Please click your browser's Back button, review the questions, and fill out any empty fields."

14. Highlight this text and select Format | Font to bring up the Font dialog box.

15. Change the font color to red and set the font style to bold. Click OK when you have finished with the font settings.

NOTE

Step 15 is not required for the setup to function properly, but it will show as an obvious error when the user sees it.

16. Switch to HTML view, position your cursor directly above the text you input in step 13, and add the following script to your HTML:

```
<% If Request("Name")="" Or Request("Age")=""
   Or Request("Location")=""
   Or Request("Dogs")="" Then %>
```

This script will check your form to make sure each field has been completed. As you can see, the script checks each form field name to see whether a value has been entered. If a value has not been entered, it will print the error you input. It will also print the form.

Next, you'll want to set up the form so it contains any fields that have been entered. This way, the user will not have to repeat the entries.

17. Switch back to normal view and select the Name text box.

18. Select Format | Properties from the menu bar to bring up the Text Box Properties dialog box.

19. Type the following script in the Initial Value field and click OK:

```
<%=Request.Form("Name")%>
```

20. Repeat steps 18 and 19 for each form field.

That takes care of the error-processing part of the problem. Now you'll want to set up the page so that a successful entry will print to a file and give the user a thank-you message. To complete this aspect, continue to the next steps.

21. Switch back to HTML view and move your cursor one line after the </FORM> tag. Insert the following scripting:

```
<%
Else

Const ForAppending = 8
Set File =
  CreateObject("Scripting.FileSystemObject")
Set survey =
  File.OpenTextFile(Request.ServerVariables
    ("APPL_PHYSICAL_PATH")
    + "\_private\survey.txt",
        ForAppending, True)
survey.WriteLine
  "Name: " + Request.Form("Name")
survey.WriteLine
  "Age: " + Request.Form("Age")
survey.WriteLine
  "Location: " + Request.Form("Location")
survey.WriteLine
  "Dogs: " + Request.Form("Dogs")
survey.Close
Set survey = Nothing
%>
```

Here, the < % Else %> script tells the system that these operations are to be performed if all the fields are filled in. You then input a script that creates a file on your system and writes each form field to its own separate line.

Switch back to the normal view, and you will see that a Microsoft Script Editor tag appears where you have just entered this scripting. If you do not see this tag, press CTRL-/ to turn on Reveal Tags. Move your cursor directly below the icon and type some thank-you text for your visitors who complete the survey. Your page should look like the one shown here:

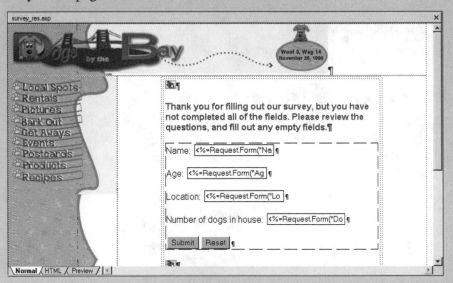

You now need to add one more item to the page so that the scripts will work properly. This item is the <% End If %> script. Switch back to HTML view and add this directly below the thank-you text you have input:

```
%>
<p>Thank you for filling out our survey!</p>
<% End If %>
```

Save your page and test it by not filling in all the fields and submitting the form. If you have set it up correctly, you should receive the error message you created. Then, fill in the missing field(s) and submit the form again. You should now see your thank-you message. Check the text file you specified, and you'll see that the submitted contents of the form now appear in the text file.

Behind the Scenes of the Script

Now let's take a look at what the rest of the ASP script is actually doing. As we previously discussed, the initial If statement checks the contents of the form fields to see whether any of them contain no text (""). If any of the fields are empty, we display an error message and allow the user to fill in the missing information.

When all fields have been completed, the submitted information is written to a text file within the Web's _private folder. But how do we get the correct path of this folder? To accomplish this seemingly easy task, we must use the ASP method Request.ServerVariables( ). By passing this method the APPL_PHYSICAL_PATH server environment variable, we in turn receive the physical path of the Web on the server's hard drive. By appending the path of the _private folder and the name of the destination file, we create a completely portable script (versus hard-coding the physical path of the _private folder).

Armed with this understanding, you'll find that the OpenTextFile( ) method of the File object begins to look a little less intimidating. Within its parentheses, we provide the physical path of the file we want to write to. We use the ForAppending parameter to specify that we want to open the file and add information to its existing contents, and we insert the Boolean value True, indicating that the server should create the file if it does not already exist.

The OpenTextFile() method returns a new File object. By beginning your statement with Set survey =, we take the returned object and name it survey for future referencing. As a matter of fact, we do just that in the next statement when we write

```
survey.WriteLine "Name: " + Request.Form("Name")
```

In this statement, we use the WriteLine method of the File object named survey to physically write "Name: " and then the appended user-submitted value. We then repeat this statement for each of our form fields and complete the process with the survey.

Using the Close command method closes the file we have just written to. If we don't close the file when we are done writing to it, the file might become corrupted. After we close the file, we then issue the command Set survey = Nothing. This releases the File object from our survey object variable and frees up the memory that it occupied.

And lest we forget, all this functionality we just used was made possible by the FileSystem object (FSO). We use the FSO to create a new TextStream object when we used the statement

```
Set File = CreateObject("Scripting.FileSystemObject")
```

The resulting TextStream object was placed in the File object variable, which we used when opening our survey.txt file, writing to it, and closing it.

Finally, regardless of whether we ended up making the user complete the submitted information or successfully wrote it out to the survey.txt file, we must end our Visual Basic If…Then statement by entering an **End If** statement. This tells the server's VBScript interpreter that we have finished with our conditional code.

By now you can easily see the usefulness of this type of simple Web application. In Chapter 12, we'll take things up a level by submitting, editing, and viewing information in a database.

Incorporating Cookies into Your Pages

Cookies are a great resource you can use to accomplish many tasks, such as tracking where visitors go on your site. But that is only the start. The capabilities of cookies are quite incredible. Using this functionality in your ASPASP, you can track items saved to a shopping cart, save commonly used information (such as usernames and passwords), and customize your sites based on user interaction.

Now, I am sure you have heard many things about cookies that do not show them in the best light. However, this attitude toward cookies is pretty unwarranted. When a site uses cookies, it simply uses your browser application to write information to a text file on your computer that it can read later, but that is about as far as it can go. Any other information that a cookie wants to obtain from you must be supplied by you. Additionally, users can disable the use of cookies on their systems. Because the browser is the application that actually reads and writes cookies, you may determine a user's cookie-enabled setting using the Navigator.cookieEnabled function. This is a client-side function (that is, it must be run in the user's browser application), but its result can easily be stored in a hidden form field and then passed to the server. This can be accomplished using the following method:

```
<script language="JavaScript"> <!--
document.write('<input type="hidden"
   name="AllowsCookies"
    value="' + navigator.cookieEnabled + '">');
//--> </script>
```

Cookies are fairly basic in implementation, but they have some strong capabilities. The basic syntax behind the implementation of cookies is

```
Cookies(cookie_name)(key)
```

When working with cookies, you deal mainly with the Response and Request objects.

Using the Response Object with Cookies

The Response object is used to send information to your user's computer. With the Response object, you send out a text file that contains the cookie information. This information can later be retrieved using the Request object.

When working with the Response object, the server checks the client to see whether the cookie being sent has been sent before. If it already resides on the client, it is simply updated. If it does not exist, it is passed on to the client and created. The following syntax outlines the basic text of a response cookie being sent from the server to the client:

```
Response.Cookies(cookie_name)[(key)|.attribute] = value
```

If a key is specified, the cookie is said to be a *dictionary* (it contains one or more key=value pairs). If a key is not specified, the cookie simply contains a single piece of information.

Cookies also have optional attributes and take the following form:

```
(cookie name).attribute
```

Used individually or in combination, these attributes provide greater control over how cookies are handled. These attributes are defined as follows:

- ▶ **Domain**   Indicates that this cookie may only be read by the server at the domain that created it. Using this write-only attribute prevents others from looking at your cookies.

- ▶ **Expires**   Indicates the date or time the present cookie will expire. Be sure to use this write-only attribute if you want the user's information to remain longer than your user's current session. If you want the information to expire at the end of the current session, do not use this attribute.

- ▶ **HasKeys**   Specifies whether there is a dictionary for this cookie. You may use this read-only attribute to determine whether the cookie has keys (making it a dictionary) or is just a single piece of data.

- ▶ **Path**   Specifies that the cookie should be sent only to requests to this path. If this write-only attribute is not set, the application path is used.

- ▶ **Secure**   Specifies whether the cookie is secure. When set to true, this write-only attribute prevents the cookie from being read via unsecured connections.

By combining key attributes when creating cookies, you gain much control over their capabilities. Attributes are combined in the following manner:

```
<%
Response.Cookies("User") ("Name") = Request.Form("Name")
Response.Cookies("User") ("BDay") = Request.Form("BirthDay")
Response.Cookies("User").Domain = "mydomain.com"
Response.Cookies("User").Expires = "December 31, 2000"
Response.Cookies("User").Path = "/www/myhome/"
Response.Cookies("User").Secure = FALSE
%>
```

This example stores the user's name and birthday in a cookie using the keys Name and BDay. Additional cookie attributes are set in the following statements.

Using the Request Object with Cookies

The Request object is used to obtain information that has been written to your user's computer using either the Response object or a form. The Request object only has the ability to read information, so it must work in conjunction with a cookie that has already been set up on a system. As an example of how this may be used, suppose you have personalized your page to have the user's name appear each time he or she enters the page. Using the Request object, you instruct the server to check the user's computer to see whether the cookie containing the user's name appears on the system. If it does, the cookie reads that information and processes it to display the user's name on the page. If it does not, you can display a form asking the user to enter his or her user name. The form would then be processed using the Response object, and the information would be stored on the user's computer.

The basic syntax of the Request object is as follows:

```
Request.Cookies(cookie_name)
```

To read our cookie's information back during a later session, we would use code similar to the following:

```
UserName = Request.Cookies("User") ("Name")
BirthDay = Request.Cookies("User") ("BDay")
```

This example reads the user's name from the cookie into a UserName variable and the user's birthday into a BirthDay variable. If the specified cookie doesn't exist on the user's system, the returned value is nothing.

Summary

In this chapter, we have taken a look at much of the theory associated with ASP, along with some basic implementations of it. Using the information in this chapter, you will be able to move into the next chapter, which takes a more in-depth look at some of the advanced aspects of developing with ASP.

Although we have not covered all the information associated with the theories behind ASP, we have touched on many of its key components. Along with that, you have seen how to implement a number of ASP techniques using FrontPage. If you are interested in the theory behind ASP, many resources are available to you. The best one is the Microsoft Web site, which contains reference documentation for ASP, along with many code examples.

Integrating Active Server
Pages into Your Webs

IN THIS CHAPTER:

Connect to Databases

Use ASP to Query Databases

Work with ASP Components

In Chapter 11, we looked into the theories behind Active Server Page (ASP) technology, along with how to incorporate some basic features of ASP into your Webs. In this chapter, we take an in-depth look at incorporating some of the more advanced features of ASP into your Webs. ASP has become one of the most used interfaces on the Web for interactive content, and implementing ASP-based pages is not as difficult as you might think, especially if you are familiar with SQL. As we move through each topic in this chapter, you will gain a good understanding of how to work ASP into your pages using FrontPage. You will also find that FrontPage already makes use of some aspects of ASP, and you will see how to maximize these features.

As you read through the sections in this chapter, you will gain firsthand knowledge on how to create active pages using ASP technology. We'll take an in-depth look at the ASP components and their implementation, along with how to maximize the database capabilities already in FrontPage through the use of scripting in your ASP pages.

ASP and Your Database

In Chapters 9 and 10, we discussed how to set up a database connection on your system, along with how to use FrontPage to integrate a database into your Web. Here, I want to take this one step further by showing you how to use ASP to connect and manipulate your database. This is accomplished using the Database Access Component.

The Database Access Component is a component much like the ones discussed earlier in this book, but it extends the server component capabilities much further. This component allows you to access ActiveX Data Objects (ADO), which were introduced in Chapter 9. Through the use of ADO, you can access and manipulate information in your databases.

Using ADO

In Chapter 11, we discussed the basics of ADO. Now we will take a look at incorporating the various objects we discussed into your Webs.

Making a Connection to Your Database

The main object necessary for making your data source connections is the ADO Connection object. This object, like the other server components, must be set prior to working with the data source. To create a database Connection object for an external data source (a database that is not contained within your FrontPage Web), follow these steps:

1. Set up a data source on your system for a database on your computer. For information on setting up a data source, see "Setting up an ODBC Data Source on the Server" in Chapter 9.

2. Open a page in your Web that you want to connect to the database.

3. Switch to HTML view and position your cursor directly below the <BODY> tag.

4. Type the following script:

```
<% Set MyConnection = Server.CreateObject("ADODB.Connection")
MyConnection.Open "MyDSN" %>
```

Looking at this code, you will see that we named the connection (MyConnection) and then instructed it to open the database referenced by the Data Source Name, MyDSN. This assumes you already have the database set up and MyDSN as a DSN on your system.

If you're working with a database that you have imported into your Web, you would substitute the name "MyDSN" for Application("*DatabaseConnectionName_* ConnectionString"), where *DatabaseConnectionName* is the name you gave the connection when importing the database into FrontPage. By doing so, you tell the server to look at the connection string for the data source as set up in your global.asa file when you imported the database and created your data connection. In the following examples, we'll be working with an Access database contained within a FrontPage Web. We'll therefore use this method to access our data source.

Performing Queries

Once you have made a connection, your next step is to perform a query on the database. This is accomplished by creating a Recordset object and populating it with an SQL statement that queries the database.

TIP

If you are simply performing queries on your database and displaying your results on a page, I strongly suggest that you use the FrontPage Database Results Wizard. This wizard performs the same tasks that will be outlined in this section, but you do not need to incorporate any code into your pages. FrontPage takes care of all the coding and offers quite a bit in the way of customizing your layout.

The example we are working with here is an Access database that contains company contact information. We will be accessing the database and displaying the contact information on a page in table format. To follow along, use the sample database company.mdb on the CD-ROM. Here are the steps to follow:

1. Create a new FrontPage Web using the Empty Web template.

2. Import the sample database (company.mdb) from the CD-ROM into your new Web.

3. When prompted to add a database connection, enter the name **MyConnection** in the Add Database Connection dialog box.

4. When prompted whether to store the database in the fpdb folder, click Yes. FrontPage then finishes importing the database into the new fpdb folder and creates a global.asa file containing the new database connection information.

5. Create a new blank page and switch to the HTML view.

6. Move to the blank line following the <BODY> tag and insert the following script into your page:

```
<% Set MyConnection = Server.CreateObject("ADODB.Connection")
MyConnection.Open Application("MyConnection_ConnectionString")
Set MyRecordset = MyConnection.Execute("SELECT * FROM Employees") %>
```

Here, we have created a Connection object named MyConnection, opened the data source specified in Application("MyConnection_ConnectionString"), and created a Recordset object named MyRecordset using the Connection object's Execute command. The SQL statement within the Execute command instructs the data source that we want everything in the Employees table retrieved using the SELECT statement.

NOTE

The Set Recordset = Connection.Execute(SQL) method used here is great for performing quick queries because it returns a read-only, forward-only Recordset. If you need more control over how your Recordset is created, you would use

```
Set MyRecordset = Server.CreateObject ("ADODB.Recordset")
```

to create your Recordset object and then the

```
recordset.Open Source, ActiveConnection, CursorType,
LockType, Options
```

method to populate your Recordset.

This retrieves our data, populating our Recordset, named MyRecordset, but does not display our results. The next steps will complete the script so that we can display our results.

7. Position your cursor on the line directly below the script you just entered and press ENTER to create a new blank line.

8. Select Table | Insert | Table and insert a table 400 pixels wide with two rows and three columns. Set Cell Padding to 3 and Cell Spacing to 0.

9. Switch back to the Normal editor view.

10. In the top row of the table, type the following headings in the three cells: Name, Phone, and Email. Select the row and press CTRL-B to boldface the text.

11. Switch back to HTML view to insert the calls to the Recordset object that will display our results.

12. Starting with the second table row (second <TR> tag), position your cursor at the beginning of this line, press the ENTER key to create a new blank line, and insert the following ASP code:

```
<% Do Until MyRecordset.EOF %>
```

13. Next, position your cursor in the first table column of the second row (the first <TD> tag within second <TR>), highlight the   code, and type

```
<% =MyRecordset ("Name")%>
```

14. Position your cursor in the second column, highlight the   code, and type

```
<% =MyRecordset ("Phone")%>
```

15. Position your cursor in the third column, highlight the   code, and type

```
<% =MyRecordset ("Email")%>
```

16. Moving down a few lines, position your cursor before the </TABLE> tag and press ENTER a few times to create some blank space.

17. Within the blank space just created, enter the following code:

```
<%
   MyRecordset.MoveNext
   Loop
%>
```

When you are finished, the code within the <body> tags should look something like this:

```
<% Set MyConnection = Server.CreateObject("ADODB.Connection")
MyConnection.Open Application("MyConnection_ConnectionString")
Set MyRecordset = MyConnection.Execute("SELECT * FROM Employees") %>
```

```
<table border="0" cellpadding="3" cellspacing="0" width="400">
  <tr>
    <td width="33%"><b>Name</b></td>
    <td width="33%"><b>Phone</b></td>
    <td width="34%"><b>Email</b></td>
  </tr>
<% do until MyRecordset.EOF %>
  <tr>
    <td width="33%"><% =MyRecordset("Name")%></td>
    <td width="33%"><% =MyRecordset("Phone")%></td>
    <td width="34%"><% =MyRecordset("Email")%></td>
  </tr>
<%
  MyRecordset.MoveNext
  Loop
%>
</table>
```

18. Save the file to your Web, calling it emplist.asp, and then preview it in your browser. The results should look like those shown in Figure 12-1.

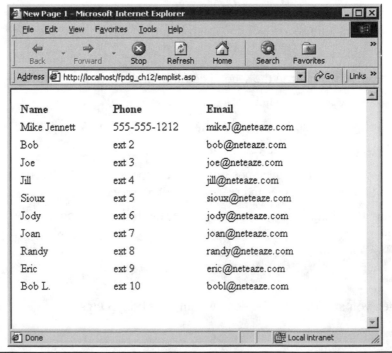

Figure 12-1   *A sample company contact list created from a custom query*

Adding Records to a Database

Querying a database is a great thing for displaying your information, but what if you want your users to update that information from the Web? Well, this is accomplished using a standard form you can create in FrontPage and a separate ASP document. It really is not that difficult a proposition, especially if you have had no trouble in the chapter so far.

TIP

If you are simply adding entries to your database, I strongly suggest that you use the FrontPage Form to Database option. This option makes it easy to link to a database on your system, and it even allows you to create a database if you have not already created one. For information on sending your form results to a database, see "Sending Form Results to a Database" in Chapter 10.

You've already imported the database and created a data connection to it, and the information about the data connection is stored in the global.asa file that was created along with the database connection. Continuing from the previous example, here are the steps to follow:

1. Create a new page in your Web.

2. Within the page, create a form with three text boxes—Name, Phone, and Email. Insert text descriptions before each text box. Your form should now look like the one shown in Figure 12-2.

3. Right-click inside the form and select Form Properties from the pop-up menu. This brings up the Form Properties dialog box.

4. In the Form Properties dialog box, set the Where to Store Results option to Send to Other.

5. Click the dialog box's Options button to bring up the Options for Custom Form Handler dialog box; then set the Action field to update.asp and the Method field to POST.

6. Close the Options for Custom Form Handler dialog box and the Form Properties dialog box by clicking OK on each.

7. Switch to HTML view, insert a space before the </FORM> tag, and enter the following code:

   ```
   <input type="hidden" name="EmployeeID" value="0">
   ```

8. Finally, save your page as editadd.asp.

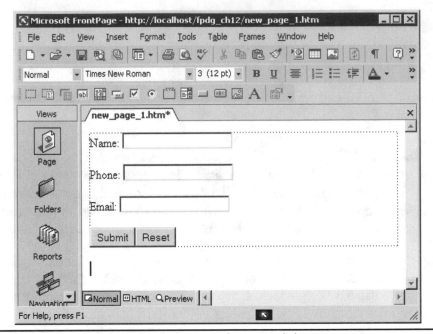

Figure 12-2   *A new form page with three text boxes and descriptive text*

NOTE

An example of the completed page, named editadd1.asp, can be found on the CD-ROM.

We now need to create the script for actually adding our records. This script will take the information from the form fields and append them to our database. Here are the steps:

1. Create a new page within your Web.

2. Switch to HTML view and delete all the code within the page, leaving a totally blank screen.

3. Enter the following ASP code:

```
<%
Const adOpenDynamic = 3, adLockOptimistic = 3

Set MyConnection = Server.CreateObject("ADODB.Connection")
MyConnection.Open Application("MyConnection_ConnectionString")

Set MyRecordset = Server.CreateObject ("ADODB.Recordset")
```

```
sql = "SELECT * FROM Employees " _
    & "WHERE EmployeeID = " & Request.Form("EmployeeID")
MyRecordset.Open sql, MyConnection, adOpenDynamic, _
    adLockOptimistic

If Request.Form("EmployeeID") = 0 then      _
    MyRecordset.AddNew
End If

MyRecordset("Name")  = Request.Form("Name")
MyRecordset("Phone") = Request.Form("Phone")
MyRecordset("Email") = Request.Form("Email")
MyRecordset.Update

MyRecordset.Close
Set MyRecordset = Nothing
MyConnection.Close
Set MyConnection = Nothing
%>
```

4. Save this page with the name update.asp

NOTE

An example of the completed page, update.asp, can be found on the CD-ROM.

When you open the editadd.asp page in your browser, enter the name, phone number, and e-mail address of a new employee. Then, when you click the Submit button, the form sends this information to the update.asp page. In turn, that page opens a data connection and creates an empty recordset that is linked to the Employees table of the database. Because we hard-coded a value of 0 for EmployeeID in the editadd.asp page, our script adds a new record to the recordset and proceeds to take the information from our fields and insert it into the new record. We don't have to worry about the EmployeeID field because it is configured as an AutoNumber field in our database (each new record automatically gets assigned a new number, one higher than the last record in the table). Finally, our new record is written back to the database when we issue the Update command. Because we have finished with our data Connection and Recordset objects, we can close them and set them to nothing, thus freeing up the memory they occupied on the server.

When we opened our data connection, we used the Application ("MyConnection_ ConnectionString") property to retrieve the connection string from our global.asa file. The server had already read the settings in this file when we made our first page request and returned the proper string.

When we created our Recordset object, we set its type to adOpenDynamic so that it can be updated. We also set the record to lock so that no one will overwrite our record during the update phase. This is done using the adLockOptimistic method, which locks the record as soon as the Update method is used and then unlocks it when the update has been completed.

Go ahead and try it out by previewing the editadd.asp page in your browser. When you submit your information to the update.asp page, it is written to the database and nothing else happens. To view the results, you would have to open the database in Access directly or create a data-viewing page. We'll do just that and more in the next section.

Updating Records in a Database

Updating records in your database through the use of a browser is easily accomplished using ASP. We'll start this phase by creating a page to view our employee records. To accomplish this, we'll use the Database Results Wizard. We'll then link that page to editadd.asp and make a few changes to that page to allow us to display a selected employee record.

To create the page for viewing employee records, follow these instructions:

1. Create a new blank page within your Web.

2. Select Database | Results from the Insert menu. This opens the Database Results Wizard.

3. Within step 1 of the wizard, select Use an Existing Database Connection and select MyConnection in the drop-down list. Proceed to step 2 of the wizard.

4. In step 2 of 5, select the Employees table as the record source. Proceed to step 3 of 5.

5. In step 3 of 5, click the More Options button and then the Ordering button within the More Options dialog box that's displayed.

6. Within the Ordering dialog box, double-click the Name field in the Available Fields list to move it to the Sort Order list. Click the OK button to close this dialog box.

7. Back in the More Options dialog box, check the Limit Number of Records Returned field and type **5** in the adjoining field.

8. Click OK again to return to the wizard and proceed to step 4 of 5.

9. In step 4 of 5, select Table – One Record per Row as the formatting option and check all three boxes below this option. Proceed to step 5 of 5.

10. In step 5, select Split Records into Groups and type **5** in the Records per Group field.

11. Click the Finish button to complete the wizard and create the display region for your database results.

    Now that we've created the display page, we need to make a couple of final modifications to complete this process.

12. Right-click the <<EmployeeID>> text and select Hyperlink from the pop-up menu.

13. In the Address field, enter **editadd.asp** and then click the Parameters button.

14. In the Hyperlink Parameters dialog box, click the Add button to display the Add Parameter dialog box.

15. Select EmployeeID from the Name drop-down list. The text <%=FP_FieldURL (fp_rs,"EmployeeID")%> should appear in the Value field.

16. Click OK in this and the two preceding screens to return to the Normal page view.

17. In the editor's normal view, move to just below the table containing our database results region and type **Add New Employee**.

18. Highlight that text and click the Hyperlink button on the Standard toolbar.

19. In the URL field, type **editadd.asp?EmployeeID=0** and click OK.

20. Save this page as viewempl.asp.

    Next, we need to make a few adjustments to our previously created editadd.asp page.

21. Reopen the editadd.asp page and switch to the HTML view.

22. Enter the following script between the <BODY> and <FORM> tags:

```
<%
Dim MyConnection, MyRecordset, sql
Dim EmployeeID, EmpName, EmpPhone, EmpEmail
EmployeeID = Request.QueryString("EmployeeID")
If EmployeeID > 0 Then
  Set MyConnection = Server.CreateObject("ADODB.Connection")
  MyConnection.Open Application("MyConnection_ConnectionString")

  sql = "SELECT * FROM Employees WHERE EmployeeID = " _
    & Request.QueryString("EmployeeID")
  Set MyRecordset = MyConnection.Execute(sql)
  If Not MyRecordset.EOF Then
```

```
        EmpName = MyRecordset("Name")
        EmpPhone = MyRecordset("Phone")
        EmpEmail = MyRecordset("Email")
    End If
    MyRecordset.Close
    Set MyRecordset = Nothing
    MyConnection.Close
    Set MyConnection = Nothing
End If
%>
```

23. Now locate the hidden field, EmployeeID, you previously added to this form, and change the value from "0" to <% = EmployeeID) %>.

    We now need to bind our text boxes to the data from our Recordset.

24. Move up to the text box input field called Name and add the following to the input tag:

    ```
    value=<% =EmpName %>
    ```

25. Repeat step 24 for the Phone and Email text box input fields, substituting "EmpName" with "EmpPhone" and "EmpEmail," respectively.

26. That's it! Just save your page and you're ready to test it.

TIP

To make the update.asp page switch back to the employee viewer page, just insert the following code at the end of the update.asp page before the final %> tag:
```
Response.Redirect("viewempl.asp")
Response.End
```

After the update is finished, this code will take users back to the viewer page, and they'll see their results. The update.asp file contains this code and is available on the CD-ROM.

Active Server Components

When you install ASP on your system (included with Internet Information Services and Personal Web Server), you are given a great set of components for creating dynamic content within your site. This part of the chapter takes a look at some of the key components you will most likely work with if you are planning on using Active Server technology.

Advertisement Rotator Component

As you well know, advertising is commonplace on the Web and is almost a necessity for any commercial Web site. Even if it does not generate much revenue, it aids in brand name recognition, known as "Top of Mind," whereas seeing the name over and over again will induce recognition. In the industry, it can cost large sums of money to purchase and maintain certain programs, and this has led to advertising systems being out of the reach of many developers. With the Advertisement Rotator, however, you can implement random rotating ads on your pages without the need for an expensive system. Furthermore, it is not that difficult to implement. The main aspect of setting up the rotator is the scheduling file necessary for the rotator to work.

Scheduling File

The scheduling file is simply a text file that contains schedule information for your advertisements. It specifies all the information the server needs in order to process the ads, such as where the images are, the URLs for the ads' home pages, and a weight associated with the ads (how often the ads are displayed). Here is an example of a schedule file:

```
REDIRECT /asp/before.asp
WIDTH 540
HEIGHT 50
BORDER 0
*
banners/spotlight.gif
http://www.spotlightstudios.com
interactive solutions for what's next
50
banners/humane.gif
http://www.scvhumane.org
Humane Society
10
```

Now that you have seen an example of a schedule file, here is what it all means:

▶ **REDIRECT /asp/before.asp**   Specifies a file that you want the click directed through prior to going to the ad's home page. This allows you to implement tracking capabilities into your rotator.

▶ **WIDTH 540**   Specifies the default width of the ad.

▶ **HEIGHT 50** Specifies the default height of the ad.

▶ **BORDER 0** Specifies the weight (width) of the border around the ad. (In this case, there is no border.)

▶ * This is the separator needed between global settings and individual ads.

▶ **banners/spotlight.gif** Specifies the location of a graphic.

▶ **http://www.spotlightstudios.com** Specifies a home page for the ad.

▶ **interactive solutions for what's next!** Allows for alternative text display.

▶ **50** Indicates the weight for this ad (that is, the number of times it should be displayed in relation to the other ads in the rotator). All the numbers in your schedule are added together, and the system assigns a percentage based on the total number.

Implementing the Rotator

Once you have created your schedule file, you simply need to reference it in your pages. Here are the steps to follow:

TIP

If you create a separate file containing the rotator implementation information, you can then simply use a "file includes" statement and include the file in your page (for example, <!-- #include file="filetoinclude.asp" --> or <!-- #include virtual="/path/filetoinclude.asp" -->). This way, you do not have to enter the entire string into each page, and you only have to change it once if you need to make adjustments.

1. Open a page in your Web (for this example, we will use adbanner.asp found on the CD-ROM).

2. Switch to HTML view and position the cursor where you want your ads to appear.

3. Type the following server-side ASP script:

```
<% Set AdRotate=Server.CreateObject( "MSWC.AdRotator" ) %>
<% = AdRotate.GetAdvertisement("schedule.txt") %>
```

As you can see, we have set our object (AdRotate) and then we call the schedule file (schedule.txt).

4. Save your page as an ASP page by selecting Active Server Pages from the Save as Type drop-down menu in the Save As dialog box. Then, preview the page in your browser.

When the server runs this script, it will automatically select a random image, based on the weighting factor you have assigned to each image within the schedule file. This image is then inserted into your page, along with its associated URL and message. However, you will notice that the URL shown on the image does not directly relate to the URL you input into your schedule file. The URL begins with the redirect filename you placed at the beginning of the schedule file, and has the URL appended afterward, as shown here:

```
before.asp?url=http://www.spotlightstudios.com&image=banners/spotlight.jpg
```

To get the viewers to the final destination of this advertisement, you need to now add some code to your redirect page that will parse this information and send them on their way. You may be asking, Why don't we just send them straight to the page for the ad? This can be done by not using the redirect functionality of the Advertisement Rotator; however, this functionality gives you the ability to track the number of visitors who are actually clicking through on the ads.

To create the redirect page, follow these steps:

1. Create a new page in your Web.

2. Switch to HTML view and type the following code after the <BODY> tag:

```
<%
Set Location = Request.QueryString("url")
Select Case Location
Case "Spotlight"
Location = http://www.spotlightstudios.com
Case "Humane"
Location = http://www.scvhumane.org
End Select
Response.Redirect Location
%>
```

3. Save this page as before.asp by selecting Active Server Pages from the Save as Type drop-down menu in the Save As dialog box.

You have now put into place all the pieces you need to display and track your ads.

Browser Capabilities Component

With browser technology expanding by leaps and bounds, it is no wonder we want to incorporate dynamic features into our Webs. With today's browsers, we can generate pages that move, jump, and sing—but it does come at a price. There are still a great number of people who use older browser technology, and if we are not careful, our sites can leave much of our targeted audience out in the cold.

As this problem has become more and more of an issue, a number of solutions have come about, but the most prevalent solution has always been to create two versions of sites—one for the bleeding-edge group and one for those who still use snail mail as their main means of communication. This, needless to say, is not a solution that is happily accepted by today's developers. Fortunately, with the Browser Capabilities component comes a new and much more palatable solution.

The Browser Capabilities component allows you to create a single page containing the latest features supported by browsers, with a component set up to detect the browser and display only those aspects of the page that the browser is capable of viewing.

For this example, we are going to incorporate some of the key features that the Browser Capabilities component has to offer. This way, you can get a good look at each of the requests you can make. This example creates a page that checks the browser and returns all the pertinent information about it. Here are the steps to follow:

1. Create a page within your Web.

2. In the normal view, type **Browser Capabilities Test** and set it to the Heading 3 style.

3. Type some identifying information about what the page will do so your users will know why they are there. For this example, type the following: **This page will inform you as to what browser you are currently using, along with the features supported by the browser.**

4. Now we need to set up the component for use. To do so, switch to HTML view and enter the following scripting, just after the previously entered text (before the </body> tag):

```
<% Set capabilities = _
    Server.CreateObject("MSWC.BrowserType") %>
```

This creates a new instance of the Browser Capabilities component so that we can make calls to it from our page. Once this is set, we can begin entering the various items we want to check for within the browser. For this example, we are going to set the scripts within our text so that we can give the user some supporting information rather than simply displaying the responses from the server. Also, we are going to make some changes to the standard responses so they are a bit more informative.

5. Add the following text and scripting to your page, just below the script you just entered:

```
You are viewing this site with version
<% =capabilities.Version %>
of the <% =capabilities.Browser %> browser.</p>
```

In this part of the page, we have added a descriptive sentence that includes calls to our object requesting two items:

▶ **Version of the browser being used**   <% =capabilities.Version %>

▶ **Name of browser being used**   <% =capabilities.Browser %>

When we make the call, we receive the following from Internet Explorer:

```
You are viewing this site with version 5.0 of the IE browser.
```

We are now going to check the browser for capabilities.

6. Move your cursor down another line and add the following scripting:

```
<% If capabilities.Frames = True Then
    Frames = "Supports Frames"
Else
    Frames = "Does not support Frames"
End If
If capabilities.Cookies = True Then
    Cookies = "Supports Cookies"
Else
    Cookies = "Does not support Cookies"
End If
If capabilities.Tables = True Then
    Tables = "Supports Tables"
Else
    Tables = "Does not support Tables"
End If
    If capabilities.BackgroundSounds = True Then
    BGS = "Supports Background Sounds"
Else
    BGS = "Does not support Background Sounds"
End If
If capabilities.ActiveXControls = True Then
    AXC = "Supports ActiveX Controls"
Else
    AXC = "Does not support Active X Controls"
End If
If capabilities.JavaApplets = True Then
    Java = "Supports Java Applets"
Else
```

```
    Java = "Does not support Java Applets"
End If
If capabilities.VBScript = True Then
    VB = "Supports VBScript"
Else
    VB = "Does not support VBScript"
End If
If capabilities.JavaScript = True Then
    JS = "Supports JavaScript"
Else
    JS = "Does not support JavaScript"
End If
%>
```

As you can see from the code, we have added checks for the major features of the browser. We have also added a statement that converts the response to some logical text, such as "Supports Java Applets." We did this because we will be writing this code out to the page in the following steps.

7. Move your cursor down another line below the scripting you have just entered and then type the following text:

```
Your Browser <% Response.Write(Frames) %><BR>
Your Browser <% Response.Write(Cookies) %><BR>
Your Browser <% Response.Write(Tables) %><BR>
Your Browser <% Response.Write(BGS) %><BR>
Your Browser <% Response.Write(AXC) %><BR>
Your Browser <% Response.Write(Java) %><BR>
Your Browser <% Response.Write(VB) %><BR>
Your Browser <% Response.Write(JS) %>
```

The information calls for each of the attributes we set up in our earlier script and instructs them to be written on the page.

8. Save your page with an .asp extension.

Now view the page in your browser. Although your results may be different, depending on the browser you are using to view the page, your page should resemble the one shown in Figure 12-3.

NOTE

This sample page, named browsertest.asp, can be found on the CD-ROM.

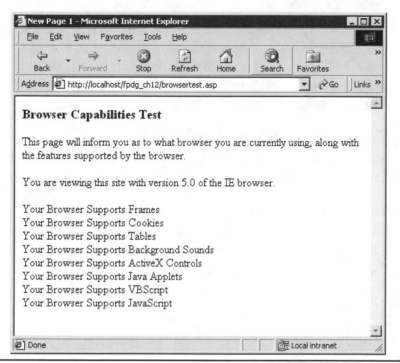

Figure 12-3   *An example of browser capabilities in Internet Explorer*

TextStream Component

Like the Database Access Component, the TextStream Component allows you to access files other than HTML and ASP files. You may have noticed in the "Hands On: Creating a Validated Survey with ASP" example in Chapter 11 that we wrote our results to a text file. This was completed using the TextStream Component, so if you performed that Hands On exercise, you already have some experience working with it.

When working with the TextStream Component, you actually make calls to the FileSystem object. Upon making those calls, you can then create, edit, and open text files with your code.

NOTE

The examples shown in this section are based on a system running FAT32. If you are running a system on NTFS, you will need to give "Write" to the IUSR machinename account on the server for the directory where you create/write the files. For this reason, it is probably a good idea to limit read/browse access to this directory.

Creating Files with the TextStream Component

To create a text file using this component, you make a call to the FileSystem object using the CreateTextFile call. To do so, follow these steps:

1. Open a page in your Web.

2. Switch to HTML view and enter the following scripting directly below the <BODY> tag:

```
<% Set File = CreateObject("Scripting.FileSystemObject")
Set textfile =
File.CreateTextFile(Request.ServerVariables("APPL_PHYSICAL_PATH") _
   & "\_private\newfile.txt", True) %>
```

3. Save your file to the current Web with an .asp extension and preview it in your browser.

NOTE

An example of this file, named createtextfile.asp, is located on the CD-ROM.

Now when you view this page in the browser, the server creates the text file _private\newfile.txt, overwriting any existing file with the same name. You may have to refresh your Web in FrontPage to see the file. If you'd rather not overwrite existing files, simply change the True attribute at the end of the File.CreateTextFile call to False. As previously discussed, we use the Request.ServerVariables("APPL_PHYSICAL_PATH") function to return the physical path of our root Web and then append the local path and filename to make our code portable.

Appending and Editing Existing Files with the TextStream Component

Creating a text file is one thing, but being able to add text within that file is where this component really shines. Using the TextStream Component, you have the ability to open your files (creating them if they do not yet exist) and add information to them. This capability goes hand in hand with using forms in your ASP pages.

Using a form, you can instruct the page to take the information from that form and write it to a file. Looking at the following example, you will see that we write to the file using the following scripting:

```
<%
Const ForAppending = 8
Set file = CreateObject("Scripting.FileSystemObject")
Set textfile = _
  File.OpenTextFile(Request.ServerVariables _
  ("APPL_PHYSICAL_PATH") & "\_private\newfile.txt", _
  ForAppending, True)
textfile.WriteLine "Name: " & Request.Form("Name")
textfile.WriteLine "Age: " & Request.Form("Age")
textfile.WriteLine "Location: " & Request.Form("Location")
textfile.WriteLine "Dogs: " & Request.Form("Dogs")
textfile.Close
Set textfile = Nothing
%>
```

NOTE

This sample code can be found in the file writetofile.asp on the CD-ROM.

In this script, we used the FileSystem object to create our text file, but we also added code for the purposes of writing information to this file. If you look at the line that includes our text file path, you will see that we have added the constant ForAppending (8). This addition is used to specify the input/output mode of our FileSystem object reference, which is, in this case, the mode for adding data onto the end of the file. We also added another optional argument to the statement, True, which specifies that the server should create the file if it does not already exist. The OpenTextFile method uses the following syntax:

object.OpenTextFile(filename[, input/output mode[, create[, format]]])

These optional arguments are explained here:

▶ **Input/output mode**   Allows you to specify that the file is to be opened by ForReading (1), ForWriting (2), or ForAppending (8). In our example, we are adding information to the file, so we have set the mode to ForAppending. To make our statement more readable, we also declared the ForAppending constant value instead of using the number 8.

▶ **Create**   A value of True here causes the specified file to be created if it does not exist. A value of False causes an error to be generated if the file does not already exist, and the file is not created. If not specified, this argument defaults to False.

▶ **Format**   Allows you to determine the format in which the file is viewed. When working with the format, you can specify whether the file is opened. TristateFalse means to open the file as ASCII (0), TristateTrue specifies Unicode (-1), and TristateUseDefault specifies the system default (-2). TristateUseDefault is the default setting when this option is not specified.

NOTE

Once again, you may either declare the constants for these attribute options, as we did in our example, or just enter their numeric values.

After opening your file, you can use the following methods for writing to the file:

▶ **Write**   Writes the specified string to your text file.

▶ **WriteLine**   Writes the specified string to your text file and adds a line break.

▶ **WriteBlankLines(*x*)**   Writes *x* number of blank lines to the file.

Once you have finished writing to your file, you should use the following methods to clean things up:

▶ **Close**   Closes your text file. Failing to properly close an open file may result in corruption to the file and its data.

▶ **Set *file* = Nothing**   Destroys the FileSystem object reference you created (where *file* is your FileSystem object) and frees up the memory it occupied.

TIP

For additional information on the FileSystem object, check out Microsoft's Scripting site at http://msdn.microsoft.com/scripting.

Summary

In this chapter, we have taken an in-depth look at Active Server Pages and their uses on the Web. Upon completion of this chapter, you should have a good understanding of ASP technology, along with some hands-on knowledge of how to implement various aspects of ASP. Obviously, this chapter does not cover every aspect of ASP—that would easily fill a book this size. This chapter has, however, touched on the major topics and shown you some good techniques for using this technology within your FrontPage Webs.

This chapter references many of the topics in Chapters 9, 10, and 11 because ASP has some great qualities when it comes to database interaction and development. Using the information in this chapter in conjunction with what you learned in the previous three chapters will give you the knowledge necessary to create dynamic database-driven sites that use ASP technology to its fullest potential.

PART

III

Beyond HTML

Extended Technology for Your Webs

IN THIS CHAPTER:

Learn the Differences Between ActiveX and Java

Incorporate ActiveX into Your Sites

Incorporate Java into Your Sites

Gain a Working Understanding of Plug-In Technology

As browser technology moves forward, so do the underlying applications that help provide active content on our Web sites. Many of these technologies now have their plug-ins tied directly to the browsers and need no external assistance to perform correctly. Other technologies still need the assistance of plug-ins to allow the applications to perform within the browser.

Along with the rampant use of plug-in technology is the use of ActiveX and Java technology. ActiveX has been Microsoft's answer to Java—a cross-platform application development language. Unfortunately, the display capabilities of ActiveX are integrated into the Internet Explorer browser only and will only work in Netscape via the use of a plug-in. This may cause you to refrain from using ActiveX on the public Internet because, unlike Java, it is platform dependent. But for those of you creating sites for specific groups—especially if you are an intranet developer—ActiveX can offer a wide range of capabilities for integrating Windows-based applications into your Webs.

In this chapter we will take a look at ActiveX, Java, and plug-ins. We will discuss their pros and cons, and you will gain the knowledge necessary to incorporate these technologies into your pages.

ActiveX and Java

The first part of this chapter introduces ActiveX and Java technologies. This information will help you to better understand the workings of the two technologies as we move through the chapter.

About ActiveX

ActiveX finds its roots in Microsoft's Object Linking and Embedding (OLE) technology, which was developed to allow different applications on your computer to share objects, such as text and graphics, and also to share process information. Delving a little deeper, OLE is based on Microsoft's Component Object Model (COM) technology. Whenever you're dealing with OLE or ActiveX controls, you're working with COM objects. To understand what I am talking about, you only have to take a look at the OLE capabilities of IE. When opening a spreadsheet in Internet Explorer, Excel is started and incorporated into the browser's display window. This, obviously, is only one demonstration of OLE, but it gives you a quick example of what ActiveX technology can do.

This technology can also be seen in previous chapters of this book, especially in Chapter 11, where we discuss the use of objects when working with Active Server Pages. Although these server-side objects are usually not ActiveX objects, they are all COM objects. Therefore, they share a common implementation with ActiveX objects. Through the use of ActiveX, you can program your pages to work with other data on your computer—a database, some sort of media-transfer application, or a simple text file.

Now that you have a basic understanding of OLE, let's take a look at how ActiveX works with the Web. If you know much about the Java programming language, you will have no problem understanding the ActiveX model. ActiveX is basically Microsoft's equivalent to Java. When you're working with an ActiveX control, it is much like incorporating a Java applet into your Web, with the exception that ActiveX is geared to work with Microsoft's technologies. As a matter of fact, Java applets can also be wrapped within an ActiveX interface and function just like any other native ActiveX control. But that's well beyond the scope of our discussion here.

ActiveX being a Microsoft-centric technology is the greatest drawback to incorporating ActiveX technology into your Webs on the Internet. ActiveX will only work on Windows-based systems, and, even then, it will only work with the Internet Explorer browser, unless you use a plug-in. Working on this concept, you can see one way in which ActiveX and Java differ: Java is a language directed toward the opening of standards for the Internet, whereas ActiveX is more of an extension of Windows-based technology. We'll get into a deeper discussion of the differences between the ActiveX and Java technologies later in this chapter.

About Java

Java was introduced by Sun Microsystems in the early stages of today's Web. When first introduced, it was touted as the application development tool of the masses—a programming language that would revolutionize the industry and allow developers to create their applications on a single platform but have them run on any platform. However, as many developers have found out over the last few years, Java has a number of great uses, but it has fallen behind on the client side as a number of other technologies have usurped it. It is still a very valuable solution, however, especially on the server side.

Java's byte-code implementation allows you to "code once, run anywhere," as common source code is compiled "just in time" (known as *JIT*) on the computer running the byte-code. These compilers, known as *Java Virtual Machines*, allow the same code to be used on a variety of operating systems. Each time a Java applet or application is run, it is compiled by the computer it's running on.

Java allows you to create anything from simple image-switching applets, as seen in the FrontPage hover buttons, to complex database application interfaces. We will not go into the details of the Java programming language, but we will take a look at how to incorporate Java applets into your Webs using FrontPage.

ActiveX Versus Java

You may be asking yourself whether you should use ActiveX or Java in your Webs. If you are, you should take a look at your deployment environment and some of the fundamental differences between ActiveX and Java. First of all, ActiveX is Microsoft platform dependent. This means it will only work on Windows-based machines, and furthermore, it will only work in the Internet Explorer browser, unless you use a plug-in. This is in contrast to Java, which has been developed to work on any operating system without the need for a plug-in of any sort.

Along with the platform dependency issue, you need to take a look at security factors involved with using the two technologies. If you are using ActiveX technology, you need to be aware that this technology can interact directly with the operating system. This inherently creates a security hazard because anytime an ActiveX control is used, the operating system may be directly affected.

NOTE

Though there are security risks involved with ActiveX technology, the controls developed must be digitally signed by their authors. This gives you some recourse if a developer creates a dangerous control that gets onto your system.

Of course, this direct interaction may be exactly what you need. Using ActiveX controls, you can directly read and write to the user's hard drive. You can also directly interface with other COM objects, making use of this technology's great interactive capabilities. Microsoft Office Web Components make great use of ActiveX controls within an intranet environment.

In contrast, Java applets work only within the Java Virtual Machine, which lives in the browser. Although there are some security risks involved with Java applets, they are far less intrusive than ActiveX because they have no inherent method of reading or writing to the user's hard drive. Nonetheless, many system administrators have Java applets turned off on their browsers system-wide. This would cause any Java applet you incorporate into your Webs to be ignored by the browser when your pages are opened.

If you don't already, you should understand the difference between Java applications, JavaScript, and Java applets. Java applications run on a client computer and normally send and retrieve all their data from a server. Java applets are almost identical to Java applications, with the exception that they cannot run without a hosting application such as a Web browser. Although the syntax of Java and JavaScript are similar, JavaScript is not a subset of Java. JavaScript is a scripting (macro) language that usually runs in a browser and is contained within a Web page.

With these concepts in mind, you can make your decision about whether to use ActiveX or Java within your Webs—or even possibly decide not to use either. If you are going to use one of these technologies, I suggest you keep the following guidelines in mind:

▶ **ActiveX**   Use ActiveX technology when you are working within an environment where all viewers will be working on a Windows platform and using browsers capable of displaying the contents of your controls. A prime example of this is a private intranet.

▶ **Java**   Use Java applets if you are creating for an environment that is cross-platform in nature, such as the Internet. Using Java gives you the ability to display your applets on a variety of operating systems.

Integrating ActiveX Technology into Your Webs

In the next sections we will take a look at how FrontPage handles ActiveX technologies and how you can incorporate these controls into your Webs. I will also show you some behind-the-scenes information regarding how FrontPage incorporates the code necessary for ActiveX controls to work within your pages.

Adding ActiveX Controls in FrontPage

FrontPage makes adding ActiveX controls to your Webs an easily accomplished task and comes complete with a set of controls at your disposal.

CAUTION

Some of the accompanying ActiveX controls may only be distributed to individuals who have a current Office license.

To add an ActiveX control to your Web, follow these steps:

1. Position your cursor where you want the control to appear.

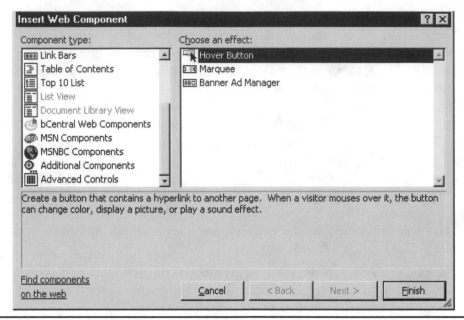

Figure 13-1   *The dialog box used for inserting Web Components into your site*

2. Select Insert | Web Component. This brings up the Insert Web Component dialog box shown in Figure 13-1.

3. From the Component Type pane, select Advanced Controls. You will now see the ActiveX Control icon appear in the right-hand pane.

4. Select ActiveX Control from the list and click Next. You are now presented with an updated Insert Web Component dialog box, which lists the various ActiveX controls available on your system. Figure 13-2 shows this dialog box.

5. Choose the control you want to insert from the list of available controls and click Finish. The selected control is now inserted into your page, and it's ready to be configured.

NOTE

Just because an ActiveX control appears in the list does not mean you are licensed to reuse or distribute the control. Always verify licensing requirements and restrictions before distributing ActiveX controls.

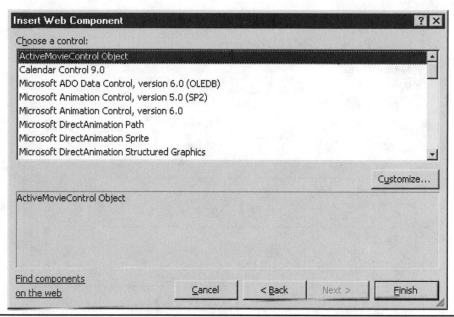

Figure 13-2   *The updated Insert Web Component dialog box, which is displayed after you click the Next button*

Configuring ActiveX Controls

Once you have inserted a control into your Web, you will want to configure its properties to set up various aspects of the control. The options dialog box is available by selecting the control and then selecting Format | Properties from the menu bar or, more commonly, by just double-clicking the control itself. The options dialog box that appears will depend on the control you have inserted. The following sections detail two of the common tabs found within the options dialog box. You should, however, always consult the documentation of the control you're working with.

Object Tag

The Object Tag tab, shown in Figure 13-3, allows you to specify many of the attributes associated with your control. Each option available to you is outlined in the following list:

▶   **Name**   Specifies a name for the control that will allow scripts to reference it.

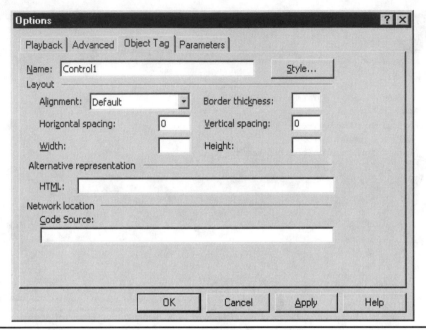

Figure 13-3 *The Object Tag tab of an ActiveX control's Options dialog box*

▶ **Alignment**   Specifies the alignment of the control within your page or the paragraph it resides in.

▶ **Border thickness**   Determines the size of the border around the control. Leaving this field blank instructs the system not to display a border.

▶ **Horizontal spacing**   Specifies the number of pixels you want between the control and the other elements of your page on the horizontal axis.

▶ **Vertical spacing**   Specifies the number of pixels you want between the control and the other elements of your page on the vertical axis.

▶ **Width**   Specifies the width of the control in pixels.

▶ **Height**   Specifies the height of the control in pixels.

▶ **Alternative representation**   Specifies an alternate object or text to be displayed for browsers not supporting ActiveX technology. This field allows you to enter HTML source code for adding a Netscape plug-in or other replacement for non-ActiveX-enabled browsers.

NOTE

Be sure to include an alternative representation because Netscape browsers do not support ActiveX technology unless a special plug-in is installed in the browser.

► **Network location**   Specifies the location of the control on the server. This is a critical property because it tells the client browser where to go to download the control if it does not already exist on the client machine.

Parameters

The Parameters tab allows you to set additional parameters that relate to your specific control. The parameter settings will differ depending on the control you have inserted into your page.

Many of the controls you work with need to have specific parameters edited before they can perform correctly. An example of this would be if you were to insert the Windows Media Player control. Once you insert this control, you need to specify the source of the media you want to play within the Media Player. This is accomplished by editing the parameters for that control.

To edit specific parameters, follow these steps:

1. Insert a control into your page.

2. Double-click the control. This brings up the ActiveX control's Options dialog box.

3. Click the Parameters tab to bring up the parameter options.

4. Select the parameter you want to edit and click Modify. This brings up the Edit Object Parameter dialog box shown here:

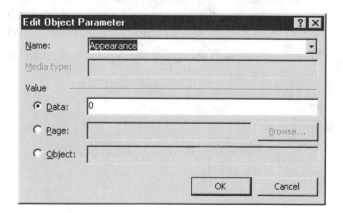

5. Select the options you want and click OK.

When working in the Edit Object Parameter dialog box of the Windows Media Player control, you have the following options you can configure:

► **Name**   Specifies the name of the current parameter and allows you to select from all the available parameters for the control.

► **Media type**   Specifies the type of media being used.

► **Value**   Specifies a value to be associated with the parameter. This is used for items such as the Filename parameter, where you would specify the file to be played in the Media Player, as well as other parameters, such as simple on/off option parameters.

Customizing the Insertable ActiveX Control List

While inserting a control into your page, you may have noticed the Customize button on the Insert Web Component dialog box shown in Figure 13-2. This button allows you to customize the controls that appear in the dialog box, and this customization is accomplished by following these steps:

1. Select Insert | Web Component. This brings up the Insert Web Component dialog box shown in Figure 13-1.

2. From the Component Type pane, select Advanced Controls. You will now see the ActiveX Control icon appear in the right-hand pane.

3. Select ActiveX Control from the list and click Next. You are now presented with the updated Insert Web Component dialog box, which lists the various ActiveX controls available on your system, as shown in Figure 13-2.

4. Click the Customize button. This brings up the Customize ActiveX Control List dialog box, shown here:

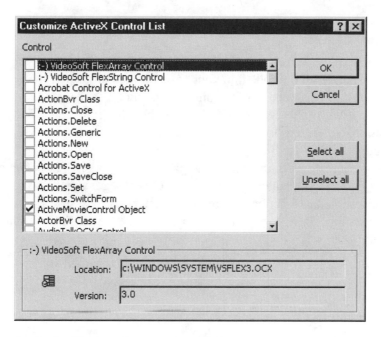

5. Select the ActiveX controls you want displayed in the dialog box by checking or unchecking them in this list. When you click OK, the selected controls appear in the list on the Insert Web Component dialog box.

NOTE

Although you'll likely have many controls listed in the Customize ActiveX Control List dialog box, you won't necessarily be able to use them all. ActiveX controls are used heavily by many Windows applications. Because of their shared nature, a single copy of each control exists on a computer, and one or more, possibly unrelated, applications use the same control. Because these controls are registered in your system registry, they appear in this list. However, as you'll soon discover, many controls require specific design-time licenses, and you won't be able to use these controls in your pages without purchasing them and obtaining their respective licenses.

Behind the Scenes

When you insert an ActiveX control into your Web, FrontPage takes the necessary steps to incorporate all the code into your page for the control to function properly. This code consists of a number of settings, including those that are used to display the control. Earlier in this chapter we discussed how to set up and modify the object tag and parameter settings for an ActiveX control. These settings are used to display and configure your control.

If you have inserted a control into your page, it will consist of two main attributes: Object tag and the Param tags. The Object tag is the main tag used for the control's insertion and functions. Param (parameter) tags are specific to the control and specify settings for its operation. A snippet of code may look something like this:

```
<object
classid="clsid:22D6F312-B0F6-11D0-94AB-0080C74C7E95"
id="MediaPlayer1" width="286" height="225" codebase=
http://activex.microsoft.com/activex/controls/mplayer
  /en/nsmp2inf.cab#Version=5,1,52,701 >
  <PARAM NAME="FileName"
      VALUE="http://server/path/your-file.asx">
  <PARAM NAME="AnimationatStart" VALUE="true">
  <PARAM NAME="TransparentatStart" VALUE="true">
  <PARAM NAME="AutoStart" VALUE="true">
  <PARAM NAME="ShowControls" VALUE="1">
</object>
```

The preceding snippet is part of the Windows Media Player control. As you can see, all the properties of the control are specified in the Object tag. This tag displays the following attributes:

▶ **classid**   This attribute identifies the control to Windows by specifying the control's GUID (Globally Unique Identifier). This unique hexadecimal number corresponds to a matching number in the client computer's registry. This number will be the same on each machine upon which the control resides. If the control is already on the client computer, the matching registry entry tells Windows where to find the control and how to implement it. If the control does not exist in the user's registry, it is automatically downloaded, registered, and then run.

▶ **id**   An identifying name for the control that you use when writing a script that accesses the control. This name can be anything you like as long as it conforms to the proper naming conventions (such as no spaces, no numbers or special characters at the beginning, and so on).

▶ **codebase**   The location on the network where users who do not already have the control may download it. This operation can be handled automatically by Internet Explorer if the user's browser security settings for the specified location allow it.

▶ **width**   The width of the control as it appears in the page.

▶ **height**   The height of the control as it appears in the page.

▶ **type**   The type of encoding used for the object. This tells the browser application what to do with the control.

▶ **param**   These name/value pairs specify information, such as source file and behavior instructions, that the control needs to perform its desired operation properly.

Integrating Java Applets into Your Webs

In this section, we will take a look at how FrontPage handles Java applets and how you can incorporate them into your Webs. I will also show you some of the behind-the-scenes information regarding how FrontPage incorporates the code necessary for applets to work within your pages.

Adding Java Applets in FrontPage

Although FrontPage does not include a selection list of Java applets for your use as it does for ActiveX controls (discussed earlier), incorporating Java applets into your Webs is still easy to do. This task is accomplished by following these steps:

1. Open a page within your Web.

2. Select Insert | Web Component. This brings up the Insert Web Component dialog box shown in Figure 13-1.

3. From the Component Type pane, select Advanced Controls. You will then see the Java Applet icon listed in the right-hand pane.

4. Select Java Applet from the list and click Next. The Java Applet Properties dialog box now appears, as shown in Figure 13-4.

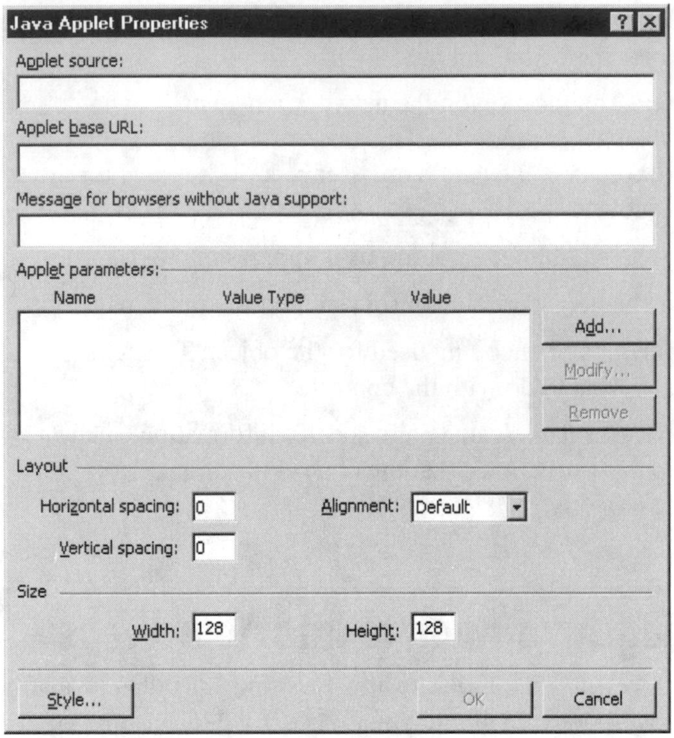

Figure 13-4 *The Java Applet Properties dialog box, used to insert applets into your page*

5. Type the source code for your applet in the Applet Source field. This is the actual class file used for the applet.

6. Type the base URL for the applet in the Applet Base URL field. This URL points to the server on which the applet is stored so it can be downloaded by the browser.

7. In the next field, enter a message to be displayed in non-Java-capable browsers. This is much like the <NOFRAMES> text you would insert for browsers that do not support frames.

8. Determine the layout and size formatting of your applet and enter these values in their respective fields. These values will determine how your applet is displayed on the page when viewed.

Notice we have skipped a step here (that is, the insertion of your applet's parameters). The parameters determine a variety of display and functional issues that relate to an applet and will differ depending on the applet you are inserting into your page. For this reason, we will not go into which parameters to set and so forth. I will, however, take you through the motions of setting up your parameters in the following steps.

9. Click Add to bring up the Set Attribute Value dialog box, shown here:

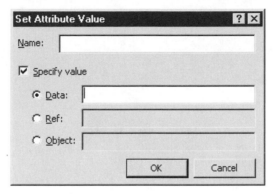

10. Enter the name for the attribute you are adding. If you would like to specify a value for this attribute at this time, check Specify Value and enter the appropriate value for your attribute.

11. Click OK to close the dialog box. Repeat steps 9 and 10 until all your parameters are set.

12. Once you have completed setting up your applet, click OK to close the Java Applet Properties dialog box.

You will now see the FrontPage placeholder inserted for your applet on your page, as shown in Figure 13-5.

Java Applets Included with FrontPage

In addition to giving you the ability to add your own Java applets, FrontPage includes a couple of its own applets, although their implementation is somewhat masked. These semi-hidden applets are the Hover Button and the Banner Ad Manager applets. Each may be inserted into your pages by selecting Insert | Web Component from the menu bar and then selecting the desired component/applet.

Microsoft considers these Java applets to be "components" because of their customization interfaces. As you can see when inserting either one, FrontPage displays built-in dialog boxes that make the configuration process easier for the

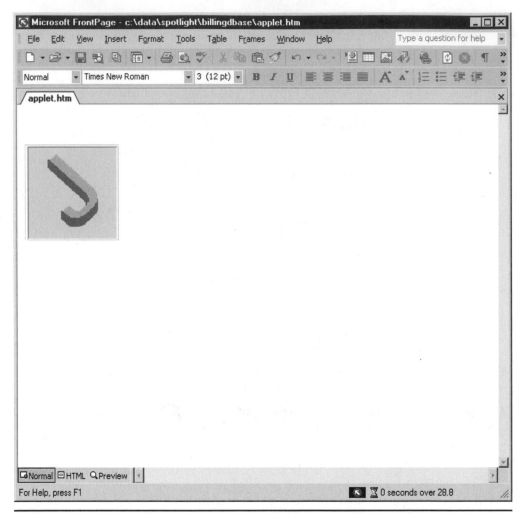

Figure 13-5 *Example of the Java applet placeholder inserted by FrontPage*

general user. After completing this configuration, just switch to the HTML view and you'll see that these components are really Java applets. For example, the Hover Button applet code is as follows:

```
<applet code="fphover.class" codebase="./"
    width="120" height="24">
```

```
    <param name="color" value="#000080">
    <param name="hovercolor" value="#0000FF">
    <param name="textcolor" value="#FFFFFF">
    <param name="effect" value="glow">
    <param name="text" value="Home">
    <param name="url" valuetype="ref" value="index.htm">
</applet>
```

Behind the Scenes

When you incorporate a Java applet into your page, it is inserted using the
<APPLET> and <PARAM> tags. These tags are automatically inserted by
FrontPage using the information you entered in the Java Applet Properties dialog
box (Figure 13-4). The main tag necessary for your applet is the <APPLET> tag, the
attributes of which instruct the browser as to where your applet code exists and the
layout of the applet on the page. The <PARAM> tag, on the other hand, incorporates
the properties associated with the display and functions of the applet. Both of these
tags are outlined in the following list:

▶ **<APPLET>**   Contains the code source and the base URL for your applet,
   along with the layout information necessary for the display of the applet on
   your page. The <APPLET> tag encompasses the <PARAM> tags, where all
   parameters fall prior to the </APPLET> tag. Here's an example of an
   <APPLET> tag:

```
<applet width="128" height="128" code="Banners.class"
codebase="http://www.myWeb.com" hspace="3" vspace="5"
  align="absmiddle">
```

▶ **<PARAM>**   Contains a specific parameter associated with your applet.
   You can have any number of parameters within your applet each set out by its
   own <PARAM> tag. These parameters are based on the applet itself and may
   include items such as the font, color, URL, and other parameters that affect the
   applet. Here are some examples of <PARAM> tags:

```
<param name="font" value="Arial">
<param name="fps" value="40">
<param name="pause" value="0">
<param name="repeat" value="10">
<param name="size" value="14">
<param name="style" value="Bold">
<param name="textColor" value="Black">
```

Now, if you put all of these tags together, you would have the complete applet code necessary for the applet to function properly, and it would look similar to this:

```
<applet code="Banners.class" codebase="./"
    align="baseline" width="350" height="20">
<param name="font" value="Arial">
<param name="fps" value="40">
<param name="pause" value="0">
<param name="repeat" value="10">
<param name="size" value="14">
<param name="style" value="Bold">
<param name="textColor" value="Black">
</applet>
```

This is a simple example of how an applet is incorporated into your page, and it does not take into account any of the intricacies of the actual class files necessary for the applet. These class files are the real meat of the applet and are well beyond the scope of this book.

Incorporating Plug-Ins into Your Webs

Plug-ins have become an indispensable piece of today's Web technology. You see them throughout a variety of Web sites, adding interactivity and expanded capabilities. The idea behind the use of plug-ins is that you can create content that browsers do not natively support. For example, you can create a Macromedia Flash movie, insert it into your Web, and have it viewed directly in the browser by your users. The use of a plug-in or "helper application" is necessary when the client browser does not directly support the media you have incorporated into your Web.

As mentioned earlier in this chapter, a plug-in is necessary for viewers using the Netscape browser to view any ActiveX component you have incorporated into your Web. Now, although you may want to avoid using ActiveX if you are working in a cross-browser environment, you do have the capability of allowing your viewers to make use of the technology with the use of a plug-in.

This part of the chapter takes a look at how plug-ins work in the browser environment and gives you some tips for incorporating plug-in-based applications into your Webs.

Using FrontPage to Incorporate a Plug-In

Incorporating plug-ins into your Web is automated through the use of FrontPage. The following sections show you how to incorporate a plug-in into your page and provide information on modifying the data associated with the plug-in.

Adding a Plug-In to Your Page

Inserting a plug-in into your page is accomplished by following these steps:

1. Position your cursor where you want to insert the plug-in on your page.

2. Select Insert | Web Component. This brings up the Insert Web Component dialog box shown in Figure 13-1.

3. From the Component Type pane, select Advanced Controls. You will now see the Plug-In icon appear in the right-hand pane.

4. Double-click Plug-In to bring up the Plug-In Properties dialog box, shown in Figure 13-6.

5. Type the media filename you want incorporated into your page into the Data Source field. This is not the name of the plug-in but rather the file you want the plug-in to use. Your browser's configuration and the encoding type of the file will determine which plug-in is used to work with different media types.

6. Type alternative text that will display for those browsers that do not currently have the plug-in installed in the "Message for browsers without plug-in support" field.

TIP

You may want to include a link where browsers can obtain the plug-in in your alternative text (or in some other part of your page).

7. Set the height and width for the file that will be displayed on your page using the plug-in.

8. Specify whether you want your plug-in displayed in the browser window when an individual views the page. If you check Hide Plug-In, your plug-in will not appear on the page.

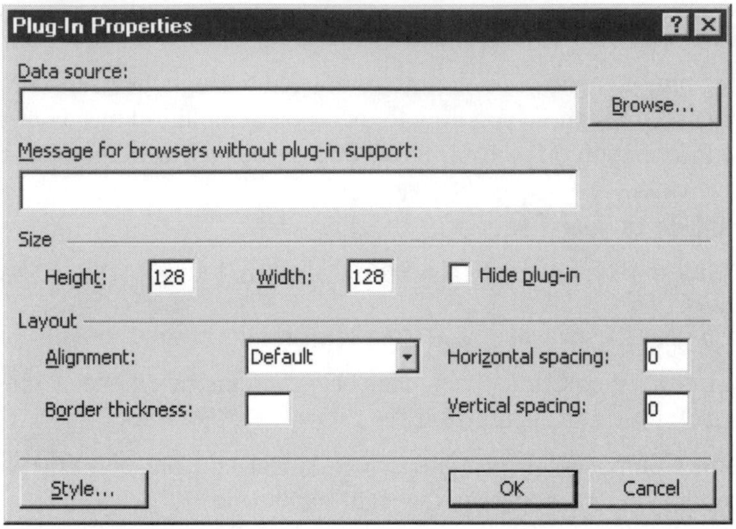

Figure 13-6   *The Plug-In Properties dialog box, used to insert and modify plug-ins in your pages*

9. Select the layout properties and optional style attributes for your plug-in and then click OK. The plug-in is now inserted into your page, and a representative image is displayed.

Setting the Plug-In Properties

Once you have inserted a plug-in into your page, you may find that you need to modify its properties. This is accomplished by following these steps:

1. Double-click the plug-in image on your page. This brings up the Plug-In Properties dialog box, shown in Figure 13-6.

2. Modify the properties to suit your needs and click OK. The new properties will now take effect.

Incorporating Alternative Messages

When working with plug-in technology, you should always include alternative messages to display in browsers that do not currently have a plug-in installed for the data you are attempting to transmit to the browser. This alternative text works much the same as the <NOFRAMES> tag—it displays only if the plug-in is not available to the viewer. Also, I recommend that you incorporate information about what would be displayed if the plug-in were installed as well as a link directing viewers to where they can obtain the plug-in.

An alternative message can be incorporated into your plug-in setup using one of two methods. You can simply incorporate the message using the Plug-In Properties dialog box (discussed in the previous section), or you can incorporate it directly into your code. The first method is the simpler of the two, but the second method is recommended because you will have an easier time entering long strings of information.

TIP

If your page is plug-in based—meaning that all that appears is the information in the embedded file—be sure to include alternative navigation in your text. This way, robots will still be able to index your pages even if you have plug-in-only content.

To incorporate your alternative message directly into your code, follow these steps:

1. Insert the plug-in as specified in the earlier section "Adding a Plug-In to Your Page."

2. Select the plug-in by clicking it once.

3. Switch to HTML view. You will see that the plug-in code is selected.

4. Move your cursor to the end of the <EMBED> tag and type the **<NOEMBED>** tag.

5. Type the alternative text you want incorporated into your page. This text can be of any length and can include any number of HTML tags.

TIP

If you are incorporating this text in a plug-in area that has a specific width and height, you will want to enter an amount of text that will not exceed that specification so that your page formatting will not be affected.

6. When you have finished entering your alternative text, type **</NOEMBED>** to close the tag.

Now, when viewers without the plug-in look at your page they will see the alternative text you have entered.

Behind the Scenes

To incorporate a plug-in into your page, FrontPage simply inserts the <EMBED> tag into your code. The <EMBED> tag does just what it says it does: It embeds a filename into the page. When the browser loads the page, it sees the <EMBED> tag and launches the plug-in associated with the file's MIME type. Along with launching the plug-in, the browser interprets the attributes associated with the tag for the display of the embedded file.

Along with the <EMBED> tag, FrontPage also inserts the <NOEMBED> tag into your code if you have specified an alternative representation for the plug-in. This tag works much like the <NOFRAMES> tag—it only displays when the plug-in is not available and allows you to incorporate alternative content to display.

Here's an example of how a substitute for the Windows Media Player plug-in might be used:

```
<Embed type="application/x-mplayer2" pluginspage=
"http://www.microsoft.com/windows95/downloads/
 contents/wurecommended/s_wufeatured/mediaplayer/default.asp"
          src="http://server/path/your-file.asx"
          Name=MediaPlayer
          ShowControls=1
          Width=360
          Height=180

    >
    </embed>
```

As you can see in the preceding example, additional information has been added to FrontPage's simple plug-in implementation. Although this code is not always necessary, it often increases the probability that your targeted media will display properly and should be used whenever possible. The additional tags you can use are as follows:

▶ **type**   The encoding type of the plug-in to be used to display the media specified in the src attribute

▶ **pluginspage**   A URL where the user may download the plug-in for use

▶ **name**   An object name used to identify this particular plug-in when performing scripted activities

Mixing Things Up to Create Cross-Browser Compatibility

As you've seen in this chapter, it's quite easy to implement ActiveX controls, Java applets, and plug-ins within your FrontPage Webs. Of course, a problem arises when you must choose which technology to use for the broadest browser compatibility. Well, the answer to that nagging question is a mixture of the technologies.

Just as ActiveX controls only natively run under Internet Explorer, plug-ins are usually browser specific and take the form of a DLL (Dynamic Link Library) file—a set of functions compiled into a binary file that provides access to those functions. A plug-in extends the browser's capabilities but is usually not a standalone application itself. An exception to this is the helper application, which is often capable of running within multiple browsers, often through the use of a browser-specific plug-in.

In order to display cross-browser-compatible extended media formats that are not directly supported by browsers, you must either use a Java applet or a combination of an ActiveX control <OBJECT> tag and a plug-in <EMBED> tag. Because many extended media files do not yet have Java applet–based viewers available, the latter, more complex choice is usually required.

As we have previously discussed, ActiveX controls are implemented using <OBJECT> </OBJECT> tags. Anything that lies between those tags is considered to be part of the object declaration. In the traditional forgiving nature of HTML, Internet Explorer ignores anything within these tags that it does not understand. On the other hand, Netscape's browsers do not understand the <OBJECT> </OBJECT> tags and ignores them along with any included object parameters. Therefore, to make your extended media cross-browser compatible, simply insert your plug-in's <EMBED> </EMBED> tags within the <OBJECT> </OBJECT> tags, and everybody's happy.

Here's an example of this method using Microsoft's Media Player, which we've been working with so far in this chapter:

```
<OBJECT ID="MediaPlayer"
  classid="CLSID:22d6f312-b0f6-11d0-94ab-0080c74c7e95"
CODEBASE="http://activex.microsoft.com/activex/
    controls/mplayer/en/nsmp2inf.cab#Version=5,1,52,701"
  standby="Loading Microsoft Windows Media Player
  components..."
  type="application/x-oleobject">
```

```
        <PARAM NAME="FileName" VALUE="
            http://server/path/your-file.asx">
        <PARAM NAME="AnimationatStart" VALUE="true">
        <PARAM NAME="TransparentatStart" VALUE="true">
        <PARAM NAME="AutoStart" VALUE="true">
        <PARAM NAME="ShowControls" VALUE="1">

        <Embed type="application/x-mplayer2"
pluginspage="http://www.microsoft.com/
            windows95/downloads/contents/wurecommended/
            s_wufeatured/mediaplayer/default.asp"
        src="http://server/path/your-file.asx"
        Name=MediaPlayer
        ShowControls=1
        Width=360
        Height=180
    >
    </embed>
</OBJECT>
```

As you can see, we've simply inserted the plug-in's <EMBED> tags within ActiveX <OBJECT> tags. By using this method, both Microsoft and Netscape browsers will be able to properly display your content.

Finding ActiveX Controls

Several ActiveX controls are readily available on the Internet for you to download and incorporate into your pages. These controls have already been developed and simply need to be downloaded from their respective locations and installed on your machine.

The following list provides some great resources for ActiveX controls and documentation on the Internet. Some are free for noncommercial use, and others are shareware:

▶   **Microsoft COM technologies**   http://www.microsoft.com/com/activex.asp
    Contains information on ActiveX, along with resource sites.

▶   **CNET ActiveX site**   http://www.activex.com
    Contains a great number of ActiveX controls you can download and incorporate into your pages.

▶ **Microsoft Site Builder component development site**
http://www.microsoft.com/com/tech/activex.asp?RLD=18
The Site Builder Network has some great tutorials on how to build ActiveX
components.

▶ **BrowserWatch, ActiveX Arena!**
http://browserwatch.internet.com/ activex.html
This is a great list of ActiveX controls you can download.

Finding Java Applets

Many Java applets are readily available on the Internet for you to download and
incorporate into your pages. These applets have already been developed and simply need
to be downloaded from their respective locations and installed on your machine.

The following list provides some great resources for applets and documentation
on the Internet. Some are free for noncommercial use, and others are shareware:

▶ **Sun Microsystem's applet site**   http://java.sun.com/applets/
Demonstration applets from the source.

▶ **JavaPowered.com**   http://www.javapowered.com/
Lots of great downloadable Java applets update frequently.

▶ **FreewareJava.com**   http://www.freewarejava.com
This site includes a number of applets and tutorials.

Summary

In this chapter we have taken a look at some technologies you can use in FrontPage.
The first is the incorporation of ActiveX controls into your Webs. As you learned in this
chapter, integrating ActiveX controls into your sites can be easily accomplished, and
FrontPage gives you complete control over the layout and property settings for the
controls. This chapter also includes links to a number of Web sites where you can obtain
further information about ActiveX controls and download custom-built controls.

Along with discussing the ActiveX controls, we have detailed how to incorporate
Java applets into your Webs using FrontPage. Upon completing this chapter, you
should have a basic understanding of both ActiveX and Java, along with the
knowledge necessary to incorporate these technologies into your pages.

In the last part of the chapter, I have shown you how to incorporate plug-in-based applications into your pages and create cross-browser-compatible implementations using a mixture of ActiveX control declarations and embedded plug-in declarations. Although many third-party programs come equipped with their own software for incorporating their plug-ins into your pages, it is nice to know that FrontPage has taken the usage of plug-ins into consideration and made it easy to incorporate them into your Webs.

Introducing the
Microsoft Script Editor

IN THIS CHAPTER:

Get to Know the Script Editor

Debug Your Code

Work with COM Objects

One of the most incorporated items, outside of HTML, in Web pages today is the client-side script. For the most part, developers incorporate JavaScript into their sites to add interactivity and to extend DHTML capabilities. For those who are looking to an Internet Explorer–only audience, there is also the use of VBScript in pages. In the release of FrontPage 2000, Microsoft made a huge advance by incorporating the Microsoft Script Editor into the package. With the release of FrontPage 2002, Microsoft has extended that step by enhancing the interface and capabilities of the Microsoft Script Editor, making it even easier to incorporate custom scripting into your pages.

This tool not only gives you the ability to incorporate scripts but also offers features to assist you in the development of those scripts. For developers, this tool allows you to easily develop and customize complex scripts within the FrontPage environment. For novices, this editor gives you the tools you need to begin creating your own scripts and making your pages that much more dynamic.

This chapter gives you the information you need to begin using the Script Editor to add another level of creativity and functionality to your Webs. This chapter is also a precursor to Chapter 15, where we take a look at JavaScript and VBScript and how to incorporate them into your Webs.

NOTE

When working with the Script Editor, you may find options and tools that simply do not make sense or seem to have no purpose. This is because these options are related to the upcoming release of Visual Studio .NET. At the time this book was written, this product was not yet released.

Origins of the Script Editor

The Script Editor is a powerful tool that allows you to add and modify VBScript and JavaScript when working with FrontPage. This tool has many advanced features. For the purposes of this book, we will cover the basics of the editor and how to work with it when incorporating scripting into your pages.

If you are familiar with Microsoft's Visual InterDev, you already know quite a bit about the Script Editor. Basically, the Script Editor is a limited version of the Microsoft Development Environment (MDE). Microsoft has taken the MDE, disabled some of its features, and included it as the Office Script Editor. For instance, when you're working with HTML documents created in FrontPage or other Office applications, the Script Editor does not support the "Design" view, which is the standard WYSIWYG editor that comes with the full version of MDE. The main reason this is done is to protect Office-generated code that the Script Editor might not be able to display graphically. FrontPage itself also provides a warning before switching from HTML view to the WYSIWYG editor when it does not understand—or cannot graphically display—a document's code. The Script Editor's lack of Design view support for FrontPage documents is not really a problem, though. Because it is linked directly to FrontPage, there is no need for the WYSIWYG editor within the Script Editor. If you choose to create a new page within the Script Editor, Design view is available until you edit the page within FrontPage or another Office application. However, when saving the page, you will not have the opportunity to publish it to your Web server. For these reasons, you will likely want to work solely within the Source and Quick views for creating and inserting your code when using the Script Editor.

Now, you may be wondering whether you should simply use Visual InterDev for your script creation since the MDE comes equipped with a WYSIWYG editor that allows you to create your scripts and incorporate them using a layout tool. Well, some serious programmers may say this is the best route to take, but if you are creating graphically complicated Webs and want to take advantage of FrontPage's many Web Components, you will appreciate the design, layout, and automation capabilities of FrontPage.

Working with the Script Editor

When you are working with a page in your Web that you want to add scripting to, you simply select Tools | Macros | Microsoft Script Editor from the menu bar. This will launch the Script Editor and display the page you are currently working on within a window in the editor, as shown in Figure 14-1. You can then add your script to the page and save it, automatically updating the page in FrontPage.

When you move back into the FrontPage environment, you will see an icon representing your script in the Normal view with Reveal Tags turned on. Another nice feature is that the link between FrontPage and the Script Editor is bidirectional and always hot (active) while the document is open in both applications. Therefore, changes made to a page in either program are immediately reflected in the other.

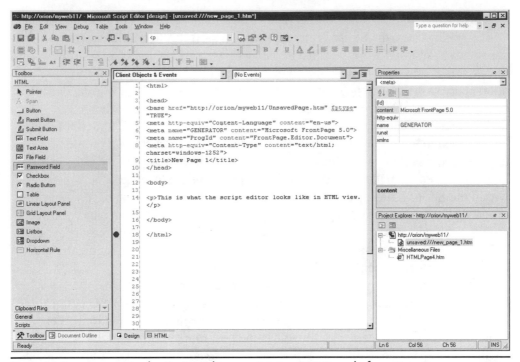

Figure 14-1   *A page in the Script Editor containing HTML code from FrontPage*

Script Editor Windows

When working within the Script Editor, you will work with various windows that you need to be aware of in order to use the application to its fullest extent. These windows allow you to view your code and organize the files you are working with.

Source Editor Window

The Source Editor is where you will do the bulk of the work associated with incorporating existing scripts and, more importantly, writing your own scripts. This view contains all the elements of your HTML page that have been brought over from the FrontPage environment. Within the Source Editor (refer to Figure 14-1), you will see your code much as you would see it when working in the FrontPage HTML view. For detailed information on working in the Source Editor, see "Working with the Source Editor," later in this chapter.

Project Explorer

The Project Explorer allows you to view the various files you have open within the Script Editor. This is a tree-based interface, shown in Figure 14-2, that allows you to view and select the files you are incorporating code into within the Script Editor. You use this window to collapse or expand the various groupings of files you are working with and to select various files for opening in the Source Editor.

Properties Window

The Properties window displays all the design-time properties associated with the currently selected item. When working with an item, you can specify many of the parameters associated with it in this window. You will see that the properties list adjusts depending on the item you have selected. If no item is selected, the default DOCUMENT properties title appears in the drop-down menu. To work with and adjust other properties, you can select them in one of your views or simply select them from the drop-down list that appears in the Properties window. If you want to adjust a specific property for an object, simply click the text box next to that property in the window and adjust the property value.

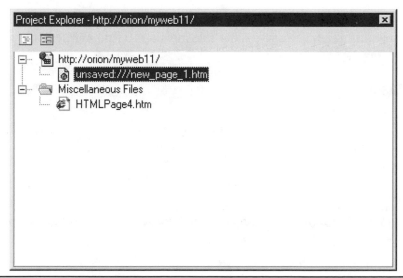

Figure 14-2   *Example of the Project Explorer window in the Script Editor*

Toolbox Window

You will notice that I make reference to the Toolbox extensively in this chapter. The Toolbox is a dynamic window that contains various tabs filled with tasks and procedures. The most basic of these is the HTML tab of the Toolbox. From this tab, you can drag and drop various HTML elements directly into your page. This assists you in speeding the process of implementing common HTML elements you will be working with.

But the Toolbox does not stop there. This window will come in very handy if you use the Script Editor a lot. You will see in the section "Adding Controls to the Toolbox," later in this chapter, that this window allows you to add your own custom buttons to it. These buttons can contain items such as commonly used scripts that you want to store for use in your documents.

Script Editor Menus

The Script Editor also contains a number of menus that allow you to perform functions within the program. These menus are your main tools for completing operations, and each menu is described here, along with the various functions associated with it.

File Menu

The File menu is much like many other File menus you find in Microsoft products, and it contains the following command options:

- ▶ **New File**   Brings up the New File dialog box, allowing you to create a new file in the editor.

- ▶ **Open File**   Brings up the Open File dialog box, allowing you to open an existing file.

- ▶ **Close**   Closes the current file.

- ▶ **Save**   Saves the current file.

- ▶ **Save Selected Item As**   Brings up the Save a Copy dialog box, allowing you to specify a different name and location for the file.

- ▶ **Save All**   Saves all currently open files.

- ▶ **View in Browser**   Opens the current file in the default browser.

- ▶ **Browse With**   Brings up the Browse With dialog box, allowing you to select the browser you want to view the file in, along with display options for viewing.

▶ **Page Setup**   Brings up the Page Setup dialog box, allowing you to specify settings, such as the width and height when printing the page within the editor.

▶ **Print**   Prints the current document.

▶ **Exit**   Closes the editor.

Edit Menu

The Edit menu consists of the standard Microsoft editing commands. But it also contains some commands that are specific to the Script Editor when you're working in the source view. These commands are explained here:

▶ **Paste as HTML**   When you're pasting text from a graphical viewer such as your Web browser or a Word document, all of the text's HTML and style formatting information is pasted along with the text. Using the Paste as HTML option inserts the copied text without any formatting information.

▶ **Cycle Clipboard Ring**   Places the next bit of code from the clipboard ring into the document at the present cursor location.

▶ **Insert Script Block**   Contains Client and Server options, allowing you to insert a script block of the selected type within your document. The Server option is only available when you're working with pages that have an .asp extension.

▶ **Insert File as Text**   Brings up the Insert Text dialog box, allowing you to select a file to insert into your page at the current cursor location.

Advanced Menu   The Advanced menu option contains the following set of commands for use within the editor:

▶ **Tabify Selection**   Replaces character spaces with the appropriate number of tabs corresponding to your tab settings and the number of spaces.

▶ **Untabify Selection**   Replaces tabs with the corresponding number of spaces based on your tab settings.

▶ **Make Uppercase**   Changes the selected text to uppercase.

▶ **Make Lowercase**   Changes the selected text to lowercase.

▶ **Delete Horizontal White Space**   Removes extra space characters from the selected lines.

▶ **View White Space**   Displays invisible characters using dots for spaces and arrows for tabs. This makes it much easier to view and manipulate the exact formatting of text.

▶ **Word Wrap**   Wraps the text of the current document to fit in the window without the need for horizontal scrolling.

▶ **Incremental Search**   Allows you to search through the current document using the search box on the menu bar.

▶ **Increase Line Indent**   Increases the indent of the current line by a single tab.

▶ **Decrease Line Indent**   Decreases the indent of the current line by a single tab.

Bookmarks Menu   Bookmarks contain a subset of commands. The Bookmark commands allow you to set placeholders within your documents, which you can quickly jump to later within the Script Editor, the same way HTML bookmarks allow you to jump to specific locations within a page in your browser. Here are the commands:

▶ **Toggle Bookmarks**   Sets a placeholder (bookmark) on the page for future reference.

▶ **Next Bookmark**   Moves you to the next bookmark within your file.

▶ **Previous Bookmark**   Moves you to the previous bookmark within your file.

▶ **Clear All Bookmarks**   Removes all the bookmarks you have created in your file.

▶ **Add Task List Shortcut**   Adds an arrow to the selected line, notating a needed task.

NOTE

Bookmarks only exist during the document's current editing session. Once closed, all bookmarks within the document are lost.

Outlining Menu   The Outlining menu option contains the following set of commands for use within the editor:

▶ **Hide Selection**   Allows you to select and hide a block of text in your code.

▶ **Toggle Outlining Expansion**   Expands or contracts the currently selected outline item.

▶ **Toggle All Outlining**   Expands or contracts all outlined items.

▶ **Stop Outlining**   Turns off outlining.

▶ **Stop Hiding Current**   Removes outlining from the current selection.

IntelliSense Menu   The IntelliSense menu option contains the following set of commands for use within the editor:

▶ **List Members**   Displays a drop-down menu that lists all the available properties and methods associated with a specific object. This allows you to scroll through the list without the need for opening the Properties dialog box or reference materials. Pressing the spacebar selects the currently highlighted item.

▶ **Parameter Info**   Displays information relating to the parameters of an initial function or statement.

▶ **Complete Word**   Finishes typing a word once you have entered enough of the text for the system to recognize which word it is you are typing.

View Menu

The View menu contains commands that allow you to toggle on and off the various windows in which you work when using the editor. The commands found in this menu are fairly self-explanatory because they refer to the various windows in which they display. I will not describe each of these commands here, but you will find information regarding the windows they display throughout this section.

Debug Menu

The Debug menu gives you the power to fix problems within your scripts before deploying them. Within this menu are a number of commands used for debugging your scripts. They are described here:

NOTE

Several of the Debug menu options are only visible while you're running the current page in debug mode (using the debugger). Others are only visible when you're not in debug mode.

▶ **Window**   Allows you to toggle the display of the various debug-related display windows (non-debug and debug mode).

▶ **Start**   Runs the code and attaches the debugger (non-debug mode).

▶ **Start Without Debugging**   Runs the script without debugging (non-debug mode).

▶ **Continue**   Resumes execution of the page code from the current breakpoint (debug mode).

▶ **Stop Debugging**   Stops running the current document (debug mode).

▶ **Detach All**   An advanced debugging option that has little meaning to FrontPage users. See the Processes option in this list for more information (debug mode).

▶ **Restart**   Stops any currently running debugging session and begins it again after rebuilding (debug mode).

▶ **Break All**   Allows you to temporarily stop the debugging process without ending the session (debug mode).

▶ **Processes**   This advanced option displays the Process dialog box. This is a remnant of the Script Editor's original parent, Visual Studio, and is used when you're debugging server-based COM components—a subject well beyond the scope of this book (non-debug and debug mode).

▶ **Show Next Statement**   Makes the Script Editor jump to the statement that will be executed next within a script that is running in break mode. This line is simply displayed but not yet executed (debug mode).

▶ **Step Into**   Runs your code one statement at a time through each function call (non-debug).

▶ **Step Over**   Moves to the next line of code and runs it without following through to any function calls (non-debug).

▶ **Step By Line**   Runs the code line by line (non-debug and debug mode).

▶ **Step By Statement**   Runs the code by each script statement (non-debug and debug mode).

▶ **Set Next Statement**   Allows you to force a script running in break mode to jump to another location within the current function or event. This handy feature lets you temporarily skip problematic code without having to make any changes. It also allows you to back up and run statements again (debug mode).

▶ **Run To Cursor**   Begins the execution of your code up until the current cursor position (non-debug and debug mode).

▶ **Quick Watch**   Displays the Quick Watch dialog box, allowing you to quickly add watched (monitored) expressions and variables to the Watch window (debug mode).

▶ **New Breakpoint**   Brings up the Breakpoints dialog box, allowing you to add and modify breakpoints (non-debug and debug mode). This dialog box is discussed later in the chapter.

▶ **Clear All Breakpoints**   Removes all breakpoints from the current document (non-debug and debug mode).

NOTE

Server-side script debugging (for Active Server Pages) is only available when you're working with pages being hosted on Internet Information Services. Pages stored on your hard drive or hosted on any of the Personal Web Servers do not support server-side script debugging. Client-side script debugging is supported on any server implementation.

Table Menu

Your Table menu works much like the Table menu found in FrontPage, with obvious limitations. The commands in this menu give you the ability to insert tables and make modifications to them once they are placed on the page. A particularly nice feature of the Script Editor's Insert Table dialog box is the ability to specify common cell attributes when you're creating a table. This eliminates the need to create the table and then go back and select the table to configure options such as cell alignment.

Tools Menu

The Tools menu contains commands used to set up your environment within the program. Within this menu you have the Customize Toolbox and Options commands. These commands are discussed later in this chapter.

Windows and Help Menus

These two menus are the standard ones found in most Microsoft programs. Among the helpful features found here include some that are missing from FrontPage, such as the ability to cascade and tile multiple windows, to split the current window into two concurrent views, and to close all windows without closing the application.

Adding Controls to the Toolbox

The Script Editor's Toolbox, shown in Figure 14-3, displays many of the basic tools you need when working within your code. It consists of various tabs that allow you to add items to your code simply by selecting an item and dragging it onto your page or by double-clicking an item to insert it at the cursor's location. One of the great features of the Toolbox is the ability to add various ActiveX controls to it for use within your documents. This is accomplished by following these steps:

1. Select the tab on the Toolbox where you want your new control to appear by clicking it with your mouse.

Figure 14-3 *The Script Editor's Toolbox*

2. Select Tools | Customize Toolbox from the Script Editor menu bar. This brings up the Customize Toolbox dialog box, shown in Figure 14-4.

3. Select the ActiveX control you want to add to the Toolbox by checking the box corresponding to the item. Then click OK. Your new control now appears on the Toolbox.

NOTE

Just because a control appears in the ActiveX Controls list doesn't mean you can use it. This list encompasses all the controls currently installed on your computer, many of which require special licenses to be used or redistributed. Consult the control's documentation for further information on restrictions and/or limitations.

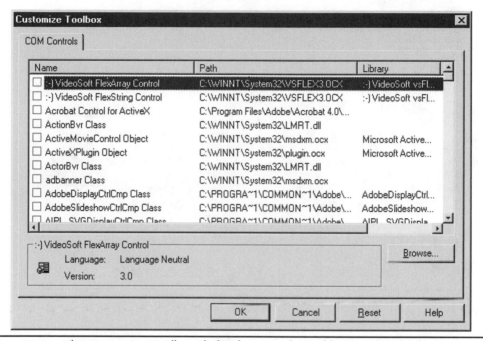

Figure 14-4   *The Customize Toolbox dialog box, used to add ActiveX controls to your Toolbox*

We'll cover other Toolbox customization features later in this chapter.

Setting the Script Editor Options

When working in the Script Editor, you are presented with a default look and feel, along with a standard layout for your code. This may suit your needs just fine, but you may find that you want to modify various aspects of the layout. This is accomplished via the Options dialog box, shown in Figure 14-5. To open the Options dialog box, simply select Tools | Options from the menu bar. Within this dialog box you can set various options.

Environment

Your Environment settings determine the look and feel of the Script Editor. Within this section, various subcategories allow you to specify how your system will display information. Those categories, and their settings, are outlined here.

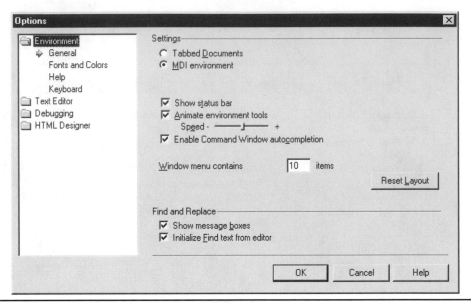

Figure 14-5   *The Script Editor's Options dialog box*

General   The General settings determine the overall settings for the editor itself:

▶ **Tabbed Documents**   Allows you to select a tabbed document interface, instructing the Script Editor to show the documents in a tabbed format for easy switching. This setting takes effect the next time you launch the Script Editor.

▶ **MDI Environment**   Allows you to select a Multiple Document Interface (MDI). This setting takes effect the next time you launch the Script Editor.

▶ **Show Status Bar**   Allows you to toggle the status bar on and off.

▶ **Animate Environment Tools**   Determines whether tool displays are animated and at what speed.

▶ **Enable Command Window Autocompletion**   If this option is checked, the editor will attempt to complete your commands for you while you type.

▶ **Window Menu Contains X Items**   Allows you to determine the number of open items that will display in the Windows menu list before being relegated to the More Windows dialog box. Optional values range from 1 to 24.

▶ **Reset Layout button**   Returns all settings to the default.

▶ **Show Message Boxes**   Displays the Find and Replace message boxes.

▶ **Initialize Find Text from Editor**   Prefills the Find field in the Find and Replace dialog box with text you have selected in the page.

Fonts and Colors   The settings in this category allow you to set up different fonts, colors, and backgrounds for the various types of text items appearing in your editor window. If you don't care for the editor's default color coding, you can change it to suit your needs.

Help   The settings in this category specify the language and collection you want to use for the Script Editor's help system.

Keyboard   The settings in this category specify the various shortcut keys you use to launch commands from the keyboard.

Text Editor

The Text Editor settings allow you to specify how your text-editing window is set up for use in the system. Within this category are various subcategories you can use to specify how your editor looks and works. These categories and their commands are outlined here.

General   The General category allows you to configure the following settings:

▶ **Go to Selection Anchor after Escape**   Instructs the system to move the cursor to the last position it was in when you select a block of text and press ESC on your keyboard.

▶ **Drag and Drop Text Editing**   Allows you to select a block of text and drag it to another location within the document.

▶ **Include Insertion Point Movements in Undo List**   Instructs the system to include various insertion points you have placed when working with the Undo list.

▶ **Automatic Delimiter Highlighting**   Instructs the system to automatically highlight the various delimiters.

▶ **Selection Margin**   Adds a slight margin between the text displayed in the editor and its left border.

▶ **Indicator Margin**   Instructs the system to display the left margin, which contains various markers (such as breakpoints) within your document.

▶ **Vertical Scrollbar**   Displays the vertical scroll bar in the Editor window.

▶ **Horizontal Scrollbar**   Displays the horizontal scroll bar in the Editor window.

All Languages   The All Languages category contains two subcategories, General and Tab, that have the following settings:

▶ **Auto List Members**   Displays an onscreen prompt to help you complete a statement you are entering in the editor. This IntelliSense feature allows you to enter the beginning of a statement, and then it presents you with a pop-up list of options for completing the statement. You may then use your arrow keys to scroll through the displayed list and press the spacebar to insert your selection into the page.

▶ **Parameter Information**   Displays an onscreen prompt instructing you as to what parameters can be used with the function statement you are typing.

▶ **Enable Virtual Space**   Allows you to have a selection that passes the end of your code line either in the vertical or horizontal space.

▶ **Word Wrap**   Turns word wrap on or off for all languages.

▶ **Line Numbers**   Instructs the system to display line numbers in the margins.

▶ **Navigation Bar**   Instructs the system to display the navigation bar for all languages.

▶ **Indenting**   Sets the indentation for your text within the editor when you press ENTER for each new line. If you select None, when you press ENTER, the next line begins at the left margin, regardless of your current tabbed indentation. When you select Block, the next line begins at your current tabbed indentation, and when you select Smart, the next line's indentation level is determined based on the function of the current line. For example, if the current line contains a Do While statement, the next line will automatically be indented one more tab. This option is not available in the HTML and Text options, and it only applies to the general Tab settings area.

▶ **Tab Size**   Specifies the number of spaces associated with each tab.

▶ **Indent Size**   Specifies the number of spaces associated with indentation within your code.

▶ **Insert Spaces**   Instructs the editor to use spaces rather than tabs when indenting your code.

▶ **Keep Tabs**   Instructs the editor to use tabs rather than spaces when indenting your code.

Within the Text Editor options are various settings you can assign to each type of document/language you are working with. For the purposes of this book, I will outline the General and All Languages options under this category. Each of the underlying options has language-specific settings that will further allow you to customize how specific aspects of your page appear within your views. They are described next but exclude the basic options discussed previously in this section.

CSS   The options for Cascading Style Sheets (CSS) fall under two categories that are not covered by the General and Tabs attributes. They consist of CSS-specific properties and format properties. The values found under these subsections are described here:

▶ **Show Statement Completion Popups**   Instructs the system to show various options for completing your statements while you type.

▶ **Show Property Description Tooltips**   Instructs the system to show possible property options while you type.

▶ **Detect Errors**   Instructs the system to automatically alert you to errors while entering values.

▶ **Detect Unknown Properties**   Instructs the system to automatically alert you to CSS properties you have typed that are unknown to FrontPage.

▶ **Detect Invalid Values**   Instructs the system to automatically alert you to invalid CSS values.

▶ **Style**   The Style attributes determine how the CSS code will display within your style sheet page. You have three specific options for display under the style properties: Compact Rules, Semi-expanded, and Expanded. The choice you make here has no effect on the actual styles you develop; it only determines how they will display on the page. When you select one of the available options, you will see an example of that display type in the Preview area of the dialog box.

▶ **Capitalization** The Capitalization setting determines how your code will be capitalized within the style. Here you have the option to instruct the system to display your code as entered, in lowercase, or in uppercase. Once again, this has no effect on the actual style; it is simply a determinate of how the text displays within the style.

HTML The HTML-specific options fall under two categories that are not covered by the General and Tabs attributes. They consist of the format and HTML-specific properties, whose options are described here:

▶ **Line Breaks** Allows you to instruct the system to insert hard line breaks before and/or after the beginning and end of each HTML tag inserted into the document.

▶ **HTML Tag Capitalization** Instructs the system to automatically set the case of entered and generated HTML tags based on your selection.

▶ **Apply Formatting** Instructs the system to automatically apply your selected formatting based on the option you select. If you do not select one of the available options, formatting will not be applied to the document.

▶ **HTML Validation** Instructs the system to automatically validate your HTML code.

▶ **Statement Completion** Instructs the system to give you pop-up tips concerning the code you are typing. You can set this to give tips for both HTML and scripting statements.

▶ **Auto Insert** Instructs the system to automatically insert a closing tag for each opening tag you enter and to surround your HTML values (for example, width="xx") with quotation marks.

Debugger

The Debugger settings allow you to set the global options for debugging your code within the editor. Debugger contains the General subcategory, along with the JIT (Just In Time) settings. The General settings contain basic global options for debugging. The JIT settings allow for debugging outside the editor environment. If errors are found, you are notified and asked whether you want to begin the debugging process. To use this feature, you must set the Enable JIT Debugging option. Also, you can connect the debugger to your scripts so that you can debug without having to run the script from the editor by selecting the Enable Attach option.

HTML Designer

The HTML Designer settings are used for determining the display attributes of the Design mode of the Script Editor. Because you will be working in conjunction with FrontPage, you will not need to set these options.

Working with the Source Editor

When working within the Source Editor, you have many tools to make your script creation painless. These tools are designed to make it easy to work with the code and also to automate much of your code generation.

Color Coding

Within your code you will see a variety of colors, which are designed to make reading and editing your code easier. Although the Source Editor assigns default colors to many aspects of the code, you can set the colors according to your own preferences via the Text Editor's Font and Color settings, found in the Options menu. (For more information on setting your options, see "Setting the Script Editor Options," earlier in this chapter.)

Automatic Word Completion and Function Help

The Script Editor has some great automation tools built in to help you in writing your scripts. These tools help you by completing basic scripting words, displaying available methods and properties for an item, and displaying the various functions associated with an item. All these functions will work to your advantage whether you are an experienced programmer or just starting out with scripting. Here is a description of each:

► **Complete Word**   You use this function by typing a partial word, such as **Msg**, within a VBScript client-side script area and then selecting Edit | IntelliSense | Complete Word (ALT-RIGHT ARROW). If you have typed in enough information, the editor will automatically complete the word for you.

► **Parameter Info**   Displays complete function declarations, providing you with a blueprint for completing your statement. Continuing with the previous example, type **Msg** within a VBScript client-side script area and press ALT-RIGHT ARROW to have the editor complete the function name MsgBox. Next, type an opening parenthesis (, and the entire MsgBox function declaration will be displayed in a ToolTip with the prompt argument displayed in bolded text. If the Parameter Info option is turned off in the Options dialog box, you may also display this information with the Edit menu's Parameter Information option. You will also see that as you type the rest of the statement, the current argument will always be displayed in bold text, telling you exactly where you are in the statement, as shown here:

```
17  MsgBox (
18  MsgBox (prompt, [buttons], [title], [helpfile], [context])
19  </script>
```

▶ **List Members**   You use this function by selecting an object and then selecting Edit | IntelliSense | List Members from the menu bar. This brings up a drop-down list containing all the properties and methods available for the selected object, as shown in the following illustration. When the Auto List Members option is turned on (Options | Text Editor | All Languages dialog box), you may also type the name of an object and simply type a period (.) to display the list.

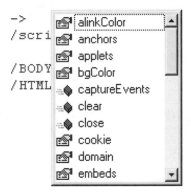

▶ **Context Sensitive Help**   Displays context-sensitive help. If you're still unsure how to use a function call, simply click anywhere within the function name and press F1 to display context-sensitive help on the selected function. Because the Script Editor contains both VBScript and JavaScript references, you'll likely find what you're looking for within the excellent help system.

Incorporating Breakpoints

Breakpoints are like bookmarks you set in your script that instruct the application to stop and enter the debugging break mode when they are encountered. These points allow you to specify exact lines within your script where you want execution to halt and debugging to begin.

Inserting and Removing Breakpoints

To insert a breakpoint in your script, follow these steps:

1. Move to the point in your script where you want the breakpoint set.
2. Click the left margin. You will see a red dot appear in the margin. This specifies that a breakpoint has been set.

   To remove the breakpoint, simply click the dot in the margin, and the point will disappear.

TIP

The F9 key also toggles breakpoints on and off for the current line, showing or hiding the same red dot in the left margin area.

Working with the Breakpoints Dialog Box

The Breakpoints dialog box, shown in Figure 14-6, allows you to view all the breakpoints within the current document. You bring up this dialog box by selecting

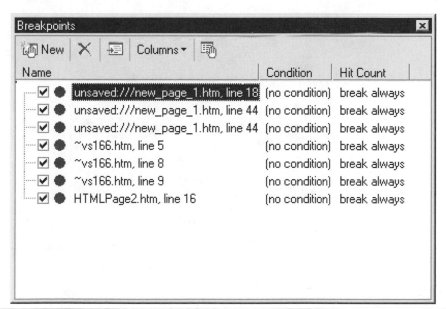

Figure 14-6 *The Breakpoints dialog box is used to display breakpoints within a document.*

Debug | Windows | Breakpoints from the menu bar. Within this dialog box, you can view all your breakpoints as well as remove, enable, and disable each point.

Along with these capabilities, you can view a specific breakpoint's properties and add new breakpoints to your document.

Adjusting Breakpoint Properties

The Breakpoint Properties dialog box, shown in Figure 14-7, allows you to adjust the properties associated with a specific breakpoint within your document. To open the Breakpoint Properties dialog box, simply right-click a breakpoint and select Breakpoint Properties from the drop-down menu.

Once inside the dialog box, you have the following options, which you can edit:

▶ **File/Function tabs**   These tabs display the current filename and function, respectively, along with the line number and character placement.

▶ **Condition**   Brings up the Breakpoint Condition dialog box, allowing you to specify a condition in which the code should stop execution. Once you have

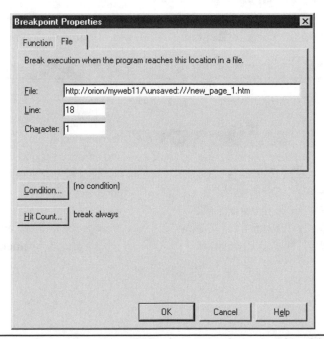

Figure 14-7   *The Breakpoint Properties dialog box is used to adjust breakpoint properties.*

entered a condition, you can specify how that condition should be handled by selecting either Is True or Is Changed. Selecting Is True causes the system to stop if the specified condition is true. Selecting Is Changed causes the system to stop if the specified condition has changed. If no condition is entered (default), the script execution will be halted each time the breakpoint is reached.

▶ **Hit Count**   Brings up the Breakpoint Hit Count dialog box, allowing you to specify when the system is to stop the code execution if the criteria within this section are met.

▶ **When the Breakpoint Is Hit**   Allows you to set an equation that instructs the system when to stop execution on this breakpoint. Select an equation parameter and then select the number to be associated with that equation. The code execution will stop when that parameter is met.

▶ **Reset Hit Count button**   Resets the hit count for the current breakpoint.

Adding a New Breakpoint in the Breakpoints Dialog Box

You can add a new breakpoint to your code simply by clicking in the left margin, but you can also add a breakpoint by clicking the New button in the Breakpoints dialog box, reached by clicking Debug | Windows | Breakpoints on the menu bar (Figure 14-6). This brings up the New Breakpoint dialog box, which contains the same functions as the Breakpoint Properties dialog box discussed earlier.

Hands On: Using Breakpoints

Now that you've seen how to configure breakpoints, let's put a simple one to use. Here are the steps to follow:

1. Create a new blank HTML page in FrontPage and open the Script Editor.

2. Locate the <body> tag and place the cursor on the line immediately following it.

3. Right-click this blank line and select Insert Script Block | Client from the pop-up menu. This inserts the basic beginning and ending scripting tags within your code.

4. Move to the blank line within the script block (after the <!— line and before the —> line) and enter the following code:

```
dim MyVar1, MyVar2, MyVar3
MyVar1 = 1
MyVar2 = 2
MyVar3 = MyVar1 + MyVar2
```

5. Click the gray margin area just to the left of the third line of code. A red dot is displayed, indicating that a breakpoint has been set on that line of code.

6. Now click Debug | Start on the menu bar to run your code. If you are asked to save the page, click Yes to save it.

After briefly opening a browser window to display the page, the Script Editor returns to view and displays your code with a yellow arrow on top of the breakpoint indicator dot, as shown here:

```
16
17  <script language="vbscript">
18  <!--
19  dim MyVar1, MyVar2, MyVar3
20  MyVar1 = 1
21  MyVar2 = 2
22  MyVar3 = MyVar1 + MyVar2
23  -->
24  </script>
25
```

Move your mouse over MyVar1 in your code. As you can see, a ToolTip pops up, displaying the value of MyVar1. This immediate-value ToolTip is part of the Script Editor's IntelliSense features and is a very useful and convenient debugging tool.

Now move your mouse over MyVar2 in the line containing the breakpoint. As you see, an immediate-value ToolTip is displayed, telling you that the variable MyVar2 is empty. This is because the breakpoint has stopped the running code before executing this statement. Pressing F11 allows you to step into the next line of code. After doing so, you'll see that the immediate-value ToolTip now reads MyVar2 = 2.

Pressing F5 resumes execution of the script. After completing the code execution, the browser window returns to the forefront of your display. You can simply close that window now that we've finished this example.

Inserting COM Controls into Your Pages

The Script Editor makes it easy to incorporate COM controls into your pages. Although this can also easily be done within FrontPage, you may find it necessary to incorporate them within the editor if you are working with other scripts at the time.

Basically, the Script Editor has all the COM controls on your system already available. However, they are not set up to use by default. To access them, you simply need to add them to your Toolbox. You can then drag them onto your page and begin working with them.

As previously mentioned, just because a control appears in the COM Controls list doesn't mean you can use it. This list encompasses all the controls currently installed on your computer, many of which require special licenses to be used or redistributed. Consult the control's documentation for further information on restrictions and/or limitations.

Adding a COM Control to the Toolbox

To add a COM control to your Toolbox, simply follow these steps:

1. Select the tab on the Toolbox where you want to add your control.

2. Select Tools | Customize Toolbox from the menu bar. This brings up the Customize Toolbox dialog box, shown previously in Figure 14-4.

3. Select the COM control you want to work with and click OK. If your control does not appear in the dialog box, click the Browse button to select the path for the control.

Your COM control now appears in your Toolbox and can be dragged onto the page.

Working with COM Control Properties

Once you place a COM control on your page, you will want to adjust the properties for that control. To do so, right-click within the object code and select Properties. The Properties window, shown in Figure 14-8, displays the properties associated with that control. You can then move throughout the various properties and assign the necessary information to each for the control to function properly.

This method of setting control properties has definite advantages because all control properties are already listed for you. Instead of manually entering each of them in the source code, you may simply browse the list and adjust the settings for the properties as needed.

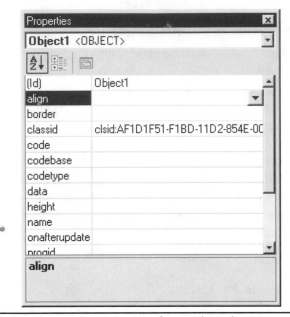

Figure 14-8   *A window displaying properties for a selected item*

Hands On: Customizing Your Toolbox

One of the great features of the Toolbox is the ability to customize it by adding your own tabs and code links. This is especially useful if you want to perform tasks such as creating a script library for use with your documents. You can create the script once and then add it to your Toolbox. Then when you want to use the script at a later date, you simply drag it onto your page, and the script appears in your code.

A perfect example of a script that you will likely use repeatedly is the common browser detection script. By adding it to your Toolbox, you may simply drag it onto pages whenever you need to use it.

To add a script function to the Toolbox, simply follow these steps:

1. Open a page to create your code. For this example, we will be creating a simple submit button message that informs users their information has been submitted.

2. From the HTML tab of the Toolbox, drag a button onto your page. The following code will appear:

```
<INPUT type="button" value="Button"
 ID="button1" name="button1">
```

3. Position your cursor directly below this code and select Edit | Insert Script Block | Client from the menu bar. This will insert the following code into your page:

```
<SCRIPT LANGUAGE=vbscript>
<!—


-->
</SCRIPT>
```

4. Add the following to the <SCRIPT> tag:
Event="onClick" For="button1"

5. Inside the arrow markers, type the following code:

```
MsgBox "Your form has been submitted"
```

Once you have completed steps 1 through 5, your page should look like this:

```
<INPUT type="button" value="Button"
 id="button1" name="button1">
<SCRIPT LANGUAGE=vbscript Event="onClick"
 For="button1">
<!--
   MsgBox "Your Form has been submitted"
-->
</SCRIPT>
```

That takes care of creating the script to add to your Toolbox. Now you'll need to create a new tab to house this script. To do so, follow these steps:

6. Right-click the Toolbox. This brings up a pop-up menu.

7. Select Add Tab from the pop-up menu. You will see a text area appear at the bottom of the Toolbox.

8. Type **Scripts** in the text area and press ENTER. Your new tab is now added to the Toolbox.

9. Select your new tab by clicking it with your mouse. You will see the default pointer appear.

Now you need to add your new script to your new tab.

10. Highlight the button and script code you just created and drag it onto your new tab. Once you let go of your mouse button, your item appears on the Toolbox with the title "HTML Fragment," as shown here:

You now need to change the name to something representing the actual content.

11. Position your cursor over your new script and right-click to bring up a pop-up menu.

12. Select Rename Item from the pop-up menu. The current name is highlighted.

13. Type **Submit Message** and press ENTER. Your new name is now saved on the Toolbox.

Now, whenever you want to add this script to your code, you simply drag it onto the page.

Editor Views

If you are working with large documents containing quite a bit of HTML and scripting, you will really like the HTML Outline and Script Outline features that come with the editor. These views allow you to quickly jump to a particular spot within your code that contains an HTML tag or a script you have inserted.

HTML Outline

The HTML Outline allows you to view all your HTML tags in a treelike hierarchical
fashion. It also allows you to quickly jump to any of those tags within your document
by selecting them from the tree. You view the HTML Outline by clicking the
Document Outline tab, which will normally be in the same window as your Toolbox,
and clicking the HTML Outline button at the top of the view. If it's not already visible,
you may display the HTML Outline tab by selecting View | Other Windows |
Document Outline from the menu bar (or simply by pressing CTRL-ALT-T). When
you click the tab, the HTML Outline appears with all your tags, as shown here:

To jump to a particular tag within the outline, simply click it. You will then be
moved to that tag's position within the HTML page.

Script Outline

The Script Outline displays all the scripts on your current page, just like the HTML
Outline, but it also gives you a listing of all the available scripting objects within
your page. Using this outline, you can quickly navigate to any script on your page.
You can also specify events for any scripting element on your page and create event
handlers for those scripts.

You view the Script Outline by clicking the Document Outline tab, which will
normally be in the same window as your Toolbox, and clicking the Script Outline
button at the top of the view. If it's not already visible, you may display the Script
Outline tab by selecting View | Other Windows | Document Outline from the menu
bar (or simply by pressing CTRL-ALT-T) and clicking the Script Outline button at the

top of the view. When you click the button, the Script Outline appears with all your scripts and the available objects, as shown here:

TIP

You may also locate your position within the Script Outline at any time while working within the source code by right-clicking anywhere within your script and selecting Synchronize Document Outline from the pop-up menu.

To insert an event handler for any Document (current page) or Window (browser) event, simply locate the event within the Script Outline and double-click it. Doing so inserts the proper event handler routine into your page at the current location of the cursor. You may then add whatever code is necessary to accomplish your task.

Script Only and Full HTML Views

Along with the Outline views described earlier, this latest version of the Script Editor comes equipped with the new Script Only and Full HTML views. These two views come in very handy because they allow you to hide aspects of your page while you are working so that you can keep your information organized and accessible. If you select the Script Only view, the editor window will shift to hide all content on the page that does not appear within script blocks.

To switch to the Script Only view, simply select View | Show Script Only, or you can click the Script Only View toggle button at the top left of your editing window. Once in the Script Only view, click the Full HTML View toggle button to display all of your code.

Summary

In this chapter, we have taken an in-depth look at using the Script Editor to incorporate scripts into your Webs. As you have seen, the inclusion of the Script Editor in the FrontPage product has made scripting an easier task than ever. It allows those who do not know scripting to quickly incorporate scripts into their pages, along with giving even the most advanced scripter the ability to automate many tasks.

   After completing this chapter, you should have a good understanding of the Script Editor's windows, menus, Toolbox, and other features and a good grasp of how to work with them to make your life that much easier.

Working with Scripting Technologies

IN THIS CHAPTER:

Learn the Difference between JavaScript and VBScript

Create Scripts for Use in Your Webs

Add Interactivity to Your Webs with Scripts

W e know FrontPage offers many great tools for creating Webs that scream as well as function on a business level. What you may not know is that FrontPage uses scripting technology to facilitate many of these functions. This use of scripts has become common on the Web, and you will find some sort of scripting in just about any high-level site. This chapter covers some of the scripting technology out there and how to incorporate it into your Webs.

With client-side scripting, you can take your Web to another level. No longer do you need access to server-based CGI scripts to create dynamic effects on your pages or to process and validate forms used in your site. Through the use of scripts, you can perform these functions within the viewer's browser by inserting code directly into your HTML pages. This code is then interpreted by the browser, and the proper functions are performed.

Throughout this chapter, you will find both JavaScript and VBScript examples to get you started on incorporating scripts into your pages. We will also take a look at these two technologies and why you might want to choose one over the other.

JavaScript Versus VBScript

As you begin this chapter, you may be wondering what scripting language you should use. It is pretty simple to determine what language you want to use based on your target environment. If you are developing for an environment in which individuals will be using a Netscape browser, you should not use VBScript because none of the Netscape browsers directly support VBScript. If, however, you are developing solely for an IE audience, such as in an intranet environment, you may find that VBScript is the answer you are looking for, especially if you are already familiar with Visual Basic.

When we look at the two scripting languages, we can see that JavaScript is accepted in all the newer browsers, including IE. With this knowledge in mind, you will find that developing for the viewer's browser with JavaScript is a pretty safe bet.

HTML Object Model

If you are new to scripting, you know how difficult it can be to learn and keep up with all the HTML and scripting language elements, along with the proper syntax necessary to create scripts in a text editor. For this reason, Microsoft has added what is called *IntelliSense* support to its Script Editor. This capability allows you to begin typing a statement within <script> tags, and the editor will give you a list of options that enable you to complete that statement by simply typing a period (.) after typing the name of an object. For example, say you want to specify certain aspects of your page using JavaScript, such as the link colors. Instead of needing to know the various methods associated with this, you can simply type **document.**, and all the available methods, collections, and properties will appear in a drop-down list, as shown here:

You can then select the method you want. For this example, you would select the property LinkColor from the drop-down list. This support makes writing scripts easier than ever. It doesn't quite write scripts for you, but it does help jog your memory and lead you in the right direction. When you're entering script function statements, the editor makes further use of this technology by providing function parameter information in a ToolTip. This can be another great timesaver, removing the need to check documentation for the proper syntax of function calls. As we move into the section on the Script Editor, you will want to keep this capability in mind because it will save you a great deal of time when writing your scripts.

Developing with VBScript

VBScript is a Microsoft technology born out of Visual Basic for Applications. Because it is a scripting language, it does not have all the capabilities of Visual Basic. It is, however, fairly easy to read and write and can be integrated directly into your pages. VBScript provides many of the capabilities of JavaScript, and then some. Just remember that it is a Microsoft technology, and because of this, it is not compatible with browsers outside the Internet Explorer realm.

Even though VBScript has drawbacks in the compatibility department, it is a powerful language that allows you to integrate items such as ActiveX controls and Active Server Pages into your Webs. This part of the chapter takes a look at VBScript and how to incorporate it into your pages using the Microsoft Script Editor.

Displaying Date and Time Information

Using VBScript's inherent functions, you can easily display information about the current date and time within your pages. Some of these functions are described in the following list:

▶ **Now( )**   Returns the current date and time, formatted according to the user's Short Date and Time settings within the Control Panel's Regional Settings applet.

▶ **DateDiff**(*interval, date1, date2* [*,firstdayofweek*[*, firstweekofyear*]])   Returns the number of intervals between two specified dates. An *interval* is part of a date, such as months (mm), days (dd), years (yy), or weeks (w), or part of a time designation, such as hours (h), minutes (m), or seconds (s). Optionally, the first day of the logical week and/or year may be specified when you're working with nonstandard calendars.

▶ **Year**(*date*)   Returns the numeric year of a valid date value or string.

▶ **Month**(*date*)   Returns the numeric month of a valid date value or string.

▶ **MonthName**(*month* [*,abbreviate*])   Returns the month name, optionally abbreviated (Boolean value), based on the numeric month specified.

▶ **Day**(*date*)   Returns the numeric day of the month value from a valid date string or value.

▶ **Weekday**(*date* [*,firstdayofweek*])   Returns the numeric day of the week value from a valid date string or value. Optionally, the first day of a logical week may also be specified.

▶ **Time( )**   Returns the current time, formatted according to the user's system Locale settings.

▶ **Hour**(*time*)   Returns a numeric hour (0–23) from a valid time string or value.

▶ **Minute**(*time*)   Returns a numeric minute (0–59) from a valid time string or value.

▶ **Second**(*time*)   Returns a numeric second (0–59) from a valid time string or value.

Now that we have all this powerful time/date information available, let's put some of it to use. Suppose you want to make sure you remember the birthday of an important person in your life. Using VBScript's date and time functions, we can easily create our own birthday countdown page. We'll tell ourselves the current date and time and then tell how many days, hours, minutes, and seconds remain until the big day. For this example, I've used my wife's birthday (I hope I get it right in the code). Here are the steps to follow:

1. Create a new blank page within FrontPage.

2. Open the Script Editor by clicking Tools | Macro | Microsoft Script Editor from the menu bar.

3. Move to the line just following the <body> tag and insert a script block by right-clicking the page and selecting Script Block | Client from the pop-up menu. By default, VBScript is the default client-side scripting language; therefore, the argument LANGUAGE=vbscript will be displayed within the <script> tag. If you've changed this option, edit this argument as necessary to specify VBScript as your scripting language.

4. Move to the blank line following the <!— comment tag within the scripting block and insert the following code:

```
dim CurDate, DayPart, days, hours, minutes, seconds

CurDate = Now()

DayPart = Hour(CurDate)
If DayPart < 12 then
    Document.Write "Good morning!  "
ElseIf DayPart < 17 then
    Document.Write "Good afternoon!  "
Else
    Document.Write "Good evening!  "
End If

days = DateDiff("d", CurDate, "3/4/2001")
hours = DateDiff("h", CurDate, "3/4/2001")
minutes = DateDiff("n", CurDate, "3/4/2001")
seconds = DateDiff("s", CurDate, "3/4/2001")

Document.Write "It is now " & CurDate & _
" and Kim's birthday is getting close...<br><br>"
Document.Write "That's only " & days & _
" Days until her birthday!<br>"
Document.Write "That's only " & hours & _
" Hours until her birthday!<br>"
Document.Write "That's only " & minutes & _
" Minutes until her birthday!<br>"
Document.Write "That's only " & seconds & _
" Seconds until her birthday!<br>"
```

5. Now preview your new birthday counter from the Script Editor by clicking Debug | Start or by pressing F5. The resulting page should look like this:

Good afternoon! It is now 2/7/01 1:22:56 PM and Kim's birthday is getting close...

That's only 25 Days until her birthday!
That's only 586 Hours until her birthday!
That's only 35141 Minutes until her birthday!
That's only 2108415 Seconds until her birthday!

TIP

To preview a current page in IE without first saving it, use the Script Editor's Debug | Start (F5) method to open the page within the browser instead of using the Preview In Browser method. Understand, however, that all links to external references will be broken because the editor creates a temporary copy of the page (in the temp directory) and does not update local/unqualified references, such as /images.

In this example I used the Document object's Write method to dynamically place text on the page when it is loaded in the client browser. You can easily incorporate this functionality within static text anywhere within a page.

NOTE

Because we used VBScript to accomplish this, the page will be blank when viewed in Netscape browsers.

To keep your page code a little cleaner, or to create reusable code, you can also place the code we entered within a subroutine and simply call it anywhere it is needed within the page. This is accomplished by beginning the code with a declaration, such as Sub CountDown( ), and ending the code with an End Sub statement. The resulting subroutine declaration would appear as follows:

```
<SCRIPT LANGUAGE="VBScript">
<!--
Sub CountDown()
<script code appears here...>
End Sub
-->
</SCRIPT>
```

Although not necessary, you might also move the code to the header section of your page, thus keeping your display code a little cleaner. You could then call this subroutine anywhere within the page by inserting another script block and using the single line Call CountDown.

Using VBScript with Forms

According to Microsoft, the primary purpose of client-side scripting within a Web page is to "create event procedures for controls." Although some people might disagree with this statement, no one can deny that VBScript provides powerful capabilities for working with controls. In this section, we'll take a look at how VBScript can be used to work with and manipulate standard HTML form controls.

We'll use some of the functions in our birthday countdown page example to demonstrate some simple form element control features. In this example, we're going to create a simple form with two text boxes and a single button. We'll then write a little script and tie it to the button. Each time the user clicks the button, the current time and date will be displayed in the text boxes. In order to easily identify our form controls, we'll also use the id="<name>" property. The following steps detail how this is done:

1. Create a new blank page within FrontPage.

2. Add two single-line text boxes to the page. (FrontPage automatically places these text boxes in a new form and inserts Submit and Reset buttons unless you have disabled the Automatically Enclose Form Fields Within A Form option within the Page Options | General tab. If you have disabled this feature, you will need to add a single button manually.)

3. Delete the Reset button (if one exists).

4. Double-click the Submit button to display the Push Button Properties dialog box and then change the Button Type option to Normal and the Value/label field to read "Display Time and Date." Click OK to save your changes and close the dialog box.

5. Now open the Script Editor and view your form's source code.

6. Delete the method and action arguments from the opening <form> tag and add the text **language="vbscript" id="MyForm"** to the tag. The id property makes it easy to reference the form later.

7. Delete the entire SaveResults WebBot tag (the first line following the <form> tag).

8. Locate the first text box <input> tag and add the property **id="txtTime"** anywhere within the tag. Again, the id property allows for easy reference to the control later.

9. Locate the second text box <input> tag and add **id="txtDate"** anywhere within the tag.

10. Locate the button <input> tag and add **onclick="Call ShowTimeDate"** anywhere within the tag. Your code should now look like this:

```
<form language="vbscript" id="MyForm">
  <p><input type="text" id="txtTime" name="T1" size="20"></p>
  <p><input type="text" id="txtDate" name="T2" size="20"></p>
  <p><input type="button" value="Show Time and Date"
onclick="Call ShowTimeDate" name="B1"></p>
</form>
```

Now it's time to write the ShowTimeDate subroutine, which will be called when the form button is clicked. Follow these steps:

1. Move to a blank line preceding the <form> tag (location really doesn't matter here, but we want to be consistent so that our work matches). Add a new script block by right-clicking and selecting Script Block | Client from the pop-up menu.

2. Move to the blank line in the middle of the script block and insert the following code:

```
Sub ShowTimeDate()
    MyForm.txtTime.value = Time()
    MyForm.txtDate.value = _
        Month(Now()) & "/" & Day(Now()) & _
        "/" & Year(Now())
End Sub
```

By referencing MyForm.txtTime.value, we are using the id properties of the form object and first text box control to specify that we want to access the value of that individual control. We then use the VBScript Time( ) function to return the current time. Because the Now( ) function returns both the date and time, we have to do a little string manipulation for our second text box to piece together the different parts of the date without including the time.

3. Press F5 within the Script Editor to try your routine out. When the user clicks the form button, it will call the ShowTimeDate subroutine. In turn, this subroutine will then fill in the text boxes with the current time and date, respectively.

Because our script is triggered by the user clicking the button, it is considered event-driven code and does not automatically run when the page is loaded. As such, the script will run each time the user clicks the button, refreshing the display without having to reload the page.

Developing with JavaScript

JavaScript is helping to transform the Web for everyday developers who do not want, or have the ability, to use server-side programming. It also has allowed developers to create dynamic effects and powerful programs that work completely on the client side, freeing server resources and allowing information to be transferred in a quick and easy manner. Although we are working with JavaScript in this chapter, we will by no means tackle the language itself, because this is well beyond the boundaries of this book. What we will be looking at are some great JavaScripts you can use for your Webs, along with how to implement them using FrontPage.

The following sections display, by example, some of the functionality you can add to your sites with JavaScript. All these scripts are also included on the accompanying CD-ROM so that you can modify them for your own use.

JavaScript Versus JScript

While working with the Script Editor, you may notice quite a few references to JScript. It is important that you know that JScript and JavaScript are not the same thing. Although they are closely related, they have been developed with different technologies and have some distinct differences.

First of all, JavaScript has been developed in cooperation between Netscape and Sun Microsystems, and JScript has been developed by Microsoft. Like many other implementations by Microsoft, JScript has some distinct differences that have been incorporated for use only with the Internet Explorer browser. For this reason, I strongly suggest not using JScript if you are deploying in a cross-browser environment, because the JScript implementation does not cover all aspects of JavaScript. This is to say that some of the features available in JavaScript, especially in the newer versions of the language, are not supported in the JScript implementation.

Using JavaScript with Forms

FrontPage offers some great capabilities when it comes to using forms for collecting data and transferring it to other locations. This is all accomplished using some sort of server-side technology, though. In this section we will look at some client-side forms that allow you to accomplish particular tasks. The first script we will look at is used for navigation purposes. This script allows you to redirect the user to a new page based on a selection from a drop-down menu. This is a fairly simple script, but it is very powerful when it comes to site navigation. The second script is a simple calculation form that works much like a formula would in an Excel spreadsheet. This script has a number of uses and can be altered to fit your needs.

Navigation Form

You've probably seen a Web site that make use of one or more drop-down lists containing various areas of the site. When you select one of those areas, and possibly click an associated button, you are sent directly to that page. This is a simple use of JavaScript that works much like hyperlinks do within the page, and although it is easy to implement, it can be a very powerful navigation tool for your site.

In many of the sites I have developed, I have used this script for navigational items. Sometimes this is used for the primary page, where we want quick links to the main topics within the site. At other times, I include the table of contents for a long, multipage document within this form and attach it to every page. This way, when users are deep within a document, they can simply select a new chapter and jump directly to it. Although you can accomplish the same effect using a navigation bar, this script allows you to contain all your links within a restricted space that is unobtrusive to the user but still available when needed.

The incorporation of this drop-down menu into your page is accomplished in two steps. The first is to insert the script into your page, and the second is to create the form that links to the script. To insert this style of navigation, follow these steps:

1. Open a page in your Web.

2. Create the layout for your page, leaving room for where you want the drop-down menu to appear.

3. Select Tools | Macro | Microsoft Script Editor from the menu bar. This launches the Script Editor program with your current HTML shown in a window.

4. Move your cursor directly above the </head> tag and insert the following script:

```
<script language="JavaScript">
<!--
function leapto(menu)
   {
   var links = menu.dest.selectedIndex;
   if (links == 0)
      alert("You must first select an area.");
   if (links >= 1)
      { document.location = menu.dest.options[links].value; }
```

```
      }
//-->
</script>
```

5. Still working in the Script Editor, move down to where you want your actual drop-down list displayed.

TIP

Although you can create your form using FrontPage, it is better to work in the HTML for this script because you are not assigning an action to your form, which is something that FrontPage really wants to do.

6. Insert the following HTML, which will constitute your drop-down menu:

```
<form name="menu">
<select name="dest" size="1">
<option value>-- Click for List of Topics--- </option>
<option value="faq.html">Frequently Asked Questions</option>
<option value="support.html">Support</option>
<option value="products.html">Products</option>
</select> <input type="button" value="Jump"
    onclick="leapto(menu)">
</form>
```

NOTE

Replace the options listed here with the pages you want your menu to link to within your Web.

7. In the Script Editor, select File | Save.

8. Switch back to FrontPage. If you haven't already saved the page prior to step 7, FrontPage will display a Save As dialog box. If this is the case, enter a name for the page and save it.

You may now test the form in your browser. When you select an item from the list and click Jump, the script instructs the browser to load the associated page. Notice that if you do not select an item, you are presented with the error "You must first select an area." This error can be customized to say anything you want it to.

Optionally, you may also eliminate the need for a Jump button altogether by using this code in the <select> tag:

```
<select name="dest" size="1" language="JavaScript"
   onchange="leapto(menu)">
```

By adding a language attribute and the onchange event handler, you specify that any change made to the menu's current selection triggers the leapto( ) function.

NOTE

Because some older browsers don't support the onchange event within drop-down menus, you might want to implement the best of both worlds by including a Jump button and an onchange event handler within the <select> tag.

Order Form Calculator

Calculations within your page can add great value to your Web. This is especially true if you are creating client-side shopping carts and the like. Although we will not go into the detail necessary to create shopping carts or other complex applications, this section will show you how to incorporate a simple calculation form in your page.

This example creates a basic order form that calculates the price of an order based on each item ordered. It also adds the appropriate sales tax for the items in the form. To implement this example, follow these steps:

1. Create a form on your page by selecting Insert | Form | Form. This will insert a basic form on your page with Submit and Reset buttons. You can remove the buttons because we will not be using them.

2. Right-click inside the form's border and select Form Properties from the pop-up menu.

3. In the Form Properties dialog box, type **calcform** in the Form Name field and click OK. This gives the form a name that we will reference from our script.

4. Select Table | Insert | Table from the menu bar. This brings up the Insert Table dialog box shown here:

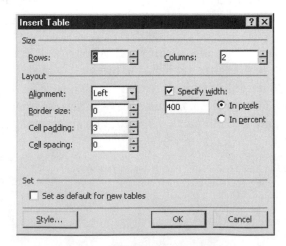

5. Create a table with three columns and seven rows, setting Border Size to 1 and Cell Padding to 2.

6. In the top three cells, enter the following headings: Quantity, Price, and Total.

   Now we want to create the input cells for our items.

7. Insert a text box in each of the cells in the second, third, and fourth rows by selecting Insert | Form | Text Box.

8. In the second column, type the words **Subtotal**, **Tax**, and **Total** in the fifth, sixth, and seventh cells.

9. Highlight these three cells and right-click over them. Then select Cell Properties from the pop-up menu.

10. Set the Horizontal Alignment field to Right and click OK to close the dialog box.

11. Position your cursor in the third column of each of these rows (fifth, sixth, and seventh) and insert a one-line text box by following the procedure in step 7. When you are finished, your table should look like the one shown here:

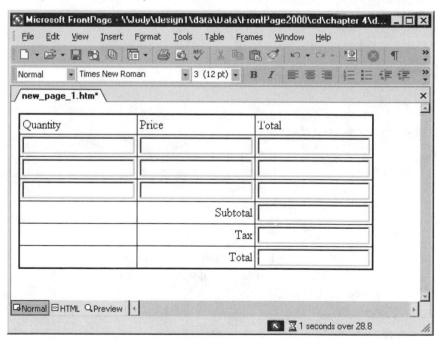

   Now it is time to insert our script. To do so, continue on with the next steps.

12. Select Tools | Macro | Microsoft Script Editor from the menu bar. This launches the Script Editor program with your current HTML shown in a window.

13. Position your cursor within the <head> tag and insert the following script:

```
<SCRIPT>
function dp(price)
{
    string = "" + price;
    number = string.length - string.indexOf('.');
    if (string.indexOf('.') == -1)
       return string + '.00';
    if (number == 1)
       return string + '00';
    if (number == 2)
       return string + '0';
    if (number > 3)
       return string.substring(0,string.length-number+3);
return string;
}
function calculate()
{
document.calcform.total1.value =
dp((document.calcform.price1.value)*
(document.calcform.quantity1.value))
document.calcform.total2.value = dp
((document.calcform.price2.value)*
(document.calcform.quantity2.value))
document.calcform.total3.value =
dp((document.calcform.price3.value)*
(document.calcform.quantity3.value))
document.calcform.subtotal.value =
dp(eval(document.calcform.total1.value) +
eval(document.calcform.total2.value) +
eval(document.calcform.total3.value))
document.calcform.tax.value =
dp((document.calcform.subtotal.value)*0.175)
document.calcform.total.value =
dp((document.calcform.subtotal.value)*1.175)
}
</SCRIPT>
```

Now all that is left to do is to link our form to our script, and we have
our price calculator. To complete this operation, continue with the
remaining steps.

14. Switch back to FrontPage and right-click the first text box in the table, under
    Quantity. This will bring up a drop-down menu.

15. Select Form Field Properties from the drop-down menu to bring up the Text
    Box Properties dialog box shown here:

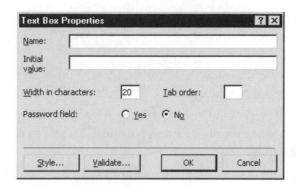

16. In the Name field, type **quantity1** and click OK.

TIP

Although this is the proper way to change the text box properties in FrontPage, it is much easier to go into HTML view and change the Name attribute associated with each text box. If you are comfortable working in the HTML view, this will save you quite a bit of time when you have numerous fields to change, as in this example.

17. Repeat steps 14, 15 and 16, incrementing the number at the end of the names to read quantity2 and quantity3, respectively, for the two remaining text boxes in the Quantity column.

18. When you have finished with the Quantity column, move on to the Price and Total columns and repeat steps 14, 15 and 16, substituting "price" and "total" for "quantity" in their respective columns and adding the appropriate number to the end of the field names (price1, price2, price3 and total1, total2, total3).

19. Once you have changed the names for each of your text boxes, switch to HTML view and add the following code to the quantity and price fields, just after the Name attribute:

```
ONCHANGE="calculate()"
```

This instructs the system that we want the form to calculate every time a value of any text box is changed.

20. Upon completing each column, you'll notice that your text, in HTML view, looks similar to this:

```
<TR>
<TD><INPUT type="text" name="quantity1"
    ONCHANGE="calculate()"></TD>
<TD><INPUT type="text" name="price1"
```

```
          ONCHANGE="calculate()"></TD>
<TD><INPUT type="text" name="total1"></TD>
</TR>
```

We now have everything we need for the form to function properly, except we have not yet linked our Subtotal, Tax, and Total fields, which we will do next.

21. In Normal view, right-click the field to the right of the word Subtotal and select Form Field Properties from the pop-up menu. This brings up the Form Field Properties dialog box.

22. In the Name field, type **subtotal** and click OK.

23. Repeat steps 21 and 22 for the Tax and Total fields, substituting "tax" and "total," respectively.

Those are all the steps you need to create this calculation form. Save your page and preview it in your browser to see your form at work.

TIP

The form we created assumes that the tax you want to assess is 8.5 percent. If you want to change this, simply move to the following line in the script and change the number to the tax you want your form to calculate:
*document.calcform.tax.value = dp((document.calcform.subtotal.value)*0.085)*

Creating Dynamic Text with JavaScript

Text has pretty much been a constant within Webs. When you want to add dynamic elements, you usually accomplished it using an image or some sort of server-side include function. JavaScript now gives you the ability to add dynamic text to your pages that works in a cross-browser environment, without the need for images or server-side includes. Although many scripts allow you to accomplish dynamic effects, we'll focus on just one here. It uses cookies to find out whether the user has been to the page before, and then it selects a text string to display from a list, based on the user's last visit. Using this script, you can cycle users through all your strings before they see the first one again.

Inserting Generated Quotes

A great JavaScript that I use for certain sites inserts a new text string each time a page is accessed by a visitor. In the original implementation, these text strings were famous quotes, but you can replace them with any string you want. This script makes use of cookies to inform the browser that the visitor has been to the page before and also to instruct the browser as to which text string in the sequence to bring up.

To insert this script into your pages, follow these steps:

1. Open a page in your Web.

2. Create the layout for your page, leaving room where you want the text to appear.

3. Select Tools | Macro | Microsoft Script Editor from the menu bar. This launches the Script Editor program with your current HTML shown in a window.

4. Move to the <head> area of the page and insert the following script:

```
<SCRIPT LANGUAGE="JavaScript"><!--
var quoteList = new Array(
    "This is my first text string",
    "This is my second text string",
    "This is my third text string",
    "This is my fourth text string"
    );
function getCookie(name) {
    var search = name + "="
    if (document.cookie.length > 0)
        { // if there are any cookies
        offset = document.cookie.indexOf(search)
        if (offset != -1) { // if cookie exists
            offset += search.length
                // set index of beginning of value
            end = document.cookie.indexOf(";", offset)
                // set index of end of cookie value
            if (end == -1)
                end = document.cookie.length
                return
unescape(document.cookie.substring(offset,
                end))
            }
        }
    }
function setCookie(name, value) {
    document.cookie = name + "=" + escape(value)
    }
function quote() {
    i=getCookie("ETUQuoteCount");
    if (i==null)
        i=0
    else
        i=parseInt(i)
        i = i % quoteList.length;
        j = i++;
        setCookie("ETUQuoteCount",i);
        return quoteList[j]
```

```
    }

// --></SCRIPT>
```

5. Move your cursor to the position where you want the text strings to appear and insert the following script:

```
<SCRIPT LANGUAGE="JavaScript"><!--
document.write(quote());
// --></SCRIPT>
```

6. Move to the portion of the script where the text strings reside. This code will look like the following:

```
"This is my first text string",
"This is my second text string",
"This is my third text string",
"This is my fourth text string"
```

7. Change these lines, adding or removing existing lines as necessary, to reflect the text you want to appear in your pages.

NOTE

Be sure to include a comma at the end of each text string, except the final text string.

8. In the Script Editor, select File | Save.

9. Switch back to FrontPage and save your file.

Those are all the modifications necessary for this script to function within your pages. You can now test the script in your browser. Each time the page loads, you will see a new text string appear.

Creating Image Rollover Effects with JavaScript

Rollovers, the effect of an image or text changing when the mouse rolls over it, have become an integral part of Web site navigation today, giving you the ability to alert users to links, jazz up your pages, and deliver explanatory content on the fly. I don't know how we ever worked with sites before their introduction. Now, this is not to say you need to use rollovers within your Webs. Just like any other technology, they can be detrimental if used improperly. However, when used properly, they can add some flare that really makes your site something to be seen and used.

The following topic deals with a simple image switch that works much like the Hover button discussed in Chapter 5 of this book, but all the integration is done on the client side using JavaScript.

Changing the Images on a Rollover

Many different scripts have been developed to allow for rollover events that change an image within a page when users move their mouse pointers over that image. Some are long, and some are short, but they all accomplish the same final outcome, which is to switch the image. For this reason, we are first going to go with the short end of scripting. You'll learn how to change your images with a minimum amount of scripting. This script involves inserting code into the link itself, which is then referenced by the image. Because the majority of rollovers are used in conjunction with links, this method seems to make a lot of sense.

To incorporate a simple rollover into your page, follow these steps:

1. Open a page in your Web.

TIP

It is a good idea to have both images you are planning to use already created and placed within your Web. This way, you simply need to reference them when implementing this script.

2. Insert the initial image you want to appear on the page when first loaded.

3. Select the image and turn it into a hyperlink.

4. Switch to HTML view and add the following scripting to your hyperlinked image's anchor (<a>) tag:

```
onMouseOver='rollover.src="image2.gif"'
    onMouseOut='rollover.src="image1.gif"'>
```

When you have finished with this step, your code should look something like this:

```
<a href="page.html" onMouseOver='rollover.src="image2.gif"'
onMouseOut='rollover.src="image1.gif"'>
```

Notice that we have used both single (') and double (") quotes to enter a string of text that contains quotes itself.

We now want to modify the image tag to make use of the scripting we have just inserted.

5. Move to your <img> tag and add the following to your code:

```
name="rollover"
```

When you have finished, your code should look like this:

```
<img src="images/image1.gif" name="rollover" border="0">
```

6. Save your page. You can now view it in the browser to see the script work.

That is all there is to it. Using this method, you don't have to incorporate a long string of code to create rollovers. The downside is that the secondary (rollover) image isn't loaded until the user moves his or her mouse over the primary image. Also, if you use the same images in several places within your page and need to make changes, you have to change the code in each location where you've used those images.

Although a little more complicated, the following method allows the browser to load all the images at one time, delaying the initial load of the page but smoothing the image rollover events when they take place. In general, the larger your images are, the more important it is to preload them.

To incorporate advanced multiple-image rollovers into your page, follow these steps:

1. Create a new page within FrontPage and insert all primary (normally displayed) images that you wish to use. For this example, insert at least two images. As mentioned in the previous example, you should already have imported all the images you will be working with into their desired location (normally, the images folder).

2. Assign the appropriate hyperlinks to the images.

NOTE

Even if you don't want to use an image as a hyperlink, you still should make it a hyperlink with a dummy target URL of "javascript:void(0);" to maintain compatibility with Netscape's browsers.

3. Open the Page Properties dialog box by selecting File | Properties and move to the General tab. Under the Design-time control scripting options, set the Client option to JavaScript. Click OK to close the dialog box.

4. Now open the page in the Script Editor by clicking the Tools | Macro | Microsoft Script Editor menu option.

5. Move to (or create, if necessary) a blank line just preceding the </head> tag and insert a new client-side script block. Because we set the page's default client-side scripting option to JavaScript in step 3, the script block is inserted with the language set to JavaScript.

6. Move to the blank line in the middle of the script block and insert the following code (note that I will "comment" on each line of this code because of its complexity):

```
window.onerror = null;
var bOK = 0;
var bName = navigator.appName.substring(0,8);
var bVer = parseFloat(navigator.appVersion);
if (bName == "Netscape" && bVer >= 3)
    { bOK = 1; }
if (bName == "Microsof" && bVer >= 4)
    { bOK = 1; }
if (bOK) {
//only do this if we've determined
//that the browser can handle it
    roImages = new Array(4);
//total number of images being used in all rollovers

    for (i=0; i<(roImages.length); i++)
      //step through the entire array…
        {roImages[i] = new Image();      }
     //set the current array element to a new Image() object
    roImages[0].src = "images/btn1-up.gif"; //preload all images
    roImages[1].src = "images/btn1-dn.gif";
    roImages[2].src = "images/btn2-up.gif";
    roImages[3].src = "images/btn2-dn.gif";
}
function rollover(roName,roImageIndex) {
    if (bOK) {
        document.images[roName].src =
        roImages[roImageIndex].src;
    }
}
```

Setting the window.onerror property to null instructs the browser to suppress all JavaScript error dialog boxes. This ensures that your users won't see JavaScript errors caused by your own code as seen in the following code line:

```
window.onerror = null;
```

The bOK variable will be used to store a true (1) or false (0) value, indicating whether the user's browser can support both JavaScript and the onMouseOver and onMouseOut events, which are required to perform image rollovers as seen in the following code line:

```
var bOK = 0;
```

In the following code we retrieve the first eight characters of the user's browser name and store it in the bName variable:

```
var bName = navigator.appName.substring(0,8);
```

Next we get the primary version number of the browser. Because application versions contain more detail than we need for our purposes, we convert the version to an integer and drop any subversion and build elements from the version as seen with this code:

```
var bVer = parseFloat(navigator.appVersion);
```

If the first eight characters of the browser name are "Netscape" and the primary version is at least 3—the minimal version that meets our code's requirements—we set the bOK variable to true (1) as seen here:

```
if (bName == "Netscape" && bVer >= 3)
    { bOK = 1; }
```

If the first eight characters of the browser name are "Microsof" and the primary version is at least 4, we set the bOK variable to true (1), because the browser meets our code's requirements as shown here:

```
 if (bName == "Microsof" && bVer >= 4)
    { bOK = 1; }
```

Note that the code never gets run unless we've determined that the user's browser can handle our code. Also, the line roImages = new Array(4); is the first line of code in this script that you'll need to modify each time you use it in a page. Just change the number 4 to the total number of images you'll be using. This is all taken care of in the following lines of code:

```
if (bOK) {
//only do this if we've determined
//that the browser can handle it
    roImages = new Array(4);
//total number of images being used in all rollovers

    for (i=0; i<(roImages.length); i++)
      //step through the entire array…
        {roImages[i] = new Image();      }
      //set the current array element to a new Image() object
```

The following code shows one of the major advantages of using this method of image rollovers. By setting the source value of each of our image objects in our script, all images will be preloaded and cached by the browser when the page is loaded. That way, they are waiting for us when it comes time to use them. Of course, if you use the same image more than once, you only need to load it a single time and then reference it accordingly in the rollover function call. The following lines of code are where this is handled:

```
roImages[0].src = "images/btn1-up.gif"; //preload all images
roImages[1].src = "images/btn1-dn.gif";
roImages[2].src = "images/btn2-up.gif";
```

```
        roImages[3].src = "images/btn2-dn.gif";
}
```

Ending our script is the unitary function of our implementation—the *rollover* function. Whenever we call this function, we'll pass it the name of the image we want to change and the roImages array index that we want to load in its place. Once again, we check to make sure the user's browser can handle our script (bOK is true) before running the image-changing code. Once we're sure our code won't blow up the browser, we set the source (src) property of the *document* object's *images* collection's image to the cached image that we want to load. We use the name property (roName) of the image whose event handler is calling the function as a key value to identify which of the document's images we want to change. We'll also pass the roImages array index for the image that we want to display as handled by the following code lines:

```
function rollover(roName, roImageIndex) {
    if (bOK) {
        document.images[roName].src =
        roImages[roImageIndex].src;
    }
}
```

TIP

This is a perfect example of a script that can be added to the Script Editor's toolbar for repeated use, because the number of images and the names of the image files themselves are the only items that change. See "Hands On: Customizing Your Toolbox" in Chapter 14 for detailed instructions on adding HTML fragments to the Toolbox for later use.

This may all seem a little complicated at first, but through using this script, you'll grow to appreciate the simplicity of its implementation. Now that we've entered all of our script, it's time to use it within our image tags. Here are the steps to follow:

7. As in the previous example, we need to add a name parameter to each of the images we'll be changing with the rollover function. Locate the first image (<img>) tag and add the attribute name="RollOver1". Your code should now appear something like this:

```
<img src="images/btn1-up.gif" name="RollOver1"
width="48" height="46" border="0">
```

Repeat this step for each of your images, incrementing the number (last character) for each image.

8. To trap the required events that will trigger our rollover function, we need to place our event handlers in the anchor (<a>) tag of each hyperlinked image. As you see, when an image is set as a hyperlink, the <img> tag is surrounded by the <a> (anchor) tag of the hyperlink. Within the first image's <a> tag, add the following text:

```
onMouseOut="rollover('RollOver1',0)"
onMouseOver="rollover('RollOver1',1)"
```

This tells the browser to call the *rollover* function whenever the mouse moves off or over the image. In each case, we pass the name attribute of the image ('RollOver1') to tell the function which image to change. We also pass the index of the member of the roImages array that contains the cached image we want to load. Your code should now appear something like the following:

```
<a href="linkedpage.htm"
onMouseOut="rollover(' RollOver1',0)"
onMouseOver="rollover('RollOver1',1)">
<img src="images/btn1-up.gif" name=" RollOver1"
width="48" height="46" border="0"></a>
```

Repeat this step for each of your images, incrementing the image array index to match the image you want to load for each event.

That's it. Now save and preview your page to view your new image rollovers.

Summary

In this chapter, we have taken an in-depth look at scripting for your Webs. Throughout the various sections, we have looked at the basics of JavaScript and VBScript, including some of the reasons to use one over the other. Included are various examples, which can be found on the CD-ROM accompanying this book, that cover some of the more popular functions associated with scripting.

After completing this chapter, you should have a good understanding of how to incorporate scripts into your Webs, along with the basic knowledge necessary to decide when and how to incorporate scripts into your pages.

FrontPage 2002's VBA Scripting Engine

IN THIS CHAPTER:

Understand the VBA Scripting Engine

Create Macros for FrontPage

Customize the FrontPage Interface

A long with the integration of FrontPage into the Office suite of tools has come the ability to create macros and other design-time scripts using the popular Visual Basic for Applications language (VBA).

In this chapter, we'll cover the Visual Basic editor and the FrontPage object model. I'll also give you lots of examples of how you can use these items to create both simple macros and more complex applications. However, we won't get into a high-level study of the Visual Basic programming language. As you might expect, that subject is far too vast to be covered in a single chapter, and I highly recommend that you obtain one or more of the many great Visual Basic programming guides available. Although those of you with Visual Basic programming experience will get the most out of this chapter, anyone interested in customizing FrontPage will gain understanding through plenty of useful examples.

The Visual Basic Editor

Differing from the VBScript and JavaScript used in Web pages, FrontPage's Visual Basic editor allows you to write scripts that affect the way FrontPage's design-time environment operates. This code only runs inside the FrontPage development environment and is not associated with or stored in individual Web pages or sites.

Although FrontPage shares this common language, its implementation still differs considerably from that of other Office applications:

▶ FrontPage's VBA code is associated and stored with FrontPage and is always available, regardless of the current Web site or page. You can think of this as a single, persistent project.

▶ FrontPage's object model differs from those of other Office applications in that it has no inherent Application object. To work with the Application object (properties, events, and methods), you must create your own class of the type FrontPage Application.

▶ Code written for/with FrontPage's VB editor cannot be compiled using the Office Developers Edition (ODE). This may change, though, in a future version of FrontPage.

To write, debug, and maintain VBA script, FrontPage includes the VB 6.3 editor. Although somewhat different in appearance and operation, this development environment holds many similarities to the Microsoft Script Editor. Let's start by reviewing the components of the Visual Basic editor.

Editor Windows

When working in the editor, you will work with a variety of windows. These windows are described here, along with the functions they allow.

Project Explorer

The Project Explorer, shown in Figure 16-1, works as your guide to all the elements contained within your current project. Within this window, you will find references to all the Forms, Modules, and Classes residing in your project, and it works much like the tree views you are used to working with in the FrontPage Folder view. If you take a look at the Project Explorer, you will see that the current project name appears at the top of the tree, with the various elements of the project found below it.

When working with the Project Explorer, you have access to the following elements:

▶ **Project elements**   All the elements found within your project, including UserForms, Modules, and Class Modules

▶ **View Code**   An option that switches to the Code window and displays the code associated with the selected item

▶ **View Object**   An option that allows you to view a visual representation of a form

▶ **Toggle Folders**   An option that toggles the display to list elements within their associated folders or in alphabetical order

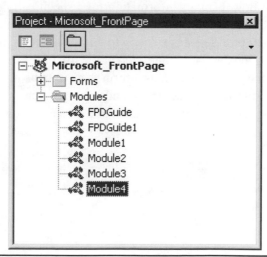

Figure 16-1   *The Project Explorer window, displaying elements of the current project*

This tree gives you quick and easy access to the elements within your project. If you want to modify an element, such as a form, you simply need to click that element, and all the available properties for it will appear in the Properties window. Furthermore, if you have a variety of windows open on your screen, you can bring the selected element to the front by clicking the View Object or View Code button on the Project Explorer.

Properties Window

The Properties window, shown in Figure 16-2, displays all the information relating to a selected item within your project. Properties associated with a selected item will vary depending on what that item is, but the properties themselves can be seen much as any other properties you would work with in FrontPage. However, rather than having to open a specific Properties window in FrontPage, you can simply select the item and have all its associated items displayed for editing.

The window itself contains two views so that you can organize your properties for viewing:

▶ **Alphabetic** Allows you to view properties in alphabetical order

▶ **Categorized** Allows you to view properties based on their functions within the object

When working with properties, you will find that the majority of the information is fairly self-explanatory. This is to say that most properties contain an explanatory name, along with a drop-down list showing the various options available for that property.

The Properties window displays information for a specifically selected item. This item can be an overall UserForm, Module, Class Module, or an item within a form, such as a button or text box. The easiest way to tell what item's properties you are viewing at is to take a look at the name found at the top of the Properties window. Furthermore, if you have an item such as a form that contains numerous interior items, such as drop-down boxes, text areas, and so on, you can select each one's properties by clicking the arrow found in the name area at the top of the window. You can then select the item whose properties you want to view.

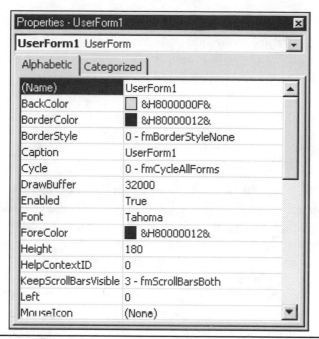

Figure 16-2   *The Properties window, displaying project information*

TIP

Along with the ability to view a selected item's properties, you can also view properties that are shared by multiple items within a group. This can come in handy if you have like items within a single form and want them to contain the same characteristics. For example, say you have two drop-down boxes within a form and want them to share color characteristics. To accomplish this, you would select both drop-down lists by clicking each one while holding down the CTRL key. You will then see their shared characteristics appear in the Properties window. Now, when you make a change to a color property, it will affect both drop-down boxes.

Object View

Object View windows allow you to graphically build, edit, and preview UserForms. In Visual Basic, you create windows (UserForms) visually by dragging and dropping elements into and within the UserForm. This drag-and-drop design capability is what gives Visual Basic the *visual* portion of its name. Visual Basic also allows you to manipulate forms and controls through code at runtime, giving you the best of both worlds.

Code View

Very similar to the Microsoft Script Editor, Visual Basic Code View windows provide you with a highly intuitive, color-coded editor. These Code View windows contain two drop-down boxes—the object selector and the event selector. These selectors not only let you navigate through existing code but also serve to list all scriptable controls and their corresponding events within the current UserForm. They also serve as sub/function selectors within Modules and Class Modules.

Within the main editor area of the Code View windows, Microsoft has incorporated complete color coding, real-time syntax checking, auto-indenting, and IntelliSense capabilities.

Object Browser

Although not displayed by default, the Object Browser (opened by pressing F2) is an indispensable reference and debugging tool (see Figure 16-3). Because the primary object that you'll be manipulating within FrontPage's VBA engine is FrontPage itself, you need to know and understand how its object model is built. The Object Browser is your window into the structure and contents of that and other objects accessible to you through Visual Basic.

When you first open the Object Browser, it displays <All Libraries> by default. To make it easier to find FrontPage-specific information, you'll likely want to select one of the two FrontPage-specific reference libraries:

▶ **FrontPage**   Contains reference information on the FrontPage Application object model. This is the object model that is used to control the FrontPage application, with the exception of HTML editing functions. In previous, nonintegrated versions of FrontPage, this would have been the FrontPage Explorer.

▶ **FrontPageEditor**   Contains reference information on the FrontPage page editor. This is the object model that is used to work with HTML pages within the editor.

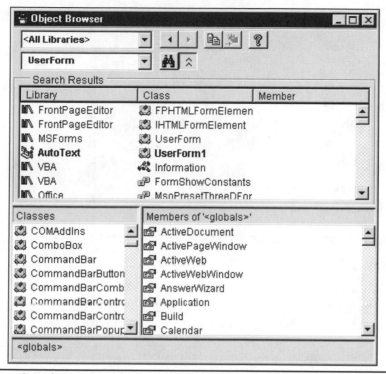

Figure 16-3   *The Object Browser, displaying object model information*

After selecting the proper reference library, you can browse through the classes and their associated members in the dual list views in the middle of the screen. As you select a class in the left pane, the view on the right is updated to display the selected class members. Additional information can also be displayed on many classes and their members by pressing F1 to open the matching context-sensitive help system.

Object Window

The Object window, shown in Figure 16-4, is where you will create the forms for your project. This window appears when you insert a form into your project by selecting Insert | UserForm from the menu bar. Once you have inserted a form into your project, you can begin adding elements to it using the controls found in the Toolbox, discussed next.

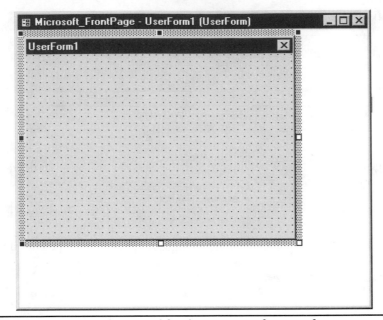

Figure 16-4   *The Object window, used for the creation of project forms*

Toolbox

Your Toolbox appears whenever you are working with a UserForm. This box, shown here, allows you to add various elements to your form:

Adding Pages to the Toolbox   Along with the standard controls in your Toolbox, the editor gives you the ability to add new pages and tabs to the Toolbox. These pages will help you organize the tools you are working with so that they are easily accessible when you are working with a form.

To add a page to your Toolbox, follow these steps:

1. Right-click an area of the Toolbox outside the Controls tab and select New Page from the pop-up menu. This automatically adds a new tab titled New Page to your Toolbox. You will notice that the tab contains a default pointer and no other controls.

2. Once you have added your page, you will want to assign a name to it. You can accomplish this by right-clicking the New Page tab and selecting Rename from the pop-up menu. This brings up the Rename dialog box, shown here:

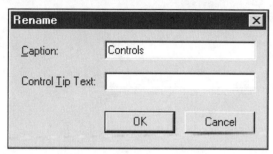

3. Type the name you want the tab to have and then type in any Control Tip text you want associated with the tab.

TIP

The Control Tip text you assign to the tab will appear when you move your mouse over the tab name. If you have several tabs in your Toolbox, this text can be used to identify the tab you want—it works in the same manner as ToolTips.

4. Click OK to accept your new changes.

Adding Custom Items to the Toolbox   Once you have created a set of tabs for your toolbox, you will want to populate them with commonly used controls. This way, you will have them available whenever you need them. For this example, we will simply be changing some basic properties associated with a Button control to turn it into an OK button. This is a simple example, but it will show you the process necessary to add controls to your Toolbox:

1. If you do not already have one displayed, insert a UserForm by selecting Insert | UserForm from the menu bar. This will place a standard form on your page and cause your Toolbox to appear.

2. Drag a standard button onto your form. It will appear as shown here:

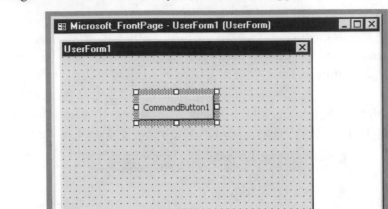

3. Select the button by clicking it once. You know it is selected when the anchor points appear around it.

4. Move to the Properties window and type **cmdOK** in the Name field and **OK** in the Caption field. You will see the change take place immediately on your button.

5. Now move to the tab you created in the previous section and drag the button from the form onto your tab. You will see the button appear on the tab, just as it appears in the standard set of controls.

   Because the button does not have any distinguishing features in the Toolbox, you will want to customize it so that a Control Tip appears when you move your mouse over it. Continue on to accomplish this.

6. Right-click your new button within the Toolbox and select Customize New CommandButton from the pop-up menu. This brings up the Customize Control dialog box, shown here:

7. Type in a tip that will allow you to easily remember what this button is used for. Then click OK.

Now, whenever you add this customized command button to a form, it will have the default name "cmdOK" and caption "OK".

TIP

You can also change the display associated with your control by loading a custom icon or by editing the picture using the Load Picture and Edit Picture buttons.

Code Window

The Code window, shown in Figure 16-5, is a text editor where you will do the bulk of your coding work. Along with standard text-editing capabilities, the Code window offers a great many built-in tools that will make your coding go more quickly and smoothly.

There are two ways in which you can launch the Code window when working in the Visual Basic editor. First, you can select View | Code from the menu bar. Second, you can simply double-click a form, and the window will appear.

TIP

If you want to move to a particular procedure within the Code window, you can do so by clicking the visual representation in the Object window. For instance, if you are working with a button and want to move to the button's associated code, double-click the button, and the cursor will automatically move to the button's code.

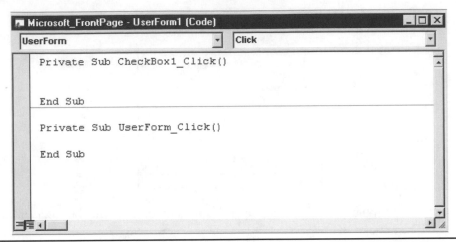

Figure 16-5   *The Code window is an editor that allows you to view and edit code associated with your project.*

Toolbars

Along with the windows you see in the editor, a number of toolbars allow you to quickly access features of the product. If a toolbar is not present on your screen, you can access it by selecting View | Toolbars and selecting the toolbar you want displayed from the list. The following sections take a look at each of the toolbars and their associated functions.

Standard Toolbar

Many of the basic functions you will find in the menu bar commands are provided on the Standard toolbar, shown here and described in Table 16-1. Although you can work with all these functions by using the menu bar, the toolbar gives you quicker access.

Button	Name	Description
	View FrontPage	Switches you back to the FrontPage interface.
	Insert	Allows you to insert a UserForm, Module, Class Module, or procedure into your project.
	Save	Saves all changed files associated with the project.
	Cut	Cuts the selected text or control from the editor.
	Copy	Copies the selected text or control from the editor.
	Paste	Pastes the text or control from your clipboard to the editor.
	Find	Brings up the Find dialog box, allowing you to search through your code for a text string.
	Undo	Cancels the previous change.
	Redo	Reinserts the change you have undone.
	Run Sub/ UserForm	Begins processing the current subprocedure or form.
	Break	Pauses the current process.
	Reset	Stops the current process.
	Design Mode	Allows you to enter or exit the design mode. The design mode is your development time when no processes are running.

Table 16-1 *Commands Found on the Standard Toolbar*

Button	Name	Description
	Project Explorer	Activates the Project Explorer window.
	Properties Window	Activates the Properties window.
	Object Browser	Activates the Object Browser window.
	Toolbox	Activates the Toolbox window.
	Help	Launches the Visual Basic editor's help system.

Table 16-1   *Commands Found on the Standard Toolbar* (continued)

Debug Toolbar

Most of the commands found in the Debug menu are also on the Debug toolbar, shown here and described in Table 16-2. Through the use of this toolbar, you are given quick access to your controls while preparing to debug, and while debugging, your applications.

Button	Name	Description
	Design Mode	Allows you to enter or exit the design mode. The design mode is your development time when no processes are running.

Table 16-2   *Commands Found on the Debug Toolbar*

Button	Name	Description
▶	Run Sub/ UserForm	Runs the current project for debugging purposes and replaces any current project registration information.
∥	Break	Pauses the project and switches you into the break mode for purposes of examining the project.
■	Reset	Completely stops the current project and resets the call stack.
🖐	Toggle Breakpoint	Turns on or off a breakpoint on the current line of code.
	Step Into	Continues execution of the code one line at a time.
	Step Over	When a statement contains a call procedure, this control executes the call procedure as a unit and then steps to the next statement in the procedure.
	Step Out	Processes the remaining lines of the current procedure, based on the current position of the cursor within the code.
	Locals Window	Activates the Locals window and displays all the variables within the current stack, along with their values.
	Immediate Window	Activates the Immediate window and displays debugging information.
	Watch Window	Activates the Watch window and displays all the current watch expressions.
👓	Quick Watch	Activates the Quick Watch dialog box, displaying the current value of a selected expression within your project.
	Call Stack	Activates the Call Stack dialog box, listing all procedures that have begun but have not been completed.

Table 16-2   *Commands Found on the Debug Toolbar* (continued)

Edit Toolbar

The Edit toolbar, shown here, is only active when you are working in the Code window. The functions available in this toolbar are the same as some of those in the Edit menu, along with some extra functions that can come in very handy when you are editing. Table 16-3 shows each toolbar button and describes its function.

Button	Name	Description
	List Properties/ Methods	Displays, via a pop-up list, all the available properties and methods for an object you have inserted via the Code window.
	List Constants	Displays, via a pop-up list, all the available constants for a property you have inserted via the Code window.
	Quick Info	Displays the syntax prototype for a variable, function, statement, method, or procedure you are working with in the Code window.
	Parameter Info	Displays tips within the Code window about available parameters for use with a statement or function.
	Complete Word	Completes a word you have begun typing in the Code window. Once you have entered enough characters for the editor to recognize the word, you can use this command to complete it.
	Indent	Indents the code based on the next available tab.
	Outdent	Moves the current code back to the previous tab.
	Toggle Breakpoint	Turns on and off the breakpoint for the current line.

Table 16-3 *Commands Found on the Edit Toolbar*

Button	Name	Description
	Comment Block	Adds comment marks to the selected text.
	Uncomment Block	Removes comment marks from the selected text.
	Toggle Bookmark	Turns on and off the bookmark for the current line.
	Next Bookmark	Moves the cursor to the next bookmark within the code.
	Previous Bookmark	Moves the cursor to the previous bookmark within the code.
	Clear All Bookmarks	Removes all bookmarks from the code.

Table 16-3   *Commands Found on the Edit Toolbar* (continued)

UserForm Toolbar

In contrast to the Edit toolbar, the UserForm toolbar, shown here and described in Table 16-4, is only available when you are working in the Object window. This toolbar allows you to manipulate various objects you have inserted into your forms.

Button	Name	Description
	Bring to Front	Brings the currently selected object to the front of the form.

Table 16-4   *Commands Found on the UserForm Toolbar*

Button	Name	Description
	Send to Back	Sends the currently selected object to the back of the form.
	Group	Groups selected objects within a form.
	Ungroup	Ungroups selected objects within a form.
	Align	Aligns objects within the form.
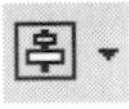	Center Horizontally/ Vertically	Determines the position of the selected objects in reference to the vertical and horizontal axes.
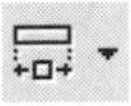	Make Width Same Size	Allows you to select multiple objects and set their widths to the same settings.
 100%	Zoom	Resizes the form display to the selected percentage. This does not affect the actual size of the form, but only the display of the form within the development environment.

Table 16-4   *Commands Found on the UserForm Toolbar* (continued)

Visual Basic Editor Options

The Visual Basic editor comes with standard settings for the working environment. Through the use of the Options dialog box, you can specify changes to these settings to suit your needs. To access the Options dialog box, simply select Tools | Options from the menu bar. Within the Options dialog box are four tabs, which we discuss here.

Editor Tab

The Editor tab, shown here, is the main area for setting up your working environment.

Here are the settings you can use in this tab:

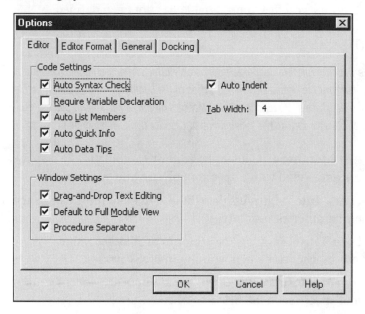

▶ **Auto Syntax Check**   Instructs the editor to automatically check your code for errors while you are working in design mode. Using this option will help you while working because the system will constantly check your code as you work. The only downside to this feature is that it displays a dialog box every time it finds an error in your code, forcing you to click OK or Help each time the dialog box is displayed. This can be very helpful for the novice programmer, but experienced developers will likely want to turn this feature off. When this feature is deactivated, errors in code syntax are still displayed in red, but the warning dialog box is not displayed.

▶ **Require Variable Declaration**   Requires you to declare all your variables prior to using them in your code. This is a great feature that will save you quite a bit of time in the long run because it will minimize errors within your project caused by typos. If this feature is turned off and you mistype a variable name, VB will assume that it is a new variable and will continue without generating an error, thus making debugging potentially very difficult. With this feature enabled, you must declare (DIM) all variables before using them; otherwise, VB will notify you that your variable has not been defined.

NOTE

*The Require Variable Declaration option only affects new UserForms, Modules, and Class Modules by inserting the Option Explicit instruction at the beginning of the code. If you enable this option while UserForms, Modules, and Class Modules already exist in your project, you must manually enter **Option Explicit** as the first line of code for this feature to be activated.*

▶ **Auto List Members**   Causes the editor to automatically display a listing of all members associated with a specific object while you type.

▶ **Auto Quick Info**   Instructs the editor to display information about functions and their parameters as you type.

▶ **Auto Data Tips**   Instructs the editor to display the value of a variable you have your mouse over when working in break mode.

▶ **Auto Indent**   Instructs the editor to automatically indent your code based on the indent specified in the first line of code.

▶ **Tab Width**   Sets the number of spaces for each tab in the editor.

▶ **Drag-and-Drop Text Editing**   Allows you to drag and drop various objects between windows.

▶ **Default to Full Module View**   Allows you to view all the procedures contained within a new module in a single list.

▶ **Procedure Separator**   Adds a line separator between each procedure when you're working in full module view.

Editor Format Tab

The Editor Format tab, shown here, determines how the text within your Code window will appear. Using this tab, you can assign specific colors, fonts, and sizes to the elements of your code. Leaving the default settings will not affect the way your project works, but you may want to customize it to suit your preferences.

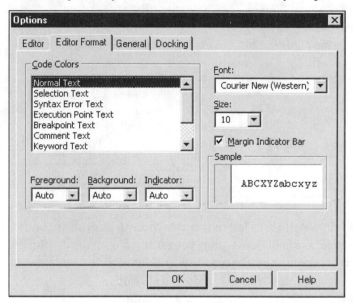

General Tab

The General tab, shown here, allows you to customize how the program works in respect to various aspects of development. Within this tab, you can set the attributes shown next.

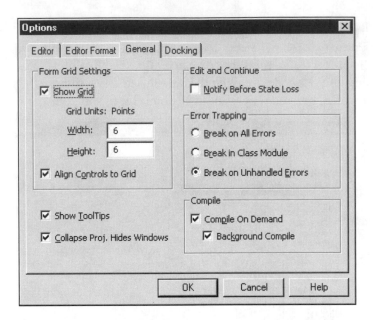

▶ **Form Grid Settings**   Determines the spacing of grids on your forms. The grids appear as small dots within your form. Using these settings, you can determine the spacing between your grid lines, along with whether you want your objects to align with the grids you specify.

▶ **Show ToolTips**   Instructs the editor to display ToolTips for items shown on the screen.

▶ **Collapse Proj. Hides Windows**   Determines whether items are automatically hidden when a project is collapsed in the Project Explorer window while the project is running.

▶ **Edit and Continue**   Instructs the editor to display a message before resetting the module-level variables for running a project.

▶ **Error Trapping**   Determines how the editor will handle errors within a project. With these options, you can instruct the system to break on all errors, break on Class Modules, or break only on unhandled errors (errors for which you have not incorporated an error handler).

▶ **Compile**   Determines how the program will compile your projects. Within this section, you can instruct the system to compile when needed and to compile in the background while you continue working. Be careful when enabling the Compile On Demand option, because this will not report errors in code until it is run—potentially causing errors to go untrapped.

Docking Tab

The Docking tab in the Options dialog box, shown here, allows you to configure which windows within the environment are dockable and which are not. *Docking* allows the window to be positioned along the screen borders, which helps with the organization of your project window.

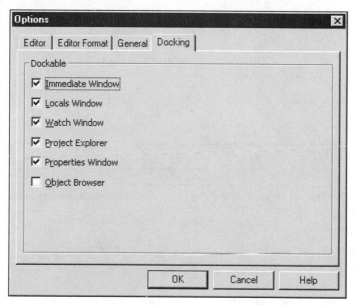

Setting Project Properties

If you have worked with Visual Basic, you know that the properties you set for your projects in the program are much more complex than the properties available to you when working with the Visual Basic editor. However, there are some basic property settings that you will want to assign to your project, along with some security settings. These settings are determined by using the Project Properties dialog box (see Figure 16-6).

To open the Project Properties dialog box, select Tools | (project name) Properties from the menu bar. Once you are inside the Project Properties dialog box, you will

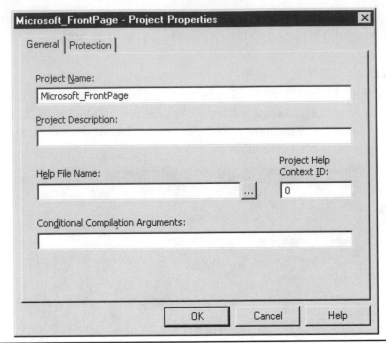

Figure 16-6 *The Project Properties dialog box, used to determine the basic settings for your project*

see two tabs. The first is the General tab, which is shown in Figure 16-6, and the second is the Protection tab, shown in Figure 16-7.

Project Properties, General Tab

The General tab allows you to specify some of the basic properties for your project. Within this tab, you can set the following options:

▶ **Project Name**   The name you will associate with your project.

▶ **Project Description**   A brief description of the project and what it does.

▶ **Help File Name**   The name of the help file, if any, that will be associated with your project.

▶ **Project Help Context ID**   The context-sensitive help ID that will be called to bring up help when the project's object library is selected.

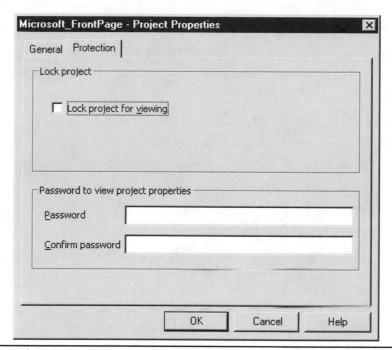

Figure 16-7   *The Project Properties dialog box's Protection tab, used to set up security for your project*

▶ **Conditional Compilation Arguments**   Conditional text that is associated with arguments in your code. When you compile your code, the conditional argument will be matched with the argument within the code, and the compilation will be based on that argument.

Project Properties, Protection Tab

The Protection tab sets up basic security for your project. When you look at this tab, you will see a single check box titled Lock Project for Viewing. If you check this box, you will then need to enter and confirm a password to be used before the project is made available for viewing. Using this option allows you to redistribute your code without allowing others to view the code itself.

Importing Files into the Editor

You may find you want to import specific Visual Basic files into your project for use with the current code you are creating. Working with the Visual Basic editor, you can easily accomplish this by following these steps:

1. Select File | Import File from the menu bar. This brings up the Import File dialog box—a standard Windows dialog box.

2. Move to the directory containing your file and select it.

3. Click OK to import the file into your project.

Exporting Files from the Editor

Once you have created a project form, Module, or Class Module, you can export it from the editor. To accomplish this, follow these steps:

1. Select the file you want to export in the Project Explorer.

2. Select File | Export File from the menu bar. This brings up the Export File dialog box—a standard Windows dialog box.

3. Move to the directory where you want to place the file and then export the file.

NOTE

You will notice that the system automatically recognizes the file format you are working with when you export.

Debugging Your Projects

Breakpoints are markers you set in your script that instruct the application to stop and enter the debugging mode when encountered. These markers allow you to specify exact lines within your script where you want debugging to begin, and they are set by following these steps:

1. Move to the point in your script where you want the breakpoint set.

2. Click the left margin. You will see a red dot appear in the margin. This specifies that a breakpoint has been set.

To remove the breakpoint, simply click the dot in the margin, and the point will disappear.

FrontPage Macros

In FrontPage, a *macro* is simply a VBA subroutine with no arguments. A *subroutine* is a type of procedure, or a "named sequence of statements executed as a unit," that does not return anything. FrontPage macros are stored and run within FrontPage and are not Web specific. You create macro subroutines within a Module in FrontPage's Visual Basic editor using the following syntax:

```
Sub MacroName()
[ …procedure code… ]
End Sub
```

When you run a macro, the procedure code between the Sub and End Sub statements is executed by FrontPage's VBA scripting engine. This code is used to perform simple actions directly or to start more complex processes.

Hands On: Creating the "Hello World" Macro

Let's start by creating a simple macro that displays a dialog box with the message "Hello World." Here are the steps to follow:

1. From FrontPage, open the Visual Basic editor by selecting Tools | Macro | Visual Basic Editor (or by pressing ALT-F11).

2. In the Project Explorer window, click the + symbol next to the Modules item to display the default Module1 item. Double-click Module1 to display it in the Code Editor window.

3. In the Module1 Code window, enter the following code:

```
Sub SayHello()
   MsgBox "Hello World"
End Sub
```

4. Save your work by clicking the File | Save menu option (or the disk button on the toolbar).

That's it. You've just created your first FrontPage macro. Close the VB editor and return to FrontPage. Now that we've created a macro, we need to run it. There are two primary ways of running a macro within FrontPage. For this example, we'll run our macro from the macros list. Here are the steps:

1. Click the Tools | Macro | Macros menu option to display a list of available macros.

2. Highlight the SayHello macro we just created and click Run.

3. A dialog box pops up with the message "Hello World."

When you run the SayHello macro, our SayHello subroutine is executed. The VBA command MsgBox in our procedure instructs FrontPage to display a message box with the command's message argument "Hello World."

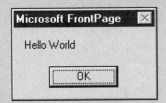

Of course, this is the simplest of examples, but you should now have a basic understanding of how to create and run macros with FrontPage. We'll get into much more complicated and useful macro/application examples as we proceed, but first, let's cover the other direct method of executing macros.

Customizing Toolbars and Assigning Macros

As you create and use macros, you may find that the previously described method of opening the macros list and running the desired macro is somewhat tedious. To make commonly used macros more accessible, you can create your own custom toolbars and add command buttons that run specific macros.

To begin customizing FrontPage's toolbars, follow these steps:

1. Within FrontPage, right-click anywhere within an existing toolbar and select Customize from the pop-up menu. This displays the Customize dialog box, shown in Figure 16-8.

2. Move to the Toolbars tab and click the New button.

3. Enter a name for your new toolbar, such as MyToolBar (Custom1 is the default, but it's not very meaningful), and click OK to create the new toolbar. Your new toolbar will then be displayed as shown here:

   Now that we've created a new toolbar, we need to add a control button to it that we'll use to run our macro.

4. Switch to the Commands tab within the Customize dialog box and scroll down the list under Categories to the Macros item. Select this item, and the macro command options will be displayed in the Commands list.

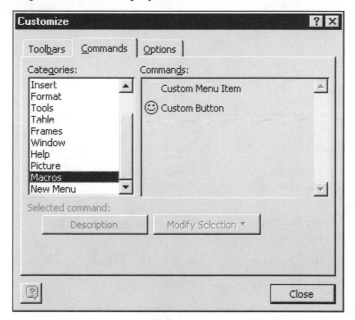

The two options available to be assigned to macros are Custom Menu Item and Custom Button. As their names imply, Custom Menu Item is normally used to add a new command to a menu, and Custom Button is used to add a command button to a toolbar. For this example, we'll be using the Custom Button option.

5. To add a new custom button to our new toolbar, just drag it from the Commands list and drop it into place on the toolbar, as shown here:

   Now that we've added a new control button, we need to further customize it.

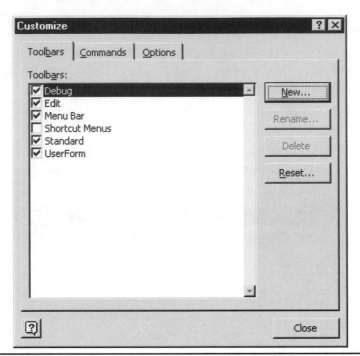

Figure 16-8 *The Toolbars tab of the Customize dialog box, used for adding and editing toolbars associated with your interface*

6. Right-click the button to display the customization pop-up menu. The options are as follows:

   ▶ **Reset**   Resets all options to their defaults (those of a new button).

   ▶ **Delete**   Deletes the button or menu item.

   ▶ **Name**   Assigns a name to the button or menu item. This is the text that is displayed in a menu item and the ToolTip (and, optionally, the text that is displayed for a command button).

TIP

Inserting an ampersand (&) before a single letter in a menu item's name causes the letter that follows to act as a keyboard accelerator. This has no effect on command buttons unless the Text Only or Image And Text display option has been selected.

   ▶ **Copy Button Image**   Copies the button's current image to the clipboard.

- ▶ **Paste Button Image**   Pastes a previously copied button image onto the current button.

- ▶ **Reset Button Image**   Resets the button image back to the default smiley-face image.

- ▶ **Edit Button Image**   Opens the button editor, where you can customize the current button image.

- ▶ **Change Button Image**   Opens the button image selection dialog box, where you may select another image to assign to the button.

- ▶ **Default Style**   Sets the display style of the control to that of a button with no text.

- ▶ **Text Only (Always)**   Sets the display style of the control to text only. This text is what was entered in the Name option.

- ▶ **Text Only (in Menus)**   Sets the display style of the control to text only, when it is being used in a menu.

- ▶ **Image and Text**   Sets the display style to show an image and text together.

- ▶ **Begin a Group**   Inserts a group separator (line) before the current control. This option is only available when there is more than one command control on a toolbar or menu.

- ▶ **Assign Macro**   Opens the macros list, where you can choose a macro to assign to the control. Once assigned, the selected macro will be executed whenever the control is clicked.

NOTE

Unfortunately, there is currently no way you can assign keyboard accelerators to macros, command buttons, or menu items that make use of the CTRL key, as you can in some other Office applications.

Let's go ahead and assign our SayHello macro to our new button. To do so, follow these steps:

1. Right-click the button to display the customization menu.

2. Select the Assign Macro option and then select the SayHello macro from the macros list.

3. Close the Customize dialog box and click the new command button. A dialog box displays with the message "Hello World," just as it did when we ran the macro from the macros list.

Now that we've covered the creation of a simple macro and the two primary methods of running macros (we'll cover a third method later), you need to know how to access the components within FrontPage.

The FrontPage Object Model

When you're writing VBA code that interacts with FrontPage, it's important to understand the FrontPage object model and its structure. To control FrontPage, you must reference FrontPage's objects and collections and make use of their properties and methods.

NOTE

Some objects are also collections, and some objects can only be referenced as objects within their collections.

Application

The Application object is the highest-level object within the FrontPage object model hierarchy. This object always exists while FrontPage is running, and there is only one Application object, even when multiple copies of FrontPage are running.

The Application object is also the only object that generates events. These events include OnAfterPageSave, OnAfterWebPublish, OnBeforePageSave, OnBeforeWebPublish, OnPageClose, OnPageNew, OnPageOpen, OnWebClose, and OnWebNew. We'll cover each of these events in more detail, along with examples of how to trap and use them, later in the "Trapping FrontPage Application Events" section.

WebWindow

A WebWindow object is an individual instance of the FrontPage interface, of which multiple instances can exist within the single FrontPage Application object. In other words, each copy of FrontPage that is running represents an individual WebWindow object. All WebWindow objects are contained in the zero-based WebWindows collection. The ActiveWebWindow object references the WebWindow object that is currently active. Use the ActiveWebWindow object to control the current instance of the FrontPage program interface. Here's an example:

```
Application.WebWindows(index).WebWindow or Application.ActiveWebWindow
```

Web

A Web object represents either a disk-based or server-based Web. All Web objects within a FrontPage Web are contained within the zero-based Webs collection. For each Web object, there exists a WebWindow object, but because the same Web can be open in more than one WebWindow (FrontPage instance) at a time, there is not necessarily a separate Web object for each WebWindow object. The ActiveWeb object references the Web object within the ActiveWebWindow. Here's an example:

```
Application.Webs(index).Web or Application.ActiveWeb
```

PageWindow

The PageWindow object is a member of the zero-based PageWindows collection, which contains all the open page Editor windows in the specified WebWindow (FrontPage instance). The ActivePageWindow object is used to access the PageWindow object that is currently active. Use the ActivePageWindow object to control the active page Editor window within the active instance of FrontPage. Here's an example:

```
Application.WebWindows(index).PageWindows(index).PageWindow or
Application.ActiveWebWindow.ActivePageWindow
```

ActiveDocument

The ActiveDocument object allows you to access the Microsoft FrontPage Page object model elements. These elements are used to interact programmatically with the source code of HTML pages. Use the Document object to reference the Page object model elements within the ActivePageWindow. Here's an example:

```
Application.ActiveDocument or
Application.ActiveWebWindow.ActivePageWindow.Document
```

CommandBars

The CommandBars object/collection provides access to the CommandBars collection of all toolbars and menus (visible or not) within FrontPage. Using the CommandBars object/collection, you can control the display of existing toolbars and menus, create new toolbars and menus, customize toolbars and menus, and delete user-defined toolbars and menus. The CommandBarControls object provides access to the Controls collection, which represents all the controls within the specified CommandBar object. Here's an example:

```
Application.CommandBars(name).Controls(name)
```

Themes

The Themes object/collection provides access to the Theme objects within FrontPage or an individual FrontPage Web. The Application.Themes collection references all the themes available to FrontPage. The Web.Themes collection references only the theme(s) that exist within the specified Web.

```
Application.Themes(index) or ActiveWeb.Themes(index)
```

Controlling FrontPage with VBA

Now that we've covered some of the common objects and collections within the FrontPage object model, you should begin to see how we can reference the various components that make up the application. But to actually control FrontPage, we must use these objects' properties, methods, and events. We'll cover many of these implementations through practical examples.

NOTE

All code examples are available on the accompanying CD-ROM. Within the VB editor, import the file FPDGuide.bas to load the examples' code.

Working with Command Bars and Controls

Although the implementation of the VBA scripting engine within FrontPage 2002 has improved greatly over the previous release, there are still some areas that have no directly programmable interface. In these situations, we are forced to take a slightly regressive approach and write code that interacts with the FrontPage user interface itself, mimicking the actions of a human user.

Hands On: Using Macros to Add Functionality

Still missing in this release of FrontPage are the Save All and Close All options. If you're like me and often edit multiple pages at a time, closing each page can sometimes be a redundant, if not arduous, task. We can add this feature to FrontPage by creating a simple macro.

A page that is open in a FrontPage Editor window is referenced by its PageWindow object. Although the ActivePageWindow object always references the current page, we need to access all the PageWindow objects if we are to save and close each open page. To do so, we need to use the PageWindows collection to step through all the PageWindow objects and use the PageWindow.Close method to close and optionally save the individual pages. By adding the True argument to the Close method, we'll also instruct FrontPage to save each page before closing it (if unspecified, this method defaults to False, meaning don't save before closing).

To create the macro, use the following code in your project.

```
Sub SaveCloseAll()

  Dim pPage As PageWindow

  On Error Resume Next

  For Each pPage In ActiveWebWindow.PageWindows
    pPage.Close True 'close the currently referenced page
  Next

  Set pPage = Nothing

End Sub
```

TIP

To make this macro close all files without saving them, simply change the Page.Close True statement to Page.Close False. I won't show this simple change here, but it is included as the CloseAll subroutine in the FPDGuide.bas module.

After creating the SaveCloseAll macro, you'll likely want to create a toolbar button to activate it within FrontPage. See the earlier section "Customizing Toolbars and Assigning Macros" for details.

Opening a New WebWindow

In order to programmatically open a new WebWindow, we will access the New Window menu command. To run a toolbar or menu command, we can use the following code:

```
Application.CommandBars("toolbar name").Controls("control name").Execute
```

NOTE

In this release of FrontPage, Microsoft has added the ability to open additional instances of FrontPage using the WebWindows.Add method. Although it is no longer necessary to mimic command button clicks to accomplish this, I'll still cover it here because it provides an excellent example of manipulating the FrontPage environment using VBA.

Let's create a simple macro that clicks the New Window command and opens a new copy of FrontPage. To do so, just add the following subroutine within a Module (such as Module1):

```
Sub OpenNewWindow()
  Application.CommandBars("Window").Controls("New Window").Execute
End Sub
```

Try it out in FrontPage itself by running the macro using the macros list. When you run the OpenNewWindow macro, a new copy of FrontPage (WebWindow) is opened with the current Web loaded.

This code works great right now, but it can easily be broken when users customize their menus and toolbars. After all, if the New Window command is removed or simply moved to another toolbar or menu, our location-specific code will no longer work. To avoid these potential problems, we should instead rely on the Control object's ID property.

Every built-in control in FrontPage has a unique identifying number that may be read by checking its ID property. To get a control's ID, follow these steps:

1. Make sure the control currently exists on a menu or toolbar. Controls must be accessed as members of the CommandBars collection's Controls collection.

2. In the VB editor's Immediate window, type the following code and press ENTER at the end of the line:

```
? Application.CommandBars("Window").Controls("New Window").ID
```

3. The number 303 is then displayed on the following line. This is the ID property for the New Window command.

Regardless of where you place the control, or even if you remove it from all menus and toolbars, it still maintains the unique ID property of 303.

Now that we have a way to consistently reference a particular control, we need to deal with the problem that it may not be part of any CommandBars collection (it is not on any menu or toolbar). To handle this, we can either search for it using the CommandBars collection's FindControl method or, better yet, programmatically create a new temporary CommandBar object and add the desired control to that command bar. Using this second method, we guarantee that the control will be where we'd like it to be, and we can then delete the temporary CommandBar object when finished. This is exactly what we'll do in the following code example:

```
Sub RunMenuCommand(iMenuID As Long)

  'Ignore any errors (such as the menu ID not valid)
  'On Error Resume Next

  'Create our own temporary commandbar to hold the control
  With Application.CommandBars.Add

    'Add the control and execute it
    .Controls.Add(Id:=iMenuID, temporary:=True).Execute

    DoEvents   'allow the control execution to complete
               'before deleting the control

    'Then delete our temporary menu bar
    .Delete

  End With

End Sub
```

When we call our RunMenuCommand subroutine, we'll pass it the ID of the control we want to execute. This subroutine is also reusable in any Office application and can be called many times within the same program. As you can see, we've also used the VB With/End With statement to avoid redundant code.

NOTE

It is very important to include the DoEvents statement between the creation/execution and deletion of the control. If you exclude this line, you stand a high risk of crashing FrontPage as it tries to delete a control that it is still in the process of executing.

Now that we have a somewhat foolproof way to execute a toolbar or menu command, without fear that users have customized their system and broken our code, we can simplify our OpenNewWindow subroutine and put our safer code to use. Because you'll likely soon forget that the New Window control's ID property is 303, I recommend that you create a constant for this item and place it in the Declarations section of your Module, like this:

```
Const fpmNewWindow = 303
```

Then, edit your OpenNewWindow subroutine to read as follows:

```
Sub OpenNewWindow()
  RunMenuCommand fpmNewWindow
End Sub
```

I'm sure you're starting to see that by creating a single menu/toolbar command execution subroutine (RunMenuCommand), you can now make calls to any of the FrontPage menu or toolbar commands quite easily. Just check the control's ID property, create a meaningful constant for that control's ID, and pass it to the RunMenuCommand subroutine whenever you need to execute it.

NOTE

You may have noticed that unlike our other subroutines, RunMenuCommand is not listed in the macros list and cannot be directly run from FrontPage. This is because it requires a control ID to run. When clicking a button or menu command, you cannot pass any arguments. So whenever your subroutines have one or more arguments, they are not macros.

The State Property

Although everything we've done so far works great for most toolbar buttons and menu commands, there's an exception that deserves consideration. This exception is the command button that maintains a persistent state (on or off). An example of this is the View menu's buttons. When you click a button in the top two sections of the

View menu, the button stays in the on (down) position. Conversely, when you click one of these buttons that is already in the down position, it reverts to the up (off) position. Whenever you execute one of these buttons, it toggles to the opposite position. For this reason, we need to check the State property of these buttons before executing them if we are to know the resulting action.

In the next example, we want to open a new copy of FrontPage and also hide the Views bar and folder list, making the entire window available for editing a page. To do so, we'll take our previous OpenNewWindow macro and extend it to close the Views bar and folder list if, and only if, they are currently displayed.

Let's start by creating a procedure that tells us the current state of a command button. To accomplish this, we'll create a function instead of a subroutine. The only difference between a subroutine and a function is that a function has a return value, whereas a subroutine (sub) does not. Here's the code:

```
Function GetMenuCommandState(iMenuID As Long) As Integer

  With Application.CommandBars.Add

    'Add the control and check its state property
    GetMenuCommandState = .Controls.Add(Id:=iMenuID).State

      DoEvents

      'Then delete our temporary menu bar

    .Delete

    End With

End Function
```

In this example, we pass our function the ID property of the control we want to check, just as we did in the RunMenuCommand sub. Additionally, we add the As Integer return declaration to tell VB that the function will return a value of the type Integer. As you can see, we create a new temporary ControlBar and add the desired control. We then substitute the Execute method for the State property and set the function equal to that value. Now, we can use this function whenever we need to check the state of a command button. VBA includes two internal state constants that make performing comparisons more readable. They are msoButtonUp and msoButtonDown.

Creating a Full-Screen Page Editor Window with a Single Click

In FrontPage, the state of toolbar and menu command buttons is persistent throughout the entire application. Although changes made to these controls are only immediately seen in the WebWindow where they occur, they become the new standard for all subsequently opened WebWindows, even after FrontPage has been closed and reopened. For this reason, it would be very handy to be able to open and close all ancillary windows with the single click of a toolbar button. Although FrontPage does not directly offer this ability, through menu and toolbar customization, we can programmatically handle it quite easily. To do so, we'll create two macros that allow us to show or hide both windows.

Checking the ID property of the Views Bar and Folder List buttons, we can now add two new constants to the Declarations section of our Module:

```
Const fpmFolderList = 1077
Const fpmViewsBar = 2504
```

Now that we have the IDs of these command buttons, all we need to do is check their current state and execute or ignore them, as necessary. First, let's create a macro to hide both windows:

```
Sub HideViews()

  If GetMenuCommandState(fpmFolderList) = msoButtonDown Then
    RunMenuCommand fpmFolderList
  End If

   If GetMenuCommandState(fpmViewsBar) = msoButtonDown Then
    RunMenuCommand fpmViewsBar
  End If

End Sub
```

In this macro, we use the GetMenuCommandState function that we previously created to return the state of the button in question. If the button's state is equal to msoButtonDown (on), we execute the control to toggle it off. This procedure is repeated for each of the two controls.

To display both views, we'll create a second, very similar macro that executes the command buttons if their state is equal to msoButtonUp (off):

```
Sub ShowViews()

  If GetMenuCommandState(fpmViewsBar) = msoButtonUp Then
```

```
   RunMenuCommand fpmViewsBar
End If

If GetMenuCommandState(fpmFolderList) = msoButtonUp Then
   RunMenuCommand fpmFolderList
End If

End Sub
```

Although the functionality of these two subs is so close that a programmer's first instinct may be to create a single sub and pass it the value of the desired action, keep in mind that a macro cannot accept any attributes.

NOTE

We could also have created a single procedure that accepts a show or hide attribute and performs the desired action, thus simplifying the calls, but we still need to create a separate show and hide attribute without the macros that call such a unified procedure.

Opening the Current Page in a Full-Screen Window

FrontPage 2002's single-window interface has many benefits, but there may be times when you want to open a page in a separate window, without any ancillary windows getting in the way. Building on our previous examples, we'll now do just that.

In review, we've so far discussed how to close open pages, how to open new WebWindow objects (copies of the FrontPage user interface), and how to hide or show both the Views Bar and Folder List windows through VBA code. The final requirement to complete our current goal is to programmatically open a particular page in another running copy of FrontPage (WebWindow). Here's what we need to accomplish so that our task will be complete:

1. Because we want to open the page within the active page Editor window in a new copy of FrontPage, we need to check to see whether there is a page open in an Editor window. If there is, we can proceed. If not, we'll just open a new WebWindow object without trying to load a page.

2. If we do have an active page in an Editor window, we'll get and store its address (URL) using the ActivePageWindow.File.URL property.

3. If the page has had changes made to it since it was opened for editing (ActivePageWindow.IsDirty property), we'll give the user the option of

saving the page and proceeding, proceeding without saving the page, or just canceling the whole operation.

4. If the user selects one of the first two options, we'll proceed and create a new WebWindow object using the RunMenuCommand subroutine we previously created. We'll also close the active page in the original ActivePageWindow.

5. Next, we'll obtain a reference to our new WebWindow object using the WebWindows.Count property. WebWindows(WebWindows.Count – 1) is our newly opened copy of FrontPage.

6. Once we have a reference to our new WebWindow object and know the address (URL) of the page we want to open, we'll create a new PageWindow (Editor window) within the WebWindow using the PageWindow.AddURL method after closing the default new_page_1.htm document that FrontPage always creates at startup.

7. Finally, we'll hide the Views Bar and Folder List windows in our new WebWindow and activate our new full-screen window.

Here's the actual OpenInNewWindow subroutine, which is included in FPDGuide.bas:

```
Sub OpenInNewWindow()

   Dim NewWindow    As WebWindow
                     'WebWindow object variable
   Dim FileToOpen   As String
                     'address of the page we want to open
   Dim Response     As Integer
                     'user response to our save first question
   Dim msg          As String
                     'the question we ask to obtain a response


   On Error Resume Next 'ignore any errors

   'if there isn't an active page to open in
   'the new window, just open the window
   If ActiveWebWindow.PageWindows.Count = 0 Then
     RunMenuCommand fpmNewWindow
   'MenuID 303 - open a new WebWindow
     Exit Sub 'since there's no page to open, get out
   End If
```

```
'get the address of the page we want to
'open in the new WebWindow
FileToOpen = ActivePageWindow.File.URL
'get the full path of the file to be opened

'if the page has been altered,
'offer to save it before proceeding
If ActivePageWindow.IsDirty Then
   msg = "Would you like to save the
current page before reopening it in a new window?"
   Response =
MsgBox(msg, vbQuestion Or vbYesNoCancel, "Save Current File")
   Select Case Response
      Case vbYes 'save and close
        ActivePageWindow.Close True
      Case vbNo  'close without saving
        ActivePageWindow.Close False
      Case vbCancel  'cancel the whole thing
        Exit Sub
   End Select
Else
   ActivePageWindow.Close False
   'if the page hasn't been altered, just close it
End If

'open the new WebWindow
RunMenuCommand fpmNewWindow
'MenuID 303 - open a new WebWindow

'create a reference to the new WebWindow object
Set NewWindow = WebWindows(WebWindows.Count - 1)

NewWindow.ActivePageWindow.Close False
'close the new_page1.htm document

NewWindow.PageWindows.Add FileToOpen
'open the page in our new WebWindow
HideViews 'hide the Views Bar and Folder List if shown
NewWindow.Activate
'activate the new WebWindow to bring it to the front

Set NewWindow = Nothing
'clean up our WebWindow reference variable

End Sub
```

Trapping FrontPage Application Events

As was briefly mentioned in our discussion of the FrontPage object model earlier in this chapter, the Application object provides a method of monitoring FrontPage-generated events. For those of you not familiar with the concept, an *event* is simply a notification that something has happened or is about to happen.

Within other Office applications, there is always at least one default object that is separate from the application itself and has events. Examples of this are the WorkBook and WorkSheet in Excel, the Normal.dot template in Word, and the MDB database itself, in Access. Unfortunately, FrontPage 2002 has no such default document to store event-driven code. For this reason, we must roll our own for FrontPage's Application object by creating a Class Module and using the WithEvents statement. Let's take a look at exactly how this is done.

First, we need to create a new Class Module. To do so, just right-click anywhere within the VB editor's Project window and select Insert | Class Module from the pop-up menu. The editor then creates a new Class Module named Class1 and opens it in the Code Editor window. You'll notice that only two properties of the new class are displayed in the Properties window.

Moving to the Code Editor window, add the following code in the Declarations section at the top of the code:

```
Dim WithEvents e_fp As FrontPage.Application
```

The WithEvents statement tells VBA that the variable being declared is an object variable that will trap and handle events triggered by an ActiveX object. In this case, e_fp is the object variable, and FrontPage.Application is the ActiveX object whose events will be handled. We've done this in a Class Module because this is the only place the WithEvents statement can be used.

Now that we've created a variable that can trap and handle the events that the FrontPage application generates, we need to create an instance of the variable in the Initialize event handler of the class. To accomplish this, add the following code below the variable declaration:

```
Private Sub class_initialize()
    Set e_fp = Application
End Sub
```

Whenever we create a new instance of our class, the class_initialize subroutine is automatically run, creating an instance of our WithEvents object variable, thereby tying it into the application's events.

To trap and handle the application's events, we need to declare them. To save time, let's import a class file from the CD-ROM that contains all the FrontPage application event declarations. To import this file, right-click anywhere in the Project window and select Import File from the pop-up menu. Browse to the CD-ROM's Chapter16 folder and select the cFPEvents.cls file. After importing the class file, double-click it to open it in an Editor window.

In addition to the code we entered in our new class file previously, you can see that each of the FrontPage application events has been declared for you. In each of the event declarations, I've also added a message box statement that will notify you of each event as it occurs.

The final steps to activating and using our event handler class are to declare a new instance of it within a macro and create a separate macro that destroys that instance. In a Module file, you would add the following code to the Declarations section.

NOTE

This code is already included in the file FPDGuide.bas, which you imported earlier in the chapter. To use the included code, uncomment the commented code in the Declarations area and the EnableEvents subroutine.

```
Dim FPEvents As cFPEvents
```

Next, add the following two macros:

```
Sub EnableEvents()
  Set FPEvents = New cFPEvents
  'create a new instance of the event
End Sub
```

```
Sub DisableEvents()
  Set FPEvents = Nothing 'destroy the event
End Sub
```

To test our new event-handling code, save your work and return to FrontPage. Run the EnableEvents macro and perform any of the following: open an existing Web, create a new Web, close a Web, open a page, create a new page, save a page, or close a page. As you can see, each of these actions triggers an Application event, firing off a message box announcement when each event handler routine is run. Using these event handlers, you can now monitor many user actions within FrontPage and respond to them accordingly.

Hands On: Creating and Using the FrontPage Auto Start Macro

Although there's no way to prevent FrontPage from creating the default new_page_1.htm page when first opened, we can at least automatically remove this pesky file as soon as it is created. We can also automatically activate our FrontPage Application event-handler code and display the Views bar and folders list, which we may have closed the last time we ran FrontPage. To accomplish these tasks, we'll use the FrontPage Auto Start add-in and Auto_Start macro.

In a Module, add the following subroutine:

```
Sub Auto_Start()
  On Error Resume Next 'ignore errors
  ActivePageWindow.Close False
  'close the default page created by FrontPage
  ShowViews 'display the Views Bar and Folder List
  EnableEvents
  'create and activate our event handling class
End Sub
```

Now save your work, close FrontPage, and restart it. If you've installed the Auto Start add-in, the Auto_Start macro automatically runs, closing the default page, displaying the Views Bar and Folder List windows, and activating the event-handler class.

TIP

Remember, to prevent the Auto_Start macro from running at startup, just hold down the SHIFT key while FrontPage opens. To prevent the event messages from being displayed, comment out the call to the EnableEvents subroutine.

NOTE

To disable the event notification messages, either comment out the MsgBox calls or the EnableEvents call in the Auto_Start subroutine.

Using Add-Ins

An *add-in* is a program (DLL) that extends the capabilities of its target application. It is beyond the abilities of FrontPage or its VBA implementation to create add-ins, but third-party developers offer a growing variety of these feature-extending tools. One example is the FrontPage Auto Start add-in by Business Modeling Solutions (http://www.BMSLtd.co.uk). You'll find this add-in, complete with commented source code, on the book's CD-ROM in the BMS folder and can install it by running FPAutoStart.exe.

NOTE

Although not required, you'll need to install the add-in if you want to run this section's sample code. To work with the add-in's source code, you'll need the full version of Visual Basic 6.0 or the Office XP Developer Edition.

One of the surprisingly missing features within FrontPage 2002 is the ability to automatically run a macro when the application is first started. The FrontPage Auto Start add-in does just that. When FrontPage is first opened, the add-in simply runs a macro named Auto_Start if it exists. You can also prevent the Auto_Start macro from being run by holding down the SHIFT key while FrontPage is loading.

UserForms and the FrontPage Editor Object Model

In addition to the subroutines and functions we've created in Modules and Class Modules, FrontPage's VBA implementation includes the ability to create and use UserForms (windows and dialog boxes) that improve our ability to interact with the user. *UserForms* (we'll just refer to them as *forms* from now on) are containers that house controls such as command buttons, text boxes, and labels.

Creating a form is quite simple. Within the VBA editor's Project window, right-click and select Insert | UserForm from the pop-up menu. The editor then creates a new form and opens it in the graphical Editor window. A control can then be placed on the form by clicking it within the Toolbox and then drawing the selected control on the form.

Let's start our exploration of forms by again creating a simple "Hello World" macro. We'll use code similar to that in our previous example, but this time we'll place it within a form, trigger it using a command button, and display our message in a text box.

The "Hello World" UserForm

To begin this example, open FrontPage and proceed to the Visual Basic editor. Once there, right-click in the Project window and select Insert | UserForm from the pop-up menu. Then continue with the following steps:

1. Locate the CommandButton control within the Toolbox. Click once to activate the command button and then click and drag a rectangle on the form to create a new button.

2. Locate the TextBox control (represented by ab|) in the Toolbox, activate it, and then draw a new text box on the form. Your form should now look something like the one shown in Figure 16-9.

3. Double-click the CommandButton1 control to open a Code Editor window. Note that a new CommandButton1_Click event-handling sub is automatically created. This is the procedure that will be run when the user clicks the button at runtime.

4. Within the CommandButton1_Click event procedure, add the following code:

```
Private Sub CommandButton1_Click()
  TextBox1.Text = "Hello World"
End Sub
```

5. Close the Code Editor window and click a single time on the form to make it the active window. You will note that the focus rectangle moves around the outside of the form.

6. Now press F5 to run the form.

7. Click the command button, and the message "Hello World" is displayed in the text box.

8. Delete the text in the text box and click the command button again. As you can plainly see, our code is run each time the CommandButton1_Click event is triggered.

9. Close the form by clicking the X in the upper-right corner of the form.

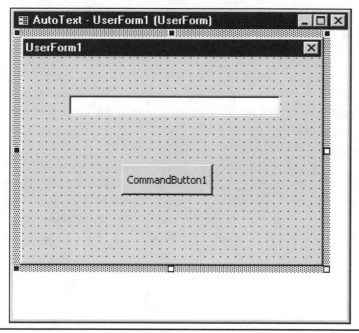

Figure 16-9   *A UserForm containing text area and a command button*

Running a UserForm from the FrontPage User Interface

Switch back to FrontPage and open the macros list. You'll note that our new
UserForm is absent from the listing. Although we just ran our simple form application
by pressing F5 within the VB editor, it is not possible to directly open a form in such
a manner within FrontPage. Instead, we must create a helper macro
(a subroutine with no arguments) to launch our form within FrontPage.

Switching back again to the VB editor, open Module1, scroll to the bottom
of the existing code, and append the following procedure:

```
Sub RunSayHello()
  UserForm1.Show
End Sub
```

Once again moving back to FrontPage, open the macros list and run our new
RunSayHello macro. As you can see, the macro is executed, displaying UserForm1.

Summary

This is probably one of the most complex chapters of the book. Not only were you introduced to an extended feature of FrontPage 2002, but you were also shown how to change the functionality of FrontPage itself. If you are a Visual Basic programmer, you already have a good grasp of many of the topics covered in this chapter. If, however, you're a developer who has not had much experience with VB, the examples shown here will give you a basic understanding of what you can accomplish.

The best part of the Visual Basic editor is that it allows us as developers to include functionality in FrontPage that is useful to us. We can customize the tool to our needs and save time in development. With the information you have found here, you should be well on your way to creating a custom environment that will help speed your products to market.

Working with Web Servers

IN THIS CHAPTER:

Understand Server Extensions

Work with a Web Server

Work with the SharePoint Team Services

T hroughout this book, we have talked about how you can create compelling and dynamic Webs through the use of FrontPage 2002. You have also seen that many features of this product are made possible through the use of servers equipped with the FrontPage Server Extensions and SharePoint. Without these products, your Webs would simply be a group of HTML files just like any other set of documents. But by using these products, you can publish your Webs and add extended capabilities to them.

Folders Versus Webs

Web site is one of the most commonly used yet misunderstood terms within the world of the Internet. This lack of understanding has led to great confusion over why anyone would want to use a Web server. After all, you can easily create complete Web sites and simply store the source files on your hard drive until you are ready to transfer them to your public Web server using FTP. In fact, this is how many Web developers handle this process.

This may be fine if you are developing a small site that offers only static content and requires no server interaction whatsoever. But doing so while using FrontPage as your development tool wastes much of the program's ease of use and functionality. An analogy to this scenario would be using Microsoft Word as your word processor and then saving all your documents as simple text files. Although Word is quite capable of operating in this limited way, doing so wastes much of its functionality, limiting your ability to create quality documents.

When you save your files directly to your hard drive and then view them with your browser, you simply read the files, displaying the information exactly as it is contained within the HTML source. The browser reads the file, just as Notepad reads a text file stored on your hard drive. Although this method of previewing HTML documents is arguably the most efficient in many cases, it can also be quite limiting.

When you save your files to a Web server, you let the server handle the storage and retrieval of the files, adding the ability to manipulate the information sent to the browser at the time of retrieval. Instead of directly reading the file, the browser makes a request to the server to dish up the information encompassed by the source file. The server then reads in the file, handles any server-side processing, and then transmits the resulting information to the browser for display. FrontPage's Web Components (WebBots), ASP documents, and many Java applets require such server-side interaction to function. For you to properly test pages that incorporate these technologies, the pages must be accessed through a Web server, not simply read directly from your hard drive.

Now that we've discussed some differences between simple folders and server-based Web sites, we can give a meaningful definition to a Web. A *Web* is a collection of files within a common network location (URL) that is accessible through a Web server. Inherent to the Web server is the ability to dynamically modify and/or create the information returned to the requesting client, making the Web site a true client-server application.

By applying this knowledge and thinking of a Web site as an application (or object), instead of just a group of files, you can begin to appreciate why it is to your advantage to develop your sites using a Web server.

Using Windows Internet Information Services

If you plan to work with a Web server on your system, your best bet is to work with Windows Internet Information Services (IIS). IIS comes with Windows 2000 and is part of the option pack of Windows NT. If you are working on Windows 95/98, you can work with the Personal Web Server, but for the purposes of this discussion, we will be looking at IIS running under Windows 2000.

With the release of Windows 2000, Microsoft has integrated IIS into the main computer-management application. This makes it easy to locate on your system and allows you to manage many other aspects along with your Web server. This type of integration comes in very handy when you are working with large-scale projects that include e-mail and FTP, and it becomes even more appealing when you are working with add-ons such as the SharePoint Team Services or Commerce Server, because everything is right there at your fingertips. For those of you familiar with the Microsoft Management Console, you will see that all the features found there are now under the Computer Management dialog box, shown in Figure 17-1.

To reach the IIS area of Computer Management, follow these steps:

1. On your Desktop, right-click the My Computer icon.

2. Select Manage from the pop-up context menu. This brings up the Computer Management dialog box shown in Figure 17-1.

3. In the tree, expand Services and Applications. You will see Internet Information Services listed as a sub-item.

4. Click Internet Information Services. You will now see all the Internet services currently running on your system.

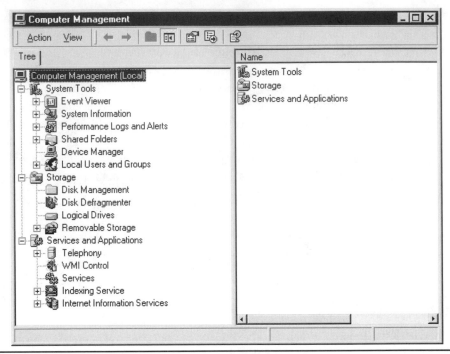

Figure 17-1 *The Computer Management dialog box, used to manage many aspects of your system*

You are now ready to begin working with IIS. The following topics take a look at the core knowledge you will need to operate IIS and begin creating dynamic sites right on your machine.

Web Sites and Virtual Directories

When working with IIS, you have the ability to create Web sites and virtual directories on your system. Although these two items have many similar qualities, they are inherently different in the way IIS works with them. The following list describes these items as well as provides information relating to when to use them:

▶ **Web site** When you create a new Web site, you are creating a site that is connected to the name or IP address for the machine you are working with. IIS gives you the ability to create any number of sites on your system. Windows 2000 Server allows multiple sites with their own IP addresses to run on a single server. On Windows 2000 Professional, you can only have one site active at any given time. The Web site you create should be used to house an entire site, such as your company's Web site. Once this is in place, you can put any number of virtual directories below it that contain company information, such as contact information, billing databases, and so on.

NOTE

There are ways to create multiple Web sites on a single server machine containing more than one IP address, but this falls outside the coverage of this book.

▶ **Virtual directory**   A virtual directory is a sub-directory of a selected site. This directory can be housed anywhere on your computer or another computer within your network and is simply a pointer to the directory containing the information you want displayed under the site. The use of a virtual directory allows you to create sub-directories for a site on your system, where the URL would look something like this:

```
http://localhost/virtual_directory_name/
```

The following topics outline how to create a site and a virtual directory on your system.

Creating a New Web Site in IIS

To create a new Web site on your system, follow these steps.

NOTE

The example shown here works with Windows 2000 Server. If you are working with Windows 2000 Professional, you only have the ability to create subwebs. The creation of subwebs works the same way as the creation of Webs, but your display options will be different.

1. Open Computer Management, as outlined earlier in this chapter.
2. Right-click Internet Information Services and select New | Web Site from the drop-down menu. This brings up the Web Site Creation Wizard.

3. Click the Next button on the opening screen to begin working with the wizard. You will now be presented with the Web Site Description dialog box, shown here:

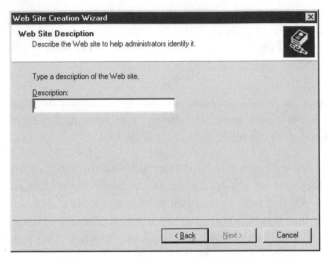

4. Type a description for your new Web site in the Description field. The description will display in IIS later on, so you should type something of meaning in this field.

5. Click Next to proceed to the IP Address and Port Settings dialog box, shown here:

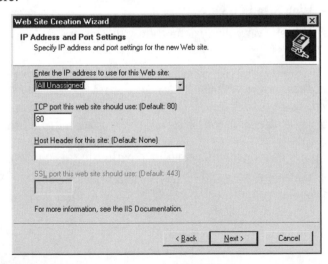

6. Select the IP address to be used for this Web site. If you only have one IP address associated with your system, you can leave this as the default.

7. Leave the TCP Port and Host Header fields at their defaults and click Next. This brings up the Web Site Home Directory dialog box, shown here:

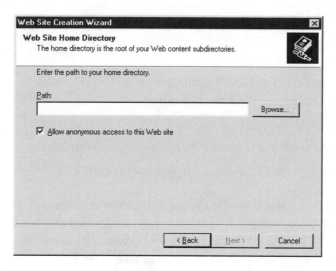

8. Enter the path for the directory containing the content you will be using for this Web site. If you do not know the path, click Browse to find the directory on your system.

9. If you want to allow anonymous access to your Web site, meaning anyone can view the content, leave the check box for anonymous access checked.

10. Click Next to bring up the Web Site Access Permissions dialog box, shown here:

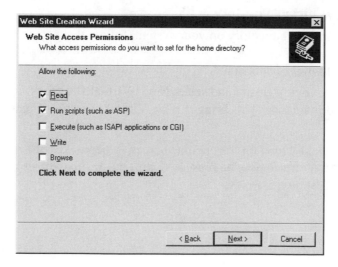

11. Check off the items you want to allow for this Web site. Here is a description of each:

   ▶ **Read**   Allows browsers to view the contents of this Web site

   ▶ **Run scripts (such as ASP)**   Instructs the Web site to allow script-based pages to run on the site

   ▶ **Execute (such as ISAPI applications or CGI)**   Instructs the Web site to allow applications to run on the site

   ▶ **Write**   Allows write access to the Web site

   ▶ **Browse**   Allows directory browsing on the Web site

12. Click Next and then Finish to complete the creation of your new Web site.

You will now see your Web site appear as a subset of Internet Information Services in the Management Console. You may also notice that next to your Web site's description is the word *Stopped*. This is because IIS already has a default Web site running on your system, which means that your new Web site is not currently running. To change this, follow these steps:

1. Right-click the Web site titled Default Web Site and select Stop from the drop-down menu.

2. Right-click your new Web site and select Start from the drop-down menu.

Your Web site is now active and can be viewed in your browser.

Creating a New Virtual Directory in IIS

To create a new virtual directory on your system, follow these steps.

1. Open Computer Management, as outlined earlier in this chapter.

2. Right-click your Web site and select New | Virtual Directory from the drop-down menu. This brings up the Virtual Directory Creation Wizard.

3. Click the Next button on the opening screen to begin working with the wizard. You will now be presented with the Virtual Directory Alias dialog box, shown here:

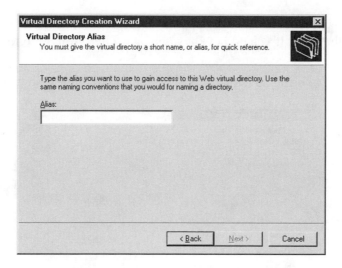

4. Type a name you want associated with your virtual directory in the field provided. This name will be used by your Web site to display the information found under this alias. For example, if you typed in **MyDocuments** as the alias, the Web site would display information found under this alias when a viewer types in the following URL:

   `http://localhost/MyDocuments/`

5. Click Next to bring up the Web Site Content Directory dialog box, shown here:

6. Enter the path for the directory containing the content you will be using for this virtual directory. If you do not know the path, click Browse to find the directory on your system.

7. Click Next to bring up the Access Permissions dialog box, shown here:

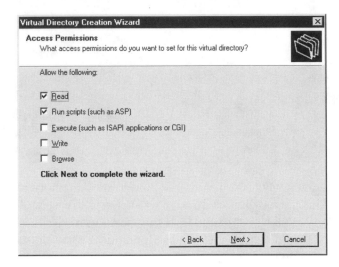

8. Check off the items you want to allow for this virtual directory. Here is a description of each:

   ▶ **Read**   Allows browsers to view the contents of this directory

   ▶ **Run scripts (such as ASP)**   Instructs the directory to allow script-based pages to run on the site

   ▶ **Execute (such as ISAPI applications or CGI)**   Instructs the directory to allow applications to run

   ▶ **Write**   Allows write access to the directory

   ▶ **Browse**   Allows directory browsing on the directory

9. Click Next and then Finish to complete the creation of your new virtual directory.

You will now see your virtual directory appear as a subset of your Web site in the Management Console.

NOTE

If the physical location of the virtual directory you create resides on another computer within your network, you may also be prompted for authentication credentials.

FrontPage Server Extensions: What Are They and Why Should You Use Them?

Server Extensions allow you to use many advanced features found in FrontPage, such as form processing, search capabilities, and FrontPage Web Components (WebBots). Without the FrontPage Server Extensions, these features simply won't work. For this reason, you should be sure to install the Server Extensions on the server where you will be hosting your site.

Along with the capabilities mentioned, the FrontPage Server Extensions offer you some key capabilities when developing and administering your Webs:

▶ **Web authoring**   Use of the FrontPage Server Extensions within your Web allows you to create and maintain a clean development environment for your project. Whenever you make a change to an item in your Web—for instance, the name or location of a page or image—the FrontPage Server Extensions automatically update all links to the changed item throughout your Web. The extensions also allow you to generate and maintain standard navigation bars throughout your Web.

▶ **Web administration**   Server Extensions allow authorized users to set permissions for Webs without needing to be a system administrator on the server. Through the use of the extensions, you can set permissions for authors, administrators, and visitors throughout your Web.

▶ **Web functionality**   Forms, discussion groups, hit counters, and search capabilities are all handled by the FrontPage Server Extensions. Through their use, you can incorporate this extended functionality into your Webs without the need for any programming on your part.

Along with the documentation that comes with the FrontPage Server Extensions, Microsoft has an online resource kit called SERK (Server Extension Resource Kit).

This kit gives you all the information you will likely ever need about configuring and using the FrontPage Server Extensions. At the time of this writing, you can find it at http://office.microsoft.com/frontpage/wpp/SERK/.

Installing the FrontPage Server Extensions

You can always obtain the latest version of the FrontPage Server Extensions from the Microsoft Web site at http://www.microsoft.com/frontpage. Once you have downloaded the extensions, simply follow the instructions in the program to complete the installation. The FrontPage Server Extensions are included with FrontPage and are also incorporated into the new SharePoint Intranet Portal Server. When installing FrontPage, either as a stand-alone application or as part of Microsoft Office XP, you are prompted to install the Server Extensions if the setup application finds a Web server installed on your computer. Regardless of where and how you obtain them, you'll be pleased to find that the installation of the extensions is an extremely simple process.

Working with Webs

The FrontPage Server Extensions make use of a Web's structure to enable various features for your pages. This part of the chapter instructs you on how to set up Webs that can make use of the FrontPage Server Extensions to enable many of the extended features offered by FrontPage. When working with FrontPage Server Extensions, you have the ability to

▶ Configure properties for individual Webs and subwebs, such as performance, e-mail options, scripting language defaults and execution permissions, and logging,

▶ Create and delete Webs and subwebs,

▶ Convert folders into subwebs and subwebs into folders,

▶ Recalculate the hyperlinks within a Web or subweb,

▶ Open a FrontPage Web for editing (if FrontPage has been installed on the local system), and

▶ Add new Web and subweb administrators.

Adding Server Extensions to a Web

To take advantage of the Server Extensions capabilities, you must first add them to your Web. If you had a Web server installed on your computer when you installed FrontPage, you may have already installed the FrontPage Server Extensions. If not, follow these steps:

1. Open Computer Management, as shown earlier in this chapter.

2. Right-click the Web you want to add extensions to and select All Tasks | Configure Server Extensions from the drop-down menu. This brings up the Server Extensions Wizard.

3. Follow the steps in the wizard to configure your Server Extensions.

That is all it takes to extend your Web and begin taking advantage of everything FrontPage has to offer. As I mentioned previously, you'll be pleased to discover that this process is very straightforward and simple.

Removing Extensions from a Web

There may come a time when it is decided that a Web on your system no longer needs the Server Extensions installed on it. Through the use of the Computer Management applet, you can easily remove the extensions from the Web, while keeping the Web and its contents intact. However, if you remove Server Extensions from a Web, you will no longer have the capabilities offered by the extensions. This is to say that any features of the Web that make use of the extensions will no longer function properly. For this reason, it is a good idea to make sure you do not—and will not—be using any functionality that needs the Server Extensions prior to removing them.

If you find out later that you have made a mistake, you can easily put the Server Extensions back on the Web.

NOTE

Server Extensions can only be removed from a root Web. Removing extensions from a root Web will cause the extensions to be removed from all the root Web's subwebs. Before doing so, it is always a good idea to convert any subwebs into folders. Failure to do so may cause problems if you choose to later reapply the FrontPage Server Extensions to the Web.

To remove Server Extensions from a Web, follow these steps:

1. Right-click the root Web you want to remove the extensions from. This brings up a drop-down menu.

2. Select Task | Remove Server Extensions from the drop-down menu. You are presented with the following dialog box, asking you to confirm that you want to remove the extensions:

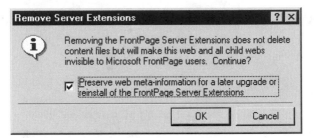

NOTE

Notice that the dialog box has a check box asking if you want to retain the Web meta-information. Retaining this information will allow you to easily add Server Extensions back to this Web at a later date.

3. Click OK to confirm that you want to remove the extensions.

Server Extensions are now removed from the current root Web and all its subwebs.

Adjusting Performance Attributes

One thing you will hear people say time and time again is that it takes a long time to access data on the Web. Although there are many factors that make this so, IIS gives you some capabilities that will speed access to the information contained within your Webs. This is accomplished by adjusting the performance attributes set up for your Web.

When you set the performance attributes, IIS accommodates the data within your Web by setting aside a certain amount of cache. Setting up the performance attributes properly will allow the FrontPage Server Extensions to set aside the proper amount of cache so that your Web will respond quicker. You set the performance attributes for your Web through the following steps:

1. Right-click the Web to bring up a pop-up context menu.

2. Select Properties from the menu. This brings up the Default Web Site Properties dialog box, shown in Figure 17-2.

3. Within the Default Web Site Properties dialog box, select the Server Extensions tab. This brings up the Server Extensions options shown in Figure 17-3. You will see a drop-down list box titled Performance. From this box, you can select a standard setting based on the number of pages within your Web, or you can set up custom settings by continuing on to the next step.

4. Select Use Custom Settings from the Performance drop-down box. This causes the Settings button to appear in the dialog box.

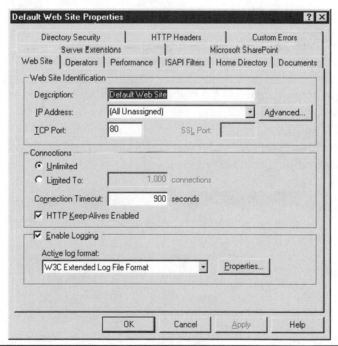

Figure 17-2   *The Default Web Site Properties dialog box*

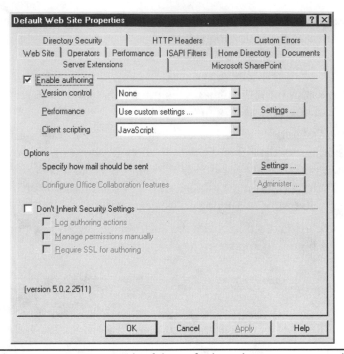

Figure 17-3   *The Server Extensions tab of the Default Web Site Properties dialog box*

5. Click the Settings button next to the Performance text box to bring up the Performance dialog box, shown here:

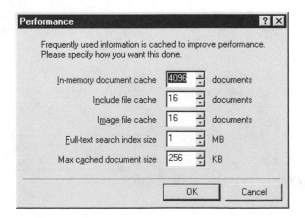

6. Specify the amount of disk space you want cached for each of the items found in the dialog box and then click OK.

7. Click OK to close the Default Web Site Properties dialog box.

That is all there is to tuning your Web for faster performance.

Setting Default Script Languages

Setting the default client scripting language in IIS is much like setting it in FrontPage through the Web Settings dialog box. Most likely, this will not be an issue for you because you will probably use the setting in FrontPage rather than this one, but it is a good idea to be aware of this setting in case you want to set it for a company-wide intranet or have multiple people working on Webs you are administering.

By default, IIS will specify JavaScript as the client scripting language, because it is the most widely accepted scripting language. You may find, however, that you want to modify a specific Web, or your entire Web, to use VBScript. With IIS, you can specify exactly which Webs have which scripting language associated with them by making the following changes to the property settings. Here are the steps to follow:

1. Right-click the Web whose scripting language you want to change and select Properties from the pop-up context menu. This brings up the Default Web Site Properties dialog box for your Web (refer to Figure 17-2).

NOTE

If you are adjusting properties in a subweb, your Default Web Site Properties dialog box will look slightly different from the one shown in Figure 17-2.

2. Within this dialog box, select the Server Extensions tab. This brings up the Server Extensions options shown earlier in Figure 17-3.

3. Select the scripting language you want from the Client Scripting drop-down list box and then click OK.

4. Click OK to close the Default Web Site Properties dialog box.

Your Web is now set up for the specified client scripting language.

Enabling E-mail from Your Webs

A great aspect of the Server Extensions is that they allow you to enable e-mail capabilities in your Webs. This allows you to create forms that send e-mail directly from your Web pages. Before this capability will function properly, you must set up the e-mail options in IIS. This is accomplished by following these steps:

1. Right-click the root Web and select Properties from the pop-up context menu. This brings up the familiar Default Web Site Properties dialog box, shown previously in Figure 17-2.

2. Within the Default Web Site Properties dialog box, select the Server Extensions tab. This brings up the Server Extensions options shown in Figure 17-3.

3. In the Options section, click the Settings button next to Specify How Mail Should Be Sent. This brings up the Email Settings dialog box, shown here:

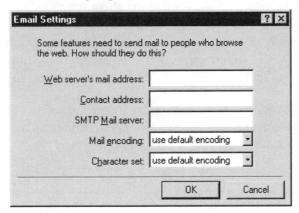

4. Specify the Web server's e-mail address in the required field. This is usually a POP address. If you do not know it, contact your system administrator.

5. Type a contact e-mail address for the server.

6. Specify the SMTP server you will be using. If you do not know it, contact your system administrator.

7. If you are not familiar with the next two options, Mail Encoding and Character Set, it is best that you leave them at their default settings. If you have specific settings you want, select them from the drop-down lists.

8. Click OK to save the settings.

9. Click OK to close the Default Web Site Properties dialog box.

If you have specified all the settings properly, you are all set to begin using the e-mail capabilities of the FrontPage Server Extensions. It is a good idea to test this using a form created in FrontPage once you have set it up.

Working with the SharePoint Administrator

The SharePoint Administrator is a Web-based administration system that allows you to configure all aspects of your SharePoint Team Services as well as all the underlying SharePoint-based Web sites you create. The administrator is available if you have installed the SharePoint Team Services on your system, and it is accessible by following these steps:

1. On your Desktop, right-click the My Computer icon.

2. Select Manage from the pop-up context menu. This brings up the Computer Management dialog box, shown previously in Figure 17-1.

3. In the tree, expand Services and Applications. You will see Internet Information Services listed as a sub-item.

4. Click Internet Information Services. You will now see all the Internet services currently running on your system.

5. Right-click Microsoft SharePoint Administration and select Browse from the drop-down menu.

This brings up the Microsoft SharePoint Team Services Administration home page, shown here:

Microsoft SharePoint
Server Administration

The links below take you to administration pages where you can specify the rights available for roles, set installation defaults, such as whether Web document discussions are turned on or off, and reset user passwords.

    ⊞ Set list of available rights
    ⊞ Set installation defaults
    ⊞ Reset user password
    ⊞ Reset MSDE Database password

Virtual Servers

The following virtual servers are available on this machine. To perform site administration tasks for a virtual server, click the virtual server name. To specify configuration settings for a virtual server, click **Administration**. To Extend Microsoft SharePoint to a virtual server, click **Extend**. To upgrade to the latest version of Microsoft SharePoint, click **Upgrade**.

Name	URL	Version	
Default Web Site	http://orion	5.0.2.2511	Administration
myweb	http://orion	5.0.2.2511	Administration
extended site			Extend

Once you have launched the SharePoint Administrator, you have the ability to configure a number of aspects associated with the server. These are overall settings that will determine how the server works on your system.

> **NOTE**
>
> *Depending on your system configuration, you may have slightly different options from the ones shown in these topics. The topic discussions assume that you are running Windows 2000 Server.*

Extending a Standard Web to a SharePoint Web

The SharePoint Team Services allows you to convert existing Web sites into SharePoint Web sites quickly and easily. This gives you the ability to take an existing site, such as your current intranet, and add to it the features and flexibility available with the SharePoint Team Services without having to start from scratch. To do so, follow these steps.

1. Install the SharePoint Team Services on your system.

2. Launch the SharePoint Administrator.

3. From the SharePoint Team Services Administration home page, look for your current Web site under the Virtual Server heading.

4. At the end of the line containing your server name, you will see the word *Extend*.

5. Click Extend. This brings up the Extend Virtual Server with Microsoft SharePoint page, shown here:

6. Specify an administrator account or leave the default.

7. Select the type of site you want. If you want to keep your existing home page, select the second option.

8. Click Submit.

SharePoint will now begin the process of converting your site and adding the SharePoint features. Once completed, the Administration screen will reappear, with your site showing under Virtual Servers and containing the new SharePoint information.

Setting Rights on the Server

When you set rights on a server, you give various users the rights to perform specific tasks. The SharePoint Administrator makes setting up these rights easy through the use of its Web interface:

1. From the SharePoint Team Services Administration home page, click Set List of Available Rights. This brings up the Set List of Available Rights page, shown here:

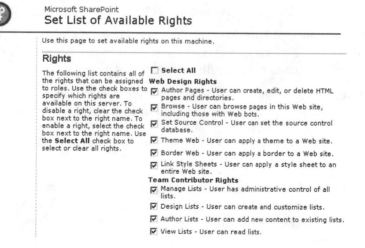

2. Select rights for each type of user on the server by checking the available check boxes next to each function. For example, if you want team contributors to have the right to design their own lists, you would check the Design Lists box under Team Contributor Rights.

3. Once you have checked all the rights you want users to have on the server, click Submit to have the settings take effect.

NOTE

If you want all rights enabled on your server, simply check the Select All box and click Submit.

Setting Installation Defaults

The installation defaults are the settings that will be assigned to each new virtual server that is SharePoint enabled. Setting these defaults allows you to control a base setup for each virtual server on your system, thus eliminating the need to set up basic functionality each time you create a new virtual server.

When you set the installation defaults, you have the following setup options available to you:

▶ **Database Settings**   Allows you to specify the default database settings for the server, which include the server name, username, and password. You can also check Use Local MSDE Database Server, instructing the server to use the Microsoft Data Engine rather than SQL Server as your default, which works well for smaller computers such as desktops.

▶ **Web Document Discussions**   Instructs the server whether or not discussions will be available on the server, where the files for those discussions are to be stored, and when to delete discussion topics.

▶ **Web Subscriptions**   Instructs the server whether or not subscriptions (an e-mail notification feature available to send out mail when changes are made to a site) will be available on the server. This allows you to determine what the notifications will be based on and when they will be sent out to subscribers.

▶ **Usage Analysis**   Instructs the server as to whether you want default logging analysis enabled for the server. If this feature is turned on, you have the ability to set when the logs are to be analyzed as well as if and when the logs should be deleted.

▶ **Server Health**   Instructs the server to run tests to ensure that all aspects are performing correctly as well as to verify that documents on your Web site are properly synchronized.

▶ **Mail Settings**   Instructs the server how mail is to be handled. This is very important because the configuration of the mail server allows the system to enable the various e-mail-based features of the SharePoint Team Services.

▶ **Security Settings**   Instructs the server as to what the default security settings should be. Here you have the choices to log the actions of authors, require SSL (Secure Socket Layer) for authoring, and determine whether authors can upload executables (.exe files) to the server.

To set up the installation defaults, follow these steps.

1. From the SharePoint Team Services Administration home page, click Set Installation Defaults. This brings up the Set Installation Defaults page, shown here:

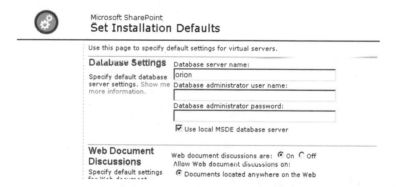

2. Enter the default settings you want for your virtual servers and click Submit to have these defaults stored.

Resetting Passwords

The SharePoint Team Services allow administrators complete access for creating new passwords for users as well as for your MSDE, if it's set up on your system. To create new passwords, follow the steps in the following topics.

Resetting User Passwords

Once you have begun working with the SharePoint Team Services, you may run into a situation where a user on the system forgets their password. The administration console makes taking care of this problem a snap; simply follow the steps shown next and your user will have their new password in no time.

1. From the SharePoint Team Services Administration home page, click Reset User Password. This brings up the Reset User Password page, shown here:

2. Select the virtual server this user is associated with from the drop-down list.

3. Type the name of the Web this user is associated with in the Web Name field.

4. Type the person's username in the User Name field.

5. Type and confirm the new password for this user and click Submit.

The new password is now assigned to the user you have specified.

Resetting the MSDE Password

You may find, at some point, that you are unable to find or remember the password you set up for your MSDE (Microsoft Data Engine). Using the SharePoint administration console, you can easily reset this password so that you once again have access. Here are the steps:

1. From the SharePoint Team Services Administration home page, click Reset MSDE Database Password. This brings up the Reset MSDE Database Password page, shown here:

Microsoft SharePoint
Reset MSDE Password

Use this page to reset the MSDE password.

Reset MSDE Password

Enter the new password and confirm to change the MSDE password.

MSDE server:
orion

New password:

Confirm new password:

Submit   Cancel

2. Type and confirm the new password for your MSDE and click Submit.

The new password is now assigned.

Summary

Upon completing this chapter, you should have a good grasp of what a Web really is and the basic principles associated with administering your server-based Webs using Computer Management and the SharePoint Team Services. This chapter has shown you step-by-step processes associated with the most common tasks in administering Webs. If you are an experienced administrator, this chapter will simply serve as a quick reference. But if this is your first time administering a site, you will find this information invaluable as you get started in using all the extended features available to you in FrontPage.

Index

NOTE: Page numbers in italics refer to illustrations or charts.

INTERNATIONAL CONTACT INFORMATION

AUSTRALIA
McGraw-Hill Book Company Australia Pty. Ltd.
TEL +61-2-9417-9899
FAX +61-2-9417-5687
http://www.mcgraw-hill.com.au
books-it_sydney@mcgraw-hill.com

CANADA
McGraw-Hill Ryerson Ltd.
TEL +905-430-5000
FAX +905-430-5020
http://www.mcgrawhill.ca

GREECE, MIDDLE EAST,
NORTHERN AFRICA
McGraw-Hill Hellas
TEL +30-1-656-0990-3-4
FAX +30-1-654-5525

MEXICO (Also serving Latin America)
McGraw-Hill Interamericana Editores S.A. de C.V.
TEL +525-117-1583
FAX +525-117-1589
http://www.mcgraw-hill.com.mx
fernando_castellanos@mcgraw-hill.com

SINGAPORE (Serving Asia)
McGraw-Hill Book Company
TEL +65-863-1580
FAX +65-862-3354
http://www.mcgraw-hill.com.sg
mghasia@mcgraw-hill.com

SOUTH AFRICA
McGraw-Hill South Africa
TEL +27-11-622-7512
FAX +27-11-622-9045
robyn_swanepoel@mcgraw-hill.com

UNITED KINGDOM & EUROPE
(Excluding Southern Europe)
McGraw-Hill Education Europe
TEL +44-1-628-502500
FAX +44-1-628-770224
http://www.mcgraw-hill.co.uk
computing_neurope@mcgraw-hill.com

ALL OTHER INQUIRIES Contact:
Osborne/McGraw-Hill
TEL +1-510-549-6600
FAX +1-510-883-7600
http://www.osborne.com
omg_international@mcgraw-hill.com

LICENSE AGREEMENT

THIS PRODUCT (THE "PRODUCT") CONTAINS PROPRIETARY SOFTWARE, DATA AND INFORMATION (INCLUDING DOCUMENTATION) OWNED BY THE McGRAW-HILL COMPANIES, INC. ("McGRAW-HILL") AND ITS LICENSORS. YOUR RIGHT TO USE THE PRODUCT IS GOVERNED BY THE TERMS AND CONDITIONS OF THIS AGREEMENT.

LICENSE: Throughout this License Agreement, "you" shall mean either the individual or the entity whose agent opens this package. You are granted a non-exclusive and non-transferable license to use the Product subject to the following terms:

(i) If you have licensed a single user version of the Product, the Product may only be used on a single computer (i.e., a single CPU). If you licensed and paid the fee applicable to a local area network or wide area network version of the Product, you are subject to the terms of the following subparagraph (ii).

(ii) If you have licensed a local area network version, you may use the Product on unlimited workstations located in one single building selected by you that is served by such local area network. If you have licensed a wide area network version, you may use the Product on unlimited workstations located in multiple buildings on the same site selected by you that is served by such wide area network; provided, however, that any building will not be considered located in the same site if it is more than five (5) miles away from any building included in such site. In addition, you may only use a local area or wide area network version of the Product on one single server. If you wish to use the Product on more than one server, you must obtain written authorization from McGraw-Hill and pay additional fees.

(iii) You may make one copy of the Product for back-up purposes only and you must maintain an accurate record as to the location of the back-up at all times.

COPYRIGHT; RESTRICTIONS ON USE AND TRANSFER: All rights (including copyright) in and to the Product are owned by McGraw-Hill and its licensors. You are the owner of the enclosed disc on which the Product is recorded. You may not use, copy, decompile, disassemble, reverse engineer, modify, reproduce, create derivative works, transmit, distribute, sublicense, store in a database or retrieval system of any kind, rent or transfer the Product, or any portion thereof, in any form or by any means (including electronically or otherwise) except as expressly provided for in this License Agreement. You must reproduce the copyright notices, trademark notices, legends and logos of McGraw-Hill and its licensors that appear on the Product on the back-up copy of the Product which you are permitted to make hereunder. All rights in the Product not expressly granted herein are reserved by McGraw-Hill and its licensors.

TERM: This License Agreement is effective until terminated. It will terminate if you fail to comply with any term or condition of this License Agreement. Upon termination, you are obligated to return to McGraw-Hill the Product together with all copies thereof and to purge all copies of the Product included in any and all servers and computer facilities.

DISCLAIMER OF WARRANTY: THE PRODUCT AND THE BACK-UP COPY ARE LICENSED "AS IS." McGRAW-HILL, ITS LICENSORS AND THE AUTHORS MAKE NO WARRANTIES, EXPRESS OR IMPLIED, AS TO THE RESULTS TO BE OBTAINED BY ANY PERSON OR ENTITY FROM USE OF THE PRODUCT, ANY INFORMATION OR DATA INCLUDED THEREIN AND/OR ANY TECHNICAL SUPPORT SERVICES PROVIDED HEREUNDER, IF ANY ("TECHNICAL SUPPORT SERVICES"). McGRAW-HILL, ITS LICENSORS AND THE AUTHORS MAKE NO EXPRESS OR IMPLIED WARRANTIES OF MERCHANTABILITY OR FITNESS FOR A PARTICULAR PURPOSE OR USE WITH RESPECT TO THE PRODUCT. McGRAW-HILL, ITS LICENSORS, AND THE AUTHORS MAKE NO GUARANTEE THAT YOU WILL PASS ANY CERTIFICATION EXAM WHATSOEVER BY USING THIS PRODUCT. NEITHER McGRAW-HILL, ANY OF ITS LICENSORS NOR THE AUTHORS WARRANT THAT THE FUNCTIONS CONTAINED IN THE PRODUCT WILL MEET YOUR REQUIREMENTS OR THAT THE OPERATION OF THE PRODUCT WILL BE UNINTERRUPTED OR ERROR FREE. YOU ASSUME THE ENTIRE RISK WITH RESPECT TO THE QUALITY AND PERFORMANCE OF THE PRODUCT.

LIMITED WARRANTY FOR DISC: To the original licensee only, McGraw-Hill warrants that the enclosed disc on which the Product is recorded is free from defects in materials and workmanship under normal use and service for a period of ninety (90) days from the date of purchase. In the event of a defect in the disc covered by the foregoing warranty, McGraw-Hill will replace the disc.

LIMITATION OF LIABILITY: NEITHER McGRAW-HILL, ITS LICENSORS NOR THE AUTHORS SHALL BE LIABLE FOR ANY INDIRECT, SPECIAL OR CONSEQUENTIAL DAMAGES, SUCH AS BUT NOT LIMITED TO, LOSS OF ANTICIPATED PROFITS OR BENEFITS, RESULTING FROM THE USE OR INABILITY TO USE THE PRODUCT EVEN IF ANY OF THEM HAS BEEN ADVISED OF THE POSSIBILITY OF SUCH DAMAGES. THIS LIMITATION OF LIABILITY SHALL APPLY TO ANY CLAIM OR CAUSE WHATSOEVER WHETHER SUCH CLAIM OR CAUSE ARISES IN CONTRACT, TORT, OR OTHERWISE. Some states do not allow the exclusion or limitation of indirect, special or consequential damages, so the above limitation may not apply to you.

U.S. GOVERNMENT RESTRICTED RIGHTS: Any software included in the Product is provided with restricted rights subject to subparagraphs (c), (1) and (2) of the Commercial Computer Software-Restricted Rights clause at 48 C.F.R. 52.227-19. The terms of this Agreement applicable to the use of the data in the Product are those under which the data are generally made available to the general public by McGraw-Hill. Except as provided herein, no reproduction, use, or disclosure rights are granted with respect to the data included in the Product and no right to modify or create derivative works from any such data is hereby granted.

GENERAL: This License Agreement constitutes the entire agreement between the parties relating to the Product. The terms of any Purchase Order shall have no effect on the terms of this License Agreement. Failure of McGraw-Hill to insist at any time on strict compliance with this License Agreement shall not constitute a waiver of any rights under this License Agreement. This License Agreement shall be construed and governed in accordance with the laws of the State of New York. If any provision of this License Agreement is held to be contrary to law, that provision will be enforced to the maximum extent permissible and the remaining provisions will remain in full force and effect.